Defining *Deutschtum*

The New Cultural History of Music

Defining *Deutschtum*

DAVID
BRODBECK

Political Ideology, German

Identity, and Music-Critical

Discourse in Liberal Vienna

OXFORD
UNIVERSITY PRESS

Oxford University Press is a department of the University of
Oxford. It furthers the University's objective of excellence in research,
scholarship, and education by publishing worldwide.

Oxford   New York
Auckland   Cape Town   Dar es Salaam   Hong Kong   Karachi
Kuala Lumpur   Madrid   Melbourne   Mexico City   Nairobi
New Delhi   Shanghai   Taipei   Toronto

With offices in
Argentina   Austria   Brazil   Chile   Czech Republic   France   Greece
Guatemala   Hungary   Italy   Japan   Poland   Portugal   Singapore
South Korea   Switzerland   Thailand   Turkey   Ukraine   Vietnam

Oxford is a registered trademark of Oxford University Press
in the UK and certain other countries.

Published in the United States of America by
Oxford University Press
198 Madison Avenue, New York, NY 10016

© Oxford University Press 2014

Library of Congress Cataloging-in-Publication Data
Brodbeck, David, author.
Defining Deutschtum : political ideology, German identity, and music-critical discourse in liberal
Vienna / David Brodbeck.
pages cm. — (The new cultural history of music series)
Includes bibliographical references and index.
ISBN 978–0–19–936270–7 (hardback : alk. paper)   1. Musical criticism—Austria—
Vienna—History—19th century.   2. Music—Austria—Vienna—19th century—History and
criticism.   I. Title.
ML3880.B893 2014
780.94361309034—dc23
2013050579

This volume is published with the generous support of the Donna Cardamone Jackson Endowment
of the American Musicological Society, funded in part by the National Endowment for the Humanities
and the Andrew W. Mellon Foundation.

9 8 7 6 5 4 3 2 1
Printed in the United States of America
on acid-free paper

For Leonora

CONTENTS

PREFACE AND ACKNOWLEDGMENTS

Twenty-five years ago I began to work on Brahms's Third Symphony for an essay slated to appear in *Brahms and His World*, published in 1990 in connection with the first Bard Music Festival.[1] In the early stages of this research I did what any other young scholar of Brahms would have done by reading what the composer's biographer Max Kalbeck had to say about the work. There I learned that Brahms composed the symphony in the summer of 1883 while residing in a lovely apartment in Wiesbaden, living, as he explained in a letter to his friend Theodor Billroth, "quite charmingly," as though he were "trying to imitate Wagner."[2] In the footnote that Kalbeck attached to this quotation was another passage taken from the same letter, wherein Brahms cheered Billroth's efforts, along with those of their mutual friend Eduard Hanslick, in opposing the opening in Vienna of a Czech-language school. The footnote concluded with Kalbeck's take on why Brahms had decided to summer in Germany that year instead of in his adopted home of Austria: "The liberal German in Brahms was up in arms against Austria's escalating Czech-Clerical special-interest politics." A bit further on, this time in connection with the symphony's early reception, Kalbeck reported again Brahms's displeasure with the "anti-German politics of the government" and the "priestly machinations" that were a part of it.[3] But

---

[1] David Brodbeck, "Brahms, the Third Symphony, and the New German School," *Brahms and His World*, ed. Walter Frisch (Princeton: Princeton University Press, 1990): 65–80.

[2] Max Kalbeck, *Johannes Brahms*, rev. ed., 4 vols. in 8 (Berlin: Deutsche Brahms-Gesellschaft, 1915–21; rpt., Tutzing: Hans Schneider, 1976), 3: 381.

[3] Ibid., 3: 402. We shall return to this episode in Chapter 5.

though he suggested (somewhat implausibly, in my view) that the discouraging political situation in Habsburg Austria caused an upsurge in Brahms's patriotic feelings at this time toward Bismarck's Germany, he made no serious attempt to explain how the composer's political and ideological allegiances as a German liberal could be detected in the symphony at hand. Instead Kalbeck was quick to note how contemporaneous musical conditions in Vienna had also raised Brahms's ire and with that moved to a discussion of purely musical partisanship along the familiar Brahms-Bruckner (and, by extension, Brahms-Wagner) divide.

Kalbeck's foray into Austrian domestic politics was intriguing, but it was not clear how it might lead me to a deeper understanding of the music of the Third Symphony, which was my concern at the moment. And so I simply made a mental note to ponder the political Brahms at some later date. I took my immediate cue instead from the composer's typically cutting remark to Billroth about imitating Wagner and settled on the theme of my essay. There I explored how Brahms emulated certain techniques associated not only with Wagner but also with that other leading light of the New German School, Liszt. These emulations I saw not as acts of homage, but rather, especially with respect to Liszt, as pointed commentary. In other words, like Kalbeck, I focused on musical partisanship and left out of my account "the German liberal" Brahms and the "anti-German politics" and "Czech-Clerical special-interest politics" that vexed him.

In a sense, the genesis of the book at hand can be traced back to that early reading of Kalbeck's discussion of Brahms's Third Symphony, although I could never have imagined at the time writing a book such as this one. Owing largely to the work of Leon Botstein and Margaret Notley beginning around 1990, Brahms's liberal politics and indeed the musical culture of what we shall call Liberal Vienna soon became topics of considerable scholarly interest.[4] Knowing that the members of the Vienna Philharmonic typically chose their own programs, about ten years ago I began to wonder about the degree to which those programming decisions may have been influenced by the liberal culture in which they were made. To what extent were the Philharmonic players catering to the sensibilities of their liberal subscribers? To what extent did the programming decisions reflect the influence of the city's liberal music critics? And I was curious to discover how, if at all, the national politics of the day—the German liberals lost their accustomed hold on power in the central government in 1879, were replaced by a coalition

---

[4] I briefly discuss the work of these scholars in the Introduction.

dominated by Czech and Conservative-Clerical parties, and never regained their once dominant position—played out in those decisions.

To begin, I made an inventory of the new music by Austrian composers performed in the Philharmonic's subscription concerts during the 1880s and 1890s. It was not surprising to learn that the works of Brahms, an establishment darling, were heard more often than those by any other composer, even though his challenging music was respected more than loved by the Viennese. Standing in second place was a now largely forgotten figure, Robert Fuchs, a professor at the Vienna Conservatory and "a splendid musician," as Brahms put it, in whose music "everything is so fine and so skilful, so charmingly invented, that one is always pleased."[5] This was the kind of cozy music the Viennese could really warm up to. Cozy is not the word to use in describing the monumental symphonies of Anton Bruckner, and yet this composer held third place, largely on the basis of his increasingly frequent appearances in the programs in the final decade of the century. But already by the early 1880s he had his ardent champions, especially among a younger generation that was slowly becoming more influential. This left two other composers on the "top five" list, Antonín Dvořák and Carl Goldmark. Given the political circumstances of the period, with the Czechs threatening traditional German hegemony and the simultaneous rise of political and eventually racialist anti-semitism, the frequency with which the music of a Czech composer and an assimilated Jewish composer was performed drew my attention and seemed worth a closer look. As the book took shape, my topic expanded considerably in several directions. But these are the basic questions with which I began, and they remained guiding ones throughout.

Growing from an extended engagement with late Habsburg social and political history, as well as with the writings of Vienna's leading musical critics of the last forty years of the nineteenth century, this book now places front and center topics of the sociopolitical kind that I had earlier left unaddressed after stumbling upon Kalbeck's brief discussion of Brahms's politics. I have since learned that liberalism was not a static ideology at this time and place, and as a result that in "German Vienna" there was no single, universally held notion of what it meant even to be a German. Moreover, I have discovered that Vienna's music critics often tell us as much about these kinds of issues as they do about matters more purely musical. My aim in this book, then, is to reveal the very great extent to which contemporary political ideology and political developments on the ground were tied to questions of German identity in

[5] Quoted by Robert Pascall in s.v., "Robert Fuchs," *Grove Music Online*.

late-nineteenth-century Austria, and to show how, in turn, these questions were implicated in the musical culture and above all articulated by Vienna's music critics. This story is best told, I believe, not by reference to writings about the music of composers such as Brahms and Bruckner (or Fuchs) who in today's terminology would be described as "ethnic Germans," but rather to writings about the music of other composers—German-speaking Jews and Czech-speaking Bohemians—for whom that expression would never apply.

Some of the material in this book has appeared previously in print in different form. Chapters 1 and 7 make use of parts of "Hanslick's Smetana and Hanslick's Prague," *Journal of the Royal Musical Association* 134 (2009): 1–36 (used with permission of the publisher Taylor & Francis). Chapter 7 draws also on "*Ausgleichs-Abende*: The First Viennese Performances of Smetana's *Bartered Bride*," *Austrian Studies* 17 (2009): 43–61 (used with permission of the Modern Humanities Research Association). Chapter 5 incorporates portions of "Dvořák's Reception in Liberal Vienna: Language Ordinances, National Property, and the Rhetoric of *Deutschtum*," *Journal of the American Musicological Society* 60 (Spring 2007): 71–131 (Copyright © 2007 by the American Musicological Society. Published by the University of California Press), and "Hanslick's Smetana and Hanslick's Prague." Finally, Chapters 3 and 6 include material originally published in different form in "'Poison-flaming Flowers from the Orient and Nightingales from Bayreuth': On Hanslick's Reception of the Music of Goldmark," in *Rethinking Hanslick: Music, Formalism, and Expression*, ed. Nicole Grimes, Siobhán Donovan, and Wolfgang Marx (Rochester: University of Rochester Press, 2013), 132–59 (used with permission).

Unless otherwise noted, all translations from the German are my own. I would be remiss, however, not to acknowledge with gratitude the advice received from time to time from a number of friends and colleagues who are native German speakers, especially Anke Biendarra, Josef Eisinger, Kai Evers, and Philipp Lehmann. Another friend and colleague, Meredith Lee, provided me with an elegant translation of Robert Zimmermann's poem "Mein Böhmerland." For their expert assistance in transcribing a number of challenging passages written in *Kurrentschrift*, I thank Thomas Aigner and Frank Lehmann. I also wish to acknowledge the late Gerhard J. Winkler, who generously volunteered to share with me his transcriptions of the prose manuscripts in Carl Goldmark's hand quoted in Chapter 8. Finally, I am grateful to Ellen Langer for her translation from the Czech of two versions of the opening verses of Ferdinand Mikovec's "Ha, ty naše slunce," from his play *Záhuba rodu Přemyslovského*, and to David Beveridge and Alan Houtchens for providing me with a few other short Czech translations.

Financial support for this project was provided by a research grant from the Academic Senate Council on Research, Computing, and Libraries, University of California, Irvine, as well as by numerous faculty research and travel grants from UC Irvine's Claire Trevor School of the Arts. These grants allowed me to make three research trips to Central Europe while writing this book. In Vienna my research was facilitated by the friendly assistance of Peter Poltun (Wiener Staatsoper), Thomas Aigner (Wienbibliothek im Rathaus), Otto Biba (Archiv der Gesellschaft der Musikfreunde), Peter Stachel (Institut für Kulturwissenschaften und Theatergeschichte, Österreichische Akademie der Wissenschaften), and Silvia Kargl (Historisches Archiv der Wiener Philharmoniker). During the course of an extended stay in Vienna while on sabbatical leave in 2011, Peter and Ursula Prokop became good friends and dining and day-touring companions and gladly answered more than a few questions related to this project. It was owing to the intervention of Herr Prokop that I was able to obtain a copy from the Verein für Geschichte der Arbeiterbewegung of the speech by Victor Adler quoted in Chapter 4. I owe considerable thanks to the helpful personnel at each of the Viennese libraries in which I regularly worked: the Österreichische Nationalbibliothek, the Wienbibliothek im Rathaus, the Universitätsbibliothek Wien, and the Universitätsbibliothek der Universität für Musik und darstellende Kunst Wien.

One of the great pleasures of undertaking this project was the cause it gave me to spend time outside Vienna in those other two great capital cities of the late Habsburg era, Budapest and Prague. In Budapest, Nora Wellman (Hungarian State Opera) and Balázs Mikusi (National Széchéni Library) were most helpful in making important archival materials available to me. David Beveridge was a warm and gracious host in Prague and generously shared with me both his extensive knowledge of Dvořák and his excellent contacts in the city's libraries. Finally, to go from the large cities to the small towns of Central Europe, I want to remember here the anonymous woman who left her post in the local tourist office in Deutschkreuz, in the Burgenland region of Austria, to open for my own private tour the Goldmarkgedenkhaus Deutschkreuz Carl-Goldmark-Museum.

Over the years Celia Applegate, Styra Avins, Michael Beckerman, Steven Beller, David Beveridge, Gary Cohen, Thomas Grey, Nicole Grimes, Jonathan Hess, Kevin Karnes, Benjamin Korstvedt, and Ralph Locke read parts of this text in various stages of development. I have invariably benefited from their comments and suggestions. David Beveridge kindly took the trouble to obtain for me copies of the first edition of Hanslick's "Český houslista" (National Library of the Czech Republic) and a later reissue of his "Milostná píseň pod Wyšehradem" (Municipal Library of Prague). I am grateful to Sandra McColl for assisting me in obtaining the photograph of Ludwig Speidel reproduced as Plate II. Steven Beller has been a friendly and spirited interlocutor on the matter of Theodor Billroth's alleged antisemitism; I have learned much from our interactions even when we have not fully agreed with one another. Finally, I am profoundly grateful to Gary Cohen, professor of history and former director of the Center for Austrian Studies at the University of Minnesota, Twin Cities, for taking an interest in this project during its formative stages and for providing wise counsel as it has taken shape in the years since.

My wife, Leonora Saavedra, knows as well as I that this book would never have been completed were it not for her encouragement and support, imaginative and probing questions, and careful reading of the text. For more than twenty years she has been not only my life's companion but my scholarly inspiration and model, and I dedicate this book to her with my deepest admiration and all my love.

For places such as Vienna, Prague, Hungary, and Bohemia, I use the familiar English names. I use the German names for places with no English name in which more than one language was spoken in the later nineteenth century, even when those names are no longer in use. A list of German place names with their Czech (C), Polish (P), Slovene (S), and Hungarian (H) names follows:

Alt-Ofen	Óbuda (H)
Cilli	Celje (S)
Deutschkreuz	Németkeresztur (H)
Freiberg	Příbor (C)
Kempen	Kępno (P)
Lissan	Lišany (C)
Ödenburg	Sopron (H)
Ofen	Buda (H)
Raab	Györ (H)
Weckelsdorf	Teplice nad Metují (C)

The German writers quoted in this study frequently used German orthography when giving the proper names of Czechs. In general I make use of the Czech spelling of these names in my translations. I do, however, retain the authors' original German orthography when it seems to have been intended to make a rhetorical point. When quoting passages in German and when citing German publication titles, I invariably use the original orthography.

This applies even in the cases of the given name of Carl Goldmark, which sometimes appears with the variant spelling "Karl," and of Hans Richter, which Hanslick sometimes spells "Hanns."

Finally, I follow the growing trend among scholars writing in English to use the unhyphenated spelling "antisemitism." This not only is in keeping with the German origins of this neologism—*Antisemitismus* was coined only in 1879—but also avoids the unfortunate implication given by the more familiar hyphenated spelling ("anti-Semitism") that there once existed a threatening racial ideology of "Semitism" that needed to be combatted. In quotations, however, I retain the hyphenated spelling when used by the authors in question.

Defining *Deutschtum*

INTRODUCTION | Viennese Critics and the "Habsburg Dilemma"

Once upon a time, notably in 1848, liberals and nationalists could be allies within the Habsburg Empire, united in their shared opposition to the authoritarian, hierarchical, traditional, though not specifically ethnic centre. But later, all that tended to change. In the end virtually all the 'ethnics', including even or especially the German speakers, turned against the centre, which, however dynastic and traditional, was finally only able to rely on the support of the new men: the commercial, industrial, academic, professional meritocrats, interested in maintaining an open market in goods, men, ideas, and a universalistic open society. This was the great paradox of its terminal condition. Its loyalists were the *nouveaux riches* and the newly emancipated, often not altogether integrated and accepted, and often made to feel uncomfortable, notably if they were Jewish: all this being so, both economic and political liberalism was to their taste. They were liberal but they needed protection by the state against ethnic illiberalism.... Were the regime to be replaced by ethno-romantic, nationally specific states, the liberalism would surely lapse and the position of the newly freed and newly enriched would be grave.... In the end, the fears which had led them to be loyal Habsburg subjects proved to be only too justified.

THUS DID THE social anthropologist Ernst Gellner, in one of his final writings, describe what he called the "Habsburg dilemma."[1] This tale

---

[1] Ernest Gellner, *Language and Solitude: Wittgenstein, Malinowski and the Habsburg Dilemma* (Cambridge: Cambridge University Press, 1998), 11.

may at first blush seem fanciful, a wistful look back on a "world of yesterday" that never really existed.[2] Reality is, after all, a messy thing. In June 1848, for example, it did not take long for German liberals in Vienna to side with the Austrian crown when self-consciously Czech activists took violently to the streets of Prague. Moreover, to move from the beginning of Gellner's tale to its end, historians have become increasingly skeptical of the notion that the Habsburg Empire was doomed in its final decades by rising nationality conflicts and the political sclerosis that ensued from them—that it suffered hopelessly, in other words, from any "terminal condition."[3] Yet it is true nonetheless that Gellner's account provides a suggestive light in which to read music criticism in late-nineteenth-century Vienna. Not only were the city's principal musical institutions—the Hofoper (Court Opera) as well as the concerts of the Wiener Philharmoniker (Vienna Philharmonic), the Gesellschaft der Musikfreunde (Society of the Friends of Music), and the city's various chamber music groups— institutions of a cultural center that reflected in large measure the tastes and interests of the liberal *"nouveaux riches* and newly emancipated." The music performed in them often served as a point of departure for critical discourse that touched on—and not infrequently reflected—the various sociopolitical forces of Czech nationalism, irredentist German nationalism, and racial and political antisemitism that from the 1880s on threatened the imperial center itself.

In the midst of these many centrifugal forces, the liberal-minded Crown Prince Rudolf von Habsburg sought the support of his father, Francis Joseph I, for a proposed new project that he hoped would "communicate in both stimulating and educational fashion a comprehensive image of our fatherland and its peoples."[4] This eventually came to fruition as *Die österreichisch-ungarische Monarchie in Wort und Bild* (The Austro-Hungarian monarchy in word

---

[2] My reference here, of course, is to Stefan Zweig's *The World of Yesterday* (1942).

[3] Gary B. Cohen, "Neither Absolutism Nor Anarchy: New Narratives on Society and Government in Late Imperial Austria," *Austrian History Yearbook* 29 (1998): 37–61; idem, "Citizenship and Nationality in Late Imperial Austria," in *Nation, Nationalitäten und Nationalismus im östlichen Europa: Festschrift für Arnold Suppan zum 65. Geburtstag*, ed. Marija Wakounig, Wolfgang Mueller, and Michael Portmann (Vienna and Berlin: Lit Verlag, 2004), 201–24; and Lothar Höbelt, "'Well-Tempered Domestic Discontent': Austrian Domestic Politics," in *The Last Years of Austria-Hungary: A Multi-National Experiment in Early Twentieth-Century Europe*, rev. ed., ed. Mark Cornwell (Exeter: University of Exeter Press, 2002), 47–74. For an excellent summary of the so-called inevitability debate, see Steven Beller, *Francis Joseph* (London and New York: Longman, 1996), 3–9.

[4] Memorandum of March 1884, quoted in Regina Bendix, "Ethnology, Cultural Reification, and the Dynamics of Difference in the *Kronprinzenwerk*," in *Creating*

and image), a massive encyclopedia that appeared in twenty-four volumes between 1886 and 1902.[5] Each copiously illustrated installment of the *Kronprinzenwerk*, as the encyclopedia came to be known, comprised essays written by local experts, on topics ranging from history and geography to folklore and the arts, including music. The whole amounted to nothing less than a systematic ethnography of a far-flung empire that embraced no fewer than eleven officially recognized nationalities: Germans, Hungarians, Czechs, Slovaks, Poles, Ukrainians (Ruthenes), Slovenes, Croats, Serbs, Romanians, and Italians. Although cultural difference across regions is openly celebrated throughout, it is clear, nonetheless, that Rudolf's underlying purpose was to encourage a collective patriotism and to inculcate a belief in "the good fortune of all remaining within one Monarchy rather than embarking on the path of separate nation-states."[6]

Not surprisingly, the first volume was devoted to Vienna. Equally predictable was the decision to commission Eduard Hanslick (1825–1904), the eminent aesthetician, critic, and historian, to contribute the essay on music.[7] Hanslick, a "new man" *par excellence*, wasted little time in aligning himself with the very premises on which the monarchy rested by taking note of the music of each of the empire's predominant ethno-linguistic groups:

> Through its surpassing importance in music, Vienna is not merely the musical Imperial Capital of Austria but a powerful empire in itself. Its musical supremacy extends across the borders of the monarchy. Gentle echoes of Slavic, Magyar, and Italian tunes, enlivening and embellishing rather like miscegenation [*Racenmischung*], gently resound, without distracting from the eminently German character of Viennese music. If we imagine the entire empire of German music as though

the Other: Ethnic Conflict and Nationalism in Habsburg Central Europe, ed. Nancy M. Wingfield (New York and Oxford: Berghahn Books, 2003), 149.

[5] Die österreichisch-ungarische Monarchie in Wort und Bild, 24 vols. (Vienna: Druck und Verlag der kaiserlich-königlichen Hof- und Staatsdruckerei, 1886–1902).

[6] Bendix, "Ethnology, Cultural Reification, and the Dynamics of Difference," 159. See also the brief discussion in Philip V. Bohlman, Focus: Music, Nationalism, and the Making of the New Europe, 2nd ed. (London: Routledge, 2011), 141–43.

[7] Eduard Hanslick, "Die Musik in Wien," in Die österreichisch-ungarische Monarchie in Wort und Bild, vol. 1: Wien und Niederösterreich, part 1: Wien (1886), 123–38. For a recent account, see Peter Stachel, "'Mit wärme und lebhafter Anschaulichkeit': Eduard Hanslicks Anteil am 'Kronprinzenwerk,'" in Eduard Hanslick zum Gedenken: Bericht des Symposions zum Anlass seines 100. Todestages, ed. Theophil Antonicek, Gernot Gruber, and Christoph Landerer (Tutzing: Hans Schneider, 2010), 215–32.

it were a free federation of states, in which first this, then that land temporarily shines forth with greater brilliance—Vienna remains, in time and rank, the administrative center of this great confederation.[8]

With its striking reference to miscegenation, this account paid lip service in its own way to the idea of collective patriotism. Yet there was no doubt in Hanslick's mind about what lay in the center and what in the periphery.

Hanslick steered clear in this essay of any discussion of the music and musical life of the Vienna of his own time. Johann Strauss, Jr., makes a brief appearance at the end, but there is no mention of Johannes Brahms, Anton Bruckner, or any other living composer. Matters were somewhat different two years later, when Hanslick was called on to contribute the essay on music for a volume entitled *Wien 1848–1888*, published by Vienna's municipal government in celebration of the fortieth anniversary of Francis Joseph's imperial reign. Yet here Hanslick focused his attention in a rather descriptive, taxonomic manner on the recent history of Vienna's musical institutions rather than on composers and their works, not to speak of the heated debates that swelled up around them.[9]

In view of the state occasion that had prompted this commemorative volume, Hanslick's reluctance to write about ongoing divisive matters is understandable. By contrast, he showed no such reticence in the lively feuilletons he had been producing on a regular basis in the Viennese press for much of the same forty-year period. This body of writing makes clear where Hanslick stood, not only on the city's heated musical politics, but also from time to time on issues of state import. The work of many of Hanslick's colleagues in the field of Viennese music criticism during the second half of the nineteenth century is no less revealing on matters political and ideological. When the critic Max Kalbeck, in his monumental biography of Brahms, recalled that the 1880s had been a time when "music got mixed up in politics," he was writing as someone who had been very much in the thick of it.[10]

In the early 1990s Leon Botstein and Margaret Notley began to dig more deeply into this question, enriching our understanding of late-nineteenth-century musical culture in Vienna by giving greater due to the larger social and political contexts that helped to shape it. Botstein's signal contribution was to show how the bitter musical politics of the day ironically

---

[8] Hanslick, "Die Musik in Wien," 123.

[9] Eduard Hanslick, "Musik," in *Wien 1848–1888: Denkschrift zum 2. Dezember 1888,* ed. Gemeinderathe der Stadt Wien, 2 vols. (Vienna: Carl Konegan, 1888), 2: 303–42.

[10] Kalbeck, *Johannes Brahms,* 3: 402.

turned a contemporary social divide upside down. "Brahms's aesthetic of classi-cal continuity," he notes, "was linked with a belief in scientific progress, social emancipation, the modern nation state, and the transformation of traditional ways of life." This, of course, placed the tradition-oriented composer squarely alongside Vienna's liberal elites from the worlds of business, law, medicine, and academe. By contrast, Wagner, with his "appeal to premodern myths of com-munity"—to *Gemeinschaft*, not *Gesellschaft*—and his critique of all that the lib-erals held dear, gave direction to what Botstein calls "a radically conservative movement [among a younger generation] that sought to establish a political and cultural alternative to the cosmopolitan liberal conceits of Vienna's cultural, literary, and academic elite."[11]

Notley discerns this same social and generational divide in contemporary Viennese music criticism, particularly as it relates to Brahms and his champions in the Hanslickian camp and to Bruckner and his champions among the young Wagnerians.[12] She plausibly argues that Brahms's style suited the taste of liberal culture in part because it seemed to project typical middle-class values such as logical thinking, self-restraint, and accomplishment earned through hard work, while arguing that Bruckner's music could more easily be associated with "a non-rational cult of emotion and instinct" that she associates with Wagnerism, radical German nationalism, antisemitism, indeed, what she calls the entire "right-wing fringe."[13] After Botstein and Notley, no one is likely ever to think

[11] Leon Botstein, "Brahms and Nineteenth-Century Painting," *19th-Century Music* 14 (1990): 158. Botstein's other work in this field includes "Music and Its Public: Habits of Listening and the Crisis of Musical Modernism in Vienna, 1870–1914" (Ph.D. diss., Harvard University, 1985); and "Time and Memory: Concert Life, Science, and Music in Brahms's Vienna," in *Brahms and His World*, rev. ed., ed. Walter Frisch and Kevin C. Karnes (Princeton: Princeton University Press, 2009), 3–25.

[12] The relevant work includes Notley, "Brahms as Liberal: Genre, Style, and Politics in Late Nineteenth-Century Vienna," *19th-Century Music* 23 (1993): 107–23 (whose point of departure was the observation by Kalbeck quoted above); "Bruckner and Viennese Wagnerism," in *Bruckner Studies*, ed. Timothy L. Jackson and Paul Hawkshaw (Cambridge: Cambridge University Press, 1997), 54–71; " 'Volkskonzerte' in Vienna and Late Nineteenth-Century Ideology of the Symphony," *Journal of the American Musicological Society* 50 (1997): 421–53; and "Musical Culture in Vienna at the Turn of the Twentieth Century," in *Schoenberg, Berg, and Webern: A Companion to the Second Viennese School*, ed. Bryan R. Simms (Westport, CT: Greenwood Press, 1999), 36–71. "Brahms as Liberal" and "*Volkskonzerte*' in Vienna" reappear in revised form in Notley's *Lateness and Brahms: Music and Culture in the Twilight of Viennese Liberalism* (Oxford and New York: Oxford University Press, 2007).

[13] Notley, "Brahms as Liberal," 115; and idem, *Lateness and Brahms*, 17. For an eye-witness testimony to the musical erudition of Vienna's best liberal critics and most

that musical culture in late-nineteenth-century Vienna can be divorced from politics and society.

Yet for all that, much in this field remains to be done. As Benjamin Korstvedt has suggested, even new findings may need to be reconsidered.[14] It is most critical, in my view, to expand beyond this focus on Brahms and Bruckner and the musical politics associated with them, and to ground our discussion in a nuanced reading of liberal ideology and contemporary political tensions. The partisanship in Vienna surrounding the music of Antonín Dvořák and Bedřich Smetana was no less fierce than that attaching to the music of Brahms and Bruckner—and was, in fact, more clearly tied to pressing political concerns. The "Czech question" that so dominated late Habsburg politics and social policy merits further exploration, as it was clearly a central concern to the city's critics in their reviews of music by composers from the Bohemian crown lands. And though it certainly cannot be said that the "Jewish question" has suffered any lack of musicological attention—both Botstein and Notley, for example, rightly stress the central role played by educated Jews in Viennese liberalism and musical culture alike—this has not always been treated with the subtlety that the complex subject deserves. These, then, are the gaps in our understanding that I shall begin to fill in the pages that follow.

The Political Context

It will be useful at the outset to flesh out Gellner's tale of the "Habsburg dilemma" with which we began. The third quarter of the nineteenth century saw the German liberal nationalists rise from defeat in 1848 to ascendance during the 1860s and 1870s in all walks of Austrian public life. Two developments that were central to the liberals' initial triumphs also carried portents of difficulties that lay ahead in the years after 1880. On the one hand,

accomplished amateurs, see Arnold Schoenberg, "New Music, Outmoded Music, Style and Idea," in *Style and Idea: Selected Writings of Arnold Schoenberg*, ed. Leonard Stein, trans. Leo Black (Berkeley and Los Angeles: University of California Press, 1985), 120–21.

[14] Benjamin Korstvedt, "The Critics and the Quintet: a Study in Musical Representation," in *Anton Bruckners Wiener Jahre: Analysen—Fakten—Perspektiven. Wiener Bruckner-Studien 1*, ed. Renate Grasberger, Elisabeth Maier, and Erich Wolfgang Partsch (Vienna: Musikwissenschaftlicher Verlag, 2009), 145–66; and idem, "Reading Music Criticism Beyond the Fin-de-siècle Vienna Paradigm," *Musical Quarterly* 94 (2011): 156–210.

Prussia's resounding defeat of the Habsburg military in the Seven Weeks' War of 1866 shifted the balance of power decidedly away from the discredited aristocracy and military, two of the monarchy's traditional "pillars," to use Oszkár Jászi's famous metaphor, in favor of the new men of the middle and upper bourgeoisie who were representative, as Gellner suggests, of significant new pillars.[15] Yet, by affirming Prussian superiority in the German sphere, this defeat also shattered once and for all the old liberal dream of achieving a unification of the German people under Austrian leadership, while eventually giving stimulus to a radical *deutschnational* dream that implied breakup of the Habsburg Empire and absorption of *Deutschösterreich* into Bismarck's state. Equally significant was the *Österreich-Ungarischer Ausgleich* (Austro-Hungarian Compromise) negotiated in 1867, which established a Dual Monarchy, divided roughly along the Leitha River, whereby Hungary (or Transleithania, from the Viennese point of view) was granted autonomy in matters lying outside foreign and military policy. This not only ensured German dominance in the Austrian half of the monarchy (Cisleithania) but inevitably raised the hopes of the empire's other nationalities for achieving a degree of autonomy of their own—all of which could only be read as threatening to German liberal hegemony and the imperial center on which it rested.

In December 1867, seeking to secure the loyalty and support of the powerful *Bildungsbürgertum* (educated middle class) in this dramatically changed environment, Francis Joseph reluctantly ratified a set of five Fundamental Laws that effectively amounted to a liberal constitution. (Although the word *constitution* was not used, the Fundamental Laws came to be known as the December Constitution.) At the same time, the emperor appointed Austria's first parliamentary cabinet, the *Bürgerministerium* (Bürger Ministry).[16] The German Liberal Party (often called the Constitutional Party) had been formed six years earlier, at the beginning of the liberal thaw that followed twelve years of postrevolutionary neo-absolutism, but this loosely held coalition eventually began to splinter into various ever-changing formations that went under such names as the Progressive Club, the United Left, the German Austrian Club, the German Club, and the United German Left. The term "left" may be misleading, since the liberals' economic platform was largely one of laissez-faire capitalism. But in addition to serving as representatives

---

[15] Oszkár Jászi, *The Dissolution of the Habsburg Monarchy* (1929; reprint ed., Chicago: University of Chicago Press, 1961).

[16] Hereafter the name *Austria* will refer to the entire Habsburg Empire for the years before 1867 but solely to Cisleithania for the years thereafter.

of industry, the chambers of commerce, and high finance, the liberals also appealed to professional people, the well-educated middle and upper-middle classes, much of the bureaucracy, and those who wished to minimize the influence of the Roman Catholic Church, above all in matters related to public education. Liberal electoral dominance was ensured at first by a highly restrictive curial system that limited the right to vote to males who passed certain thresholds of income or education—the means by which, according to liberal ideology, one could demonstrate that he had acquired the level of social responsibility necessary for full civic participation. In effect, the political *Bürgertum* on which the German liberals built their successes in the 1860s and 1870s consisted primarily of Gellner's new men.[17]

The liberals' nationalist project was of the civic, not ethnic, variety, to invoke the familiar distinction most closely associated with Hans Kohn, but without the implication that the one was necessarily "good" and the other "bad," and that there could never be an overlapping between the two.[18] Writing in 1861, Johann Nepomuk Berger, a Forty-Eighter and later a member of the Bürger Ministry, could not have been more explicit in stating this mission: "The Germans in Austria...should strive not for political hegemony, but for cultural hegemony among the peoples of Austria." They should "carry culture to the east, transmit the propaganda of German intellection, German science, German humanism."[19] Herein lies a perfect representation, at least from the point of view of contemporary American multiculturalism, of what we might call the "liberal paradox." As Pieter M. Judson has argued,

[17] For a convenient overview of Austrian liberalism in the period between 1848 and 1879, see John W. Boyer, *Political Radicalism in Late Imperial Vienna: Origins of the Christian Social Movement 1848–1897* (Chicago and London: University of Chicago Press, 1981), 1–39. A more detailed account of the liberal state is found in Pieter M. Judson, *Exclusive Revolutionaries: Liberal Politics, Social Experience, and National Identity in the Austrian Empire, 1848–1914* (Ann Arbor: University of Michigan Press, 1996). Jonathan Kwan, *Liberalism and the Habsburg Monarchy, 1861–1895* (London: Palgrave Macmillan, 2013), appeared too late to be used in this study.

[18] The classic study is Hans Kohn, *The Idea of Nationalism: A Study of Its Origins and Background* (New York: Macmillan, 1944). For more recent relevant work, see Rogers Brubaker, "The Manichean Myth: Rethinking the Distinction Between 'Civic' and 'Ethnic' Nationalism," in *Nation and National Identity: The European Experience in Perspective*, ed. Hanspeter Kriesl, Klaus Armingeon, Hannes Siegrist, and Andreas Wimmer (Chur and Zurich: Verlag Rüegger, 1999), 55–71.

[19] Johann Nepomuk Berger, *Zur Lösung der österreichischen Verfassungsfrage* (Vienna, 1861), 19; quoted in translation in Carl E. Schorske, *Fin-de-siècle Vienna: Politics and Culture* (New York: Vintage Books, 1981), 117.

claims of cultural superiority were inherent in the discourse of German-Austrian liberalism from the beginning. The liberals who were defeated in 1848 but who eventually achieved their goal of constitutional government twenty years later may have espoused a set of "democratic" principles aimed at dismantling privilege by birth, encouraging free enterprise, and reducing the power of the church, but they did so within a framework of strict German elitism. The obvious contradiction embodied in this project in the context of the multinational Habsburg state was glossed over by an almost religious devotion to the idea of "culture."[20] Thus *Deutschtum* (Germanness) and bourgeois cultural values were treated as though they were one and the same: to be liberal was to be German; to be German was to be liberal. The idea of race or what would later be called ethnicity had little to do with this particular construction of social identity. Indeed, liberal nationalists—as Berger's imperative suggests—tended to treat national and class identities not as fixed categories, but as contingent ones, insofar as one could theoretically remedy inadequacies in either through education and acculturation.[21] In effect, nationalism was conceived here "as an ideology of public integration in Central and Eastern Europe, one that would eventually wipe away the backward and particularistic attitudes held by uneducated peasants and Slavs, joining them all in a great German liberal nation."[22]

Of all the monarchy's "non-German" social groups, none was more strongly attracted to this ideology than the Jews, who, as Marsha Rozenblit has noted, "rapidly modernized, shed Jewish particularisms, and embraced German culture, liberal politics, and Habsburg dynastic loyalty."[23] The liberals' defense of full citizenship rights for Jews—enshrined in the December Constitution—thus can be seen as rewarding the efforts made by urban middle-class Jews to

---

[20] I have borrowed this neat formulation from Scott Spector, "Another Zionism: Hugo Bergmann's Circumscription of Spiritual Territory," *Journal of Contemporary History* 34 (1999): 89n.

[21] Pieter M. Judson, "Rethinking the Liberal Legacy," in *Rethinking Vienna 1900*, ed. Steven Beller (New York and Oxford: Berghahn, 2001), 66–67.

[22] Pieter M. Judson, "Frontier Germans: The Invention of the *Sprachgrenze*," in *Identität Kultur Raum: Kulturelle Praktiken und die Ausbildung von Imagined Communities in Nordamerika u{n}d Zentraleuropa*, ed. Susan Ingram, Markus Reisenleitner, and Cornelia Szobó-Knotik (Vienna: Turia + Kant, 2000), 86. See also idem, "Frontiers, Islands, Forests, Stones: Mapping the Geography of a German Identity in the Habsburg Monarchy, 1848–1900," in *The Geography of Identity*, ed. Patricia Yaeger (Ann Arbor: University of Michigan Press, 1996), 385.

[23] Marsha L. Rozenblit, "The Jews of the Dual Monarchy," *Austrian History Yearbook* 23 (1992): 160.

overcome social difference by adopting German bourgeois cultural norms such as education and property ownership. Seen in this way, *Deutschtum* was a matter of "conviction and achievement."[24] And if Jews could become Germans, so too, reasoned the liberals, could ambitious members of any other group. Indeed, the German bourgeoisie tended to assume that this was the natural state of affairs, that upwardly mobile Bürger of all nationalities within the state, as they became financially successful and better educated, would perforce come to iden-tify themselves as German.[25]

Yet this project soon began to go awry. Rather than increase the ranks of self-styled Germans in the Austrian bourgeoisie, liberal reforms in education, electoral law, and rights of association only served to strengthen nationalist sen-timent among the middle classes of the non-German nationalities. The Czech bourgeoisie, for example, claiming ethnicity as the basis of its social identity, resisted the German liberal imperative, and despite common interests with the German-speaking bourgeoisie, this group—aiming to achieve what their Hungarian counterparts had won in the *Ausgleich*—focused on winning auton-omy from the powerful central bureaucracy in Vienna.[26] Thus, departing from the liberalism that they themselves had espoused in 1848, these Czech nation-alists (united at first in the Czech National Party) joined with the Bohemian nobility (the so-called Feudal Conservatives) in favoring a decentralized, federal-ist structure of government, reasoning that the Habsburgs would be more recep-tive to arguments for autonomy based on the historic rights of the Bohemian Crown (to which the nobility appealed) than to those invoking the natural right of self-determination (which would have been more in keeping with the revolu-tionary ideals of 1848).[27] To the German liberals, then, Czech nationalism came to be identified with the forces of reaction and thus to be seen as a threat to the general liberal ideals of progress and civilization.

[24] I have borrowed this apt characterization from Steven Beller, review of Pieter M. Judson, *Exclusive Revolutionaries: Liberal Politics, Social Experience, and National Identity in the Austrian Empire, 1848–1914*, in *Central European History 33* (2000): 559–60.

[25] Pieter M. Judson, "Inventing Germans: Class, Nationality and Colonial Fantasy at the Margins of the Habsburg Monarchy," in *Nations, Colonies and Metropoles*, ed. Daniel A. Segal and Richard Handler, special edition of *Social Analysis 33* (1993): 49.

[26] As Eagle Glassheim notes, for example, by the 1860s improving economic fortunes and growing middle-class status had brought Czechs to "a critical juncture in their national development. They could achieve enough of their aspirations as Czechs to obviate the need to assimilate [to Germandom]." Eagle Glassheim, "Between Empire and Nation: The Bohemian Nobility, 1880–1918," in *Constructing Nationalities in East Central Europe*, ed. Pieter M. Judson and Marsha L. Rozenblit (New York and Oxford: Berghahn, 2005), 70.

[27] Ibid., 69.

Longstanding tension between Germans and Czechs came to a head in 1879. After holding power for most of the previous twelve years, the liberals fell out of favor with Francis Joseph, above all on account of their opposition to the Austrian occupation of Bosnia-Herzegovina, which promised to increase the size of the monarchy's Slavic population and thereby threaten the Germans' hegemonic position. The emperor thereupon asked Count Eduard von Taaffe, an old friend from childhood, to head a new cabinet as minister-president and oversee new elections. After engineering the liberals' defeat at the polls, Taaffe formed a governing coalition (the so-called Iron Ring) consisting not only of conservatives, federalist aristocrats, and a small contingent of Polish nobles from Galicia, but also of a substantial bloc of deputies from the bourgeois Czech National Party, which ended its lengthy boycott of the Reichsrat (Imperial Council), as the Cisleithanian parliament was called, in order to take part in the new government. No one has described the effect of this development more succinctly than A. J. P. Taylor: "In August, 1879, Taaffe became Prime Minister. German hegemony in Austria was ended."[28]

From the start, Taaffe's government seemed to favor Slavic, and especially Czech, interests at the expense of traditional German prerogatives. In response to these setbacks, younger German bourgeois activists increasingly adopted a particularist project of German nationalism, involving a decided defense of *Nationalbesitzstand* (national property). Here we find a new kind of exclusionary process, whereby *Deutschtum* came to be defined in racial rather than cultural terms.[29] This not only exacerbated tensions between Germans and Slavs in areas of the monarchy in which both nationalities were represented in significant numbers but also fed the rise of racialist antisemitism. In Judson's provocative view, this ethno-nationalist turn represented not any failure of liberalism (as Carl A. Schorske posited in his influential *Fin-de-siècle Vienna*), but rather its most complete and logical manifestation.

---

[28] A. J. P. Taylor, *The Habsburg Monarchy, 1809–1918: A History of the Austrian Empire and Austria-Hungary* (Chicago: University of Chicago Press, 1948), 155. As Jeremy King has put it, "Almost overnight, Czech leaders shifted from organizing boycotts of the Austrian Parliament to organizing ministries" (Jeremy King, *Budweisers into Czechs and Germans: A Local History of Bohemian Politics, 1848–1948*, Princeton: Princeton University Press, 2002: 55). On Taaffe's government, see William A. Jenks, *Austria Under the Iron Ring, 1879–1893* (Charlottesville: University Press of Virginia, 1965).

[29] Pieter M. Judson, "'Not Another Square Foot!': German Liberalism and the Rhetoric of National Ownership in 19th-Century Austria," *Austrian History Yearbook* 26 (1995): 83–97.

Deutschliberal, nationalliberal, deutschnational: *Three Generations of Music Critics*

This book is set in what has been called Liberal Vienna. The term "liberal" refers, above all, to a political ideology and to the political elite that championed it. But it can also be fruitfully extended to refer to the social and intellectual leadership of the middle-class society the liberal movement was creating. Although I shall make use of both senses of the term, it is with artistic and intellectual elites within the world of music, and especially with Vienna's music critics, that I am primarily concerned.[30]

We can think of the bounds of this Viennese political-cultural milieu as extending from roughly 1861, when Francis Joseph began to move reluctantly toward allowing constitutional rule, to 1897, when the emperor, in an act that sealed the end of liberal control of Vienna's municipal government, no less reluctantly ratified the mayoral election of the Christian Social Karl Lueger, who had campaigned on an explicitly antisemitic platform. These years saw a dramatic transformation in the look of the city, as new buildings arose along the Ringstrasse, the grand circular avenue that had been laid out during the 1860s over the old glacis that had for centuries surrounded the Inner City but by then served only to separate it from the growing suburbs that lay just beyond. First to open, in 1869, was the new Court Opera Theater, built in a neo-Renaissance style. This would be followed over the next few decades by the erection of several other imposing structures, each made in imitation of one historical style or another, that together stand as a powerful visual expression of the rising liberals' conservative cultural values.[31]

Writing near the beginning of the age, Hanslick boasted that Vienna had progressed "from the patriarchal-aristocratic subjugation of art to its complete democratization."[32] This is a judgment that only a liberal elite could have made, since concert music was scarcely accessible to the broader public and opera only

---

[30] For a succinct discussion of the general cultural earmarks of Liberal Vienna, see David S. Luft, *Eros and Inwardness in Vienna: Weininger, Musil, Doderer* (Chicago and London: University of Chicago Press, 2003), 14–22. On liberal musical culture in Vienna and Brahms's leading position within it, see Notley, *Lateness and Brahms*.

[31] For an excellent introduction, see Schorske, *Fin-de-siècle Vienna*, 24–115. For a summary condemnation of the liberals' historicist taste in this regard, see Notley, *Lateness and Brahms*, 74.

[32] Eduard Hanslick, *Geschichte des Concertwesens in Wien* (Vienna: Wilhelm Braumüller, 1869), xiii. Notley, from whom I have taken my translation, quotes this telling passage from Hanslick's history of Vienna's concert life in her "'Volkskonzerte' in Vienna," 422–23, and *Lateness and Brahms*, 159.

somewhat more so. Each year, for example, the Vienna Philharmonic offered but a limited series of eight subscription concerts.[33] These were given on Sundays beginning at 12:30 in the afternoon in a season running from November through the early spring. During the 1860s the concerts took place in the Theater am Kärntnertor, which also housed the Court Opera. When the new Court Opera Theater opened nearby in 1869, the Kärntnertor-Theater was slated for demolition, and in 1870 the orchestra relocated its concerts to the magnificent large hall of the newly opened Gesellschaft der Musikfreunde, located just outside the Inner City in the Fourth District. Given the orchestra's limited number of performances each year and the relatively limited seating in the Musikverein (as the Gesellschaft der Musikfreunde was known locally), the demand for tickets was correspondingly high, as was the social status that came with the expensive subscription.[34] Thus Hugo Wolf would seem to have gotten closer than Hanslick to the elitist truth when, in a biting preview of the orchestra's 1884–85 season, he wrote:

> The public flocks to the Philharmonic not only because it has no other easy way of satisfying its hunger for music, but also because fashion dictates that one be seen there. Whoever can produce a season ticket to the Philharmonic concerts is to the unfortunates who cannot as are fat people, with their substantial shadows, to the tragic schlemiels who, casting no shadow at all, have no right to existence.[35]

Another critic put the same matter more succinctly, if with less rhetorical flourish: "The Philharmonic concerts, above all, have a place among what is fashionable within our upper middle class; it is a mark of good breeding to be a subscriber."[36]

---

[33] On the history of the orchestra, see Richard Perger, *Denkschrift: Zum Feier des fünf- zigjährigen ununterbrochenen Bestandes der Philharmonischen Konzerte in Wien 1860–1910* (Vienna and Leipzig: Carl Fromme, 1910); and Clemens Hellsberg, *Demokratie der Könige: Die Geschichte der Wiener Philharmoniker* (Zurich, Vienna, and Mainz: Schweizer Verl.-Haus, 1992).

[34] The large hall could accommodate audiences numbering just over two thousand persons, including standing room for three hundred.

[35] "Ein Monolog nacherzählt von Hugo Wolf," *Wiener Salon-Blatt*, November 1, 1884, in *Hugo Wolfs Kritiken im Wiener Salonblatt*, 2 vols. (Vienna: Musikwissenschaftlich er Verlag, 2002), 1: 58. I have adapted my translation from Hugo Wolf, *The Music Criticism of Hugo Wolf*, ed., trans., and annot. Henry Pleasants (New York: Holmes & Meir, 1978), 75.

[36] Anonymous (signed "x."), "Unser Konzertpublikum," *Fremden-Blatt*, November 25, 1888; transl. in Notley, "'Volkskonzerte' in Vienna," 442.

This situation is scarcely reflective, then, of a complete democratization of concert life as we might imagine such an idea today. But this is a "contradiction" that would not have occurred to Hanslick or probably any other critic at the time. If, as suggested above, the liberals' notion of democracy existed within a framework of German cultural elitism, then it also existed within a framework of socioeconomic exclusivity. Hanslick's claim about democracy in concert life fits within both frames. In the liberal state, full political participation was to be limited to those men—women had no political rights of their own—who embodied bourgeois cultural values such as education, independence, property ownership, and reason. And these attributes, in turn, seem a perfect description of the "new men" who, along with their wives, could be seen in the Musikverein on a Sunday afternoon.

In one perhaps unintended sense, however, Hanslick was on the mark with his talk of democracy. Although the Philharmonic consisted entirely of members of the Court Opera Orchestra, it was nevertheless independent of the court and made its repertorial and all other decisions by a vote of all its members, who delegated the organization's day-to-day management to an elected administrative committee (known as the *Comité*). The Philharmonic players, then, constituted something like one of those independent bourgeois voluntary associations that throughout the period under question, as Judson as shown, played key roles in the development of a liberal political culture outside the state bureaucracy.

It is not surprising, then, that the selection of repertoire by the Philharmonic players was sometimes bound up in matters of politics, although many other factors, of course, also came into play. This was true as well, though for different reasons, at the Court Opera. Moreover, the music-critical discourse to which these various repertorial selections gave rise frequently showed signs of political positioning. Assessing music criticism is tricky business, however. For one thing, we must be careful to assume no perfect correspondence between the critical and popular assessment of any work of art—although it must also be said that Liberal Vienna, where influential figures such as Hanslick and Ludwig Speidel (1830–1906) held forth in their roles as music and theater critic, respectively, for the establishment *Neue Freie Presse* (founded in 1864), does seem to offer something of a special case, at least for the educated social class to which these critics' writing was directed.[37] "The connection between critic and public was close," as the younger critic Max Graf recalled with barely concealed sarcasm.

---

[37] Recent work on Hanslick includes two multiauthored essay collections: *Eduard Hanslick zum Gedenken: Bericht des Symposions zum Anlass seines 100. Todestages*, ed. Theophil

Theatergoers and first-nighters...would wait several days for the appearance of Speidel's criticism, before they knew whether they liked a new play or not. There was perfect teamwork between critics like Speidel and Hanslick and newspaper readers in Vienna. Writers knew how to write, and readers knew how to read.[38]

And Graf knew of what he told. The anonymous author of one late-century feuilleton put it thus: "The Philharmonic's public is mostly reserved in judging new works. What will 'He' have to say about it? Only after 'He' has spoken does one come forth with one's own opinion with reassuring aplomb." It is surely striking that this observer saw no need whatsoever to identify the powerful Hanslick by name as Vienna's leading musical tastemaker.[39]

At the same time, we must always be mindful of the range of motivations that may have come into play in a critic's response. When, as was not infrequently the case, one critic writes that an audience had received a work warmly and another writes that it had not, we can be sure that we are not dealing with objective reporting on any given performance. Moreover, the viciously negative criticism of Bruckner during the 1880s by Max Kalbeck and Gustav Dömpke may to some degree reflect, as Korstvedt has suggested, a desire on the part of these budding young critics, both expatriate Germans, to curry favor with the powerful Hanslick.[40] The overwhelmingly negative *Bruckner-Bild* of Hanslick

Antonicek, Gernot Gruber, and Christoph Landerer (Tutzing: Hans Schneider, 2010); and *Rethinking Hanslick: Music, Formalism, and Expression*, ed. Nicole Grimes, Siobhán Donovan, and Wolfgang Marx (Rochester: University of Rochester Press, 2013). See also Kevin C. Karnes, *Music, Criticism, and the Challenge of History: Shaping Modern Musical Thought in Late Nineteenth-Century Vienna* (Oxford: Oxford University Press, 2008), 21–75; and Dana Gooley, "Hanslick and the Institution of Criticism," *Journal of Musicology* 28 (2011): 289–324. On Speidel, see Ludwig Hevesi, "Ludwig Speidel," *Biographisches Jahrbuch und deutscher Nekrolog (1906)*, ed. Anton Bettelheim (Berlin: Reimer, 1908), 193–223; idem, *Ludwig Speidel: Eine literarisch-biographische Würdigung* (Berlin: Meyer & Jessen, 1910); and Hildegard Kernmayer, *Judentum im Wiener Feuilleton (1848–1903): Exemplarische Untersuchungen zum literarästhetischen und politischen Diskurs der Moderne* (Tübingen: Max Niemoyer, 1998), 191–204.

[38] Max Graf, *Composer and Critic: Two Hundred Years of Musical Criticism* (London: Chapman & Hall, 1947), 273–74.

[39] Anonymous (signed "x."), in *Fremden-Blatt*, November 25, 1888. As Karen Painter and Bettina Varwig have suggested, cultural criticism had a greater impact on music reception than on the reception of other art forms, if only because access to live performance was so limited; see Painter and Varwig, "Mahler's German-Language Critics," in *Mahler and His World*, ed. Karen Painter (Princeton and Oxford: Princeton University Press, 2002), 267.

[40] Korstvedt, "The Critics and the Quintet," 148–53.

himself, we should note, may well be related in part to his belief that the "uneducated" composer lacked the academic qualifications for the appointment he received in 1875 to the faculty of the University of Vienna and that the subject he taught there—music theory—was, owing to its applied nature, properly a matter for conservatory training, not university study.[41] Or consider the case of Speidel, who in addition to his work for the *Neue Freie Presse* served as the music critic for the *Fremden-Blatt* (founded in 1847), another paper read widely within the educated middle class. Although this important critic championed Brahms early on, he later turned against him for what seems to have been largely personal reasons rather than any that had to do with his music.[42]

For these reasons, among others, we do well not to overestimate the value of music criticism in understanding the quotidian musical life of the past.[43] But that is not my aim. Nor is my project a reception history of the music of any given composer, although, to be sure, the critical reception of music by three composers in particular will be the subject of much discussion. Instead my interest falls primarily on the critics themselves, whom I treat as agents in the public sphere whose music-critical writing gave voice to distinct, sometimes competing ideological positions. I believe that what was often at stake in the reception of this music was the question of what did and did not count as German—and to whom.

Because of their obvious implications in this central ideological question, liberal nationalism, German nationalism, and racialist antisemitism—each touched upon in Gellner's account of the Habsburg dilemma—figured strongly in the music-critical discourse of the day.[44] Hanslick upheld traditional

---

[41] On the leading role played by Hanslick in hindering Bruckner's appointment, at least at first, see "Der General-Baß im philosophischen Professoren-Collegium," *Die Presse*, December 25, 1875. See also Manfred Wagner, "Bruckner and Hanslick," in *Eduard Hanslick zum Gedenken*, 311–12.

[42] Kalbeck, *Johannes Brahms* 2: 428. Although the *Fremden-Blatt*, the official organ of the Ministry of Foreign Affairs, did not feature arts coverage to the same degree as the political dailies, its music critic was a force to be reckoned with, as we shall see. For a dated but still useful study, see Charlotte Pinter, *Ludwig Speidel als Musikkritiker* (Ph.D.diss., University of Vienna, 1949).

[43] Leon Botstein, "The Consequences of History and Criticism," *Musical Quarterly* 94 (2011): 1–8; idem, "Music in History: The Perils of Method in Reception History," *Musical Quarterly* 89 (2007): 1–10; and idem, "Music and Its Public," 863–88. See also Korstvedt, "The Critics and the Quintet," and idem, "Reading Music Criticism Beyond the Fin-de-siècle Vienna Paradigm."

[44] Anticlericalism, by contrast, though it was a key element in liberal ideology, is less directly connected to the question of Germanness in music and in any case is rarely

deutschliberal ideology, here understood as being largely synonymous with German liberal nationalism. As long as a work evinced traits that the Prague-born Hanslick understood as German (e.g., seriousness, genuineness, or strength), he was inclined to grant its composer—even those, say, from the Czech lands—status as a German. Signs of the traditional liberal ideology that both Hanslick and Speidel professed is also evident, if only in ways that may at first seem perplexing, in their approach to music by Jewish composers. By contrast to these older German liberal critics, both of whom were Forty-Eighters, Theodor Helm (1843–1920) came of age in the 1860s, and in his role, in effect, as Hanslick's foil at the *Deutsche Zeitung*, the *nationalliberal* (or moderate German nationalist) newspaper founded in 1871 in response to evident Czech gains in Bohemia, he tended to find difference rather than similarity between works by German and Czech composers.[45] He envisioned the symphony, for example, as German *Nationalbesitzstand* rather than as a "German" genre to which composers of other nationalities could successfully acculturate.[46] Although the *Deutsche Zeitung* eventually adopted an openly antisemitic editorial policy, Helm was always relatively discreet in this regard. That cannot be said for a group of still-younger *deutschnational* (radical German nationalist) critics whose student years coincided with the rise of strongly inflected German ethno-nationalism and racialist antisemitism in the 1880s and who subsequently wrote for the upstart *Deutsches Volksblatt* (founded in 1889) and *Ostdeutsche Rundschau* (founded in 1890). Here, in the writings of critics such as August Göllerich (1859–1923), Camillo Horn (1860–1941), Hans Puchstein (1865–1937), Joseph Czerny (1869–1942), and August Püringer (1874–?), we find a full-blown *völkisch* cultural critique, rooted in Wagner's writings, whereby essentialist "German" and "non-German" traits were opposed in a set of binary oppositions that always

encountered openly in the writings with which I am concerned; for this reason, it will be addressed only in passing.

[45] On Helm, see Michael Krebs, "Theodor Helm (1843–1920): Ein Musikschriftsteller im Umkreis von Anton Bruckner" (Ph.D. diss., University of Vienna, 1999).

[46] As Judson notes ("'Not Another Square Foot!': German Liberalism and the Rhetoric of National Ownership in 19th-Century Austria," 83n), the term *Nationalbesitzstand* was frequently used metaphorically to connote "the cultural and intellectual capital of an imaginary German nation," including "not only the achievements of German speakers and their cultural institutions, but also the degree of cultivation and the moral capacity of the larger German community." To base a nationalist project on the concept of "property"—metaphorical or not—is a clear reflection of liberal ideology, in which property ownership was valued as a sign of social maturity. As we shall discover, it is in the metaphorical sense that the concept of *Nationalbesitzstand* first becomes relevant to music, although a more literal understanding of the concept would eventually come into play as well.

privileged the former against an "Other" that more often than not meant the Jews and those closely associated with them.[47]

With all these gradations and distinctions in mind, I focus in this book on the discourse found in the critical reception of new works by a select group of contemporary "Austrian" composers of either Jewish or Czech heritage. If, as we shall discover, the commingling of liberal ideals with a belief in German cultural supremacy played out most obviously in the liberals' vigorous defense of German language use in the multilingual state, something of the same thing can be seen within the high-cultural sphere in the Viennese critical reception of music by prominent "non-German" composers who lived within the monarchy's borders. This is especially evident with regard to the music of Carl Goldmark (1830–1915), a Hungarian-born Jew who made his home in Vienna, and the Czech composers Bedřich Smetana (1824–1884) and Antonín Dvořák (1841–1904).

Goldmark's first musical triumphs took place in the 1860s, coinciding with the establishment of a dominant German liberal political culture that (formally, at least) welcomed full Jewish participation. Goldmark's music would soon become ubiquitous on Viennese programs and remain in vogue over the last forty years of the century, even as the climate for Jews more generally began to chill somewhat toward the end with the rise of antisemitism. The music of the two Czech composers, by contrast, lagged some fifteen years or more behind that of Goldmark in gaining a hearing in the imperial capital, and by the time the Viennese did begin to encounter Smetana's and Dvořák's work, beginning in the 1880s, the "new men" who formed the core of the city's cultural establishment had, as a class, come to feel under siege by broad Czech advancements in the public sphere. There is a rich and complex story to be told here in what the city's music critics made of all this.

These critics published in a variety of media, including specialist music journals, literary journals, and, of course, daily and weekly newspapers. Far and away the bulk of my attention is focused on the writings that appeared in the daily political press, especially in the form of the front-page feuilleton, that characteristic Viennese genre of cultural criticism that appeared *unter dem Strich* ("below the line").[48] I am always interested in what Hanslick and

---

[47] For a convenient tabular presentation of this dichotomy, see Notley, "Bruckner and Viennese Wagnerism," 62. Notley credits Ernest Hanisch, "The Political Influence and Appropriation of Wagner," trans. Paul Knight, in *Wagner Handbook*, ed. Ulrich Müller and Peter Wapnewski (Cambridge, MA: Harvard University Press, 1992), 191.

[48] For a good introduction to this Viennese specialty with respect to music, see Sandra McColl, *Music Criticism in Vienna 1896–1897: Critically Moving Forms*

Helm had to say about a work, and because of Speidel's influence in the liberal community, I pay considerable attention, too, to his music-critical writings. Pride of place among the critics, of course, falls to Hanslick. Even before the dawning of Liberal Vienna, he had established himself as a powerful and influential figure at *Die Presse* and through his writing for other organs, and he dominated the field of music criticism—and many other spheres of musical life—right through the turn of the century.[49] It was not for nothing that he was named a *Hofrat* (Court Councilor) in 1886. Speidel was in many ways almost equally powerful as a music critic, and, like Hanslick, he was active throughout the period covered by this book. But whereas Hanslick, who descended from Czech speakers on his father's side and Jews on his mother's side, wrote in telling ideological terms on the music of Goldmark, Smetana, and Dvořák, Speidel is most interesting, as we shall discover, in his writing about Goldmark and the Jewish Question. By contrast, Helm, who enters our story about halfway through with his appointment to the staff of Vienna's most important national liberal newspaper, will draw our attention mostly on account of what he had to say about matters related to the music of the Czechs Dvořák and Smetana. Toward the end I also take up the work of the younger critics who wrote for the *Deutsches Volksblatt* and *Ostdeutsche Rundschau*, political organs, as suggested, of a very different order.[50]

In a few case studies—the first performance of Goldmark's *Die Königin von Saba* in 1875, Dvořák's Viennese debut in the fall of 1879, and the performances in Vienna of Smetana's *Bartered Bride* in the early 1890s and *Dalibor* in 1897—I aim to give fairly comprehensive consideration to the critical reception as a way of providing a snapshot of the political terrain at one key historical moment or another. Here, then, I widen my focus to include the work of a larger number of other, mostly liberal critics, including Eduard

(Oxford: Clarendon Press, 1996), 1–8. For useful thumbnail biographies of many of the critics with whom we shall be concerned and succinct characterizations of the newspapers for which they wrote, see ibid., 11–32, and Vlasta Reittererová and Hubert Reitterer, *Vier Dutzend rothe Strümpfe... Zur Rezeptionsgeschichte der Verkauften Braut von Bedřich Smetana in Wien am Ende des 19. Jahrhunderts* (Vienna: Verlag der Österreichischen Akademie der Wissenschaften, 2004), 407–37.

[49] *Die Presse* was founded in 1848 as the cultivated voice of Vienna's *Bildungsbürgertum*, loyal to the ideals of the Revolution but wary of social upheaval and ethno-nationalism. Although it continued to publish until 1896, its influence waned after 1864, when several of its editors and writers, including Hanslick, bolted and founded the *Neue Freie Presse*.

[50] The *Ostdeutsche Rundschau* began as a weekly publication in April 1890 but changed to a daily publication schedule in October 1893.

Kulke (1831–1897), Wilhelm Frey (1833–1909), Max Kalbeck (1850–1921), Albert Kauders (1854–1912), and Robert Hirschfeld (1859–1914).[51] But in general I focus on Hanslick, Speidel, Helm, and the radical fin-de-siècle critics, because I believe their work serves especially well to reveal the changes in political ideology and the contested notions of German identity in Liberal Vienna with which we are concerned.[52]

This book is organized chronologically in two large parts of four chapters each, followed by an extended epilogue. Part I covers the period, extending from the 1840s through the 1870s, that saw the emergence and eventual, albeit short-lived, triumph of Austrian German liberalism. Chapter 1 is set largely in the *Vormärz*, the period immediately preceding the March Revolution in 1848, when Hanslick, in effect, defined his Germanness during a time when he might have chosen to be Czech. Chapter 2, devoted to the young Goldmark, is similarly concerned with the embrace of a German identity. Here and elsewhere in the book, I write at some length on Goldmark's biography, not only because he remains a relatively unknown figure today, despite his earlier widespread acclaim, but also because he was a significant figure, in a way that the two Czech composers obviously were not, in the everyday social and cultural life of Liberal Vienna. Chapter 3 is set in the liberal heyday of the 1860s and 1870s, which saw Goldmark's breakthrough and reputational establishment with Vienna's liberal public in a series of works that Hanslick and Speidel struggled, paradoxically and much to the composer's dismay, to align with the liberal project. (Here the two critics' influence over the public was limited.) This is followed, in Chapter 4, by a new look at a dispute that took place at the Vienna Medical School in 1875 upon the publication of a treatise by the noted surgeon and medical professor Theodor Billroth. Although here we shall turn our attention away from

---

[51] Of this group, all but Kalbeck were Germanized Jews; Kalbeck, as we shall discover, was treated by the antisemites as though he, too, were Jewish. (One occasionally reads that Kalbeck's original family was Karpeles, a fairly common Jewish surname, but there is no documentary evidence to substantiate this identification.) On Kalbeck, a protégé of Hanslick and Brahms's future biographer, see *Max Kalbeck zum 150. Geburtstag*, ed. Uwe Harten (Tutzing: Hans Schneider, 2007). On Hirschfeld, see Botstein, "Music and Its Public," 889–926.

[52] Although he wrote perceptively on many aspects of Viennese concert life in the mid-1880s during his brief stint as the music critic for the *Wiener Salon-Blatt*, Hugo Wolf plays only a peripheral role in this study, not only because the *Salon-Blatt*, a weekly social and gossip organ, was not a daily political newspaper, but also because Wolf, for all his strongly held opinions about musical politics, had little to say about the kinds of sociopolitical issues that concern us here.

music-critical discourse, this discussion is not as far afield from our subject as it may first appear, and not only because Billroth was an accomplished musician, an intimate member of the liberal Brahms-Hanslick circle, and close to Goldmark as well. The sticking point in this controversial book was a brief passage in which the author questioned the fitness of many of his Jewish students from the Eastern provinces for the study of medicine. As I shall argue, his controversial remarks cannot be well understood unless we approach the questions of contemporary anti-Judaic and German-nationalist sentiment that they raise with nuance and sensitivity to context; this lesson will serve us well in our approach to the same questions in the case of Goldmark's reception by Hanslick and Speidel.

The four chapters of Part II are concerned with music-critical discourse in the last two decades of the century, an era, as noted, of lost German hegemony in the political sphere. The Czech Question is taken up for the first time in Chapter 5, devoted primarily to Dvořák's reception in Vienna during the 1880s. The generally less-than-enthusiastic music-critical support for the Czech composer's music at this time is viewed against the backdrop of Taaffe's pro-Slavic policies, which hastened the development of a German nationalism that diverged from the more traditional German liberalism of Hanslick, who, almost alone among Vienna's critics, made room for Dvořák in what he imagined as an ideal German liberal musical community. This divergence is seen especially clearly in the writings of Hanslick and Helm from the second half of the decade, which reveal strong ideological differences between the two critics on the question of Germanness in music. I am concerned here not only with music-critical discourse, however. A reading of materials found in the archive of the Vienna Philharmonic will allow us to gain an inside look at how political tensions between Germans and Czechs affected the orchestra's own internal programming decisions. In Chapter 6 we return to Goldmark's reception and the Jewish Question, now as this unfolded along two separate paths in the 1880s and early 1890s. The beginning of the chapter describes the composer's seeming breakthrough at last in the eyes of Hanslick and Speidel as a fully acculturated German composer; toward the end we consider the antisemitic backlash during these same years against a composer who now sat at the very center of Viennese cultural life.

The Czech Question as it was posed in the early 1890s is explored in Chapter 7. This time it is Smetana rather than Dvořák who stands front and center. What we shall discover here is that, unlike Dvořák and for reasons that may at first seem counterintuitive, Smetana found favor across the entire ideological spectrum, from traditional liberal nationalists like Hanslick, to moderate German nationalists like Helm, and on to the radical German nationalists who wrote for the *Deutsches Volksblatt* and *Ostdeutsche Rundschau*. Chapter 8 returns the focus briefly on Goldmark, who at the fin de siècle felt compelled finally to defend his self-perception as a German artist from attack by antisemitic critics who insisted that he and his music were indelibly Jewish and could never be German.[53] The epilogue is set in 1897, when, as we shall see, all the themes of this study come together at the time of Gustav Mahler's return to Vienna as the head of the Court Opera.

The issues are complex. Too often musicologists have characterized the Brahms-Bruckner critical debate of the 1880s—the focus up to now of most studies on the intersection of music and politics in late-nineteenth-century Vienna—in terms of a liberal and antiliberal divide rather than in terms of an evolving liberalism, often along generational lines, with perspectives running from the *deutschliberal* to the *nationalliberal* to the *deutschnational*.[54] It has been insufficiently recognized, on the one hand, that the older German liberal nationalists' "problem" with Czech nationalism had largely to do with their understanding of it precisely as an antiliberal ideology, and, on the other, that the younger *deutschnational* critics frequently praised Smetana as a model to be emulated by their own imagined community of "German" composers, into which, it sometimes seems, Brahms was no more welcomed than Goldmark. Finally, it has been too easy to forget the uncomfortable truth that racialist nationalism was once thought to be a progressive ideology, and so is resistant to assignment to either the left or right wings of the ideological spectrum. Examination of the work of three generations of music critics offers insight into the diverse ways in which educated German Austrians conceived of Germanness in music and understood their relationship to the "non-Germans" in their midst.

[53] For a thoughtful (and provocative) discussion of "Viennese Jewish Culture" at the end of the century as an invention of Hitler and his forerunners and after-runners, see Ernst Gombrich, *The Visual Arts in Vienna Circa 1900: Reflections on the Jewish Catastrophe* (London: Austrian Cultural Institute, 1997). As we shall see, Goldmark seems never to have imagined that he was doing anything other than German cultural work.

[54] Korstvedt stands somewhat apart here in his suggestion that we ought to read late-century Viennese criticism of Brahms and Bruckner not in terms of liberals and "others," but rather as forming part of a "larger debate of inclusion and exclusion carried out within the circle of the Viennese German-speaking Bürgertum" (emphasis in original); see Korstvedt, "Reading Music Criticism Beyond the Fin-de-Siècle Paradigm," 23–24.

PART ONE

From the *Vormärz* to the Liberal Heyday

| Hanslick's *Deutschtum*

NEAR THE BEGINNING of his autobiography, Eduard Hanslick recalls the social circumstances in which he was reared in Prague during the *Vormärz*.[1] It will be useful to quote this passage *in extenso*:

It goes without saying—nowadays one pretends not to understand this—that before the year [18]48 private as well as public education in Prague was given exclusively in the German language. Aristocracy and bourgeoisie, the entire cultivated middle classes in Prague, spoke only German and could speak only enough Czech to make themselves understood by domestic servants, workers, and peasants. Even my mother, whose parents came from Vienna, and we siblings acquired only this most basic level for use at home. I have never learned to read or write Czech, have never recited the Our Father or multiplication tables in anything other than German, have never been able to decipher a Czech theatrical handbill (which would perhaps have interested me the most). The Prague Theater [Stavovské Divadlo/Ständetheater] was German; only on Sundays at four o'clock in the afternoon, three hours before the beginning of the German performance, would there be a play in Czech. The domestic servants were sent to these Czech performances; no one

---

[1] Eduard Hanslick, *Aus meinem Leben*, 2 vols. (Berlin: Allgemeiner Verein für deutsche Litteratur, 1894; this work first appeared in serialized form in the quarterly *Deutsches Rundschau* 75 (1893).

from our circles ever went. It never occurred to anyone during my time in Prague to doubt the superiority, indeed the exclusive rights, of the Germans in matters of culture, art and science, schooling, and administration. My father commanded both a reading and writing knowledge of Czech; he made the German translation of the Czech poems composed by Tomášek. With us and with his friends, however, he spoke only German. Among these friends were the professor of humanities V. A. Svoboda, one of the most accomplished artists in the Czech language and translators from it; I also recall from my youth repeated visits from other Czech notables of that time: Palacký (who wrote his history of Bohemia, as is well known, in German, so that it would be widely read); Hanka, the famous "discoverer" of the Queen's Court Manuscript [Rukopis královédvorský/Königinhofer Handschrift]; the celebrated physiologist Purkyně; and others. I heard them speak only German with my father. Of course, since they conversed only about learned things, about art and politics, how would Czech have been adequate? Only around the middle of the forties, shortly before my departure to the University of Vienna, did Czech movements become noticeable in public, still completely innocuous and restrained; for example, a concert might contain a Czech chorus or Czech song by Joh[ann] Nep[omuk] Škroup. This was the younger brother of the theatrical Kapellmeister Franz Škroup, who has become well known and famous as a composer on account of a single song, "Kde domov můj?" ("Where is my Home?"). Joh. Nep. Škroup, on the other hand, recently deceased at an advanced age as kapellmeister at Prague Cathedral, composed frightfully much and in a mediocre manner. He was one of the first who, rejected and ignored by the German public, began to rest his cause on the newborn Czech party, that small but vocal minority. Leopold v[on] Hasner, whose period of study also fell in *Vormärz* Prague, says of these efforts: "One overemphasizes the breed [*Gattung*] so as to be able to be vain about being part of it, since as an individual one is nothing; that is national consciousness [*Nationalgefühl*]." If [in the 1840s] anyone prophesied that Prague would in 50 years have its own magnificent Czech Theater, a Czech university, a Czech Academy of Sciences(!) he would have been pronounced crazy. With these splendid achievements of the Czechs, who are coddled by the government, comes also an enmity, a spitefulness in Prague that was unknown in my youth. At that time Germans and Czechs consorted with one another in a friendly manner; the latter knew that whatever they possessed in art and science, industry, and even social graces came from German culture. Today it happens all the time in Prague that one meets old acquaintances who know German as well as we, who address us in Czech and make a violent fuss as soon as they have to think of the German word. And so the Germans in Prague must unfortunately look at it now as the first precept of peaceful self-preservation to seclude themselves as strictly as possible from all Czechs. The final stanza of an unpublished youthful poem by Robert Zimmermann characterizes perfectly our feelings at the first signs of this national discord:

> Czech or German, they say, choose your party!
> Both could easily get along in peace,
> But if you do not wish that, so be it.
> Then I shall side with my German brothers.[2]

As rich as it is in detail, this passage is misleading on a number of counts. For one thing, Hanslick gives his readers to believe that he descended from a German family in the modern, ethnic sense of the word. He not only fails to acknowledge that his father, Josef Adolf Hanslik, was the son of a Czech-speaking farmer in Lissan—note the Czech spelling of the family name—but also that his mother, Carolina Katharina Kisch, was the baptized daughter of a successful Jewish merchant. Jitka Ludvová has suggested that Hanslick's reluctance to describe his parents' background evinces a desire to avoid attack in terms of either the antisemitic or the anti-Czech rhetoric that was increasingly prevalent in fin-de-siècle Vienna.[3] Yet Hanslick's silence on the ethnic and religious background of his parents probably had more than anything to do with his self-perception as a German liberal: as I shall suggest, this was the identity that mattered most to Hanslick, and it

[2] Hanslick, *Aus meinem Leben*, 1: 15–17.
[3] Jitka Ludvová, "Několik pražských reálií k biografii Eduarda Hanslicka," *Miscellanea theatralia: Sborník Adolfu Scherlovi k osmdesátinám*, ed. Eva Šormová and Michaelou Kuklovou (Prague: Divadelní ústav, 2005), 379; German translation, "Einige Prager Realien zum Thema Hanslick," in Antonicek, Gruber, and Landerer, eds., *Eduard Hanslick zum Gedenken*, 163. Also useful on Hanslick's early biography is Jitka Ludvová, *Dokonalý antiwagnerián Eduard Hanslick* (Prague: Supraphon, 1992), 1–36; idem, "Zur Biographie Eduard Hanslicks," *Studien zur Musikwissenschaft* 37 (1986): 37–46; and Ines Grimm, *Eduard Hanslicks Prager Zeit: Frühe Wurzeln seiner Schrift* Vom Musikalisch-Schönen (Saarbrücken: Pfau, 2003), 11–104.

reflected his cultural beliefs, not his racial or ethnic heritage. Nevertheless, we have every reason to suppose that Hanslick's Czech and Jewish roots must have played their part when later, in his role as Vienna's leading music critic, he wrote about music by contemporary Czech and Jewish composers. It will be worthwhile, therefore, to explore Hanslick's early biography for what it may tell us about the formation of his social identity.

Hanslick's Prague

As Hanslick indicates at the outset of the passage from his memoirs quoted above, language use in *Vormärz* Prague had once been, above all, a marker of social class.[4] But he clouds the issue when he writes that the Czechs "knew that whatever they possessed in art and science, industry, and even social graces came from German culture"; here Hanslick is speaking not about a hierarchical relationship between the city's educated middle-class families and those persons who worked for them as domestics and the like, but about the cultural dependence of a "Czech" bourgeoisie upon a "German" one. Yet this implied bifurcation was largely nonexistent. As Gary B. Cohen has argued, in the ethnically charged fin de siècle it was all too easy—as Hanslick does here at times—to project contemporary distinctions between two consciously defined and socially separated groups back to a period before they had come into existence. The Germanized Prague in which Hanslick sets his account is overstated, and in reality one can hardly speak at all of ethnic Germans and ethnic Czechs, but merely of German speakers (in the middle and upper social strata) and Czech speakers (predominant among the workers and the petite bourgeoisie). Distinct German and Czech ethnic groups emerged only gradually in Prague from a wider "Bohemian" population that, before 1848 (and even later in many cases), showed little in the way of articulated ethnic loyalties.[5]

---

[4] As Derek Sayer has noted, in relation to the first half of the nineteenth century: "Bohemia's social divisions had been articulated as a contrast between a world language of culture, civility, and state, and a multiplicity of ignorant local vernaculars. The consolidation of written Czech [in the second half of the nineteenth century] transformed that axis of social difference into a dividing line between two national communities, each now identified and solidified by its own language." See Derek Sayer, *The Coasts of Bohemia: A Czech History* (Princeton: Princeton University Press, 1998), 113.

[5] Gary B. Cohen, *The Politics of Ethnic Survival: Germans in Prague, 1861–1914*, 2nd, rev. ed. (West Lafayette, IN: Purdue University Press, 2006), 18–23. The first chapter of Cohen's study, covering the period to 1861, is entitled "From Bohemians to Czechs and Germans."

The strong patriotic feeling that ran through Prague's educated middle class is suggested by the very name of its newspaper, *Bohemia*, which evoked the territorial-political unit that had been shared by Slavs and Germans for centuries. Paul Aloys Klar maintained the same spirit when he called his important German literary almanac *Libussa* after the legendary tenth-century Princess Libuše, revered as the founder both of the native Přemyslid dynasty and of the Czech people as a whole.[6] Moreover, as Hanslick acknowledges, his father was fluent in both of Bohemia's vernacular languages. Well versed in classical literature, aesthetics, and music, Josef Hanslik held professional employment for most of Eduard's youth in Prague's University Library, even while carrying the primary responsibility for educating his children at home.[7] (Around 1839, however, Josef entrusted Eduard's musical training to Václav Jan Křtitel Tomášek, the doyen of the city's composers, about whom it could be said that he was neither a Czech nor a German but only a Bohemian composer.[8]) Josef Hanslik's standing in the city's intellectual circles is evident from his son's listing of those who regularly visited the family home. These included several men who later played key roles in the Czech "national awakening," most notably František Palacký, known as the "Father of the Nation," but also the philologists Václav Hanka and Václav Svoboda, and the scientist Jan Evangelista Purkyně.[9] The air of cultural superiority inherent in Hanslick's observation that the language of social and intellectual discourse in his father's

---

[6] *Bohemia* was founded in 1828, *Libussa* in 1842. The patriotic significance of the names given to these organs is discussed in Jan Havránek, "The Development of Czech Nationalism," *Austrian History Yearbook* 3 (1967), 235.

[7] On Josef Hanslik, see Hubert Reitterer, "Josef Adolf Hanslik jako knihovník a satirik," *Hudební veda* 43 (2006): 385–406; rev. version in German as "Josef Adolf Hanslik als Bibliotheksbeamter und Satiriker," in Antonicek, Gruber, and Landerer, eds., *Eduard Hanslick zum Gedenken*, 139–62.

[8] Significantly, it was in *Libussa* that Tomášek published his autobiography. This appeared in six installments between 1845 and 1850.

[9] The first volume of Palacký's history was published in 1836; the whole eventually ran to five volumes in ten parts, published over some thirty years (František Palacký, *Geschichte von Böhmen: Grössentheils nach Urkunden und Handschriften*, 5 vols., [Prague: Kronberger und Weber, 1836–1867]). The Czech version, which carried the tellingly different title *Dějiny národu českého v čechách a v Moravě* (History of the Czech nation in Bohemia and Moravia), first began to appear in 1848. We shall return to some of these figures below.

salon was German—could only have been German—is transparent.[10] Yet this aging German liberal also discloses an important truth about the Prague he had known half a century earlier, namely that cultivated middle-class social identity had not yet come to be defined along rigid national lines.

The "liberal, bi-ethnic 'Bohemian' consensus of the decade that preceded the revolution of 1848," as Hillel J. Kieval has described the social and intellectual milieu in which Hanslick came of age, may best be seen in the pages of *Ost und West*, a journal of art, literature, and social life that was edited by a friend and colleague of Hanslick's father at the University Library named Rudolf Glaser.[11] The editor made plain his intentions on the opening page of the first number (dated July 1, 1837):

> The interests of the cultured nations are becoming more and more similar; more and more the spatial and spiritual distance between them is disappearing; and everything that furthers this goal is being taken up with great favor. May this also be a new literary undertaking that serves—not exclusively but chiefly—to establish a literary mediation between the Slavic East and Germany, and thereby contribute to the world literature which is still taking shape. What country would be more appropriate [to this task] than Bohemia, with its half Slavic, half German population; Bohemia, the frontier of the European East and West; a country rich in writers who are familiar with all the Slavic dialects.[12]

In the pages of *Ost und West* could be found original lyrical poetry, translations of folk poetry from the various Slavic traditions, literary criticism, theatrical reviews, and a wide range of political writing that sought to

[10] Hanslick is recalling the pre-March period, but for many of the Czech nationalists of his generation (including Smetana), German would remain the language in which serious discourse came most easily even later in the century. For a succinct account, see Sayer, *The Coasts of Bohemia*, 107–18.

[11] Hillel J. Kieval, "The Social Vision of Bohemian Jews," *Assimilation and Community: The Jews in Nineteenth-Century Europe*, ed. Jonathan Frankel and Steven J. Zipperstein (Cambridge: Cambridge University Press, 1992), 253.

[12] I take my translation from Kieval, "The Social Vision of Bohemian Jews," 279n.

encourage liberal social reform. It was in this journal and its supplement (*Prag*) that the young Eduard Hanslik made his début as a music critic.[13]

Among the other contributors to *Ost und West* were members of a group of writers known collectively as Young Bohemia. Like their counterparts in Young Germany, these men, as one of them later put it, "dreamed all the political ideals of [their] time: free forms of state, equalization of class distinctions, tolerance and peace in the realms of politics and nationalities."[14] Karel Sabina later recalled that at the time it would have been impossible to predict which identity his young contemporaries would ultimately adopt— German or Czech.[15] This was true generally among young Bohemians of Hanslick's generation. Robin Okey cites two examples in which even siblings went in opposite directions on this question. The Prague-born art historian Anton Springer grew up speaking a Slavic dialect, but "became a German as by natural power," unmoved by literature in Czech; his brother, by contrast, became an ardent Czech patriot. Similarly, Jan Evangelista Purkyně (an acquaintance of Hanslick's father, as we have seen) became a Czech national revivalist, while his brother chose a German identity.[16] It was not until the March Revolution that any sharp national division between bourgeois Germans and Czechs really came out into the open, and we may assume that the sentiments expressed in "Mein Böhmerland" (My Bohemian Land)—a poem by Hanslick's friend Robert Zimmermann that one scholar has described as a "hymn of praise to Bohemian utraquism" (i.e., German-Czech bilingualism)—provide an equally accurate representation of Hanslick's own pre-March sensibilities:

[13] Hanslick, *Aus meinem Leben*, 1: 52–56. Hanslick's first review appeared in *Prag* on November 18, 1844; he then contributed several additional concert reviews to this supplement through 1845. His last pieces for Glaser, important longer essays on Berlioz and Schumann, appeared in *Ost und West* in 1846. See Eduard Hanslick, *Sämtliche Schriften: Historisch-kritische Ausgabe*, I/i: *Aufsätze und Rezensionen 1844–1848*, ed. Dietmar Strauß (Vienna, Cologne and Berlin: Böhlau, 1993), 3–57.

[14] Alfred Meißner, *Geschichte meines Lebens*, 2 vols. (Vienna: K. Prochaska, 1884), 1: 54–55. See also Hugh LeCaine Agnew, "Czechs, Germans, Bohemians? Images of Self and Other in Bohemia to 1848," in Wingfield, ed., *Creating the Other*, 60–61; and Kieval, "The Social Vision of Bohemian Jews," 252–54.

[15] Sabina's recollection is cited in Agnew, "Czechs, Germans, Bohemians?" 60. Sabina, one of the writers whose work appeared most frequently in *Ost und West*, eventually identified as a Czech and is best known to musicians as the librettist of Smetana's first two operas.

[16] Robin Okey, *The Habsburg Monarchy c. 1765–1918: From Enlightenment to Eclipse* (New York: Palgrave Macmillan, 2001), 112; Springer is quoted there from his autobiography, *Aus meinem Leben* (Berlin: G. Grote'sche Verlagsbuchhandlung 1892), 1–2, 14–15.

Böhmerland, mein Böhmerland,	Bohemia, my Bohemian land,
Sang- und Sängerhafen,	Haven for song and singers,
Führst an deiner Mutterhand	You guide [both] Germans and Slavs
Deutsche her und Slawen;	With your motherly hand;
Weil dich Einer nicht umfaßt	Because no single one can encompass you
Mit den Liederringen.	With circles of song,
Weil du schon zwei Zungen hast	Because you already have two tongues
Soll'n dich zwei besingen.	Two shall sing your praise.
Čechenblut und deutsches Blut,	Czech blood and German blood,
Sollt Euch friedlich minnen,	You should love one another peaceably,
Kleinen Neid und bösen Muth	Remove petty jealousy and ill humor
Schlagt Euch aus den Sinnen!	From your thoughts!
Aug' in Aug' und Hand in Hand,	Eye meeting eye, hand clasped in hand,
Frisch und fröhlich Beide,	Happily and joyous together,
Böhmerland, mein Böhmerland,	Bohemia, my Bohemian land,
Eins in Leid und Freude!	United in sorrow and joy!

Mein Böhmerland (*Ost und West* 8 [September 27, 1844]),
trans. Meredith Lee

Zimmermann was not the only other contributor to *Ost und West* with whom Hanslick had close connections. Another was the bilingual poet and physician Friedrich Bach, whom we shall meet again in a different context; and still another, a colorful figure named Ferdinand Mikovec. Looking back from later in the century, Alfred Meißner remembered Mikovec as an "old German [who] wanted nothing else than to be a Czech. He worked on Czech history and archaeology, collected every possible historical inscription, provided that they were Czech, and was a poet as well as a patriotic dramatist."[17] With this last remark, Meißner probably had in mind Mikovec's four-act tragedy *Záhuba rodu Přemyslovského* (The demise of the Přemyslid dynasty), set in Prague and Olomouc in 1306, when Václav III, the dynasty's last male heir, was murdered and the throne passed briefly to Rudolf I of Habsburg. Writing in *Ost und West*, a critic identified only as "Jasoň" described the work, which opened in the Ständetheater on January 9, 1848, as "the first successful historical drama in our [Czech] language."[18] Mikovec's play also drew a long review in *Bohemia*, from which we discover that "just as the historical episodes with Dalimil are most appealing, so too is the song "Ha, ty naše slunce" ["Ah, thou, our sun"], newly composed from the Queen's Court Manuscript by Herr Hanslik, which

[17] Meißner, *Geschichte meines Lebens*, 2: 10. Mikovec's contributions to *Ost und West* included pieces on archaeological-historical matters, as well as reviews of German-language theater.

[18] *Ost und West* 12 (1848): 28.

provided genuine pleasure to every ear accustomed to original Slavic, folk-like melody."[19]

Hanslick's Vyšehrad

We shall look in vain for any mention of this Herr Hanslik of Prague in the autobiography of Hofrat Hanslick of Vienna. For the critic to have acknowledged this youthful song—let alone to have owned up to its use in what might now be viewed as a patriotic Czech play—would, of course, have meant complicating the simple picture that he wanted to draw of a Germanized pre-March Prague, while raising obvious questions about his insistence that he had never been able to speak more than simple *küchelböhmisch* (kitchen Bohemian).[20] We can in fact identify at least two extant settings by Hanslick of Czech texts: "Český houslista" ("The Bohemian Violinist") und "Milostná píseň pod Wyšehradem" ("Love Song beneath Vyšehrad").[21] Both appeared under his name in Jan Hoffmann's series *Zlatý zpěwník: Sbírka nejoblíbenějšíich zpěwů od nejwýtečnejšíich wlastenských skládatelů* (The golden songbook: a collection of the most beloved bongs by outstanding patriotic composers; see

---

[19] *Bohemia*, January 14, 1848; this review is signed "H.B."

[20] In a letter to Dvořák of June 11, 1882, Hanslick reported that he was unable to read the Czech texts of the composer's choral pieces *V přírodě* (*In Nature's Realm*), op. 63, but this does not gainsay the likelihood that Hanslick had a decent working knowledge of Czech as a native and resident of Prague forty years earlier. See Antonín Dvořák, *Korespondence a dokumenty: Kritické vydání* [*Correspondence and Documents: Critical Edition*], 10 vols. (Prague: Supraphon, 1987–2004), vol. 5: *Korespondence přijatá 1877–1884* [*Correspondence Received 1877–1884*] (1996): 387. As Cohen notes, until the 1860s or so only the very highest strata of Prague's German-speaking population failed to learn any Czech (Cohen, *The Politics of Ethnic Survival*, 19); and, given that Hanslick's father was bilingual, we may assume that as a young man Eduard knew more Czech than he was later willing to acknowledge.

[21] These songs are briefly discussed in Ludvová, "Zur Biographie Eduard Hanslicks," 43–44; idem, "Několik pražských reálií k biografii Eduarda Hanslicka," 384–86, and Grimm, *Eduard Hanslicks Prager Zeit*, 50–51 (with a reproduction of the first page of "Český houslista"). Evidently Hanslick's compositional activity was limited to the realms of song and short piano pieces. Presumably representative of his best efforts are the *Lieder aus der Jugendzeit*, a set of twelve songs selected with Brahms's assistance and published in 1882 for the enjoyment of the critic's wife. In his memoirs, Hanslick gives a brief account of his efforts at composing, but nowhere does he acknowledge the two Czech songs in question. See Hanslick, *Aus meinem Leben*, 1: 33–34, 71–74.

Fig. 1.1).[22] On September 23, 1849, Hanslick's friend Franz Balthasar Ulm took notice of the collection in a review published in *Bohemia*:

> A collection of songs by the most beloved patriotic composers, *Zlatý zpěwník*, contains among others "Český houslista" and "Milostná písen [píseň] pod Wyšehradem." H[r] E. Hanslick, the composer of these pieces, has been known for several years as a clever music critic on account of his reviews in Prague newspapers and most recently his feuilletons in the *Wiener Zeitung*.[23]

The first of these pieces (which Ulm no more than mentions in passing) is a lively, through-composed polka that might be understood as Hanslick's own "song of praise to Bohemian utraquism," inasmuch as the anonymous text is given in both Czech ("Český houslista") and German ("Der böhm'sche Musikant").[24] The "Love Song beneath Vyšehrad" is in every respect a more ambitious work. Here we encounter an ancient bard who performs in the courtly love tradition in what appears to be medieval Czech. The song is set within sight of the Vyšehrad ("high castle"), located on the rocky outcrop above the River Vltava lying just south of Prague's historic boundaries, from whence Libuše was said to have prophesied the city's founding and future glory. Ulm continues:

> The difficulty in the second poem, with its energetic-epic apos-trophe and the tender-lyrical modulation, of finding the correct, in particular national, tone is obvious. The composer mimics the rhapsodic style of the bard with extraordinary skill. Nevertheless, I would rather not decide whether the use of unison in the minor key, odd rhythms, and sudden changes of meter and key are sufficient to this demand. That the composition, considering its ingenious

---

[22] This collection carries no date, but it must have appeared before Hoffmann's death on October 1, 1849, since the title page gives the publisher as "Nákladem Jana Hoffmanna"; Hoffmann's widow took over the firm after his death and issued works under the imprint "Hoffmannová Vdova."

[23] Franz Balthasar Ulm, *Bohemia*, September 23, 1849. Although Ulm uses the newer spelling of Hanslick's name that the composer had adopted after moving to Vienna, the songs were published in Prague under the name Hanslik.

[24] As Ludvová has suggested, publication of the German text seems especially apt in this case, since the song offers two familiar aspects of an imaginary Slavdom as seen through the sympathetic eyes of Johann Herder ("Několik pražských reálií k biografii Eduarda Hanslicka," 384). Here a wandering Czech musician brings joy to others through his music, but himself dreams only of returning to his beloved homeland.

FIGURE I.I *Zlatý zpěwník, Sbírka nejoblíbenějších zpěwů od nejwýtečnějších wlastenských skládatelů*, title page. Music Department. National Library of the Czech Republic.

bearing, its poetic fragrance, diffused over the whole, necessarily has to attract is natural.[25]

The opening words of this song ("Ha, ty naše slunce") identify it as the piece that had been performed in Mikovec's *Záhuba rodu Přemyslovského* in

[25] Ulm, in *Bohemia*, September 23, 1849.

January 1848. Ulm describes a number of the stylistic means by which the composer attempted to portray this scene (Act 3, scene ii), and to that list we may add the many arpeggiated chords that appear in the piano, whereby Hanslick imitates the sound of the chronicler Dalimil's accompaniment on the harp (ex. 1.1).[26] As we have seen, the critic for *Bohemia* reported that the text was taken from the Queen's Court Manuscript, a purported medieval source that had been "discovered" by Hanka in 1817 and first published with a German translation by Svoboda a year later. In fact, the text was taken from a manuscript of similar provenance that had come to light in a separate "discovery" in 1816 and thereafter been published in a collection of *Starobylá skládání* (Ancient poems).[27] Together with several related "discoveries," these manuscripts were widely thought to contain fragments of medieval Czech poetry and thus eventually served as key sources in the Czech national awakening. Although all were subsequently proven to be forgeries by Hanka and his literary accomplice Josef Linda along the lines of Macpherson's Ossianic poetry, we have no reason to think that Mikovec or the young Hanslick questioned the poems' authenticity.[28]

There is still a mystery to be solved, however. A comparison of the poetic text of "Ha, ty naše slunce" as given in the first edition of the play (1851) with that found in the published version of Hanslick's song (performed in 1848) shows significant differences between them. Whereas the former reproduces Hanka's published make-believe, the text in the latter departs significantly from that model in nearly every line after the first. The author of the variant used in

[26] The play was unpublished when it opened, but the scene in question can be inferred from the first edition, which appeared three years later; see Ferdinand B. Mikovec, *Záhuba rodu Přemyslovského* (Prague: Pospíšil, 1851). The relatively late date of Ulm's review (September 23, 1849) suggests that Hanslick's song may also have been unpublished at the time of the play's opening.

[27] In 1829 this text was included in an omnibus edition containing both the Queen's Court Manuscript and a number of other "old Czech" poems; see *Kralodworsky Rukopis: Zbjrka staročeskych zpiewo-prawnych basnj, s niekolika ginymi staročeskymi zpiewy / Königinhofer Handschrift: Sammlung altböhmischer lyrisch-epischer Gesänge, nebst andern altböhmischen Gedichten*, discovered and edited by Waclawa Hanky/Wenceslaw Hanka, trans. Waclawa Aloysia Swobody/Wenceslaw Aloys Swoboda (Prague: J. G. Calve, 1829). It was probably this published source that led the reviewer for *Bohemia* astray when he reported that Hanslick's song had been drawn from the *Königinhofer Handschrift*.

[28] As we have seen, in his autobiography, which was written after the forgeries had been exposed, Hanslick referred to Hanka derisively as the "discoverer" of the Queen's Court Manuscript.

Hanslick's song cannot be established conclusively, but the most likely person is Mikovec himself, who, after all, was the creative force behind the rest of the play. In that case we can posit a direct connection between playwright and composer, since the one almost certainly commissioned the other to compose the music.[29] But this relation does nothing to explain the poetic discrepancy between the two versions. For that we must look ahead to the revolution and beyond.

[29] Ludvová concludes the piece most probably was written independently of the play and was suggested only later, perhaps by Wilhelm August Ambros, as suitable for use as Dalimil's song (Ludvová, "Zur Biographie Eduard Hanslicks," 44). Nevertheless, no one seems more likely than Mikovec to have revised the text in such a fashion. Despite

"German or Czech... Choose Your Party!"

On February 29, 1848, at a festive masked ball that Mikovec had organized in his role as president of the Prague art and literary society Concordia, news was received from Paris of the recent fall of the French monarchy.[30] In the March Revolution that followed Germans and Czechs at first spoke with one voice in demanding constitutional government and broader civil rights. Indeed, some fifty of Prague's writers quickly came together to issue a proclamation of national unity, so that "neither Czechs should enjoy any favor in preference to Germans, nor Germans any favor in preference to Czechs."[31] But by early April revolutionary unity had broken down along national lines, especially over the question of whether Bohemia's political future would lie in the German national state that was being planned in Frankfurt, or in a federalized Habsburg monarchy in which Czechs would dominate the province. To the Germans, Palacký's refusal to attend the Frankfurt Parliament and his participation instead in a Slav Congress in Prague cut especially deeply.[32]

Whatever might have brought Hanslick and Mikovec together in the pre-March period, the two young men would now follow very different paths. In his memoirs, as we have seen, Hanslick sought to describe what he felt at this decisive historical juncture by quoting some unpublished youthful verse by Robert Zimmermann, another native *Prager*, who had preceded Hanslick to Vienna by a few years. Two of Zimmermann's preserved poems from this period—"Den Gefallenen" (To the fallen soldiers) and "Deutschland über Alles" (Germany, above all)—are directly related to the March Revolution and were published in Vienna's *Sonntagsblätter* in 1848 (on March 19 and June 4, respectively).[33] Hanslick, who had not yet given up composition at

Hanslick's probable involvement in this sense in the making of the play, he did not travel back from the Austrian capital to see it when it opened in Prague. Throughout the early weeks of 1848 he was actively reviewing concerts for the *Wiener Zeitung*; see Hanslick, *Sämtliche Schriften*, I/i: 131–42.

[30] Meißner, *Geschichte meines Lebens*, 2: 9–15.

[31] *Bohemia*, March 23, 1848; a similar proclamation appeared in the same newspaper on April 5, 1848. Among the signatories to the two appeals was Ambros.

[32] Jeffrey T. Leigh notes the revolution in Bohemia was "essentially a civil insurrection in which battles were fought more for control of public opinion than territory, and where insurgents levelled their criticisms as often against one another as against the dynastic state." Jeffrey T. Leigh, "Public Opinion, Public Order, and Press Policy in the Neo-Absolutist State: Bohemia, 1849–52," *Austrian History Yearbook* 35 (2004): 81.

[33] Zimmermann's poem is not to be confused with August Heinrich Hoffman von Fallersleben's famous "Das Deutschlandlied" (1841), whose first stanza begins and

this stage, set at least one of these to music. In an unpublished letter of March 23, he sought to entice the Wiener Männer-Gesangverein, evidently without success, to perform his recent choral setting of "the rousing patriotic words" of Zimmermann's "Deutschland über Alles."[34]

Although Hanslick answered the call to take up arms with his fellow students in the Academic Legion in Vienna, he was more at home wielding a pen than manning the barricades, and in feuilletons that appeared in the *Wiener Zeitung* he articulates key hallmarks of the liberal ideology of universal civil liberties.[35] Hanslick was no radical democrat, however; he hewed instead to the same moderate liberal ideology as Leopold von Hasner, editor of the *Prager Zeitung*, for whom he reported in a series of increasingly grim "Letters from Vienna" throughout the summer and into the autumn of 1848.[36] The mob lynching of the hated War Minister Theodor Baillet von Latour in Vienna on October 6, in particular, seemed to take Hanslick aback; and he was wary of the growing assertiveness of the Czechs and dismissive of those on the far left:

> In the Reichstag democrats and "liberals" are angry at one another, and it is even worse between Czechs and Germans. I cannot hide the fact that the Czech deputies [František L.] Rieger, [Alois Pravoslav]

ends with the same iconic line of verse ("Deutschland, Deutschland über Alles") that serves as a refrain in each strope of Zimmermann's poem. (Despite the National Socialists' later misappropriation of Hoffmann von Fallersleben's poem for their own purposes, it, like Zimmermann's poem, expresses liberal nationalist sentiments.) Zimmermann later became the most influential Austrian philosopher of the day and Hanslick's colleague in the faculty at the University of Vienna. For a brief discussion of these poems, see Martin Seiler, "Kurt Blaukopf und Robert Zimmermann: Spuren altösterreichischer Philosophie im Werk eines Musiksoziologen der Gegenwart," *Weltanschauungen des Wiener Fin de siècle 1900/2000: Festgabe für Kurt Rudolf Fischer zum achtzigsten Geburtstag*, ed. Gertraud Diem-Wille, Ludwig Nagl, and Friedrich Stadler (Frankfurt am Main: Peter Lang, 2002), 187–88 (where the dates of publication in the *Sonntagsblätter* are erroneously given as March 17 and June 6, 1848).

[34] This unpublished letter, preserved in the Österreichische Nationalbibliothek (Handschriftensammlung 125/17–1), is quoted in Clemens Höslinger, "Eduard Hanslick in seinen Briefen," in Antonicek, Gruber, and Landerer, eds., *Eduard Hanslick zum Gedenken*, 128.

[35] "Censur und Kunst-Kritik" (Censorship and Art Criticism), published on March 24, 1848, is reprinted in Hanslick, *Sämtliche Schriften*, I/i: 56–58. Seven months later appeared "Ueber Religionsverschiedenheit" (On religious difference); we shall consider this essay at some length below.

[36] These "Wiener Briefe" appeared in the *Prager Zeitung* in several installments published between July 20 and October 19, 1848; reprinted in Hanslick, *Sämtliche Schriften*,

Trojan, Hawlíček [Karel Havlíček-Borovský] and their like-minded followers have fallen into general disapproval because of the unforgivable vehemence of their eruptions in the last session.

As for the radicals, he wrote, "Our republicans should learn...that their immature, farcical, tattered manner is not given to making proselytes out of the educated class," adding: "I always feel downright aristocratic when I come from the 'Democratic Club'."[37]

If the events of 1848 thus crystallized Hanslick's identity as a moderate German liberal, Mikovec became a true political activist on the other side of the national divide. Not only did he join the Czech majority faction in the National Committee that was formed in the Revolution's first days, but he also took a leading role in the violent June Uprising by Czech students, artisans, and workers that broke out as Palacký's Slav Congress was coming to a close.[38] After the Habsburg military commander Prince Alfred Windisch-Grätz restored order to the city and effectively ended the revolution in the Bohemian capital—moves that were widely praised by German liberals in Vienna—a warrant was issued for Mikovec's arrest, forcing him to flee to Serbia.[39]

I/i: 224–61. Hasner went on to have a distinguished political career as a liberal member of the Bohemian Diet and Austrian Imperial Council and as a cabinet minister. It may have been in connection with correspondence between the two men stemming from the revolutionary era that Hasner made the comment that Hanslick attributed to him about "national consciousness" in the passage previously cited from the critic's autobiography. Hanslick reproduces some of Hasner's letters in his discussion of this period in *Aus meinem Leben* (1: 123–33), but the comment in question is found neither among this selection nor in Hasner's own autobiography (Leopold von Hasner, *Denkwürdigkeiten: Autobiographisches und Aphorismen* [Stuttgart: Cotta, 1892]).

[37] Hanslick, in *Prager Zeitung*, September 15 and 26, 1848, repr. in Hanslick, *Sämtliche Schriften*, I/i: 241, 243.

[38] Around the time of these street skirmishes, Ambros reported on events in Prague to his friend Hanslick. "What unbelievable stupidity, brutality, wrongheadedness goes about now in the bright light of day, you would have to see for yourself to believe," he wrote. To demonstrate Prague's newly found "equality of the two nationalities" he provided his friend with a couple of ink sketches depicting three Czechs beating up one German, and three Germans beating up one Czech. Ambros's letter is quoted in Hanslick, *Aus meinem Leben*, 1: 50–52.

[39] On Mikovec, see Constant von Wurzbach, "Ferdinand Bogelislaw/Mikowec," *Biographisches Lexikon der Kaiserthums Oesterreich* (Vienna: Druck und Verlag der k.k. Hof- und Staatsdruckerei, 1868), xviii, 283–87; and Jan Novotný, "Zu den Beziehungen der slawischen Politiker zur Wiener Regierung während der Revolution

Mikovec eventually sought refuge in Leipzig, but around 1850, after the revolutionary dust had settled, he returned home to Prague. Cleared by the police of having engaged in any recent subversive activity, he subsequently became the only writer in the ensuing neo-absolutist era to win approval to begin a Czech-language literary journal. This he named *Lumír*, after the mythical Slavic bard; the first number appeared on February 6, 1851.[40] Dating from the same year was the first edition of *Záhuba rodu Přemyslovského*, which had been banned by the censors only a year earlier. It is in light of the new counterrevolution under Interior Minister Alexander Bach that we can discern a probable reason Mikovec now replaced the text of Dalimil's song, in the version that Hanslick had set, with words taken more directly from the early nineteenth-century forgery. The first six lines of verse are the key:

Ha, ty naše slunce,	Ah, thou, our sun,
Vyšegrade tvrd!	Vyšehrad strong!
Ty směle i hrdě	Bravely and proudly
na přikře stojieš,	You stand on the steep,
na skále stojieši,	Standing on the cliff,
vsem cuziem po strach!	A threat to all foreigners.

Ferdinand Mikovec, *Záhuba rodu Přemyslovského* (Prague, 1851), Act 3, scene ii;
trans. Ellen Langer

1848–1849," *L'udovít Štúr und die slawische Wechselseitigkeit: Gesamte Referate und die integrale Diskussion der wissenschaftlichen Tagung in Smolenice 27.–29. Juni 1966*, ed. L'udovít Holotík (Bratislava: Verlag der Slowakischen Akademie der Wissenschaften, 1969), 152–54.

[40] On the journal's founding, see Leigh, "Public Opinion, Public Order, and Press Policy," 96–97. Lumír—whom we shall revisit in connection with Smetana's *Vyšehrad*—was the disguise that Mikovec wore to the masked ball he had organized in Prague on February 29, 1848; Meißner, *Geschichte meines Lebens*, 2: 11–12. As editor, Mikovec published *belles lettres* and literary criticism, as well as essays on historical, genealogical, and archaeological topics. He also took steps to ensure that neither Hanslick nor his Czech songs would be forgotten, publishing in 1857 a "List of Czech Musicians, Composers, Male Singers and Female Singers Presently Living," in which an entry is reserved for none other than "Hanslik, Eduard, doctor of philosophy, native of Prague, known as a composer of several Czech songs and the author of excellent articles on music. He now lives in Vienna"; see "Seznam českých hudebníků, skladatelů, zpěváků a zpěvaček nyní žijících," *Lumír: Belletristický týdenník* 7/49 (December 3, 1857): 167. I am grateful to David Beveridge for making me aware of this citation, as well as for the English translation. Notably, Mikovec persists here in using the Czech spelling of Hanslick's surname that had been given up ten years earlier.

Ha, ty naše slunce,	Ah, thou, our sun,
Vyšehrade náš,	Our Vyšehrad,
doby české slávy,	Of the age of Bohemia's greatness,
boje naše znáš!	Thou knowst our struggles!
Na strmé stojíš skále	On a steep cliff thou standest
všem na postrach!	Offering menace to all!

Text of Hanslick's "Milostná píseň pod Wyšehradem";
trans. Ellen Langer

In the published play, Dalimil performs what pretends to be nothing more than a courtly love song from Bohemia's ancient past. The words of his opening lines are patriotic without being overtly political; depicted here is medieval glory, not contemporary national agitation. It would have been an easy matter for Mikovec to have used this original version of the poem all along, of course; and in that case, rather than commission Hanslick to write a new song, he could simply, for example, have used the popular setting by the somewhat older Prague composer František Max Kníže.[41] But in the version of the play that was first staged in January 1848, Mikovec seems to have been intent on raising Czech national consciousness in a way that was no longer advisable in the counterrevolutionary era. There the ancient symbol of Vyšehrad ("Of the age of Bohemia's greatness") had been invested with meaning relevant to the emerging Czech nationalist movement of the final years of the *Vormärz* ("Thou knowst our struggles!"). The young Hanslick thus was complicit (probably unwittingly) in the same early phase of Czech national agitation about which he would later write disapprovingly in his autobiography.[42] The older Hanslick may never have spoken about this episode, but, as we shall discover in a later chapter, he is unlikely ever to have forgotten it.

[41] The song is included in Kníže's *Five Czech Songs*, op. 21 (1819). It contains many of the same stylistic features adopted by Hanslick and so may even have served as a model to some degree for Hanslick's own song; see Ludvová, "Několik pražských reálií k biografii Eduarda Hanslicka," 384–85. Kníže was one of the composers whose work, along with that of Hanslick, was included in the *Zlatý zpěwník*.

[42] Especially remarkable in this connection is Hanslick's later remark about the "mediocre" Johann Nepomuk Škroup, who, having been "rejected by the German public," could count only on the support of "the newly born Czech party" (among whose members, of course, had been Mikovec himself).

Hanslick and the Quid Pro Quo

We should consider one other political essay by Hanslick before leaving the events of 1848. Like the dispatches he wrote from Vienna for Hasner's *Prager Zeitung*, this one, too, speaks (albeit only implicitly) to the question of Hanslick's self-perception and identity. "Ueber Religionsverschiedenheit" (On religious difference) appeared in two parts in the *Wiener Zeitung* on October 25 and 26, 1848, just as the October Revolution in Vienna was coming to its bloody end.[43] Of particular interest is the second installment of this remarkable essay, which was devoted in its entirety to the status of the Jews in the Habsburg realm. What Hanslick affirms here is the idea, widely accepted within the rising liberal middle class to which he belonged, of what David Sorkin has described as a quid pro quo: Jews could become Germans but only by giving up their distinctive Jewish ways.[44] In this view, it was only by attaining *Bildung*, the harmonious formation of the mind, body, and soul, that the Jews might be integrated into German society.[45]

Hanslick's thoughts on this matter are worth exploring at some length. He begins by asserting that contemporary "Jew hatred" (*Judenhass*), which had recently flared up in several public incidents in cities throughout the monarchy, was not an outgrowth of religious belief but was instead of a "baser nature" having to do with "money envy." This age-old prejudice toward the Jews, which Hanslick locates in the lower social classes, concerns him less, however, than do the attitudes of those in his own social class: "But now anyone who moves in better society, among the truly cultured, will have made the observation that even there a certain distaste [and] grudgingness toward the Jews prevails." Deeming "hate" an inapt expression to use to describe an attitude that had nothing to do with religious zeal or envious resentment, Hanslick searches for "a vaguer term that corresponds

---

[43] "Ueber Religionsverschiedenheit" (*Beilage zum Morgenblatte der Wiener Zeitung*, October 25 and 26, 1848); reprinted in Hanslick, *Sämtliche Schriften*, I/i: 189–201, from which the quotations in the discussion that follows are taken.

[44] David Sorkin, *The Transformation of German Jewry, 1780–1840* (Oxford: Oxford University Press, 1987), *passim*. This point is made succinctly in Steven Beller, *Antisemitism: A Very Short Introduction* (Oxford: Oxford University Press, 2007), 32–33.

[45] For a thoughtful critique of the idea that was widespread in German thinking about Jewish emancipation beginning in the later eighteenth century that the Jews were a "degenerate" race that could yet be "saved" through moral, physical, political, and physical "regeneration," see Jonathan M. Hess, "Jewish Emancipation and the Politics of Race," in *The German Invention of Race*, ed. Sara Eigen and Mark Larrimore (Albany: State University of New York Press, 2006), 203–12.

to the countless different shades and tints in which this repulsion [*umgekehrte Magnetismus*] appears." He continues:

> The Jews are only rarely received in our salons, maybe even less so in our hearts, on terms of true equality; it is no dishonor, but also no recommendation when it is said of someone that he is a Jew. It does not cross the mind of a cultured person to hate the Jews—but they are not loved.

This leads Hanslick to coin an alternative expression to help him get at the reason for the "aversion" (*Abneigung*):

> "Jew antipathy" [*Judenantipathie*]—allow me for the sake of brevity to make this distinction from "Jew hatred"—is definitely not of a religious but rather of a national, indeed even aesthetic nature. Our aversion is not to the Israelite religious community, but to the Hebraic people; we loathe, not the religion of the Jews, but rather their nationality.

The contrast Hanslick draws between Christian and Jew is not like that which divides Catholic from Protestant or a member of one European nation from that of another. Instead it is an otherness of a greater order, the contrast between Westerner and Easterner. Because they have been "removed for centuries from their far-away homeland," Hanslick explains, "the Jews have retained the stamp of their Asiatic origin and show [it to] us still in late generations of that highly favored people of the Old Testament—unfortunately, in a version that is crippled by oppression and bondage [*Druck und Knechtschaft*]." Notably, in this passage Hanslick alludes to the title of Gotthold Salomon's Passover sermon *Israels Erlösung aus Druck und Knechtschaft* (Israels's deliverance from oppression and bondage), published as a short brochure in 1829. In this sermon, Salomon, a leading liberal Jewish rabbi in Hamburg, likened the modern project of Jewish emancipation to the exodus from Egypt, and for Hanslick it cannot have been insignificant that the author's subtitle indicated that his concern was to show "how [the Jews] can achieve a more worthy position in bourgeois society."[46]

[46] Gotthold Salomon, *Israels Erlösung aus Druck und Knechtschaft, oder auf welchem Wege können wir zu einer würdigern Stellung in der bürgerlichen Gesellschaft gelangen* (Hamburg: Hartwig & Müller, 1829).

Much of what follows in Hanslick's essay concerns the cultural difference that in his view would have to be overcome during the metaphorical
exodus:

> The Jews are foreign to us nationally speaking, as cannot be otherwise
> with a people that, despite settling for centuries throughout Europe,
> has not mixed [with other peoples] and because of that maintains a
> number of internal and external peculiarities that distinguish it at
> first glance from the European-Caucasian tribe [*europäisch-caucasischer
> Stamm*].

Of these peculiarities, the external ones of "appearance, gesticulation,
facial features, [and] manner of speaking" draw the bulk of Hanslick's
attention, as these have an aesthetic dimension that is naturally of special
interest to him. Hanslick focuses on dialect, "which a Jew seldom loses
[and] ranges between softer gentleness and harsher hoarseness, strains to
stress every word, and murders the most pleasant-sounding language in
the world." And this stymies "even . . . the most well-meaning apostles of
reconciliation, [since] humanity cannot prevent aesthetics from claiming
its due."

Hanslick is forthright in acknowledging that "a large part of the
Jews' mental and physical idiosyncrasy [was] a result of their long bondage [*Knechtschaft*]" at the hands of Christians. (Here again is an allusion
to Salomon's *Israels Erlösung*, with the Jews' European Christian hosts
standing in for the Egyptian pharaohs as the oppressors.) Nevertheless, he
adds, "someone is not made straight just because another person made him
crooked." Although he concedes that there were Jews, including some of
his acquaintance, who had succeeded in straightening themselves, so to
speak, by overcoming their cultural difference, in his view those exceptions
served to prove the rule that there does exist a "complex of characteristics
we call 'Jewish'."

Hanslick sets out to illustrate his point by contrasting the man who pro-
fesses the Jewish religion but whose demeanor is unmarked by the "unpleasant" characteristics in question, to a baptized man "of decidedly Jewish
physiognomy, with a Jewish dialect and manner." In the one case, he argues,
no one would feel any aversion; in the other, no one would welcome such a
man as his "brother." Christian conversion, then, was beside the point. "If
all the Jews were to be baptized but remained unmixed as a tribe, as up to
now," he writes, "then they would seemingly come closer to the Christians,

they would have become Christian, yet remain Hebrews." And that national difference was precisely the sticking point.

Hanslick then goes on to allude to an essay from 1840 written by Heinrich Heine as a critical "memorial" to his erstwhile friend Ludwig Börne, who, like Heine, had been a liberal political writer, satirist, and radical exile living in Paris:

> A well-known German author rightly affirms that "if you poured the entire Jordan River over a Jew, he would remain a Jew," a truth that Börne expressed less delicately with the words, "If you sprinkle people with water, they do not become fleas." Certainly, holy water does nothing; in order to bring about complete social equality with the Christians the Jews would have to use a baptismal water that cleanses them of all their outer and inner infelicities, a recognition of which can be seen when Börne advised the Polish Jews to have themselves baptized with eau de Cologne.[47]

Although the two parties in this colloquy, Heine and Börne, were baptized Jews, it is evident (and notable) that Hanslick considers them both highly accomplished Germans. By making mention of both writers, he affirms that Jews *could* become Germans and indeed implies that ambitious Jews *should* become Germans.

Hanslick was not opposed to Jewish baptism—he seemed entirely indifferent on that question—but he decried as a glaring and narrow-minded injustice the state's requirement of it as a prerequisite to equality before the law. And in any case baptism was neither a necessary nor a sufficient condition for his idea of true equality. What mattered to Hanslick was instead the social question, which was a question of culture, the resolution of which he saw in intermarriage. This time he puts a more radical twist than before on Gotthold Salomon's likening of Jewish modernization to the Jews'

---

[47] In *Ludwig Börne: Eine Denkschrift* (1840), Heine recalls a conversation with Börne in which the two friends discussed the question of Jewish conversion to Christianity. "Do you believe that one's inner nature is completely altered by baptism? Do you believe that one can change lice into fleas by pouring water on them?," he has Börne asking, to which both men answered in the negative. Börne continues: "Even more repellent to me was the sight of dirty bearded Jews who came out of their Polish cloaca in order to be solicited for heaven by the Conversion Society in Berlin, and preached Christianity in their mumbling dialect and stank so horribly. It would in any case be desirable to baptize that sort of Polish lice-folk not with ordinary water but with eau de Cologne." Heinrich Heine, *Ludwig Börne: A Memorial*, trans. Jeffrey L. Sammons (Rochester, NY: Camden House, 2006), 20–21.

deliverance from slavery when he writes: "In this mixing of nationalities (not of religion) lies the truly radical salvation of Jewish suffering, since only the family connection can bring this Eastern people into a truly intimate footing with the Christian-Western nations that surround it on all sides." He continues: "Through mixed marriages all the abrasive characteristics of the Jews would be lost in the course of a few generations, and when they have become like us externally, no one will ask whether they think of the Messiah in the past or future." In this last sentence, we can see that Hanslick clearly considered himself a German as well, despite his matrilineal Jewish descent.[48]

It is tempting to read this essay in tandem with Richard Wagner's notorious "Das Judenthum in der Musik" (Jewry in music), originally published two years later, in 1850, as a two-part article in the *Neue Zeitschrift für Musik* under the pseudonym K. Freigedank.[49] It is not only tempting but also ironic. As Thomas Grey has argued, the author's animus toward Hanslick, as the most prominent representative of Vienna's supposedly unsupportive "Jewish press" during the 1860s, likely played a key role in Wagner's decision to reissue the essay in brochure form in 1869 under his own name in the form of an open letter to Maria Kalergis-Muchanow, a Polish countess, pianist, and patron of the arts.[50] To be sure, Wagner's principal interest lay

---

[48] Barbara Boisits, the only other scholar of whom I am aware who has discussed this essay, characterizes Hanslick's proposal regarding mixed marriages as follows: "From early on Hanslick avails himself of a racist discourse and draws on the idea of biological determinism. His approach to a solution effectively consists in a biological assimilation." Barbara Boisits, "'diese gesungenen Bitten um Emancipation'—Akkulturationsdiskurse am Beispiel von Salomon Sulzers Wirken am Wiener Stadttempel," in *Musikwelten—Lebenswelten: Jüdische Identitätssuche in der deutschen Musikkultur*, ed. Beatrix Borchard and Heidy Zimmermann (Cologne, Weimar, and Vienna: Böhlau Verlag, 2009): 100–1 (quoted at 101). Boisits's use of the dubious notion of biological determinism is, in my view, problematic, although our difference on this point may be more semantic than anything else. At all events, as I have argued, for Hanslick Germanness was a matter of culture, not race. What he is driving at in his call for mixed marriages is not anything having to do with biology but rather with environment.

[49] K. Freigedank [Richard Wagner], "Das Judenthum in der Musik," *Neue Zeitschrift für Musik* 33 (1850): 101–7, 109–12.

[50] Richard Wagner, *Das Judenthum in der Musik* (Leipzig: J. J. Weber, 1869). For an excellent account, see Thomas S. Grey, "Masters and Their Critics: Wagner, Hanslick, Beckmesser, and *Die Meistersinger*," in *Wagner's* Meistersinger: *Performance, History, Representation*, ed. Nicholas Vazsonyi (Rochester: University of Rochester Press, 2004), 165–89. Hereafter "Jewry in Music" will refer to the original publication of 1850; *Jewry in Music*, to its reissued form as a separate brochure. For Wagner's text,

in explaining what he called "the popular dislike of Jewry in the arts, particularly music," while Hanslick's concern had been the broader civic and social realms. Yet in a passing reference to one of the key tenets of the revolutionary project of 1848, Wagner alludes to something like Hanslick's "Jew antipathy" when he writes: "Our liberalism was a somewhat confused mental game, in so far as we proposed freedom for the Jews with no knowledge of the people [*Volk*], indeed with a distaste for any contact with it."[51] And when we come across Wagner's claim about the Jews' "unpleasantly foreign" appearance and encounter his disdainful description of "Jewish speech," we cannot help being reminded of those personal traits that Hanslick, too, saw as a dividing line between peoples from the East and West.[52]

It is important to recognize, however, that the two men reflect on these matters in ways that differ profoundly from one another. Even as Wagner acknowledges that "the peculiarities of Jewish speech...are most emphasized in the more common Jews who have remained faithful to their tribe" (*den stammtreu gebliebenen gemeineren Juden*), he claims that "the cultured Jew" can never fully lose those peculiarities, which "cling to him with an impertinent obstinacy." For Wagner there exists a chasm between Jews and Germans that cannot be bridged: any distinction that might be drawn between cultured and uncultured Jews was dissolved in his mind into an essentializing

contemporary reactions to it, and commentary, see Jens Malte Fischer, *Richard Wagners "Das Judentum in der Musik": eine kritische Dokumentation als Beitrag zur Geschichte des Antisemitismus* (Frankfurt: Insel, 2000). For two recent studies, see K. M. Knittel, *Seeing Mahler: Music and the Language of Antisemitism in Fin-de-Siècle Vienna* (Burlington, VT: Ashgate, 2010), 49–67; and David Conway, *Jewry in Music: Entry to the Profession from the Enlightenment to Richard Wagner* (Cambridge: Cambridge University Press, 2012). Hereafter I will use Conway's translation of the title. Knittel (*Seeing Mahler,* 49n.) maintains that the word *Judenthum* (or *Judentum,* to use the modern spelling) carried "menacing overtones" at the time Wagner used it, but there is no evidence to support this claim.

[51] Here and below I have adapted my translation from that given in Charles Osbourne, *Richard Wagner: Stories and Essays* (London: Owen, 1973), 23–39, mostly to avoid Osbourne's anachronistic translation of "Volk" and "Stamm" as "race."

[52] It is highly unlikely that Wagner would have known Hanslick's feuilleton. But, as David Conway has shown, he was undoubtedly familiar with a series of articles by Theodor Uhlig published in the *Neue Zeitschrift für Musik* throughout the first half of 1850 (i.e., over the months leading up to the publication of Wagner's essay in that same journal) that are full of invective against Jewish musicians and in which Uhlig attributes the supposed deficiencies in their music making to their "Jewish speech habits." See Conway, *Jewry in Music,* 258–62.

discourse of "the Jew."[53] By contrast, Hanslick makes it abundantly clear that he distinguishes between those middle-class Jews who had successfully overcome their cultural difference and those of the lower social classes who had not.

Toward the end of "Jewry in Music," Wagner, like Hanslick, invokes both Heine and Börne. But whereas Wagner offers up the former as a poet who was no true poet, as the Jewish fabricator of "poetic lies," Hanslick describes him as a "well-known German author." Börne fares somewhat better at Wagner's hands: "To become one of us...the Jew has first to renounce Judaism. Börne did this." Yet, by then alluding to the legend of the Wandering Jew, Wagner claims that this "redemption" from the "curse" of Jewry could only be achieved, as Börne's life had shown, through "self-denial," which itself could only be achieved by "the redemption of Ahasuerus—extinction [*der Untergang*]."[54] Whatever Wagner might have meant by this ominous image, Hanslick's utter indifference to religious conversion, not to speak of his call for an assimilative process facilitated by intermarriage, seem, by comparison, of a very different order. Hanslick's attitudes were anything but multicultural, but they were not, in a word, racist in the same way that Wagner's most certainly were—or, at least, would eventually become.

Just how far the two men came to stand from one another on these points is suggested by a striking passage in Wagner's late essay "Erkenne dich selbst" (Know Thyself, 1881), which could never have come from Hanslick's pen, whether in 1848 or anytime thereafter. To be sure, it may be far-fetched to imagine that Wagner had Hanslick specifically in mind when he wrote, "Let Jew or Jewess intermarry with the most distinct of races, a Jew will always come to birth."[55] But Wagner had clearly begun to think this way about Hanslick when, in the lead up to the republication of *Jewry in Music*, he learned of his bête noire's matrilineal Jewish ancestry. This news may

[53] This point is made in Thomas S. Grey, "The Jewish Question," in *The Cambridge Companion to Wagner*, ed. Thomas S. Grey (Cambridge: Cambridge University Press, 2008), 207.

[54] Osbourne translates "der Untergang" as "decline and fall." Here Conway cites Karl Marx's "On the Jewish Question" (1843), as providing a model on which Wagner could draw; see Conway, *Jewry in Music*, 262–63. For another reading of this passage, see Jeffrey S. Librett, *The Rhetoric of Cultural Dialogue: Jews and Germans from Moses Mendelssohn to Richard Wagner and Beyond* (Stanford: Stanford University Press, 2000), 256–57. See also Grey, "The Jewish Question," 208.

[55] I take my translation from "Know Thyself," in Richard Wagner, *Religion and Art*, trans. William Ashton Ellis (Lincoln: University of Nebraska Press, 1994), 271.

have come from the mouth of an unwitting Hanslick during one of Wagner's extended Viennese sojourns in 1860s.[56] Since Hanslick probably did not know "Jewry in Music" at this time, or know the identity of its author if he did, he would have had no particular reason to be discreet in Wagner's presence about his family background. However Wagner came by his newfound knowledge, he did not fail to exploit it toward his own end. In 1869, in the lengthy afterword of *Jewry in Music*, he set upon Hanslick for his "libelous" attacks against him, beginning in *Vom Musikalisch-Schönen* (*On the Musically Beautiful*), as well as for the deleterious influence he believed Hanslick's music-critical judgments to have had on other tastemakers. He also made pointed reference to Hanslick's "delicately concealed Jewish descent," as though the critic's parentage explained Hanslick's animosity toward his music.[57]

Hanslick held nothing back when, in a feuilleton that appeared in the *Neue Freie Presse* on March 9, 1869, he reviewed what he called Wagner's "repulsive book."[58] It particularly irked him that Wagner had denigrated the music of the recently deceased Mendelssohn on racial grounds: to the Viennese critic, Mendelssohn's music was no less German than, say, the poetry of Heine. Moreover, Hanslick explicitly disavowed Wagner's "lie" about his "alleged 'Judaism.'"[59] This allegation rankled, and twenty-five years later Hanslick

---

[56] Thomas Grey cites as evidence of this possibility the entry of June 27, 1870, in *Cosima Wagner's Diaries*, 2 vols., ed. Martin Gregor-Dellin and Dietrich Mack, trans. and with an introduction by Geoffrey Skelton (New York: Harcourt Brace Jovanovich, 1978, 1980), 1: 238–39. See Grey, "Masters and their Critics," 182.

[57] Wagner seems to have thought Hanslick must have known that he was the K. Freigedank who had penned the original version of *Jewry in Music* and attacked him in retaliation, an improbable supposition made even more so if, as Cosima implies in her diary entry of June 27, 1870, Hanslick mentioned his Jewish heritage to Wagner.

[58] Eduard Hanslick, "Richard Wagner's 'Judenthum in der Musik,'" *Neue Freie Presse*, March 9, 1869. We may safely take Hanslick at his word here when he avers his unfamiliarity with Wagner's essay prior to its republication in 1869.

[59] Ibid. Elsewhere in this essay Hanslick noted that he was no more a Jew than were fellow critics Ludwig Speidel and Eduard Schelle. To be sure, a handful of modern scholars have identified Speidel as a Jew; see Robert S. Wistrich, *The Jews of Vienna in the Age of Franz Joseph* (Oxford: Oxford University Press, 1989), 436; Daniel Jütte, "Der jüdische Tenor as Éléazar: Heinrich Sontheim und die La Juive-Rezeption im 19. Jahrhundert," in *Judenrollen: Darstellungsformen im europäischen Theater von der Restauration bis zur Zwischenkriegszeit*, ed. Hans-Peter Bayerdörfer, Jens Malte Fischer, and Frank Halbach (Berlin and New York: Walter de Gruyter, Max Niemeyer, 2008),

disclaimed it once more at greater length with a sardonic reference to the controversial priest Pedro de Arbués, a leader in the Spanish Inquisition:

> It would be flattering to be burned by Pater Arbuez Wagner on the same pile of wood with Mendelssohn and Meyerbeer; unfortunately I must decline this honor, since my father and all his ancestors, so far as one can trace them, were arch-Catholic peasant-sons, and, on top of that, from a region that has known Jewry only in the form of a wandering peddler.[60]

Had he lived to read this passage from Hanslick's memoirs, Wagner undoubtedly would have asserted that the author's failure to mention his mother in this connection offered unimpeachable evidence he was intent on hiding his Jewish background.[61] Yet if we dispense with notions of lies and concealment and root our discussion instead in German liberal ideology, we can gain access to a subtler, more meaningful way to consider the entire matter. Notably, when Hanslick does discuss his maternal ancestry in print, he uses that opportunity to report that he acquired his love of the theater and French literature from his beloved mother. She, in turn, as we are told, had come to it by way of her father, whom Hanslick depicts as the very epitome of the *gebildet* German, distinguished in dress and manner, devoted to learning, and an avid reader of the *Augsburger Allgemeine Zeitung*, Germany's leading political newspaper.[62] Here was the type of Jew for whom, in Hanslick's opinion, no cultured German would feel any aversion. By Hanslick's lights, his mother and maternal grandparents had become Germans, and when it came to the family connection that was what mattered to his social identity.

50–51; and Notley, *Lateness and Brahms*, 34. Speidel was not Jewish, however, and was not so identified, for example, in Wilmont Haacke, *Feuilletonkunde: das Feuilleton als literarische und journalistische Gattung*, 2 vols. (Leipzig: K. W. Hiersemann, 1943–44), the index of which, in accordance with Nazi-era practices, marks the names of all Jews with an asterisk. What we read in this book instead is the following highly disingenuous account: "Did Ludwig Speidel at any time take on the already strongly judaized face of the *Neue Freie Presse*? Never! He gave it his [own] face" (ibid., 1: 261).

60 Hanslick, *Aus meinem Leben*, 2:10.

61 For a twist on this reading, see Nicole Grimes, "'Wordless Judaism, Like the Songs of Mendelssohn?' Hanslick, Mendelssohn and Cultural Politics in Late Nineteenth-Century Vienna," in *Mendelssohn Perspectives*, ed. Nicole Grimes and Angela R. Mace (Farnham, Surrey and Burlington, VT: Ashgate, 2012), 55–58.

62 Hanslick, *Aus meinem Leben*, 1: 11–14.

In view of all this, we should not be surprised when we encounter from time to time in Hanslick's music-critical writing signs of the carefully delineated *Judenantipathie* he attributed to others in his German liberal social class. After all, for Hanslick this aversion was rooted to a large degree in aesthetics. Striking evidence of this can be found in a good deal of the critic's discourse concerning the music of Carl Goldmark, late-nineteenth-century Vienna's leading composer of Jewish descent. And so it is to that important figure we now turn.

| # Becoming a German

Goldmark and the Assimilationist Project

Seventy Jewish families have lived for a thousand years in the Ghetto of

Deutschkreuz.... In the middle stands the synagogue, at least a few hundred years

old.... The cantor who sang around fifty years ago... was named Goldmark. His

son was the famous composer Goldmark, who from a Deutschkreuz Jewish boy

became a man of international renown.... Sometimes a Jewish boy grows up, has

talent and good fortune, and becomes a Goldmark... But only sometimes. Most live

and die where they were born. That is the history of the Jews from Deutschkreuz.

—Joseph Roth, "Die Juden von Deutsch-Kreuz und die Schweh-Khilles" (1919)

O N APRIL 11, 1900, Carl Goldmark, the famous composer of the opera *Die Königin von Saba* (*The Queen of Sheba*) and numerous other once-familiar works, attended a banquet in Vienna held in honor of the seventieth birthday of Ludwig Speidel, who was then nearing the end of a long and influential career as a theater and music critic. Seated next to Goldmark on this occasion was a colleague of Speidel at the *Neue Freie Presse*, Wilhelm Goldbaum. Although the normally taciturn composer was more talkative that evening than Goldbaum might have expected, he said little about himself, but when the conversation turned to the subject of autobiography, he did open up to acknowledge, with a certain wistfulness, that writing prose no longer came easily enough to allow him ever to think of setting down his memoirs. Evidently using that as his pretext, Goldbaum marked the composer's own seventieth birthday five weeks later with a feuilleton for the *Pester Lloyd*, Hungary's leading German-language newspaper, in which he took it upon himself to offer some details about Goldmark's early life before he came to much public notice.[1]

Goldbaum was not only a respected journalist (he specialized in political reporting for the *Neue Freie Presse*) but also the author of two collections of essays in which he wrote with great sympathy about premodern Jewish life.[2] It is not surprising, then, that his sketch of the young Goldmark reads like nineteenth-century ghetto fiction. In it we find something of the same celebration of the life, customs, and manners of traditional Jewry that made the ghetto story so powerful: as Jonathan Hess has argued, by portraying "the dignity and humanity" of traditional Jewish provincial life in a world undergoing transformation by "the forces of secularization and urban migration, emancipation, and acculturation," this genre conferred a measure of bourgeois cultural respectability on the upward-striving Jews of German Central Europe in their quest to transcend the ghetto and secure a place in the modern world.[3]

Goldbaum begins by telling us that Rubin Goldmark, the composer's father and a man in whom there lived "the genius of a great singer," had once been a prosperous young tradesman in the Russian-Polish town of Lublin, halfway between Krakow and Warsaw. Rubin's business affairs decline following the death of his beloved young wife, and he eventually leaves this place of unhappy memories behind and seeks a new life with his five-year-old son Joseph to the south, in Hungary. There he marries the daughter of the cantor in the town of Pápa, and finds his own calling as a cantor in Keszthely, where Carl is born in 1830. Rubin's reputation spreads throughout West Hungary, and he eventually is called to a new position in the small town of

---

[1] Wilhelm Goldbaum, "Der junge Goldmark (Zum 18. Mai)," *Pester Lloyd*, May 18, 1900. The story about the banquet honoring Speidel is told at the end of this feuilleton.

[2] Wilhelm Goldbaum, *Entlegene Kulturen: Skizzen und Bilder* (Berlin: A. Hofmann, 1877); idem, *Literarische Physiognomieen* (Vienna and Teschen: Karl Prochaska, 1884).

[3] Jonathan M. Hess, "Leopold Kompert and the Work of Nostalgia: The Cultural Capital of German Jewish Ghetto Fiction," *Jewish Quarterly Review* 97 (2007): 581. Hess discusses Goldbaum briefly in ibid., 610–11. Goldbaum's rise from *Shtetljude*— he was born in the Prussian-Polish town of Kempen—to respected member of the German-speaking intelligentsia in Vienna is entirely typical for liberal Jews of his generation.

Deutschkreuz, near Ödenburg on the far western border with Lower Austria. But Simcha Rubin, as he is affectionately known, is not only an artistic, god-fearing cantor; he is also a clever man who serves as the community's notary. Nearly every year, he and his second wife are blessed with a new addition to their family, and though the growing size of the brood strains the family's modest resources, Simcha Rubin cheerfully marks the date of each birth in his register with a little biblical verse written alongside in clear Hebraic letters.

Among these many children, son Carl inherits the father's musical genius. The boy is especially fascinated by the sound of the violin, on which one of the members of the choir is able to perform, and he takes to singing back in his clear thin voice everything the fiddler plays. Soon he must have a cheap violin of his own. The tyke squats on the floor of the tiny family home and bows and scrapes away like a gypsy at the annual fair. He can also make himself useful, such as during Purim, when he joins in the musical festivities with his little fiddle in hand. Even with no formal training, Carl is able to play every *Nigun* and "delightfully florid melody" that his father sings to him each night. But this "ghetto idyll" and playing music by ear is no way to finding fame in the wider world. The boy's parents aim higher for their son than that he should follow in the father's footsteps to become a cantor. The Talmud says, "Teaching [Torah] comes from the sons of the poor." But Simcha Rubin understands that the sons of the poor must learn before they can teach.

And so Carl is sent off to study the violin in Vienna, where he is taken in by his older half-brother Joseph, a struggling young physician. Joseph is not impressed with the idea of his younger brother's pursuit of music as a career, however, and he is determined to put Carl on a path toward achieving a proper bourgeois profession. Private instruction in violin would be permitted, but only to ensure a proper foundation for a boy who had learned next to nothing in the "singing boondocks" in which he was reared. Attendance at the Conservatory would be permitted, too, but not to the extent that Carl should abandon himself entirely to music. Genius will not be denied, however, and Carl carries on toward his goal. With the outbreak of revolution in 1848, young Carl is sent home to Deutschkreuz. In that isolated corner of the world, he is largely spared the travails of war. True, he is twice called up to service in the military reserves, but this amounts to little more than some uneventful marching about near Ödenburg (when he proudly wears the cravat that his older sister Johanna has pressed for him), and later, after a deployment to Raab, a brief romance with the daughter of the city's cathedral choir master.

After the war, Carl returns to Vienna. With Joseph forced into exile because of his participation in the failed revolution, Carl is now free to make his own decisions. Virtually penniless, he immerses himself fully in music, studying the violin with Joseph Böhm and taking lessons in music theory with Gottfried Preyer. Meanwhile, he toils away year after year in the orchestra of the Carltheater, before returning to Hungary to play in a theater orchestra in Ofen and compose synagogue music for an Alt-Ofen cantor by the name of Wahrmann. He eventually returns to Vienna for good. His violin provides his bread, but not enough. He teaches himself to play the piano and even becomes a piano teacher, begins to compose original works, and reviews concerts for a Viennese newspaper. Finally, with successful performances of his string quartet and the *Sakuntala* Overture in 1863, his long years of apprenticeship and travel are at last behind him.

To complete the tale, the author adds a brief epilogue:

> The impressions of [Goldmark's] early years in Hungary followed him throughout his life, and like a devoted memory of his father Simcha Rubin, [and] of the cantor's daughter from Pápa who became his sweet mother, they emerged from the melodies of his finest opera [*Die Königin von Saba*], exotic, solemn, and yet compelling like the popular legend of the millennia that hovered over his cradle. His life's course leading up to the bridge over which he walked to the musical Pantheon is in its own right like a piece of that incomparably venerable legend.[4]

Although not entirely fanciful, Goldbaum's account is garbled in several details. Carl's studies with Böhm and Preyer, for example, took place already during the years when he was living with his brother Joseph. His work in the theater orchestra in Ofen occurred just after the end of the revolution, before he returned to Vienna in 1851. It was then that the young Goldmark taught himself to play the piano and composed his first original works, well before he moved one last time back to Hungary in 1858, where he collaborated with the cantor Friedmann in Pest, not Wahrmann in Alt-Ofen, in composing music for the temple services. Back in Vienna, the String Quartet was first heard in 1861; *Sakuntala*, in 1865.[5]

[4] Goldbaum, "Der junge Goldmark," 2.
[5] The chronology given in Max Kalbeck's biographical notice from 1887, which likewise stressed the importance of Goldmark's Jewish background for his mature musical style, is more accurate, but, like most early biographical notices, it incorrectly gives the date of Goldmark's birth as May 18, 1832. Max Kalbeck, "Karl Goldmark," *Deutsche Dichtung* 1 (1886–87): 204–6.

A more accurate account of the young Goldmark is found in his own memoirs. Although he had disclaimed any interest in writing such a book, in 1910, at age eighty, he set to work. This project was left unfinished at the time of his death five years later and was published posthumously in its incomplete form in 1922.[6] It is not consistent in organization. The book sets out in the form of a traditional autobiography, and in the first chapters, Goldmark works his way through his childhood, youth, and early adult years, covering the same period as Goldbaum, whose feuilleton from ten years earlier appears to have served him as a rough template, right down to the story of the cravat his sister made ready for him to wear on the march near Ödenburg. But upon reaching the point in his story of his compositional breakthrough (in the mid-1860s, where Goldbaum left off), Goldmark shifts into a different mode of narration, departing from a chronological presentation of events and instead stringing together a series of anecdotes that relate either to certain key works (above all, *Die Königin von Saba*) or else to his experiences with the leading musical personalities with whom he came into contact during his long and highly successful career.

But if at the outset Goldmark borrowed from Goldbaum's narrative, as suggested, what the composer could not abide was his friend's well-intentioned effort to root his music in his traditional Jewish upbringing. Crucial evidence bearing on this point is found not only in Goldmark's autobiography, as we shall soon discover, but also in a little-known essay, to which we shall return in Chapter 8, that appeared in the *Neue Freie Presse* in 1911. I use the depictions of Goldmark's identity, of his self-perception as a German liberal, that are found in both writings to frame and give nuance to my central concern with this composer, which has to do with the multiple ways in which the so-called Jewish Question surfaced—much to the composer's chagrin—in the discourse on his music by critics of every stripe. To fellow liberal nationalists of his own generation, not to speak of the younger antisemites who would come later, Goldmark's status as a Jew clearly played a role in how his music was understood. It is no wonder, then, that when he told his own story, Goldmark sought to efface the ghetto from Goldbaum's ghetto tale.[7]

---

[6] Karl Goldmark, *Erinnerungen aus meinem Leben* (Vienna: Rikola Verlag, 1922); English transl., *Notes from the Life of a Viennese Composer*, trans. Alice Goldmark Brandeis (New York: Albert and Charles Boni, 1927).

[7] Notably, the earliest published biographical notice, an article by Theodor Helm that appeared in the *Musikalisches Wochenblatt* in 1870 for which Goldmark supplied all the details, makes no mention of the composer's family background; see [Theodor Helm], "Carl Goldmark," *Musikalisches Wochenblatt* 1 (1870): 441–43.

A German by Culture

Goldmark's memoirs begin with a simple statement of facts: "I was born on May 18, 1830 in Keszthely in Hungary. My father was the cantor and notary of the community."[8] A few paragraphs later, he tells us that his family moved when he was four to Deutschkreuz, where "in the dual capacity of cantor and notary [his] father earned a yearly salary of two hundred florins" (12/21). Nowhere, however, do we read that the father's congregation was Jewish, nor that Deutschkreuz (or Zelem, as it was known in Yiddish-Hebrew) was one of the heavily Orthodox *Sheva Kehillot* (Seven Communities) that had been created in German West Hungary under the protection of the Esterházy family after the Jews' expulsion from Vienna in 1670.[9]

With examples such as these in mind, Péter Varga has pointed to "the discretion," not to say "the sense of shame," with which Goldmark deals with his Jewish background.[10] However that may be, this seems to me not to have been

---

[8] Goldmark, *Erinnerungen*, 11; *Notes from the Life*, 19. Hereafter quotations and other references will be cited in the text from both the German and English versions; my translations are adapted from the latter.

[9] The Seven Communities of Eisenstadt, Mattersdorf, Kobersdorf, Lachenbach, Frauenkirchen, Kitsee, and Deutschkreuz lay in Hungary until the redrawing of borders following the First World War, when they became part of the Burgenland region of present-day Austria. See Johannes Reiss, "Geschichte der Juden und jüdische Geschichte im Burgenland," in *Juden in der Stadt*, ed. Fritz Mayrhofer and Ferdinand Opll (Linz: Donau, 1999), 1–19. On Deutschkreuz, see Alfred Zistler, "Geschichte der Juden in Deutchkreuz," in *Gedenkbuch der untergegangenen Judengemeinden des Burgenlandes*, ed. Hugo Gold (Tel Aviv: Olamenu, 1970), 57–74. On Goldmark in this connection, see Gerhard J. Winkler, "'Multikulturalität' und 'Heilige deutsche Tonkunst': Komplementäre und parallele Lebensläufe aus dem historischen Westungarn," in Borchard and Zimmermann, eds., *Musikwelten – Lebenswelten: Jüdische Identitätssuche in der deutschen Musikkultur*, 267–85. Although, as Philip Bohlman has argued, the idea of the "Jewish village" more accurately captures the nature of life and cultural transactions within the Seven Communities than that of the urban ghetto, I will continue to make use of the term *ghetto* because of its broad semantic connotations during the historical period with which I am concerned. See Philip V. Bohlman, "Musical Life in the Central European Jewish Village," in *Modern Jews and Their Musical Agendas*, ed. Ezra Mendelssohn (New York and Oxford: Oxford University Press, 1993), 17–39.

[10] Péter Varga, "Deutsch-Jüdische Identitäten in Autobiografien ungarischer Juden des ausgehenden 19. Jahrhunderts," in *Mehrdeutigkeit: Die Ambivalenz von Gedächtnis und Erinnerung*, ed. Moritz Csáky and Peter Stachel (Vienna: Passagen, 2002), 106; see also idem, "'Wo gehörte ich eigentlich hin?': Deutsch-jüdisches Leben im Ungarn des 19. Jahrhunderts," in *"Swer sinen vriunt behaltet, daz ist lobelich": Festschrift für András Vizkelety zum 70. Geburtstag*, ed. Márta Nagy and László Jonácsik (Budapest: Piliscsaba, 2001), 551.

a matter of Jewish self-hatred, to invoke Sander L. Gilman's familiar analysis.[11] For Goldmark, a complete identification with German culture appears to have been entirely normal and natural and not something that necessarily required him to renounce his Jewish identity in all its dimensions. Rather than pathologizing the composer, we would do better to view his life and work from the perspective of the liberal ideology of the German cultural nation that for Jews like him was seen as both deeply liberating in theory and also full of contradictions in practice.[12]

Even Varga acknowledges that Goldmark's account of his childhood does give some evidence of his Jewish background (if only unconsciously) in the "meta-levels" of the text. It was only in Jewish communities, for example, that the father's dual role as cantor and notary would have been customary, and when Goldmark recalls how during his first impoverished years as a student in Vienna he took his noon meal each day at no charge with one of seven different charitable families (18/32), he is tacitly referring to the Jewish custom of *essen tog* ("eating days" in Yiddish).[13] But Varga is mistaken in claiming that the word *Jude* never so much as once appears in the memoirs.[14] In what is perhaps the book's most often cited passage, Goldmark recalls a social gathering from the early 1890s that turned awkward when his friend Johannes Brahms made a loud and seemingly inappropriate point of noting he was a Jew (86–87/155–57).

This episode has to do with Goldmark's modest four-voice setting of the text "Wer sich die Musik erkiest," introduced in a concert of the Gesellschaft der Musikfreunde on December 3, 1893. In a review that appeared two days later, Eduard Hanslick praised Goldmark's setting for its "quiet tonal beauty" and "expression of simple, devout naïveté," while adding that he could not verify the composer's attribution of the six-line text to Martin Luther.[15] For his part, Goldmark attributed Hanslick's doubt on this point to their mutual friend Brahms, who, during a rehearsal for the piece, had expressed in no uncertain terms (and correctly, as it turns out) his conviction that Luther was not the

---

[11] Sander L. Gilman, *Jewish Self-Hatred: Anti-Semitism and the Hidden Language of the Jews* (Baltimore and London: Johns Hopkins University Press, 1986).

[12] I am grateful to Jonathan M. Hess (personal communication) for sharing with me this perspective.

[13] Varga, "Deutsch-Jüdische Identitäten in Autobiografien," 108–110; idem, "'Wo gehörte ich eigentlich hin?'" 552–53.

[14] Varga, "Deutsch-Jüdische Identitäten in Autobiografien," 106; idem, "'Wo gehörte ich eigentlich hin?'" 551.

[15] Ed. H. [Eduard Hanslick], "Concerte," *Neue Freie Presse*, December 5, 1893.

poem's author.[16] Goldmark goes on to imply—without really saying this—that Brahms had subsequently learned otherwise and then acknowledged his error in a rude remark made several days later at a dinner party in the home of Ignaz Brüll. "Don't you think it strange," he has Brahms loudly asking the singer Eugen Gura, "that a Jew should set a text of Martin Luther to music?" The upshot, Goldmark tells us, was an estrangement between the two composers lasting several months.

In the recent musicological literature, this remark has been cited in passing as a seemingly self-evident example of the kind of "casual antisemitism" that even a staunchly liberal German such as Brahms could occasionally display.[17] Earlier writers were less circumspect. Richard Specht's account is derived from Goldmark's own, but he embroidered the story to suggest Brahms had inveighed "against the impropriety on the part of a Jew to take it upon himself to set a text by Luther to music." Putting Brahms in an even less flattering light, Max Graf has him making an utterly tactless antisemitic remark: "Wonderful text. Sorry that a Jew composed the music to it!" And when, in 1970, *The Queen of Sheba* was revived in an abbreviated form in New York, the headline over Harold C. Schonberg's preview article in the *New York Times* read: "Brahms Spoke Up—To Knock the Jew."[18]

But why should Brahms's remark, however tactless and poorly considered, be construed as evidence of antisemitism? After all, he knew Luther had indulged in the worst kind of Jew-baiting, and so he may well be forgiven for wondering why—in the increasingly antisemitic Vienna of the 1890s—Goldmark should have been moved to set what he thought were the Reformer's words to music.[19] In that light, we would do better to view Brahms's rhetorical question as an

---

[16] I am grateful to Robin A. Leaver (personal communication) for confirming Brahms's view that the text in question was not by Luther. "Wer sich die Musik erkiest" is not found in Vol. 35 (1923) of the *Weimar Ausgabe von Luthers Schriften*, nor in such collections as Martin Luther, *Luther's Lieder und Gedichte*, ed. Wilhelm Stapel (Stuttgart: Evangelisches Verlagswerk, 1950).

[17] Notley, *Lateness and Brahms*, 20–21 (an earlier version of this discussion appears in Notley, "Brahms as Liberal," 110); Korstvedt, "Reading Music Criticism Beyond the Fin-de-siècle Vienna Paradigm," 165; Leon Botstein, "Music in History: The Perils of Method in Reception History," *Musical Quarterly* 89 (2007): 4.

[18] Richard Specht, *Johannes Brahms*, trans. Eric Blom (New York: Dutton, 1927), 185; Max Graf, *Legend of a Musical City* (New York: Philosophical Library, 1945), 125; Harold C. Schonberg, "Brahms Spoke Up—To Knock the Jew," *New York Times*, March 22, 1970. Schonberg based his article on Graf's version of the story in question.

[19] In considering this possibility, it is worth noting that Brahms was the owner of an early print of Luther's *Tischreden* (*Table Talk*), in which Luther gave vent to his anti-Jewish attitudes: Martin Luther, *Colloquia oder Tischreden* (Franckfurt am Mayn, 1567), listed

instance not of casual antisemitism but of characteristic Brahmsian humor that did not go over well with the butt of the joke.

More to the point, however, is the iconic status that Luther held within the German cultural sphere. Was there a better way for Goldmark to burnish his German credentials than to set what he thought was a Lutheran text to music?[20] The inclusion of this anecdote in the memoirs demonstrates clearly enough that Goldmark was not determined to deny his Jewish heritage. But if he otherwise had little to say about that background, it may well indicate that he, no more than Hanslick, simply did not view Jewishness as the over-riding aspect of his social identity.

In one example after another in his autobiography, Goldmark soft-pedals the Jewish element in his background in favor of the German. When the author writes of having "had the good fortune not to attend school" (12/21), he can only have been referring to schooling in German, since as a boy he probably attended a *cheder* (traditional Jewish school) and in any case would have learned to read Hebrew and begun to study the Torah. What we have from Goldmark instead is the misleading report that "in the little Hungarian village there was no school for the German population," indeed that he did not even learn to read—it goes without saying that he was referring to German literacy—until he was twelve, when he received his first instruction "from Friedmann, who later became [his] brother-in-law" (13/23–24).[21]

Equally telling is the implied contrast between the quotidian existence in the ghetto (not identified as such) and the promise held out by German

---

in Kurt Hofmann, *Die Bibliothek von Johannes Brahms* (Hamburg: Karl Dieter Wagner, 1974), 73.

[20] For a study of Jewish attitudes toward Luther, see Christiane Wiese, "'Let His Memory be Holy to Us!': Jewish Interpretations of Martin Luther from the Enlightenment to the Holocaust," *Leo Baeck Institute Year Book* 54 (2009): 93–126.

[21] The reference here is to Moritz Friedmann (1827–1891). As an aspiring *hazzan*, Friedmann lived in Deutschkreuz for around four years in the mid-1840s, working as a synagogue singer, an assistant cantor to Rubin Goldmark, and a much-admired school teacher, offering instruction in Hebrew, German, and Hungarian in two elementary schools, one each for boys and girls. He eventually married Goldmark's sister Johanna and later became the chief cantor in Pest. For biographical details, see *Friedmann-Album: Zur bleibenden Erinnerung an die Feier des 25-jährigen Amtsjubiläum des Herrn Moritz Friedmann, Obercantors der israelitischen Religionsgemeinde Pest* (Budapest: Chorin & Co., 1877), 99–110; Friedmann's activities in Deutschkreuz are discussed in ibid., 101. In a heartfelt letter included in this commemorative volume, Goldmark describes himself as the cantor's "oldest friend" (ibid., 77).

culture suggested by Goldmark's one brief mention of his mother. There he writes:

> In my home village, the word poetry has not existed either as a matter of thought or emotion. The people of that place, living under the poorest of conditions, pursuing only the most basic necessities of life through their miserable work, toward which their thought and effort was (or still is) exclusively directed, had absolutely no need for intellectual-spiritual [*geistig*] enquiries. All their emotions centered in deep family affection and solidarity, as well as in deep religious devotion, and found therein their satisfaction. The concept of "art" in all its shadings, such as music, sculpture, the theater, and literature, did not exist for them. My mother was, to be sure, an eager reader but she had to do it almost secretly, since it was considered a sin to read a German book. In most households there were no books, least of all did they have music merely for its own sake. (14–15/25–26)

Goldmark may have pointed with pride to his mother's reading habits, but he says nothing at all about his father's music making, the supposed memories of which play such an important role in Goldbaum's story. Goldmark later even avers in his autobiography that, as a young boy, he "had never heard any music, in the real sense" (14/24). To be sure, he does recount a charming story about his discovery at a wedding feast of the musical properties of filled goblets and then mentions his early instruction on the violin by a member of his father's choir. But we cannot help noticing a few pages later that he defines as the decisive moment when he was set upon the course of becoming a musician nothing related to ghetto life, but rather his first experience of hearing, through the windows of a nearby church, a Catholic Mass sung in four-part harmony to the accompaniment of an organ (15–16/26–27).

Varga notes that in the autobiographies of Hungarian-born Jews who, like Goldmark, later became highly successful acculturated Germans, the first encounter with the non-Jewish world is always portrayed as an important event, as is the case here.[22] What is especially notable about Goldmark's recollection, however, is how, by failing even to acknowledge his father's music making, he tacitly places higher value on Christian "harmony" (associated

---

[22] Varga, "Deutsch-jüdische Identitäten in Autobiografien," 109; idem, "'Wo gehörte ich eigentlich hin?'" 552.

with the richly euphonic world of the church) than on Jewish "noise" (associated with the lamenting, heterophonic soundscape of the synagogue).[23]

Looking back on this formative experience, the world-famous composer surely would have harbored few romantic notions about the life of a small-town cantor. Moreover, he would have known that his father, by his final years at any rate, had come to regret his decision to become a *hazzan* rather than to pursue a career in music as an "artist." In 1863, upon learning that a younger son, Leo, was intending to follow in his professional footsteps, the aging Rubin attempted in vain to persuade the young man to choose another career instead, one that might allow "a happy existence, which can never be the case in the career of a cantor because it stems from Jews."[24] Writing again to Leo three years later, Rubin returned to the same subject: "You have chosen a calling that, with its extremely meager present, if anything carries within itself the miasma whereby any prospect of a happy future must be considered destroyed at the outset."[25] In an undated letter written shortly thereafter, Rubin adopted the age-old parental strategy of advising Leo to avoid the mistakes he had made in his own life:

> Herein you will find confirmation of the assertion I expressed in my previous [letter], that man's happiness has its roots in the recognition of his calling. I too sinned heavily against the assignment for which I was endowed. I recognized my calling as an artist, but did not exploit it, and while I could have provided a happy lot for my family, I provided for them a paltry present and sad future in shabby congregations.[26]

It is in this light that we should consider how, two decades earlier, Rubin Goldmark had done what he could to support Carl's wider musical education. The boy began formal violin studies around 1842 in nearby Ödenburg and then, two years later, was sent to Vienna to continue his studies under the tutelage of Leopold Jansa. Given what Goldmark has told us about his boyhood in Deutschkreuz, we can assume the West Yiddish-speaking youth arrived in the imperial capital without benefit of many secular educational

---

[23] I take these heavily laden terms from Ruth HaCohen, *The Music Libel Against the Jews* (New Haven and London: Yale University Press, 2011).

[24] Letter of February 8, 1863, Goldmark Family Collection, Leo Baeck Institute, New York (hereafter GFC-LBI), Box 1, Folder 1 (Correspondence addressed to Leo Goldmark and amongst family and friends, 1863–1875).

[25] Letter of February 20, 1866 (ibid.).

[26] Undated letter of late February 1866 (ibid.).

advantages. Yet by moving in with his far more worldly half-brother Joseph, the fourteen-year-old boy was in effect thrust into a world that was given meaning by the concept of *Bildung*, the ideology that for ambitious young Jews provided the means by which to assimilate into bourgeois German culture.[27] In an unpublished letter to Joseph of January 1, 1867, the composer recalls his older brother's impatience with his educational shortcomings at that early stage of his life:

> I came to you [as] a young lad from a dilapidated village. Misplaced in a circle of high intelligence, my mind could not assimilate the cultural material [*Bildungstoff*] that was presented to me quickly enough because the gap was so great. Suddenly torn from its carefree reverie, my still youthful mind was burdened by the most pressing homesickness. I was taciturn and reserved, and that annoyed you.[28]

And later, in his memoirs, Goldmark suggests something of what Joseph had tried to do to fill that cultural gap:

> I entered into a group of highly educated young men, physicians, who associated with my brother. I learned to speak pure German. The first book that my brother put into my hands was *Knigge's Practical Philosophy of Social Life*. It must have seemed quite necessary. The second was *Götz von Berlichingen*, and for my third I read *The Siege of Vienna by the Turks*. (20/35)

As Goldmark implies here, the self-cultivation demanded by *Bildung* had to do not only with development of the intellect and one's aesthetic sensibilities (Goethe's *Götz von Berlichingen*, Carl August Schimmer's history of the Ottoman siege of Vienna), but also with "appropriate modes of behavior, proper (non-Yiddish-inflected) use of language [and] the demonstration of a 'cultured' personality" (Knigge's well-known guide to etiquette, manners, and the proper conduct of life).[29] In time, as Goldmark proudly claimed, he

---

[27] Among many other studies, see George L. Mosse, "Jewish Emancipation: Between *Bildung* and Respectability," in *The Jewish Response to German Culture from the Enlightenment to the Second World War*, ed. Jehuda Reinharz and Walter Schatzberg (Hanover, NH, and London: University Press of New England, 1985), 1–16.

[28] This letter is preserved in the collection of Goldmark Family Papers, Columbia University (hereafter GFP-CU), Box 1, folder "Goldmark, Carl, 1866–1893," where it is erroneously catalogued with the dateline "Mainz (?), 1867"; the correct dateline is "Wien am Neujahrstag 1867."

[29] Leo William Riegert, Jr., "Negotiating the German-Jewish: The Uncomfortable Writing of Karl Emil Franzos" (Ph.D. diss., University of Minnesota, 2004),

indeed "acquired a good bit of philosophical insight and educational accomplishment [*philosophische Anschauung und Bildung*]."[30]

For his part, Joseph Goldmark, as suggested above, would soon become an activist in the failed Revolution of 1848 and one of only four Jews elected to the Constitutional Assembly.[31] Falsely implicated in the murder, in October 1848, of the Austrian War Minister, Count Theodor Franz Baillet von Latour, which so troubled Hanslick and other moderate liberals, Joseph fled the country and eventually took refuge in the United States, where he founded a chemical company in Brooklyn and made his fortune from an effective percussive device he had invented for munitions. On April 14, 1856, he was convicted *in absentia* of both high treason and Latour's murder and sentenced to death.[32] In his memoirs, Goldmark acknowledges his brother's political sympathies with the "radical Left" (118/213) without directly commenting on his own political sensibilities; after all, he had not yet turned eighteen at the time of the March Revolution and had been sent home to Deutschkreuz when street fighting broke out in May. Nevertheless, as he slyly notes, when he was caught up in the revolutionary crossfire in June 1849, while working as a theater musician in Raab, he was taken into custody and beaten by some Austrian soldiers when seen wearing the black Calabrian hat with cockade that had been the insignia of Vienna's Academic Legion (40/71), of which Joseph had been a leading member.[33]

9. The symbolic significance of the young Goldmark's reading of Adolph Knigge's *Über den Umgang mit Menschen* is noted in Varga, "Deutsch-Jüdische Identitäten in Autobiografien," 109; idem, "'Wo gehörte ich eigentlich hin?'" 553. The book was originally published in 1789; here I have used the title of the English translation from 1799. Goethe's *Sturm und Drang* drama *Götz von Berlichingen* would later serve as the subject of one of Goldmark's operas. Schimmer's *Wien's Belagerung durch die Türken und ihre Einfälle in Ungarn und Österreich* was published in 1845, shortly after Goldmark's arrival in Vienna.

[30] Unpublished letter of January 1, 1867 to Joseph Goldmark, in GFP-CU, Box 1, folder "Goldmark, Carl, 1866–1893."

[31] Reinhard Rürup, "Progress and Its Limits: The Revolution of 1848 and European Jewry," in *Europe in 1848: Revolution and Reform*, ed. Dieter Dowe, Heinz-Gerhard Haupt, Dieter Langewiesche, and Jonathan Sperber, trans. David Higgins (New York and Oxford: Berghahn, 2001), 758–60.

[32] *Deutsche Allgemeine Zeitung*, April 23, 1856.

[33] This account obviously differs from Goldbaum's version of Carl's experience in Raab. What matters here, however, is that by referring to the insignia of the student legionnaires, Goldmark chooses to align himself with the German liberals.

In the neo-absolutist era that followed, Goldmark continued to be dogged by his familial relation to a political fugitive. Thus while working as a poorly paid violinist in several operetta theaters, including a long stint at Vienna's Carltheater beginning in 1851, he was often "subjected to annoyances on political grounds," including frequent police searches of his rooms at night (119/214). Despite the inconveniences and hardships, these were formative years in the composer's development. As he later explained: "In the horrible years of 1848 to 1853 I endured possibly the greatest misery; through constant hunger my body fell into lingering illness, [but] I did not digress one step from my goal."[34] Not only did Goldmark soon undertake his first serious efforts at composition—he even gave a concert of his own works in March 1857 with a series of pieces that reflected the "Mendelssohn style" that was still very much in the air—but his many hours in the orchestral pit also contributed considerably to his fine understanding of the workings of the theater.[35] As we have seen, Goldmark also taught himself to play the piano during these years, and though he never became an accomplished pianist, he did build a fine reputation over the next decade as a piano teacher, above all of the young Caroline Bettelheim, later a noted soprano and the wife of the Austrian notable Julius von Gomperz.

If in looking back on this period Goldmark does nothing to minimize his allegiance to the liberal ideology of 1848, the same thing cannot be said with regard to his Jewish heritage. When the composer reports his move to Pest in 1858, he gives as the reason nothing more than certain unidentified "family considerations" (58/105). In fact, the composer had returned to Hungary in order to assist his brother-in-law Moritz Friedmann, himself recently called from Vienna to become the city's chief cantor, in reforming the music for the services there. Goldmark tells us none of this, however, but rather uses the opportunity to discuss his continued study in Hungary of the music of the German masters, above all J. S. Bach and Beethoven, and implies it was only when he returned to Vienna for good two years later that he was properly prepared at last to make headway in his chosen career.[36]

---

[34] Unpublished letter of January 1, 1867, to Joseph Goldmark, in GFP-CU, Box 1, folder "Goldmark, Carl, 1866–1893."

[35] In his memoirs, the date of this concert is given incorrectly as March 12, 1858 (*Erinnerungen*, 56; *Notes from the Life*, 101); in fact, it took place on March 12, 1857.

[36] The general nature of the "family considerations" that drew Goldmark to Pest is explained in Caroline von Gomperz-Bettelheim, *Ein biographisches Blatt* (Vienna: Carl Fromme, 1905), 10. The exact nature of Goldmark's collaboration with Friedmann, however, remains unclear. On Friedmann, see, in addition to *Friedmann-Album*, the article "Moritz Friedmann," in *Lebensbilder berühmter Kantoren, part 1: Zum 100. Geburtstage*

In the new liberal atmosphere that opened upon in the early 1860s, Goldmark began at last to build his reputation as a composer, scoring a measure of popular and critical success with works such as the String Quartet in B flat, op. 8, the String Quintet, op. 9, the Suite for Violin and Piano, op. 11, and the concert overture *Sakuntala*, op. 13. The composer now took up the Viennese café culture that he would enjoy for the rest of his life, meeting, among other notables, the young physicist Ernst Mach, and Eduard Kulke, a Germanized Jew from Moravia who made his name as the author of a number of ghetto stories and later served as a music critic for Vienna's *Fremden-Blatt* and *Das Vaterland*. At the same time, Goldmark was introduced to Brahms, with whom he eventually built an enduring, if (as implied above) not untroubled friendship, and befriended the young Wagnerians Peter Cornelius and Carl Tausig.[37] And, from December 1862 to April 1863, he reviewed concerts for the liberal *Constitutionelle oesterreichische Zeitung*, covering, among other events, Brahms's first two solo concerts in Vienna and the first of three concerts given by Richard Wagner that season in which the Viennese public was introduced to pieces from the still-unfinished *Das Rheingold, Die Walküre*, and *Die Meistersinger von Nürnberg*.[38] Especially telling

des verdienstvollen Oberkantor der Breslauer Synagogengemeinde weiland Moritz Deutsch, ed. Aron Friedmann (Berlin: C. Boas Nachf., 1918), 131–40. In his seventieth-birthday tribute to the composer, Wilhelm Goldbaum reported that during this Hungarian sojourn Goldmark had composed "Jewish Temple songs" for the Alt-Ofen cantor Wahrmann, the manuscripts of which, however, were lost; see Goldbaum, "Der junge Goldmark," 2. As suggested above, Goldbaum presumably meant Friedmann, not Wahrmann.

[37] Goldmark was among a small group of like-minded musicians with whom Brahms associated during his first season in Vienna, in 1862–63, several of whom, including Goldmark on the viola, regularly met to play chamber music together. It was to this group that Brahms entrusted an early reading of his Piano Quartet, op. 34, in its original version for string quintet; see Kalbeck, *Johannes Brahms*, 2: 52. Goldmark devotes a substantial passage in his memoirs to his relationship with Brahms; see Goldmark, *Erinnerungen,* 84–97; *Notes from the Life,* 152–74. See also David Brodbeck, "Notes from the Lives of Two Viennese Composers," *American Brahms Society Newsletter* 32/1 (Spring 2014): 1–5.

[38] Goldmark wrote under the cipher "-rk"; his reviews, published under the title "Die musikalische Woche," appeared on December 5, December 11, December 17, December 24, and December 31, 1862, and January 8, January 21, February 5, March 12, March 19, March 27, and April 4, 1863. Although Goldbaum would later claim that Goldmark reviewed concerts for two years, his activity in this realm was in fact limited to the 1862–63 season. The two Brahms reviews appeared on December 5, 1862, and January 8, 1863 (quoted in Harald Graf, "Carl Goldmark: Studie zur Biographie und Rezeption," thesis, University of Vienna, 1994, 74–77); the Wagner

of the significance of this period to Goldmark's self-cultivation is this recollection of reading Friedrich Hebbel's play *Die Nibelungen* aloud from the page
proofs with Kulke: "There are in artistic life supreme moments that rise
high above the average, everyday enjoyment of art—unforgettable impres-
sions, exaltation of the soul. To these belong my first reading of Hebbel's
Nibelungen" (78/140).[39] Similarly, Goldmark's first experience shortly thereafter of Beethoven's Ninth Symphony he described as "one of the supreme
moments in [his] intellectual-spiritual [*geistig*] life" (62/112).[40]

Although Goldmark was eager to describe his artistic and intellectual
growth during these years, he thought differently about sharing the full
nature of his work at the time as the director of a certain Viennese male chorus. As he recalled:

> In ... 1862, I directed for a while the choral society *Eintracht* [Concord],
> a group of young men who loved to sing. Once when I performed with
> them Handel's *Hallelujah Chorus*, they, in their enthusiasm, kept mov-
> ing forward so that I soon stood, not in front of them, but behind.
> Enthusiasm is irresistible and was not to be stopped. (83/149–50)

Left unsaid in this delightful anecdote about a performance of this most
"Christian" of works is that Goldmark's ensemble was a Jewish singing society—it had changed its name from the Hebrew *Sion* to the German *Eintracht*
only in 1865—and that in addition to giving public concerts it also provided music for the High Holy Days, Purim, and Chanukah in Vienna's
Leopoldstadt Synagogue.[41]

---

review, on December 31, 1862. Somewhat overstating the case, Goldmark later
claimed credit as a lonely voice of support for Wagner among Viennese critics; see
Erinnerungen, 77; *Notes from the Life*, 138–39.

[39] Kulke was a friend of Hebbel and evidently had been entrusted to read the proofs of
the play in advance of publication in 1861.

[40] The Philharmonic players performed the Ninth Symphony on January 12, 1862, and
then three more times in the next two years. Goldmark must have attended at least
one of these performances. Information regarding the orchestra's repertoire and concert
programs is provided in Perger, *Denkschrift: Zum Feier des fünfzigjährigen ununterbrochenen Bestandes der Philharmonischen Konzerte in Wien*.

[41] The earliest scholarly reference to Goldmark's work with the group of which I am
aware is *Kantor Salomon Sulzer und seine Zeit: Eine Dokumentation*, ed. Hanoch Avenary,
Walter Pass, and Nikolaus Vielmetti (Sigmaringen: Jan Thorbecke, 1985), 127.
Notably, however, already in his review of Goldmark's String Quintet, op. 9 (1862)
Eduard Hanslick described the composer as the "capable choir master (of *Sion*)"; see
Ed. H. [Eduard Hanslick], "Musik," *Die Presse*, December 18, 1862. This passage is

As the passage continues, Goldmark recounts how he once traveled with the group to a choral festival in the Lower Austrian town of Wiener-Neustadt, not far from Deutschkreuz, which he was drawn to visit now after an absence of nearly twenty years.[42] He goes on to record an abiding devotion to his Hungarian homeland, which he asserted despite his inability to speak Hungarian. What is more important, however, is that Goldmark places greater emphasis on his identity not as a Hungarian and much less as a Jew but as a proud member of the *Bildungsbürgertum*: "I have lived for sixty-seven years in Vienna, have educated myself from German sources in science and art, and in this sense I count myself among the Germans" (84/150–51). Can it be mere coincidence that this declaration of allegiance to German culture comes in the midst of the only later portion of the memoirs in which Goldmark recalls his boyhood? We could scarcely hope to find any better indication of the great distance he had traveled from the Deutschkreuz ghetto of his youth. Yet, as we shall discover, Goldmark's *Deutschtum* was by no means always a given in the minds of Vienna's leading liberal music critics.

quoted in Harold Graf, "Carl Goldmark," 34–35, but it is cited there, without reference to Hanslick, as having appeared in the Jewish periodical *Wiener Mittheilungen*, ed. M. Letteris (January 1863).

[42] His parents had long since left the town, eventually settling in Pest in October 1861. See the unpublished letter from Rubin Goldmark to Leo Goldmark of February 8, 1863, in GFC-LBI, I/1.

| Liberal Essentialism and
Goldmark's Early Reception

Music composed by Jews is not always Jewish music.
—Abraham Zevi Idelsohn, *Jewish Music in Its Historical Development* (1929)

Let us never forget that we are poor German composers.
—Carl Goldmark, letter to Franz von Holstein (1877)

GOLDMARK'S INTERNATIONAL REPUTATION was founded on two color-fully orchestrated essays in exoticism dating from the mid-1860s. The concert overture *Sakuntala* was based on a dramatization of part of the epic *Mahabharata* by the eminent Sanskrit poet Kālidāsa; the opera *Die Königin von Saba* was set to a libretto by Salomon Hermann Mosenthal that takes its historical setting (and little else) from the biblical story of the Queen of Sheba's visit to the Court of King Solomon (1 Kings 10: 1–13, largely repeated in 2 Chron. 9: 1–12).[1] As I shall suggest, the composer's choice of

---

[1] Goldmark's brilliant scores have sometimes also been seen as musical analogues of the opulent paintings of his somewhat younger contemporary Hans Makart (1840–1884), a favorite of both Richard Wagner and the Habsburg court. It is important to note, however, that Makart had not yet made his reputation by the time *Sakuntala* and *Die Königin von Saba* (most of it, at any rate) were composed; we therefore cannot speak here of any influence on Goldmark of the so-called *Makartstil*. For a recent

these subjects ought to be seen as a reflection of the broad popular interest in Orientalism among nineteenth-century Germans.[2] Yet this was by no means the understanding of certain critics and commentators in the composer's day who instead heard these works first and foremost in terms of the composer's Jewishness. This disconnect between what I take to be the composer's exoticist inclinations and the essentializing discourse seen in the music-critical reaction to which these works gave rise is explored in the pages that follow. Let us begin with *Sakuntala* before turning at somewhat greater length to *Die Königin von Saba*. Toward the end, we shall also consider the symphony *Ländliche Hochzeit* (*Rustic Wedding*). Although this once-popular work stands apart from the overture and opera in having no obvious connection to the Orient, even that did not stop one critic from hearing it in terms of the composer's putative non-German Otherness.

"A west-eastern study"?

The tale of *Sakuntala* was introduced to Europe in 1789 in an English translation by Sir William Jones. This soon became the basis for Georg Forster's German translation of 1791. Goethe responded to the appearance of the latter with his famous epigram "Willst du die Blüthe," and later acknowledged his large debt to Kālidāsa in the preface to *Faust*. When publishing the second edition of Forster's translation, in 1803, Herder included his own eulogy on Kālidāsa's drama. Goldmark evidently came to know the story, however, not in Forster's translation, but by way of Ernst Meier's later translation of 1852, which his friend Ernst Mach shared with him in 1862.[3]

Around this time Goldmark was also introduced to the Orientalist music of the French composer Félicien-César David in connection with his brief employment as the music critic for the *Constitutionelle oesterreichische Zeitung*.

---

study, see Thomas Grey, "Wagner and the 'Makart Style,'" *Cambridge Opera Journal* 25 (2013): 225–60; see also Botstein, "Brahms and Nineteenth-Century Painting."

[2] See, for example, Todd Konje, *German Orientalisms* (Ann Arbor: University of Michigan Press, 2004), and Suzanne L. Marchand, *German Orientalism in the Age of Empire* (Cambridge: Cambridge University Press, 2009). For a useful introduction within a musical context, see Carl Niekerk, *Reading Mahler: German Culture and Jewish Identity in Fin-de-Siècle Vienna* (Rochester, NY: Camden House, 2010), 178–211.

[3] Goldmark, *Erinnerungen*, 77, 96; *Notes from the Life*, 139, 173–74. There is no reason to think Goldmark would have known about Schubert's unfinished opera *Sacontala*, D. 701.

In his review of David's symphonic ode *Le désert*, performed by the Wiener Männergesang-Verein in December 1862, Goldmark praised the originality of the famous "Chant du Muezzim," even while registering his suspicion that the song was in fact "an Arabian national melody."[4] Four months later, when David's opéra comique *Lalla Rookh* was introduced at the Court Opera, Goldmark was frankly disappointed to find "little that is distinctive [in the music]," regretting in particular that David, "who [once] lived in the East and made use of it in his *Désert*," had not, with the sole exception of the "somewhat exotic" Bayadères' dances in Act I, opted to give his opera a "stronger delineation of local color."[5]

Perhaps with these Orientalist pieces by David at least vaguely in mind, Goldmark composed *Sakuntala* in May 1865. The orchestration was completed in September, and the composer then submitted the score to the Vienna Philharmonic players for performance in a *Novitäten-Probe*, the audition of new works scheduled before the start of each season to choose by a vote of the members which, if any, to include in the forthcoming programs.[6] According to Goldmark's friend Sigismund Bachrich, a cellist in the orchestra, the players' response was enthusiastic. *Sakuntala* was accepted for performance and given its première on December 26, 1865.[7] The work was published soon thereafter and quickly made the rounds throughout Central Europe.

Goldmark included a précis of Kālidāsa's drama in this published score:

> Sakuntala, the daughter of a nymph, is brought up in a penitentiary grove by the chief of a sacred caste of priests as his adopted daughter. The great King Dushianta enters the sacred grove, while out hunting; he sees Sakuntala and is immediately inflamed with love for her. A charming love-scene follows, which closes with the union (according to Grundharveri, the marriage) of both.
>
> The King gives to Sakuntala, who is to follow him later to his capital city, a ring by which she shall be recognized as his wife. A powerful priest, to whom Sakuntala has forgotten to show due hospitality in the intoxication of her love, revenges himself upon her by depriving the king of his memory and of all recollection of her. Sakuntala loses the

4 –rk [Carl Goldmark], "Die musikalische Woche," *Constitutionelle oesterreichische Zeitung*, December 17, 1862.

5 Idem, "Lalla Rookh," *Constitutionelle oesterreichische Zeitung*, April 25, 1863.

6 The autograph full score, preserved in the National Széchényi Library, Budapest, carries the inscription: "componirt vom 8. bis 12. Mai [1]865—Instrumentirt vom 8 bis 18 September [1]865—18/9 Wien, Carl Goldmark."

7 S[igismund] Bachrich, *Aus verklungenen Zeiten: Erinnerungen eines alten Musikers* (Vienna: Paul Knepler, 1914), 62–63.

ring while washing clothes in the sacred river. When she is presented to the King by her companions as his wife, he does not recognize her, and repudiates her. Her companions refuse to admit her, as the wife of another, back into her home and she is left alone in grief and despair; then the nymph, her mother, has pity on her and takes her to herself.

Now the ring is found by some fishermen and brought back to the King. On his seeing it, his recollection of Sakuntala returns. He is seized with remorse for his terrible deed: the profoundest grief and unbounded yearning for her who has disappeared leave him no more.

On a warlike campaign against some evil demons, whom he vanquishes, he finds Sakuntala again, and now there is no end to their happiness.

The work opens in F major with an introduction (Andante assai) that delineates the penitentiary grove with quiet, somber chords featuring open fifths played by the dark-hued lower strings and bassoons (ex. 3.1). The appearance of the beautiful Sakuntala in the grove can be recognized in the sensuous main theme, still in the tonic F, that follows at m. 25 (Moderato assai), performed by two solo violoncellos and a solo clarinet and featuring numerous ascending triplets (ex. 3.2). A third element is introduced when, in a modified repetition of Sakuntala's music beginning at m. 47, the solo oboe and first violins join in to perform a sweet arabesque melody, moving largely downward against a variation of the main theme that now serves as counterpoint (ex. 3.3). Through it all, the lower strings and bassoon continue to depict the sacred grove with their religious open fifths. Dushianta's arrival is suitably marked by a hunting fanfare in the brass, leading eventually to the love scene, represented in the passionate second theme in E major (Meno mosso quasi Andante), performed at first by the solo oboe and English horn over accompanying harps chords and new churning triplets in the second violins and violas (ex. 3.4).

EXAMPLE 3.1 Goldmark, *Sakuntala*, op. 13, mm. 1–8 (reduction)

EXAMPLE 3.2 Goldmark, *Sakuntala*, op. 13, mm. 25–47 (reduction)

The music in the ensuing development maps easily enough onto the episode involving Sakuntala's lost ring and Dushianta's lost memory of her as his wife; Sakuntala's rejection and loneliness are aptly portrayed in the long general pause that follows the dramatic climax. The recapitulation, in turn, beginning with the music from the introduction, restores the lovers to one another, and leads to a lengthy coda. This is announced by the "exotic" English horn on the first five notes of the main theme, setting off a lovely passage in which this triplet-based figure is delicately passed among the various solo winds (ex. 3.5). The music subsequently builds to another climax, in the tonic F, marked by an especially effective recombination of Sakuntala's two related themes, the first, with its distinctive ascending head-motif supported by the second, with its descending arabesque-like melody now played *forte* in the unison horns (ex. 3.6). Further development of the fanfare brings the overture to a jubilant conclusion.

In his memoirs, Goldmark mentions the première of *Sakuntala* in connection with Vienna's two most powerful critics, Eduard Hanslick, of the *Neue Freie Presse*, and Ludwig Speidel, of the *Fremden-Blatt*:

> This first performance was not entirely without opposition on the part of the public. In his criticism of my work Hanslick was always more disapproving than approving; the criticism of the no less influential Speidel,

EXAMPLE 3.3 Goldmark, *Sakuntala*, op. 13, mm. 47–54 (reduction)

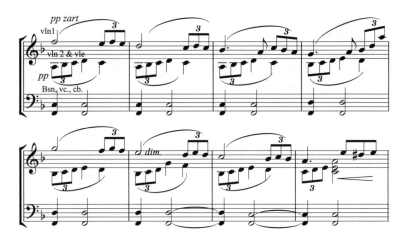

crushing. Both attacked my mind [*Gemüt*], not my composition [*Stück*]. A strong tree is not felled in one blow, but a delicate little plant is easily scrunched. The work of someone who is still little known is easily killed by such criticism. It turned out differently. The next performances took place in Budapest, Cologne (Hiller), Stuttgart (Eckert). I was invited to direct it myself by the Euterpe in Leipzig, which I did. The piece went out into the wide world. [Shortly thereafter] I began my *Queen of Sheba*.[8]

Both critics knew that Goldmark was the son of a Hungarian *hazzan*, and if not at first they would eventually come to assume on this basis that the local color used in the two works was not merely an exoticist strategic choice on the composer's part—the overture is set in India; the opera, in Palestine—but an unfortunate legacy of his "Eastern" heritage. When Goldmark complained that what had drawn the critics' disapproval was his *Gemüt*, what they imagined to be his very intellectual and mental being, he was discreetly registering resentment that his German credentials were in this way being doubted.

Yet though Goldmark certainly had reason to take umbrage at times at Hanslick's and Speidel's reception of his music, his memory with respect to the première of *Sakuntala* was, in fact, faulty. Speidel limited his comments to a single sentence, in which he described the overture as a modern and highly interesting work before briefly reporting the audience's divided reaction to it.[9] Hanslick wrote at greater length. He reported that *Sakuntala*

8 Goldmark, *Erinnerungen*, 97–98; *Notes from the Life*, 175–76.
9 sp. [Ludwig Speidel], "Viertes philharmonisches Konzert," *Fremden-Blatt*, December 27, 1865. Speidel had been much harder on Goldmark in his review of the Piano Trio in B Major; see sp. [Ludwig Speidel], "Concerte," *Fremden-Blatt*, January 12, 1864.

EXAMPLE 3.4 Goldmark, *Sakuntala*, op. 13, mm. 93–99 (reduction)

was no symphonic poem in disguise, and that although the famous Indian drama had provided the composer with his poetic stimulus, the general mood and local color, and the dramatic outlines, the music was fully understandable and independent in and of itself, without any recourse to this literary source.[10] Thirteen years later, however, Hanslick reacted very differently to the work when the Vienna Philharmonic performed it on January 13, 1878. Now he described the overture, with characteristic wit, as "an ingenious composition that...through the insatiable repetition of its main motive becomes an ingenious form of torture. The mournful character of these five closely interwoven notes follows us even in our dreams."[11] As we shall see, there was more to Hanslick's characterization of the music as mournful than meets the eye.

Speidel's attitude toward the overture likewise later soured. Consider his reactions when it was repeated in Vienna on November 22, 1868 and, then again, on January 26, 1873.[12] To be sure, both reviews included muted words of praise, but these were coupled with descriptions of the music that, with the benefit of hindsight, now seem demeaning, disturbing, even ominous. In the first review, Speidel acknowledges the brilliant complexion and impressive ornamentation of what he called Goldmark's "west-eastern study," thereby alluding to the *West-östliche Divan* (1819), Goethe's twelve books of late lyrical poems in the Persian style that stood as a symbol for the stimulating exchange and mixture between the Orient and Occident. But he describes the musical content of *Sakuntala* as "a wild marriage of the synagogue and the opera of the future" and even claims to detect in the musical ideas "strongly curved noses and sidelocks."[13] And in the second review, Speidel characterizes Goldmark as a "sensitive, intelligent artist" even as he claims that "a full

[10] Ed. H. [Eduard Hanslick], "Concerte," *Neue Freie Presse*, December 30, 1865. For an account of the reception by Hanslick of Goldmark's earlier works, see David Brodbeck, "'Poison-flaming Flowers from the Orient and Nightingales from Bayreuth': On Hanslick's Reception of the Music of Goldmark," in *Rethinking Hanslick*, 134–36.

[11] "Goldmark's 'Ouvertüre zu Sakuntala' ist...ein geistreiches Tonstück, das nur durch die unersättliche Wiederholung seines Hauptmotivs allmälig zur geistreichen Peinigung wird. Das klagende Gesicht dieser eng aneinandergeschmiegten fünf Noten verfolgt uns noch im Traume." Ed. H. [Eduard Hanslick], "Concerte," *Neue Freie Presse*, January 18, 1878.

[12] Hanslick did not attend the Philharmonic's concert of November 22, 1868. In his review of the Philharmonic's concert of January 26, 1873, he observed only that *Sakuntala* was "one of the most interesting modern orchestral works"; see Ed. H. [Eduard Hanslick], "Concerte," *Neue Freie Presse*, January 28, 1873.

[13] sp. [Ludwig Speidel], "Konzerte," *Fremden-Blatt*, November 24, 1868.

EXAMPLE 3.5 Goldmark, *Sakuntala*, op. 13, mm. 440–52 (reduction)

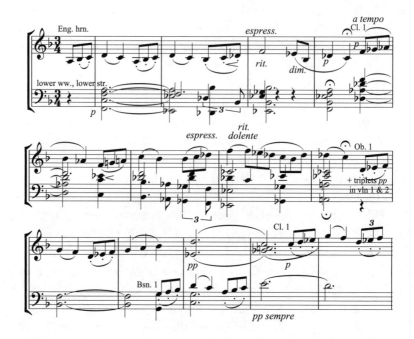

EXAMPLE 3.6 Goldmark, *Sakuntala*, op. 13, mm. 504–7 (reduction)

drop of Semitic blood has flowed into the veins of this *Sakuntala*, an echo of the joys and pains of the synagogue lives in this score."[14]

In this last comment Speidel is recycling a metaphor he had introduced three years earlier to praise (in a roundabout way, to be sure) Anton Rubinstein's musical depiction of the ancient Semites in *Der Thurm zu Babel* (*The Tower of Babel*), performed under the composer's direction in a concert of

---

[14] sp. [Ludwig Speidel], "Konzerte," *Fremden-Blatt*, January 29, 1873.

the Gesellschaft der Musikfreunde of February 20, 1870. Describing a passage featuring both the nondiatonic interval of the augmented second and a rising triplet motive recalling those that give the main theme of *Sakuntala* its distinctive character (ex. 3.7), Speidel writes:

> Rubinstein has reached deep into the synagogue for the purpose of characterization. We hear there that sobbing and exhalting *fioritura* that might be called, so to speak, Jehova's coloratura, but everything [is] so steeped in a beautiful mood and musically so pure that the composition does not continue to have a national bias.[15]

In 1878 Speidel would use similar discourse in his review of Rubinstein's *Die Maccabäer* (*The Maccabees*). Toward the end he makes a wry allusion to Wagner's *Judenbrochüre*: "There is a word to be said here about Jewry in this music" (*Hier ist nun auch ein Wort über das Judenthum in dieser Musik zu sagen*). Then taking up Leah's D-minor aria, which features the same exotic-sounding interval as the passage described above from *The Tower of Babel*, he writes: "It is evident how Rubinstein gives a musical sketch and coloring of Jewry. The procedure is rather simple: he reproduces the oriental profile, with its hooked nose, by using the augmented second" (ex. 3.8).[16]

It would be easy but misguided to view this discomforting, essentializing discourse through the lens of the racialist antisemitism—inspired, indeed, to a large degree by Wagner—that is evident in the discourse to come from certain music-critical circles in Vienna later in the century. Indeed, the term *Antisemitismus*, with all its pernicious racialist implications and directed toward the Jews alone among the Semitic peoples, would not enter the lexicon until 1879, in the immediate aftermath of the republication of Wilhelm Marr's *Der Sieg des Judenthums über das Germanenthum: Vom nichtconfessionellen Standpunkt aus betrachtet* (The victory of Jewdom over Germandom viewed from a non-confessional standpoint, 1873).[17] More to the point, nowhere does Speidel derogate the Semites as

---

[15] sp. [Ludwig Speidel], "Konzerte," *Fremden-Blatt*, February 22, 1870.

[16] sp. [Ludwig Speidel], "Hof-Operntheater," *Fremden-Blatt*, February 26, 1878.

[17] Wilhelm Marr, *Der Sieg des Judenthums über das Germanenthum: Vom nichtconfessionellen Standpunkt aus betrachtet*, 2nd ed. (Bern: Rudolph Costenoble, 1879). For a succinct account, see Alex Bein, *The Jewish Question: Biography of a World Problem*, trans. Harry Zohn (Cranberry, NJ: Associated University Presses, 1990), 593–97. As Bein notes, the term *Antisemitismus* does not appear in Marr's text, but rather first appeared in "the broadsides and press reports pro and contra Marr that his agitation inspired" (ibid., 595). Bein ties the emergence of the term also to the polemics accompanying the publication of Heinrich von Treitschke's *Ein Wort über unser Judenthum* (A word about our

an inferior race along the lines that Ernst Renan had recently proposed in his *Nouvelles considérations sur le caractère général des peuples sémitiques, et en particulier sur leur tendance au monothéisme* (New considerations on the character of the Semitic peoples, and in particular on their tendency toward monotheism).[18] And as for Speidel's stereotypes of Jewish physiognomy and dress, the composer's friend Anton Bettelheim scarcely complained about descriptions of this kind, when, clearly thinking of the music critic of the *Fremden-Blatt*, he recalled an unnamed writer who, "in a time and in a newspaper that was not at all inflamed against Jews scornfully compared Goldmark's triplets...to the sidelocks of the Polish Jews."[19] After all, Bettelheim, a distinguished writer and critic and the brother of Goldmark's former student Caroline von Gomperz-Bettelheim, could be counted among the Germanized Jews who, like Goldmark himself, were Speidel's regular readers, for whom the mostly non-German-speaking and frequently Orthodox *Ostjuden* (Eastern Jews) who began to emigrate to the city after 1867, were, to use Steven Aschheim's description, not only "brothers," but also "strangers," uncomfortable public reminders of a past best left forgotten.[20] The situation that confronts us, then, is complex and not well served by approaches holding race to be a privileged and immutable category, nor those treating antisemitism as an ideology that encompasses all varieties of anti-Jewish mentality across multiple historical eras at least without adequately distinguishing among them.[21] As I shall argue, we would do better to seek to understand Speidel's discourse of difference—and this will be true of Hanslick's rhetoric as well—within

Jewry) (Berlin: G. Reimer, 1880) and the political campaigning of the Berlin court preacher Adolf Stoecker, founder of Germany's Christian Social Party.

[18] Ernst Renan, *Nouvelles considérations sur le caractère général des peuples sémitiques, et en particulier sur leur tendance au monothéisme* (Paris: Imprimerie Imperial, 1859).

[19] Anton Bettelheim, "Goldmark-Erinnerungen," *Neue Freie Presse*, January 20, 1915; reprinted in Caroline von Gomperz-Bettelheim, *Biographische Blätter, Zum 1. Juni 1915 für Freunde gedruckt* (Vienna: Carl Fromme, 1915), 24.

[20] Steven E. Aschheim, *Brothers and Strangers: The East European Jew in German and German Jewish Consciousness, 1800–1923* (Madison: University of Wisconsin Press, 1982).

[21] On the need to differentiate among forms of anti-Judaic sentiment, see Conway, *Jewry in Music*, 9–10 and *passim*; and Leon Botstein, "The Jewish Question in Music," *Musical Quarterly* 94 (2012): 1–15. Following Bein, I will avoid the anachronistic use of the term *antisemitism* to describe anti-Judaic sentiment predating the emergence of the antisemitic movement of 1879 and beyond.

EXAMPLE 3.7 Rubinstein, *Der Thurm zu Babel*, Act I, Chorus of the Semites (beginning)

EXAMPLE 3.8 Rubinstein, *Die Maccabäer*, Act II, aria "Herr, mein Gott, so hast du mich verlassen" (beginning)

EXAMPLE 3.8 Continued

ach, die Kin-der rei - sen sie mir von— der Brust!

p

the context of traditional liberal nationalism, with its propensity for cultural elitism.[22]

German or Jewish?

Die Königin von Saba, whose origins can be traced back to the same period of the mid-1860s as *Sakuntala*, is set, as noted, to a libretto by Salomon Hermann Mosenthal based very loosely on the biblical story of the Queen of Sheba's visit to the Court of King Solomon. Goldmark completed the opera in Mosenthal's original three-act form with *lieto fine* in 1871, but the work then fell into limbo until the 1874–75 season, when, on March 10, 1875, following a long series of intrigues and significant last-minute revisions that resulted in a division of the original finale into two acts with a

[22] The inclination to collapse Speidel's rhetoric into the discourse of racialist anti-semitism, for example, limits the usefulness of Hildegard Kernmeyer's discussion of Speidel as theater critic in her *Judentum im Wiener Feuilleton (1848–1903): Exemplarische Untersuchungen zum literarästhetischen und politischen Diskurs der Moderne* (Tübingen: Max Niemoyer, 1998), 191–204. For a similar critique of Kernmayer, see Jütte, "Der jüdische Tenor as Éléazar," 50–51. Compare the recent scholarly dispute between the late K. M. Knittel and Edward F. Kravitz regarding Mahler's reception in Vienna. Knittel follows Sander L. Gilman (*The Jew's Body*, New York: Routledge, 1991) and Paul Lawrence Rose (*German Question/Jewish Question: Revolutionary Antisemitism from Kant to Wagner*, New Haven and London: Yale University Press, 1992) in stressing historical continuity among various manifestations of anti-Jewish thinking; Kravitz follows the tradition of identifying a "new" antisemitism based on race that began to take hold in the 1880s. See Knittel, "'Ein hypermoderner Dirigent': Mahler and Anti-Semitism in *Fin-de-Siècle* Vienna," *19th-Century Music 18* (1995): 257–76; Kravitz, "Mahler, Victim of the 'New' Anti-Semitism," *Journal of the Royal Musical Association 127* (2002): 72–94; and Knittel, *Seeing Mahler*, esp. 4–10.

tragic conclusion, it was finally put on the boards at the Vienna Court Opera (Fig. 3.1).[23]

This work combines certain features of midcentury grand opera in the style of Meyerbeer (the historical subject matter, the crowd and ensemble scenes, the use of local color and the ballet) with others drawn from Wagner's *Lohengrin* and *Tannhäuser* (the largely continuous dramaturgy, chromatic harmony, and limited use of recurring themes). The story is set into motion when the queen—depicted as an exotic femme fatale—seduces the courtier Assad, who has been sent by Solomon to meet her in the desert and escort her into Jerusalem.[24] The queen privately reveals her attraction to the young man, but in public she denies even knowing him. Driven to frenzy, Assad abandons his betrothed, Sulamith, daughter of the High Priest, at their wedding in the Temple and publicly declares the queen his goddess. At first condemned to death for his blasphemy, Assad is eventually banished instead to the wilderness to work out his salvation by defeating the powers of evil. There, in the end, he rejects the vile queen's entreaties and dies in the faithful Sulamith's arms during a ferocious desert storm.

[23] The extant documentary evidence belies much of Goldmark's retelling of the complex story of the opera's genesis and tortured path onto the stage (Goldmark, *Erinnerungen*, 114–29; *Notes from the Life*, 205–32). For a thorough study of the musical sources and relevant documents from the archive of the Vienna Court Opera, see Thomas Aigner, "Die Bestimmung der Skizzen, Entwürfe und Frühfassungen der Oper Die Königin von Saba von Carl Goldmark—Grundlage zur Geschichte der Entstehung des Werks" (Thesis, Universität Wien, in cooperation with the Österreichische Nationalbibliothek, 2006). The unpublished correspondence from Goldmark to his brother Joseph and between other family members, preserved in GFP-CU and GFC-LBI, likewise allows us to elaborate on and correct certain details in Goldmark's recollection. From this correspondence, for example, we know that in 1866 Joseph covered the cost of Mosenthal's fee. Moreover, Carl's letters to Joseph from 1873 and 1874 provide a fuller and presumably more accurate account than Goldmark's memoirs of the difficulties the composer faced in winning a performance of his work at the Court Opera. I discuss some of this correspondence in Brodbeck, "'Poison-flaming Flowers from the Orient and Nightingales from Bayreuth,'" 136–39.

[24] In his review of the première, Hanslick described the title character as "a kind of Egyptian Messalina." See Ed. H. [Eduard Hanslick], "Die Königin von Saba," *Neue Freie Presse*, March 12, 1875; repr. in Eduard Hanslick, *Musikalische Stationen (der "Modernen Oper" II. Theil)* (Berlin: Allgemeiner Verein für Deutsche Litteratur, 1885), 298–305 (at 300). Hanslick's reference to the sexually insatiable wife of Emperor Claudius was no doubt prompted by the recent success at the Court Theater of Adolf Wilbrandt's play *Arria und Messalina* (1874). Hanslick is using "Egyptian" as a broad-brush descriptor for the East; the ancient kingdom of Sheba seems to have been located at the southern end of the Arabian Peninsula, perhaps extending over the Red Sea into parts of present-day Eritrea or Ethiopia. In any case, in the opera the Queen is described as "the Star of Arabia."

FIGURE 3.1 Placard for the première of *Die Königin von Saba*. Picture Library. Austrian National Library.

Although the opera was enthusiastically received by the Viennese public, the initial critical reaction was a different matter altogether. "O weh!—diese Kritik," as Goldmark put it in his memoirs.[25] To be sure, Goldmark had little grounds for complaining about the opera's first review, coming from August Wilhelm Ambros in the *Wiener Abendblatt*.[26] Alone among the early critics, Ambros makes no reference to the composer's obvious stylistic debts to both Wagner and Meyerbeer; he does, however, spend a fair amount of space comparing the opera to Verdi's *Aida*, recently heard in Vienna in the previous season. The outward similarities between the two works prompted the critic to rehearse the familiar contrast between the "characteristics of the [Italian and German] musical nations" (e.g., "felicitous improvisation" vs. "lovingly detailed working out" of thematic material; "cantabile melody" vs. "concise but intellectually stimulating motives," respectively). And he concluded: "If one is asking for seriousness, solidity, depth, and careful development, then

---

[25] Goldmark, *Erinnerungen*, 130; *Notes from the Life*, 224.

[26] A[ugust] W[ilhelm] Ambros, "Goldmarks Oper: 'Königin von Saba,'" *Wiener Abendblatt*, March 11, 1875.

the author of *Die Königin von Saba* wins the day over that of *Aida*." As we shall see, not every critic seemed as willing as Ambros to place Goldmark unquestionably among the Germans.[27]

Ambros's review stands apart also on account of its relatively scanty treatment of Mosenthal's libretto, which was otherwise widely panned. For Eduard Schelle, the poem falls short not only because it is lacking any truly sympathetic figure, but also because "the atmosphere of the Old Testament Temple that streams from every pore" eventually becomes "monotonous and jaded."[28] Goldmark's old friend Eduard Kulke dismisses the libretto as a "cookie-cutter work" (*Schablonenarbeit*) whose stock characters could just as easily have had their embroilments without the interventions of the Queen of Sheba and King Solomon.[29] Johann Georg Woerz (signing himself Florestan) also questions the appearance of the character of the Queen, whom he describes as an "utterly unsympathetic title heroine, who performs a game of intrigue" with the hapless Assad. "If [Mosenthal] was to make a heartless, petulant coquette who seeks and finds a victim the central figure of the plot," he asks, "what compelled or motivated him to make this woman the Queen of Sheba and to set the entire story on biblical land?"[30] Woerz rightly observes that the opera's story has nothing in common with the biblical account that was its putative source other than "the name of Solomon, the namelessness of the Arabian queen, the place of the event, and the festivities at Solomon's court." And so he proposes an alternative explanation for why "our poet's dramatic idea [was clothed] with a seemingly historical dress":

> It will suffice to indicate that the composer probably cared most about gaining a national-Jewish subject for his début opera and that Mosenthal had no scruples about grabbing the Bible for this occasion at a weak page [and] making an opera out of what it does not say.[31]

Woerz does not tell us why he assumes Goldmark must have wanted a national-Jewish subject for his first opera, but clearly he is making a distinction

---

[27] Ibid. If, as Gundula Kreuzer has suggested, Ambros had recently been won over to Verdi's cause with respect to *Aida* and the *Requiem* primarily on the basis of the traces of German style that both works seemed to him to evince, here Ambros can perhaps be taking back some of that evaluation in the face of Goldmark's imposing opera. See Gundula Kreuzer, *Verdi and the Germans: From Unification to the Third Reich* (Cambridge: Cambridge University Press, 2010), 69–70.

[28] E[duard] Schelle, "Oper," *Die Presse*, March 12, 1875.

[29] Ed[uard] K[ulke], "Die Königin von Saba," *Das Vaterland*, March 14, 1875.

[30] Florestan [Johann Georg Woerz], "Die Königin von Saba," *Wiener Sonn- und Montags-Zeitung*, March 14, 1875.

[31] Ibid.

between this case and that, say, of the superficially similar *Aida*, which could only have been understood as an essay in exoticism. Goldmark, after all, was Jewish, while Verdi was Italian, not Egyptian or Ethiopian, and Woerz and other critics as well took that to be a significant fact. Several detected what they thought sounded like Jewish liturgical music in Goldmark's musical setting. Schelle, for example, feared the composer had been "deceived" by his "Old Testament Temple lust," leading him to go to extremes in the depiction of *couleur locale*, whereby "motives...that recall Jewish synagogue music" appear like so much "Baroque embellishment" to spoil scenes that are concerned with no particular "nationality" but rather only with the "pure, sublime human" element.[32]

For obvious reasons, critics looking for echoes of the synagogue paid special attention to the Temple Scene of Act II, during which the intended wedding of Sulamith and Assad is aborted when the queen unexpectedly appears, and the unsteady bridegroom succumbs to her erotic presence (Fig. 3.2). Introduced over the same quiet, solemn open fifths on F used to represent the penitentiary grove in *Sakuntala*, this scene commences with a brief ritualistic service of thanksgiving based on the text of Psalm 118, with responsorial singing between the High Priest and the People (ex. 3.9). Kulke's response to this passage is especially worthy of note. He challenges the composer to prove to him "that the Hebrews in Solomon's time used to sing in the way Goldmark has them sing in the Temple Scene," and he goes on to ask, "Why, then, these echoes of the synagogue, since a genuine historical coloring is not thereby achieved. Why not a four-part chorale à la Sebastian Bach?"[33] The slightly scolding tone of Kulke's comment, coming from a Germanized Jew and reading as though it were directed toward the composer himself, is telling.

Of all the work's critical naysayers, however, Goldmark singled out only two by name. "I was not prepared for the kind of thing I was to hear from Hanslick," as he wrote in his memoirs. "It was simply annihilating. Ridicule, lies, contempt! Hanslick and Speidel tried to outdo each other in their vehemence."[34] Speidel's review, in fact, could not have been more dismissive or disdainful. Weighing in on the libretto, he writes, "Every word of evaluation is superfluous. Such nonsense parodies itself." As for Goldmark's musical setting, this same

---

[32] Schelle, in *Die Presse*, March 12, 1875. See also A[ugust] Frankl, "Die Königin von Saba." *Deutsche Musik-Zeitung* 2 (1875): 10; and Kulke, in *Das Vaterland*, March 14, 1875. For a more recent, largely unconvincing attempt to develop this idea of liturgical echoes in the work, see István Kecskeméti, "Liturgical Elements in the Opera *Die Königin von Saba* (1875) by Karl Goldmark," in *Essays in Honor of Hanoch Avenary* (= *Orbis musicae*, 10, 1990/91: 229–40).

[33] Kulke, in *Das Vaterland*, March 14, 1875.

[34] Goldmark, *Erinnerungen*, 130; *Notes from the Life*, 234.

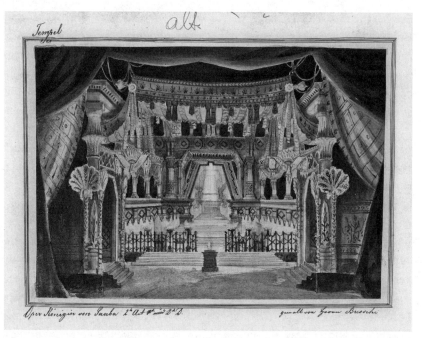

FIGURE 3.2 Carlo Brioschi's sketch for the stage design of the Temple Scene of *Die Königin von Saba*. Picture Library. Austrian National Library.

critic concluded that it evinced "a weak dramatic talent" and was "not fit to be put over the stage."[35] And then, in a flight of essentialism, Speidel adds this:

> Yet there remains a realm that is completely [Goldmark's] own, on which he stands as though on his [own] land. That is the Oriental in his music, which is an odd mixture of gypsiness and Jewishness. (Goldmark is after all an Israelite from Hungary.) He has strangely crimped melismas...that flow in triplets and double triplets and are known already from *Sakuntala*. In many a melodic phrase something nervous and obscurely sentimental can be heard whining and moaning. These are the tones of the ethos of a people that has had to endure many painful things from its god and the rest of the world.[36]

[35] sp. [Ludwig Speidel], "Hof-Operntheater," *Fremden-Blatt*, March 12, 1875.

[36] Ibid. A half-century after Speidel wrote, David Ewen would put a very different spin on some of the same essentializing observations when he defined Hebrew music as "a spirit expressed in music. That perpetual sadness, nurtured during two thousand years of the diaspora; that idealism which has kept a race alive despite the weight of centuries; that pride in one's traditions—these things are found in Hebrew music." David Ewen, *Hebrew Music: A Study and an Interpretation* (New York: Bloch, 1931), 44–45.

EXAMPLE 3.9 Goldmark, *Die Königin von Saba*, op. 27, Act II, Temple Scene (reduction): beginning

On the problems and contradictions inherent in attempts to define "Jewish music" in essentialist terms, see Klára Móricz, *Jewish Identities: Nationalism, Racism, and Utopianism in Twentieth-Century Music* (Berkeley, Los Angeles, and London: University of California Press, 2008), 2–7 and *passim* (Ewen quoted at 4).

EXAMPLE 3.9 Continued

EXAMPLE 3.9   Continued

Speidel's association of triplets with "Jewish music"—perhaps growing out of his acquaintance with the passage from Rubinstein's *Der Thurm zu Babel* cited earlier (see ex. 3.7)—would soon take on a life of its own, as we shall see. Indeed, within three years, in his review of Rubinstein's *Die Maccabäer*, Hanslick would make use of similar rhetoric when describing the scene near the beginning of the third act in which the Jews, struck down by hunger, war, and pestilence, gather outside Jerusalem to "lament and pray." Here Hanslick draws attention to "the well known Oriental unison melodies, with their dragged eighth notes and wailing triplets" (ex. 3.10).[37] And though he did not share the observation with his readers, it surely cannot have escaped Hanslick's attention that this same melody includes several instances of the interval of the augmented second, the same interval that Speidel, in his review of the opera, related to the familiar stereotype of the Jewish nose.

[37] Ed. H. [Eduard Hanslick], "Die Makkabäer," *Neue Freie Presse*, February 26, 1878: rpt. in Eduard Hanslick, *Musikalische Stationen. (Der "Modernen Oper" II. Theil)* (Berlin: Allgemeiner Verein für Deutsche Literatur, 1885), 321–30 (at 328).

EXAMPLE 3.10 Rubinstein, *Die Maccabäer*, Act III, first tableau (excerpt, vocal parts only)

Zu dir,_____ zu dir_____ fle_____ hen__

un - se - re Hän - de, un - s'rer Thrä____ nen

bitt' rer Guss, ach, uns' rer__ Thrän - en bitt' - rer Guss

Nevertheless, while Hanslick shared Speidel's concerns about the libretto of Goldmark's opera, he was kinder than his fellow critic—at least at first—to its music, singling out in particular its "passionate expression of feelings and the splendor of the [tone] painting, the distinctiveness of the Jewish-Oriental character."[38] Yet what follows makes plain his dissatisfaction with Goldmark's work as a whole. It especially troubles Hanslick that the composer seems never to operate at anything other than a fever pitch of pathos and exaltation. Notably, he finds a precedent for this tendency toward unbridled intensity—but to his way of thinking, no satisfying artistic justification—in ancient Hebraic poetry, in particular in the parallelism that is the basic rhetorical device found in the Psalms and the prophetic literature of the Old Testament, what Robert Lowth, in his *Lectures on the Sacred Poetry of the Hebrew Nation* (1788), called *parallelismus membrorum* (parallelism of members). Here the thought expressed in the first half line of verse is repeated in somewhat varied form for emphasis in the second. (For example, "They will beat their swords into ploughshares and their spears into pruning hooks," Isa. 2:4.)

We have no reason to believe Hanslick knew Lowth's work. But he clearly was familiar with the discussion of this aspect of Hebraic poetry found in *Die Poesie und ihre Geschichte* (Poetry and its history), published in 1855 by Karl Rosenkranz. Indeed, Hanslick's review continues with an unacknowledged near-quotation of Rosenkranz's account (and with the same

[38] Hanslick, *Musikalische Stationen*, 301.

illustrative pseudo-biblical verse). Here is the original passage, and following it Hanslick's paraphrase:

> The tone of Hebraic poetry becomes thereby essentially a solemn one. It immediately proclaims what it says as something momentous that is worthy of attention. Heaven shall hearken to the oration, and earth shall hear the words![39]
>
> Even in the subsidiary moments, Goldmark's tone, like that of Hebraic poetry, is a thoroughly solemn one that immediately proclaims what it says as something momentous. "Heaven shall hearken to the oration, and earth shall hear the words!"[40]

For Hanslick, this solemnity—this retention of Hebraic rhetoric, so to speak—is not a good thing in a modern opera, and he finds entirely too much of it in the work at hand, in the pathos of the singing and in the numerous orchestral interludes, which "so frequently interrupt the singing and, as it were, emphatically punctuate the singer's every phrase."[41] This is to be regretted especially because it impedes the dramatic flow. More than that, it seems lacking in good taste (always a key consideration for Hanslick): "In the affective moments Goldmark pushes passion to the extreme; the straining of the voices in the highest register and the chromatic storm in the orchestra, with its thunderous timpani and trombones and the lightning raging downward in the strings is scarcely to be outdone."[42]

It is within this context that Hanslick now declares the most prominent feature of Goldmark's music as a whole to be its "Jewish-Oriental character."[43] He acknowledges the "interestingly exotic but artistic imprint" this style had left on several earlier works, and he recognizes that its appearance was to some degree justifiable in *Die Königin von Saba* as local color (since

---

[39] Karl Rosenkranz, *Die Poesie und ihre Geschichte: Eine Entwicklung der poetischen Ideale der Völker* (Königsberg: Gebrüder Bornträger, 1855), 337–38.

[40] Hanslick, *Musikalische Stationen*, 302.

[41] Ibid.

[42] Ibid.

[43] In a recent article, Peter Stachel observes that some of the locutions found in Hanslick's review anticipate discourse that would later be understood as antisemitic, although he seems hesitant—rightly, in my view—to attribute antisemitic intent to Hanslick himself. See Peter Stachel, "Eine 'vaterländische' Oper für die Habsburgermonarchie oder eine 'jüdische Nationaloper'? Carl Goldmarks *Königin von Saba* in Wien," in *Die Oper im Wandel der Gesellschaft: Kulturtransfers und Netzwerke des Musiktheaters in Europa*, ed. Sven O. Müller, Gesa zu Nieden, Philipp Ther, and Jutta Toelle (Vienna, Cologne, and Weimar: Böhlau, 2010), 215–16.

the opera "parades a Jewish subject on its own ground").[44] Nevertheless, Hanslick finds something about the whole enterprise unsatisfying, as is evident in what seems to be his description of music from the Queen's Entrance March in Act I (ex. 3.11):

> Perhaps it is the one-sidedness of my taste, but I confess that this kind of music can only be tolerated in small doses—as an appetizer, but not the main course. Goldmark has settled down in this preference for Oriental music, with its lamenting, whining tunes, augmented fourths and diminished sixths, and the disagreeable fluctuation between major and minor, its heavily growling basses above which thousands of dissonant and small tones are crossing.[45]

Hanslick concedes that the composer made effective use of this mode in those places where the drama seems to demand it, but he complains that "this so quickly tiring and ever exotic manner" also appears in passages wherein nothing specifically "Jewish" but rather "universally human" is to be expressed.[46] What is implied, here, of course, is a binary opposition between "Jewish-Oriental" music and what, later in the review, the critic calls "European-Occidental" music. For Hanslick, one place in which the latter is required comes in the garden scene in Act II. The passage opens with a wordless siren song by the queen's slave Astaroth, a Mooress, who lures Assad to a romantic encounter with her sovereign by means of an exotic vocalise (ex. 3.12). Surely this music is intended to signify sultry, dangerous, Near Eastern female sexuality, and that is precisely how Ambros described it.[47] But in what seems to be a striking misreading of the dramatic moment, Hanslick draws attention instead to Salomon Sulzer, the famous cantor at Vienna's Stadttempel (City-Synagogue) and the compiler of *Schir Zion* (*Song of Zion*), a landmark in the reform of Ashkenazic synagogue music, published in two volumes in 1840 and 1866: "How strange the song without words...!

---

[44] Hanslick, *Musikalische Stationen*, 302–3.

[45] In the continuation of this passage, Hanslick dwells briefly on—and with evident distaste for—what he sees as Goldmark's predilection for "piercing discords" (ibid., 303).

[46] Hanslick, *Musikalische Stationen*, 303–4. As we have seen, Eduard Schelle registered the same complaint.

[47] "How extraordinarily exotic, how uncannily seductive the music becomes here. The solfeggio with which Astaroth summons Assad sounds distinctly like music from another part of the world"; Ambros, in *Wiener Abendblatt*, March 11, 1875. See also the discussion of this musical passage in Ralph P. Locke, "Cutthroats and Casbah Dancers, Muezzins and Timeless Sands: Musical Images of the Middle East," *19th-Century Music* 22 (Summer 1998): 47–48.

EXAMPLE 3.11 Goldmark, *Die Königin von Saba*, op. 27, Act I, Queen's Entrance
March (reduction): excerpts

Those are sounds that call devout Jews into the synagogue but no lover to a
rendezvous; old Sulzer in soprano clef!"[48]

Hanslick makes nothing further of the point, however, going on instead
to express his general distaste for the recent glut of operas written on exotic

---

[48] Hanslick, in *Neue Freie Presse*, March 12, 1875. Hanslick cut the last phrase, with its
direct reference to Sulzer, when adapting the review for *Musikalische Stationen*, 304.

EXAMPLE 3.11 Continued

EXAMPLE 3.12 Goldmark, *Die Königin von Saba*, op. 27, Act II, Astartoth's *Lockruf*

subjects and comparing *Die Königin von Saba* somewhat unfavorably in this regard with Verdi's *Aida*. But let us not pass so quickly over his comparison of Astaroth's siren song with Sulzer's cantorial style. As Philip Bohlman has noted, Sulzer was at the forefront of the emergence of the cantorate in a Viennese public sphere that, especially after 1848, had begun to tolerate a Jewish presence; it was this new permeability between "the sanctuary, representing the Jewish world, and the secular or public realm of the non-Jewish world" that made Sulzer's enormous fame with the public possible.[49] Thus, like countless gentiles and nonobservant Jews alike, Hanslick was drawn to witness the famous cantor sing in the City-Synagogue. This seems to have taken place in November 1865 and probably included performance of music from the soon-to-appear second volume of *Schir Zion*.[50] In a letter to Hanslick of November 28, Sulzer thanked the critic for the kind words received during his recent visit and then expressed his hope that "the foreign text, as well as the highly idiosyncratic notions characteristic of our religion" would not complicate his evaluation.[51] If this letter had been intended to ensure a favorable review, it achieved its goal. In a feuilleton that followed on March 13, 1866, Hanslick observed admiringly of Sulzer's singing that, "from the softest breadth to the most powerful tonal storm," it seemed to emanate "from the innermost place." It combined "the allure of the exotic [with] the persuasive power of true, fervent devotion" that could not but have had an effect on everyone who heard it, regardless of religion or homeland, and became "sounding fire," contrasting in every way with the "monotonously repetitive singing" that characterized the liturgical music of other faiths.[52]

[49] Philip V. Bohlman, "Composing the Cantorate: Westernizing Europe's Other Within," in *Western Music and Its Others: Difference, Representation, and Appropriation in Music*, ed. Georgina Born and David Hesmondhalgh (Berkeley and Los Angeles: University of California Press, 2000), 189–212 (quoted at 195). See also Conway, *Jewry in Music*, 133–36.

[50] The preface to the second volume of *Schir Zion* is dated 1865, but the print did not appear until early 1866.

[51] Letter from Sulzer to Hanslick of November 28, 1865, preserved in Vienna, Wienbibliothek im Rathaus, Sign. H.I.N. 34393. I have adapted my translation from Eric Werner, *A Voice Still Heard... The Sacred Songs of the Ashkenazic Jews* (University Park, and London: Pennsylvania State University Press, 1976), 216.

[52] Ed. H. [Eduard Hanslick], "Salomon Sulzer," *Neue Freie Presse*, March 13, 1866); rpt. in Hanslick, *Aus dem Concertsaal: Kritiken und Schilderungen aus den letzten 20 Jahren des Wiener Musiklebens 1848–1868* (Vienna: Wilhelm Braumüller, 1870), 401. For an interpretation of Hanslick's discourse in this feuilleton that differs subtly from my own, see Boisits, " 'diese gesungenen Bitten um Emancipation.' " My translations differ somewhat from those found in Werner, *A Voice Still Heard*, 216–17.

Hanslick subsequently moves from a description of the cantor's singing to the musical style of the newly published second volume of his *Schir Zion*. By contrast with the first volume of the anthology, which had included music by Schubert and other non-Jewish composers written in what Hanslick describes as a "German musical style," this new second volume seems to include music written by Sulzer alone that displays what Hanslick calls "a particularly Oriental-Jewish imprint." In a passage that could almost be used to describe Astaroth's "song without words," the critic explains how this character could be found "in the predominance of the recitative, which in the mouth of a cantor like Sulzer assumes the character of rapturous improvisation, in certain rhythmic, harmonic, . . . melodic main features, recurring cadenzas, and cadential formulas." Hanslick disputes the notion of "a famous recent music historian"—the implied reference here is to August Wilhelm Ambros—that the synagogue music of German Jews had, through assimilation, taken on the characteristics of German music; that of Spanish Jews, Spanish music; or that of Polish Jews, Polish music, an idea he counters by claiming that "you need only once to attend the worship service of the German, Portuguese, and Polish Jews in order to perceive, through all the differences, the similarities that are predominant in their song."[53] And what they share is precisely a "specific Oriental type that is far more reminiscent of Arabian, Turkish, [and] Persian melodies than the national music of the Germans, Portuguese, and Poles." Notably, Hanslick adds a footnote here in which he draws attention to the similarity he finds between no. 345 and other similar "laments" in Sulzer's new volume and the Arabian "Call of the Muezzin," justifying this claim to a similarity between Jewish and Arabian music by reference to recent research by Alexander Christianowitsch (ex. 3.13).[54] And this, of course, also helps to justify Hanslick's claim that Astaroth's vocalise in *Die Königin von Saba* can be likened to Sulzer's own "call to prayer."[55] In light of all these observations, Hanslick concludes by arguing: "Next to the lineament of assimilation there lives in the Jewish people an ever stronger one of stubborn adherence to national customs and traits." Although Hanslick—quintessentially urban, liberal, and agnostic—concedes this adherence to older Jewish tradition was most marked in the "lower classes of the people," in the "true, Old Guard of

---

[53] Compare August Wilhelm Ambros, *Geschichte der Musik,* vol. 1: *Die Musik des griechischen Altertums und des Orients* (1862); 3rd rev. ed. (Leipzig: Leukart, 1887), 414.

[54] Alexander Christianowitsch, *Esquisse historique de la musique arabe* (Cologne: M. Dumont-Schauberg, 1863).

[55] In this connection, it is worth noting Goldmark drew particular attention to the "Chant du Muezzim" in his review from 1862 of David's *Le désert*.

EXAMPLE 3.13 *Schir Zion*, vol. 2, no. 345

religiousness," as he puts it, he claims to recognize a "national undertone" even in *Schir Zion*, representative of "modern synagogue song."[56]

To Hanslick—here I borrow a locution from Abraham Zevi Idelsohn's discussion of the exoticized way in which gentiles (and assimilated Jews as well) tended to react in their encounters with Sulzer—the Viennese cantor's "song and singing were something foreign, un-German, and even un-European."[57] Without denying the "secular successes" of Sulzer's art, Hanslick is quick to note that its effectiveness is really limited "to the specific function of the worship service (of a minority religion, to boot)," and there is no question in his mind that such a style had no place in the concert hall or opera theater apart from providing occasional local color.[58]

With that we return to Goldmark. What was it, then, about the "Oriental" and "Jewish-Oriental" aspect of the composer's concert and operatic music that caused Hanslick and Speidel such vexation? As we have seen, in 1848, in "Ueber Religionsverschiedenheit," Hanslick had claimed the Jews were separated from "the European-Caucasian tribe" by virtue of their "internal and external peculiarities."[59] For Hanslick and his fellow liberals, the key to bridging this gap lay in the Jews' willingness to give up their traditional ways and to embrace German bourgeois cultural values. Yet, as we can now begin to understand, both Hanslick and Speidel struggled to hear Goldmark's music as fully German, one might say, fully acculturated. (They were attacking the composer's *Gemüt*, not his *Stück*, as Goldmark tactfully put it.) Indeed, the features of the composer's style that seemed to offend these critics' sensibilities the most—and, for that matter, those of Kulke as well, with his preference for Bach-like chorales over putative echoes of the synagogue—were those that might have suggested a lack of identification with the secular religion of *Bildung*, a critical component in the Germanizing process.[60]

When, toward the end of his review of Goldmark's opera, Speidel complains, "We do not live in the Orient, no palm trees shadow over us; in the land of acorns and hazelnuts such music seems...highly foreign and

---

[56] Hanslick, *Aus dem Concertsaal*, 403. Hanslick was taking his lead here from Sulzer, who, in his letter of November 28, 1865, pointed to Judaism's "highly idiosyncratic notions" precisely in connection with the music the critic had heard him perform in the City-Synagogue.

[57] A. Z. Idelsohn, *Jewish Music in its Historical Development* (New York: Holt, 1929), 254.

[58] Hanslick, *Aus dem Concertsaal*, 400.

[59] Hanslick, *Sämtliche Schriften*, I/i: 197.

[60] Speidel's reference to the sidelocks he thought he "heard" in the music of *Sakuntala* tells the same story.

depressing," the implication is that, through his "whining and moaning" music, Goldmark had resisted the "civilizing" German liberal mission and somehow remained rooted in the backward ancestral home of his Jewish forefathers.[61] Hanslick's likening of Goldmark's musical rhetoric to that of ancient Hebraic poetry and his mistaking of Astaroth's siren song as a Jewish call to prayer amounts to the same thing. Is it any wonder Goldmark bristled at the "ridicule, lies, contempt" that he read into the critics' comments? Both were striking at the very heart of his self-perception as a composer of German music.

"Come out of the Ghetto!"

Hanslick's and Speidel's naysaying did nothing, however, to harm Goldmark's growing reputation with the members of the Vienna Philharmonic. In October 1875, for example, the Philharmonic players took the step of placing the composer's *Ländliche Hochzeit* (*Rustic Wedding*) on the forthcoming season's schedule without the customary *Novitäten-Probe*—a condition to which even Anton Bruckner remained subject at this stage—and indeed before it had even been finished.[62] Although *Ländliche Hochzeit* carries the subtitle "symphony in five movements," with respect to form and genre it is neither fish nor fowl. The theme-and-variations form of the lengthy first movement is anomalous by symphonic norms, while the dimension and character of the other movements have always been seen to be more in keeping with the expectations of the suite than with those of the symphony. Moreover, although the overall title and the inscriptions given at the head of each of the movements—"Wedding March," "Bridal Song," "Serenade," "In the Garden," and "Dance"—provide the listener with poetic points of departure, the work lacks any specific program in the manner of Liszt or Berlioz.

In his memoirs, Goldmark pointedly contrasted Brahms's distaste for *Die Königin von Saba* (about which more is to come) with his admiration for the

---

[61] Speidel, in *Fremden-Blatt*, March 12, 1875.

[62] The new season was announced in mid-October 1875. In a letter of October 28, 1875, Goldmark excused himself from traveling to Pest to be in attendance at the celebration of his brother-in-law Moritz Friedmann's silver anniversary as *Obercantor* by explaining he had to remain in Vienna in order to complete his soon-to-be performed symphony; see *Friedmann-Album*, 77. That the Philharmonic players had long been well disposed toward Goldmark is evident in, among other things, their decision to perform *Sakuntala* no fewer than three times between 1865 and 1873.

symphony, which was, in Brahms's opinion, his "best work, clearcut and flawless."[63] Brahms was indignant, Goldmark wrote, that anyone should consider *Ländliche Hochzeit* a suite rather than a symphony merely because the first movement was a theme and variations rather than the usual "Sinfonieform." Brahms noted that Beethoven had included a number of variations movements in his symphonies, and he added that what is decisive in such matters in any case is the work's "symphonic character" and "symphonic working out." Insofar as this genre was seen to be a special province of German composers, it is significant that Brahms appears to have judged *Ländliche Hochzeit* to be properly symphonic. Notable, too, is Brahms's characterization of the symphony as having "arisen suddenly, like Minerva from the head of Jupiter." This remarkable allusion to "Neue Bahnen," the glowing encomium from 1853 in which Robert Schumann introduced Brahms as a composer who had "sprung fully armed like Minerva from the head of Jove," is obvious and not insignificant.

The première of the symphony, which took place during the Philharmonic's subscription concert of March 5, 1876, came in the midst of an unusually busy week in Vienna's concert halls and theaters. As a result the work did not draw as much critical attention as otherwise would have been the case. Most notably, Hanslick, whose feuilleton of March 11 was devoted entirely to the week's many operatic offerings, may well have missed the performance and in any case left no review.[64] Johann Georg Woerz, the critic for the *Wiener Sonntags- und Montags-Zeitung*, was present for the first half of the concert but had to leave to attend to other obligations before *Ländliche Hochzeit* was performed. Since Woerz could therefore take no position on the merits of the Goldmark's new work, the best he could offer his readers were secondhand reports that the symphony had been received enthusiastically by the audience and had been given some favorable critical notices.[65] Yet, citing the obligation to be evenhanded, he also acknowledged the existence of a minority view: "According to other expert opinions, ... the mood of the whole work does not correspond very well to the title, that is, to the idyllic, naïve character of the persons who would attend and the situations that would take place at a country wedding."[66] Most likely, Woerz had but one expert in mind here: Ludwig Speidel.

[63] Goldmark, *Erinnerungen*, 89–90, 122; *Notes from the Life*, 161–62, 219.

[64] Ed. H. [Eduard Hanslick], "Musik," *Neue Freie Presse*, March 11, 1876.

[65] See, for example, Ed[uard] K[ulke], "Musik," *Das Vaterland*, March 11, 1876; and E[duard] Schelle, "Musik," *Die Presse*, March 9, 1876.

[66] Florestan [Johann Georg Woerz], "Musik," *Wiener Sonn- und Montags-Zeitung*, March 13, 1876.

EXAMPLE 3.14 Goldmark, *Ländliche Hochzeit*, op. 26, I, mm. 1–39

To be sure, Speidel begins his review by praising the opening movement, the same music that had drawn Brahms's approbation, describing it as the best music Goldmark had written to date. Speidel sees a parallel between this movement and the finale of Beethoven's *Eroica* Symphony when he observes that "the theme emerges naked as it were in the basses" (ex. 3.14), and he not only notes that this simple theme is highly amenable to development, but also credits Goldmark with a "brilliant" (*geistvoll*) treatment of the many variations that follow.[67] But soon the review takes a different turn, in which Speidel gives free rein to his own imagination, creating a program for the work that seems far removed from the idyll any straightforward reading of the title and headings would seem to indicate. In particular, Speidel is disturbed that even the "Wedding March," which presumably is intended to convey a cheerful event, seems clouded by premonitions of childhood diseases, unexpected deaths, and other domestic calamities, images he finds all too strongly in evidence as well in the four shorter movements that follow. Seeking to account for these intrusions, he imagines this wedding has taken place in the wake of the great Viennese stock market crash of 1873, and so

[67] sp. [Ludwig Speidel], "Musikalische Aufführungen," *Fremden-Blatt*, March 9, 1876.

that this "rustic wedding" (*ländliche Hochzeit*) must at the same time be a "cheap wedding" (*billige Hochzeit*), the music of which therefore must not cost very much, but which brings out "all the urban sensations" in the country. And to complete the picture, he imagines this was a "non-confessional wedding" (*konfessionslose Hochzeit*) between a Jewish bridegroom and a Christian bride, in which the "Israelite member" (*israelitisches Element*) is the dominant one.[68]

After sketching this strange and unlikely scenario, the critic turns his attention squarely toward the composer himself and to the advantages he had been offered by the new liberal state in which there were no legal barriers to Jewish social advancement:

> It is remarkable, but Karl Goldmark will not come out of the ghetto. It is the old fear of persecution of the Jews that wails and whimpers, groans and sobs from his music. Were we not long ago emancipated, are we not the wood from which barons, ministers, and generals are carved? Do we not rule the world with our money? Are we not therefore potentates in the material and intellectual sphere? Away then with that anxious whining that no longer fits with our time! Dismiss from music the jargon that we have long ago abandoned in social life. We—that is, first and foremost, Karl Goldmark.[69]

It would have been one thing had Hanslick and Speidel simply discerned "orientalisms" in *Sakuntala* and *Die Königin von Saba*, with their Eastern *mise-en-scènes* and exoticist intent. But it was quite another thing, as I have argued, for them to write as though these passages manifested Goldmark's

[68] The translation "non-confessional wedding" is not entirely satisfactory. Because Austrian law prohibited civil mixed marriages, one partner in the union had to convert to the religion of the other or else to the neutral category "without religion" (*konfessionslos*); see Marsha L. Rozenblit, "Jewish Assimilation in Vienna," in Frankel and Zipperstein, eds., *Assimilation and Community: The Jews of Nineteenth-Century Europe*, 237.

[69] Speidel, in *Fremden-Blatt*, March 9, 1876. Among the Jewish nobility in Austria at this time was Julius Ritter von Gomperz, president of the Austrian Chamber of Commerce and the husband of Goldmark's former student Caroline von Gomperz-Bettelheim. In the period 1871–1879, two converted Jews were members of the country's last liberal government under Minister-President Adolf von Auersperg. Josef Unger served as a minister without portfolio; Julius Anton Glaser, as minister of justice. See Peter Pulzer, "Legal Equality and Public Life," in *German-Jewish History in Modern Times*, ed. Michael A. Meyer, vol. 3, *Integration in Dispute 1871–1918* (New York: Columbia University Press, 1997), 175.

presumed Eastern self. And now Speidel was upping the ante by supposing one could hear anxious strains of the ghetto even in *Ländliche Hochzeit*, a work that might more convincingly be characterized as "fresh" and "healthy."[70] Eventually Speidel's attitude toward Goldmark would turn around, but this would not take place until the 1880s, with the emergence in Vienna of a new racialist antisemitism that was, at bottom, different from the *Judenantipathie* seen in Goldmark's reception by Hanslick and Speidel. Some scholars have assigned a large role in this development to a controversial academic writing by Theodor Billroth, a prominent member of the Brahms-Hanslick circle. As we shall discover in the following chapter, this makes overly simple a story that is rich in complexity and nuance.

---

[70] See, for example, Eduard Schelle's account in Schelle, in *Die Presse*, March 9, 1876.

| Rethinking the "Billroth Affair"

You {are} one of the few who have correctly understood my much-denounced

book.... It has not been well understood that you can and should be harsh and

strong in the ideal, theoretical realm and yet mild and tolerant in practice.

—Theodor Billroth, letter to Wilhelm His (1876)

As we walked through the narrow, dark, and dirty streets of the ghetto and saw healthy

boys playing, Brahms remarked, "It must not be so unhealthy here," whereupon Billroth

said, "That's no proof; only the best {Auslese} remain; the frail don't survive here and die

away."

—Carl Goldmark, "Erinnerungen aus meinem Leben" (ca. 1910)

AMONG JOHANNES BRAHMS'S closest friends in Vienna was Theodor
Billroth (1829–1894), the great surgeon and professor and a fellow
expatriate from North Germany. The son of a Lutheran clergyman of Swedish
descent, Billroth was born in Bergen, on the Pomeranian island of Rügen,
then under Prussian control. The boy was only five when his father died, and
the family soon moved into the home of his paternal grandfather, the mayor
of the nearby city of Greifswald. Music was Billroth's passion from early
on, but when it came time for him to choose a career, he was persuaded by

his mother to study medicine. A mediocre student at first while attending the University of Greifswald, Billroth came into his own after transferring to Göttingen, and then established a record as a truly brilliant student in Berlin, where he earned his doctoral degree in 1852 with an original dissertation, written in Latin, on the effects of vagotomy on the lungs and the value of tracheostomy.

Billroth began his career at Berlin's Charité in 1853 and in 1860 was named professor and surgical director in Zurich; it was there he first met Brahms five years later, probably in the home of the composer Theodor Kirchner. In 1867 Billroth accepted the prestigious appointment as second surgical chair at the Vienna Medical School, two years before the composer himself took up permanent residency in the Habsburg capital. Over the next quarter century, the two men, joined by Eduard Hanslick, formed an especially tight social bond. Billroth not only was a fine pianist, discerning musical critic, and once-aspiring composer, but he could also play the viola well enough to perform chamber music as challenging as Brahms's own. When Hanslick quipped that Billroth enjoyed "an absolute *jus primae noctis*" to their mutual friend's music, he was referring to the many times when Brahms's new compositions were first tried out in musical *soirées* in the surgeon's home in Vienna's Alserstrasse.[1]

One such evening took place on November 5, 1875, when Brahms joined members of the Hellmesberger Quartet in a dress rehearsal of his Piano Quartet in C Minor, op. 60. Writing to Billroth a few days earlier, the composer confirmed the date of the forthcoming rehearsal and then added: "For your book, my very best thanks. For a passionate reader this is, however, a dangerous sort of book. You keep on reading it with care, even though

---

[1] The most substantial (if not entirely scholarly) biography is Karel B. Absolon, *The Surgeon's Surgeon: Theodor Billroth, 1829–1894*, 3 vols. (Lawrence, KS: Coronado Press, 1979–1987. See also Helmut Wyklicky, *Unbekanntes von Theodor Billroth: eine Dokumentation in Fragmenten* (Vienna: Österreichische Akademie der Wissenschaften, 1993), and Martin Nagel, Karl-Ludwig Schober, and Günther Weiß, *Theodor Billroth: Chirurg und Musiker* (Regensburg: ConBrio, 1994). For excellent summaries of the relationship between Billroth and Brahms, both written by physicians, see F. William Sunderman, "Theodor Billroth as Musician," *Bulletin of the Medical Library Association* 25/4 (1937): 209–20; and Daniel F. Roses, "Brahms and Billroth," *The American Brahms Society Newsletter* 5/2 (Spring 1987): 1–5. The published correspondence between the two men is found in *Billroth und Brahms im Briefwechsel*, ed. Otto Gottlieb-Billroth (Berlin: Urban & Schwarzenberg, 1935), which includes a substantial introductory essay. See also Hanslick, *Aus meinem Leben*, ed. Peter Wapnewski, 271–78.

it no longer concerns you."[2] Brahms referred here to Billroth's newly published treatise *Über das Lehren und Lernen der medicinischen Wissenschaften an den Universitäten der deutschen Nation* (On the teaching and learning of the medical sciences in the universities of the German nation), a self-described "cultural-historical study" that offers a comprehensive treatment of the author's views on medical education, coupled with detailed information concerning the medical-educational practices of the various German-speaking universities.[3]

In his preface, Billroth announced he would be writing frankly about the circumstances prevailing at the University of Vienna:

> It is natural that the Viennese professor likes to speak a good deal about the bright side, but also often of the dark side, of the Viennese situation. I have tried to be fair to all sides. This book has nothing to do with political geography or European statecraft; here we are dealing with the affairs of related peoples, of national cultural questions, which concern all German professors, doctors, and students, perhaps even at times ministers of education, whether they live in Russia, Switzerland, Austria, the German Empire, or elsewhere.[4]

The account of the "dark side" occurs about a third of the way through the book, in a brief excursus entitled "The Crush to Study in Vienna" (Der Andrang zum Studium in Wien).[5] In these pages Billroth expressed concern about the large size and diverse demographic makeup of the student body, which included a great number of poor, academically unprepared, mostly

---

[2] *Billroth und Brahms im Briefwechsel*, 217.

[3] *Über das Lehren und Lernen der medicinischen Wissenschaften an den Universitäten der deutschen Nation nebst allgemeinen Bemerkungen über Universitäten: Eine culturhistorische Studie* (Vienna: Carl Gerold's Sohn, 1876). The preface is dated October 1875, and it is clear that the book became available at this time. Brahms's copy is preserved in the Bibliothek der Gesellschaft der Musikfreunde in Wien (Signatur Brahms-Bibliothek 66). The English translation, somewhat abridged, appeared as Theodor Billroth, *The Medical Sciences in the German University: A Study in the History of Civilization*, trans. William H. Welch (New York: Macmillan, 1924), from which, unless no reference to that book is cited, I have adapted my own translations.

[4] Billroth, *Lehren und Lernen*, vi. This preface was omitted from the English translation.

[5] Billroth, *Lehren und Lernen*, 148–52. I cite the title of this section from the table of contents of the German edition; in the main body of the text the section carries no heading. In Welch's English translation, this excursus is (provocatively) subdivided into two sections, entitled "The Jews at Vienna" and "German Students" (*The Medical Sciences in the German University*, 105–110).

Jewish students from the eastern provinces of Hungary and Galicia. Attached to the end is a long footnote that appears to shift the terms of the discussion in an incendiary new direction. By claiming that Germans and Jews formed separate nations divided by their differing collective memories—a claim that he implicitly also makes regarding the French and other nations—Billroth appeared to invoke an unbridgeable difference at some level between Germans and the Jews in their midst, thereby evidently abrogating the quid pro quo that underlay the assimilationist project.

Billroth included this excursus with trepidation, and he soon came to regret he ever published it.[6] Consider this extraordinary letter to his friend and colleague Josef Seegen, a noted balneologist from Bohemia and the very epitome of the Germanized Jew, written on November 11, 1875, at the end of a day during which the two seem to have discussed the new book:

> I cannot get rid of the feeling...that I was unjust and distasteful toward you and do not want to lie down to sleep without asking you not to be angry with me. I'm not hard to get along with. Let's speak no more about my book. It is the only work of my life toward which I can never be objective. I know it's written in Rembrandt style, deep shadows and shiny lights, disharmoniously and abruptly biting contrasts, the mirror image of my nervous spirit....I ask you and your wife not to be angry with me! It would make me very sad! Judge me by what I do more than by what I write and chatter about.[7]

---

[6] Thus in the preface Billroth writes: "If I consider...how distressed even many colleagues who are well disposed toward me will feel that I have come to grips unsparingly with so many delicate circumstances in our German universities, indeed, that I could not spare the feelings of my best friends because I wanted to leave no doubt about my personal opinion, then the reader will understand that I publish this book with a somewhat anxious feeling" (Billroth, *Lehren und Lernen*, iv).

[7] Theodor Billroth, *Der intime Theodor Billroth: Die Billroth-Seegen Briefe*, ed. Karel B. Absolon, with Ernst Kern (Rockville, MD: Kabel, 1985), 52; published in English as Theodor Billroth, *The Intimate Billroth: The Billroth-Seegen Letters*, ed. Karel B. Absolon (Rockville, MD: Kabel, 1985), 20–21. In the English edition, the addressee is erroneously identified as Seegen's wife, Hermine. The salutation "Lieber Freund" makes the intended recipient of the letter unmistakable. Billroth's letters at this time to Frau Seegen, by contrast, begin "Verehrte Freundin." A portion of this letter is quoted in Felicitas Seebacher, *Das Fremde im 'deutschen' Tempel der Wissenschaften: Brücke in der Wissenschaftskultur der Medizinischen Fakultät der Universität Wien* (Vienna: Verlag der Österreichische Akademie der Wissenschaften, 2011), 110, but is misdated there variously as November 20 and November 29, 1875. On Seegen, see Erna Lesky, *The Vienna Medical School of the 19th Century* (Baltimore and London: Johns Hopkins University Press, 1976), 292–94.

Whatever the nature of the men's conversation that day, this was only the beginning of the troubles that Billroth's controversial comments about the Jews would bring him. In a letter of November 21, 1875, referring to a series of unflattering reviews in the liberal press, Billroth complained to the Basel surgeon August Socin that "the local political papers have seized on the explanatory notes and made it so the public thinks I've written a 500-page thick book on the Jews."[8] In the halls of the university the book soon set off partisan debate, pitting Billroth's Eastern Jewish students against his German supporters (among whom, it should be noted, were a number of Germanized Jews). This "Billroth Affair," as the contretemps came to be known in the press, culminated in an ugly fashion during Billroth's lecture of December 10, 1875, with angry cries of "Pereat!" (To hell with him!) directed toward Billroth from one side, answered by thunderous shouts of support from the other, and even reports of fist fighting that spilled out into the corridors and finally shouts of "Juden hinaus!" (Out with the Jews!).[9]

Billroth abhorred all such behavior. In an exasperated note to Seegen's wife, Hermine, also Jewish, he claimed that false reporting about the recent student disturbances only served to inspire his supporters to further demonstrations, adding, "God save me from my friends!"[10] This last remark was

---

[8] Theodor Billroth, *Briefe von Theodor Billroth*, 5th ed., ed. Georg Fischer (Hannover and Leipzig: Hannchen, 1899), 194. The reviews in question appeared in the *Neue Freie Presse* (November 11 and 18, 1875), the *Neues Wiener Tagblatt* (November 16, 1875), and *Die Presse* (November 18, 1875). Moreover, twice that month Billroth was the target of biting satire in one of Vienna's weekly humor periodicals; see *Die Bombe* 5 (November 21, 1875): 3; and ibid. (November 28, 1875): 1–2.

[9] The so-called *Pereat-Ruf* was the strongest expression for misgiving in Austrian student culture and means nothing less than what is indicated by the literal translation of "pereat" from Latin: "May he perish!" It might best be rendered into English as "To hell with him!" I am grateful to Peter Prokop (Vienna) for his advice on the ritualized language of the *Burschenschaften*. For a recent summary of the classroom disturbances, see Seebacher, *Das Fremde im 'deutschen' Tempel der Wissenschaften*, 111–17; see also Robert Hein, *Studentischer Antisemitismus in Österreich* (Vienna: Österreichischer Verein für Studentgeschichte, 1984), 17–19. Both studies cite newspaper accounts of these events. I have borrowed the title of this chapter from one of these: "Affaire Billroth," *Deutsche Zeitung*, December 13, 1875.

[10] Billroth, *Der intime Theodor Billroth*, 53; *The Intimate Billroth*, 22. Billroth's letter writing frequently extended into the early morning hours, and such seems to be the case in the letter at hand. This letter carries the date of December 10, 1875, but Billroth's reference in it to events that disrupted his lecture that day as having taken place "yesterday" suggests that it was not completed until the wee hours of the following morning.

probably made with the knowledge that the board of the Leseverein der deutschen Studenten Wiens (Reading Society of Vienna's German Students) had decided to come to his defense in a written address.[11] Responding to this turn of events in an article that appeared in *Die Presse* on December 16, Billroth took pains to explain he had not intended to provoke "conflicts" among any of the students in the university. When this response was republished a few days later as a separate brochure, he put a finer point on his disclaimer by adding a specific disavowal of "racial hatred and similar brutalities."[12]

In an extraordinary gesture of implicit regret over the damage caused by his remarks, Billroth immediately sent a copy of this brochure to Berthold Auerbach (1812–1882), the once-popular Jewish-German author with whom he had spent some pleasant hours a few months earlier while summering in Bad Aussee. Knowing he had fences to mend with a writer who, in his later years, had grown embittered by intensifying anti-Judaic sentiment in Germany, much of it inspired by Wagner, Billroth inscribed the book "To the *German* poet Berthold Auerbach in Berlin. From the author" (emphasis added). For Auerbach this gesture was too little, too late. What particularly galled him, as he explained in an open letter to Billroth, was the veneer of scientific objectivity surrounding the author's claims, as well as Billroth's invocation of Kant as the "emperor of our national, ideal Germany," all of which he saw as a perversion of the German intellectual heritage in the service of the "modern Jew baiters" from whom, as we shall see, Billroth had explicitly sought to distance his remarks.[13]

[11] On the Reading Society, founded in 1871 with the stated aim of "adher[ing] to and represent[ing] the German character of the University of Vienna at every opportunity," see William McGrath, *Dionysian Art and Populist Politics in Austria* (New Haven and London: Yale University Press, 1974), 33–52 (founding statement quoted at 33–34). This German nationalist student group included many Jews who would eventually become quite distinguished, including the medical students Sigmund Freud and Victor Adler, one of the founders of Austrian Social Democracy, and the historian Heinrich Friedjung.

[12] "Ueberreichung der Studenten-Adresse an Professor Billroth," *Die Presse*, December 16, 1875. *Prof. Dr. Th. Billroth's Antwort auf die Adresse des Lesevereines der deutschen Studenten Wien's* (Vienna: Carl Gerold's Sohn, 1875), 8. The students' address was included in ibid., 5–7.

[13] Berthold Auerbach, "An Professor Billroth in Wien," *Die Gegenwart* 9 (1876): 17–18. Auerbach quotes Billroth's handwritten inscription in the copy he had sent of his response to the Reading Society in ibid., 17. For a similar critique, see Friedrich Horn, *Offener Brief an Herrn Hofrath Dr. Theodor Billroth* (Vienna: Alfred Hölder, 1876); English transl. in Karel B. Absolon, *The Study of Medical Sciences, Theodor Billroth and*

Auerbach was not the only Jew in Billroth's acquaintance to respond to his treatise. In a speech delivered before the Reading Society on January 22, 1876, Victor Adler (1852–1918) thanked the professor for his frank discussion of the delicate problem created by the Jewish students from the eastern provinces and even granted his point that "the Jew has no part in the largest share of the history of Germany, that his *Bildung* is of today." But, insisting on the possibility of genuine assimilation, Adler goes on to argue that "tribal character is not immutable and already two generations are under the influence of the German mind." And to that he adds a cold-eyed observation: "The Jews happen to be there. They cannot be denied and form an important factor in the cultural development of the nation." Thus the German nation would have to choose either to endure "the thorn in the flesh" or "to assimilate this remnant of a tribe."[14]

Abraham Flexner: An Analysis from Past to Present (Rockville, MD: Kabel, 1986), 97–101. Auerbach's rejection of Billroth's peace offering should probably be seen in a broader context that includes Wagner. From the time of Wagner's republication of *Jewry in Music* in 1869, Auerbach had wanted to dispute it publicly, without ever finding the courage to do so. Finally, in May 1881, he did complete a polemic against the composer, entitling it "Richard Wagner and the Self-Respect of the Jews." But even then he lost his nerve and left the manuscript unpublished. See Paul Lawrence Rose, "One of Wagner's Jewish Friends Berthold Auerbach and his Unpublished Reply to Wagner's Antisemitism (1881)," *Leo Baeck Institute Yearbook* 36 (1991): 219–28. Auerbach may well have considered Billroth a less intimidating target than Wagner at which to aim his fire.

[14] A draft of Adler's speech, probably his first public address, is preserved in a manuscript held in the archive of the Verein für Geschichte der Arbeiterbewegung Wien (Adler-Archiv Mappe 7). Portions of this draft are quoted in Julius Braunthal, *Victor und Friedrich Adler: Zwei Generationen Arbeiterbewegung* (Vienna: Wienervolksbuchhandlung, 1965), 18–19; and Clemens C. Peck, " 'Paralysis progressiva': Zur Figuration des Bildungsproletariats in Jakob Julius Davids Wien-Roman Am Wege sterben," *Internationales Archiv für Sozialgeschichte der deutschen Literatur* 35 (2010): 50–51, on which I have based my corrected transcription of the original: "Es ist wahr, daß der Jude keinen Teil hat an dem größtem Teil der Geschichte Deutschlands, daß seine Bildung von heute ist...aber der Stammeskarakter ist nicht unveränderlich u[nd] bereits zwei Generationen stehen unter dem Einflusse des deutschen Geistes....Aber die Juden sind einmal da; sie lassen sich nicht leugnen und bilden einen wichtigen Factor in der Culturentwicklung der Nation. [Mir erscheint es als hätte die deutsche Nation nur die Wahl,] ob sie den Pfahl im Fleische vorzieht oder ob sie diese Trümmer eines Stammes assimilieren will." See also "The Jewish Background of Victor and Friedrich Adler: Selected Biographical Notes," *Leo Baeck Institute Yearbook* 10 (1965): 269–70; Dennis B. Klein, *The Jewish Origins of the Psychoanalytic Movement* (New York: Praeger, 1981), 52; and Jack Jacobs, *On Socialists and "the Jewish Question"*

Notably, though both the older Auerbach, who had always prided himself on his accomplishment as a *German* Jew, and the younger Adler, a decided German *nationalist*, took issue with what Billroth had written, neither accused him of racial animus.[15] By contrast, Felicitas Seebacher and many other modern scholars have come down rather harder on the surgeon on account of what they perceive precisely as a troubling racial aspect of his discussion.[16] In his book *Medicine and the German Jews*, for example, John M. Efron imputes to Billroth the claim that "Jews could never make competent physicians in the German mold" because they were separated from the Germans by a "cleavage" brought on by "blood." The medical sociologist Jonathan Imber makes the same accusation even more baldly: for Billroth, he writes, "Jews could not be Germans and therefore were unfit for medical education."[17] Such charges are not convincing; the evidence, as we shall see, simply does not support them. Even Peter Pulzer, who, in his classic study *The Rise of Political Antisemitism in Germany and Austria*, had once suggested that *Lehren und Lernen* was responsible for "draw[ing] attention to the dangers of Jewish predominance in medicine," later stepped back from that position and acknowledged that Billroth's main argument had been directed solely against those students from the East, not all of whom were Jews, who were unprepared for medical study.[18]

After Marx (New York and London: New York University Press, 1992), 86–90, all of which rely on Braunthal's study.

[15] Nancy A. Kaiser, "Berthold Auerbach: The Dilemma of the Jewish Humanist from *Vormärz* to Empire," *German Studies Review* 6 (1983): 417; and Margarita Pazi, "Berthold Auerbach and Moritz Hartmann: Two Jewish Writers of the Nineteenth Century," *Leo Baeck Institute Yearbook 18* (1973): 216. I take my characterization of Adler from Steven Beller, *Vienna and the Jews, 1867–1938* (Cambridge: Cambridge University Press, 1987), 155–62; we shall encounter another Jewish German nationalist, the historian and left-liberal politician Heinrich Friedjung, in later chapters.

[16] Seebacher, *Das Fremde im 'deutschen' Tempel der Wissenschaften*, 97–105. See also idem, "'Der operierte Chirurg': Theodor Billroths Deutschnationalismus und akademischer Antisemitismus," *Zeitschrift für Geschichtswissenschaft* 54 (2006): 317–38.

[17] John M. Efron, *Medicine and the German Jews: A History* (New Haven and London: Yale University Press, 2001), 242; and Jonathan B. Imber, Review of M. B. Hart, *The Healthy Jew: The Symbiosis of Judaism and Modern Medicine*, *Sociology* 46 (2009): 97. See also Hillary Hope Herzog, "*Vienna Is Different*": *Jewish Writers in Austria from the Fin de Siècle to the Present* (New York and Oxford: Berghahn, 2011), 17; Sherwin B. Nuland, *The Masterful Spirit—Theodor Billroth* (Birmingham, AL: Classics of Surgery Library, 1984); and Howard Markel, *An Anatomy of Addiction: Sigmund Freud, William Halstead, and the Miracle* (New York: Pantheon, 2011), 25. For an overview, see Seebacher, *Das Fremde im 'deutschen' Tempel der Wissenschaften*, 105–111.

[18] Peter Pulzer, *The Rise of Political Antisemitism in Germany and Austria* (Cambridge, MA: Harvard University Press, 1988), 245; idem, "The Return of Old Hatreds," in

Still other scholars have sought to implicate Billroth's discussion more broadly in the racialist antisemitism that was born in the *Burschenschaften* (nationalist student fraternities) of Austria's universities during the later 1870s and subsequently adopted by the radical *deutschnational* movement of Georg von Schönerer in the 1880s. In his study of the roots of National Socialism in the late Habsburg era, Michael Wladika cites the publication of *Lehren und Lernen* in the fall of 1875 as an "epochal date" in this movement.[19] Steven Beller has traced these roots back further to 1866, when any hope for achieving the failed dream of 1848 for a unified Germany that included German Austria was dashed by Prussia's defeat of the Habsburg military and Austria's subsequent exclusion on that account from the smaller unified German state that Bismarck was in the process of building. He suggests much of the German students' resentment at being exiled in this way from their imagined "homeland" was directed toward the Jews, seen "as alien figures in the German midst." The failure to achieve a pan-German unification was attributable, Beller writes, "not only to a betrayal of Germans by their rulers, but also more fundamentally to Germany's failure to achieve the 'organic' community preached by romanticism." It was easy, he notes, to make the Jews the scapegoats for this failure: they were "non-Christians, outsiders, ethnically different, heavily identified with the 'inorganic' processes of the modern economy, and the financial backers of many of [the] 'corrupt' rulers (especially the Habsburgs)."[20]

Steven M. Lowenstein, Paul Mendes-Flohr, Peter Pulzer, and Monika Richarz, *Integration in Dispute* (= *German-Jewish History in Modern Times*, vol. 3; New York: Columbia University Press, 1997), 211.

[19] Michael Wladika, *Hitlers Vätergeneration: die Ursprüng des Nationalsozialismus in der k. u. k. Monarchie* (Vienna, Cologne, and Weimer: Böhlau Verlag, 2005), 45–46. See also Hein, *Studentischer Antisemitismus in Österreich*. The standard study of Schönerer in English remains Andrew G. Whiteside, *The Socialism of Fools: Georg Ritter von Schönerer and Austrian Pan-Germanism* (Berkeley and Los Angeles: University of California Press, 1975).

[20] Steven Beller, "Hitler's Hero: Georg von Schönerer and the Origins of Nazism," in *In the Shadow of Hitler: Personalities of the Right in Central and Eastern Europe*, ed. Rebecca Haynes and Martyn Rady (London: Taurus, 2011), 43–44. As long as they were understood in cultural rather than racialist terms, the anti-Judaic aspects of this project did not foreclose participation by young Jews. As Beller has noted: "By joining the counter-culture of the radical German Nationalists, Jews were also assimilating into a culture: their rejection of their Jewish fathers should prove their credentials, that they had ceased to be Jews and had become part of the great German *Volk*." Beller, *Vienna and the Jews*, 158.

Beller argues that the students were engaged in more than a critique of the consequences of liberal modernization, however; by incorporating a racial element into their animus against the Jews, they were also embracing modernity, in that, by the 1870s, race was becoming the "modern," scientific way of viewing the various peoples of the world. The "catalyst" in the students' conversion to "modern" racial antisemitism, he writes, was Billroth, with his claim that the "cleavage" that separated Germans and Jews was not merely cultural but also based on blood. To support this claim, Beller notes that the student fraternities began to expel their Jewish members shortly after the publication of *Lehren und Lernen*.[21]

Yet the expulsion of Jews did not begin until three years after the publication of Billroth's treatise, and by then a more probable catalyst for racialist thinking had appeared in the form of an essay written by a man who was a cultural hero to the students in a way that Billroth could never be. In February 1878 the recently inaugurated *Bayreuther Blätter* included a slightly enlarged version of Richard Wagner's previously unpublished "Was ist deutsch?" ("What is German?") from 1865. Here Wagner described the Jews as "an utterly alien element" that had launched an "invasion of the German nature."[22] To be sure, this is a point he had already made in a specifically musical context several years earlier in *Jewry in Music*, with its claim that the Jews were cultural parasites who had no authentic music of their own and could only imitate the authentic music of their host cultures.[23] But in this newer essay he now also explicitly sets the Jews against the German *Burschenschaften*. Alluding to the Carlsbad Decrees of 1819, Wagner argues that when the Austrian state minister Metternich banned the nationalist

---

[21] Ibid. In an earlier formulation of this line of reasoning, Beller described Billroth as "unfortunate," thereby suggesting that although he did not quite charge Billroth with racial antisemitism, he did hold him responsible for helping to unleash it within the Viennese fraternities. See Beller, *Vienna and the Jews*, 191.

[22] Richard Wagner, *Gesammelte Schriften und Dichtungen*, 10 vols., (Leipzig, 1887–1911), 10: 36–53. I have taken my translations in this paragraph from Osbourne, *Richard Wagner: Stories and Essays*, 46, 53–54. Though Billroth had clear ties to the Reading Society of Vienna's German Students, which was essentially a debating club, he does not seem to have been affiliated with any of the student fraternities. The latter were more radical in their German nationalism than the former and came to practice a racial antisemitism that was unknown to the Reading Society before its dissolution by the government in 1878.

[23] For a thoughtful recent study, see James Loeffler, "Wagner's 'Jewish Music': Antisemitism and Aesthetics in Modern Jewish Culture," *Jewish Social Studies: History, Culture, Society* n.s.15 (2009): 2–3.

fraternities on the alleged grounds of Jacobin-inspired political subversion, that had simply allowed "the Jewish speculator who stood outside, seeking nothing but his personal profit . . . to infiltrate himself into the midst of the German people and State, and, in the end, not merely govern it, but make it completely his own." This was red flag to a bull. And it seems scarcely a matter of chance that in the same year in which "What is German?" was published *Libertas* became the first Austrian student fraternity to dismiss its Jewish members on racial grounds.

The publication of Wagner's racialist diatribe in 1878 represents, in my view, the truly epochal moment in the rise of *völkisch* antisemitism among the most nationalist elements of Vienna's student body. And even if *Lehren und Lernen* was also used by the students to give respectable cover to their racism, that alone says nothing about Billroth's intent. We shall look more closely at the subject of racialist antisemitism in Chapter 6, but for now let us consider instead what we may learn from the episode about the ideological positions on the question of Germanness and difference found within Billroth's own social class of middle-aged liberals. Margaret Notley has suggested that Billroth's controversial remarks reflect the "German nationalism and . . . attendant casual anti-Semitism" that she associates with the "political views held by Brahms and his Viennese circle."[24] She does not explore the question at any length, however. Nor does she indicate whether she means to include in this circle the likes of Carl Goldmark, Ignaz Brüll, Julius Epstein, and Anton Door, Vienna's leading Jewish musicians, all of whom were closely affiliated with the "musical Triple Alliance" (*musikalischer Dreibund*) of Billroth, Brahms, and Hanslick.[25] It is evident from the foregoing review of the literature that Billroth's excursus has given rise to a number of interpretations, some more compelling than others. We may never know exactly what meaning lurked in the Rembrandt-like shadows of the author's prose. But in what follows I will suggest that if we take care to read his controversial discussion of the Jewish students in light of the circumstances that prompted it, and read the reaction to it in Vienna's political press in light of the ideology of Austrian German liberalism, we shall at least gain a more nuanced view of the entire affair.

[24] Notley, *Lateness and Brahms*, 19–20.
[25] Hanslick, *Aus meinem Leben*, 2: 94.

A Context for the Controversy

Lehren und Lernen was written at a time when the Humboldtian model of higher education, introduced at the founding of the University of Berlin in 1810 but not fully adopted at the Vienna Medical School until 1872, had come under attack by many of Billroth's Austrian colleagues.[26] The central principle of this model was the unity of teaching and research, which held that the role of the university was to advance knowledge by original and critical investigation, not simply to transmit the legacy of the past or to teach skills. This principle reflected the university's status as an unabashedly elite institution, basically unconcerned with vocational or technical subjects. It was designed for a student body drawn from the ranks of gymnasium graduates and was especially well suited for the learned professions such as medicine and law, with their bodies of theory and knowledge that had to be kept current through research. Two other principles should be mentioned here. Academic freedom—the so-called teaching and learning freedoms (*Lehr- und Lernfreiheiten*)—meant that professors were free to deal with their subject without interference by the church or state, and also that students enjoyed free mobility from one institution to another, were under no requirement to attend lectures, and were placed under no compulsion in the order, choice, and duration of their studies other than that imposed by the final oral exams each would eventually be required to pass.[27] A third principle granted a central role in the university to the philosophy faculty (i.e., the modern faculty of arts and sciences), not only because it was the natural home for research, but also because it was through "philosophical" study that the student received *Bildung*.[28]

Because the Vienna Medical School drew large numbers of students from the non-German-speaking regions of the monarchy, many of whom lacked the academic preparation assumed by the Humboldtian model, some of the

---

[26] On the reform of Austria's universities along Humboldtian lines, see Gary B. Cohen, *Education and Middle-Class Society in Imperial Austria, 1848–1918* (West Lafayette, IN: Purdue University Press, 1996), 11–54; and idem, "Ideals and Realities in the Austrian Universities, 1850–1914," in *Rediscovering History: Culture, Politics, and the Psyche*, ed. Michael S. Roth (Stanford: Stanford University Press, 1994), 83–101.

[27] The title of Billroth's book makes obvious reference to this fundamental principle of the Humboldtian model.

[28] Among numerous studies, see Marek Kwiek, "Revisiting the Classical German Idea of the University (On the Nationalization of the Modern Institution)," *Polish Journal of Philosophy* 2 (2008): 1–24.

Austrian professors in the faculty favored reinstituting a carefully prescribed curriculum and wanted to emphasize the practical treatment of disease and to minimize "philosophical" study, fearing that to do otherwise risked turning out incompetent physicians. Fighting against this proposed backsliding, Billroth used his book to mount a vigorous defense of the Humboldtian reforms. Tatjana Buklijas has singled out two criticisms that Billroth sought to address.[29] First, in response to those who held that medical students need not study the natural sciences (taught in the philosophy faculty) because the aim of medical education was to instruct the students in treating illness, not to become scholars, Billroth argued that only those who had been trained in analytic and scientific thinking could become outstanding physicians, and that it was necessary, moreover, for physicians to be broadly educated so that they would be regarded in their communities with all due professional respect. Second, responding to critics who wanted to reestablish a fixed curriculum and compulsory lecture attendance as the best means of facilitating the learning of a student body that was drawn from a broad range of social classes and the far reaches of the vast multinational state, Billroth argued that limiting the student's learning freedom in this way would be counterproductive to the development of the self-respect of those "marked talents" for whom the system was designed; at the same time, he made no secret of his belief that it was not "possible to make energetic, industrious, intelligent physicians out of slack, lazy, stupid students, by means of school-like discipline at the universities."[30]

For Billroth, then, the "dark side" of the situation at his home university lay not with the newly adopted German model of higher education but, as noted, with the large size and diverse demographic makeup of the Viennese student body. Enrollment in the medical faculty had been steadily increasing for a number of years, fueled by expanding economic opportunities during the rising liberal tide of the 1860s and early 1870s, as well as by the new freedoms guaranteed in the liberal constitution of 1867.[31] By 1875, the year in which Billroth's book appeared, more than twelve hundred medical

[29] Tatjana Buklijas, "Surgery and National Identity in Late Nineteenth-Century Vienna," *Studies in History and Philosophy of Biological and Biomedical Sciences* 38 (2007): 766. In what follows, I largely follow Buklijas, except as noted. See also Lesky, *The Vienna Medical School of the 19th Century*, 261–73.

[30] Billroth, *Lehren und Lernen*, 149; *Medical Sciences in the German University*, 104–5.

[31] Even prior to the full emancipation of the Jews in 1867, however, medicine had long provided one path to social advancement for Habsburg Jews, who had previously been blocked from professional opportunities in the state bureaucracy.

students were enrolled in Vienna, far more than elsewhere, and, given the limited availability of suitable physical facilities, the author had reason to doubt whether all of them could be properly trained.

Beyond that concern, however, lay another that had to do with the social and economic background of the students from the Eastern lands of the monarchy, and in particular with those

> young men [who] come to Vienna, mostly from Galicia and Hungary, *most* of them Israelites, who have absolutely nothing, and who have conceived the insane idea that they can earn money in Vienna (by teaching, through small jobs at the stock exchange, by peddling matches door-to-door, or taking employment as post office or telegraph clerks in Vienna and elsewhere, etc.) and at the same time study medicine.[32]

Billroth opined that a good number of these young men, with their "entire lack of refined breeding at home and of association with educated people during their studies," had been pressured by their families to take up medicine merely for reasons of social prestige, even when they had no interest in medicine or aptitude for scientific study. With little material means at their disposal, they had no choice but to take outside employment in order to survive and so inevitably gave less than their full attention to their studies. They were also likely to have attended inferior secondary schools, and many even struggled to speak and understand the German language. How, Billroth asks, could "academic freedom and the scientific method of instruction...be accountable for failing to make good physicians out of such material?"[33]

The situation was much better, he writes, in Germany, where the ranks of the medical students were drawn from the sons of the clergy, petty bureaucrats, and school teachers, that is, from families that, notwithstanding their

---

[32] Billroth, *Lehren und Lernen*, 148; *The Medical Sciences in the German University*, 106 (emphasis added). I am grateful to Gary Cohen for his suggestion that during this period in Austrian history, the term *Israelit* was often used in polite bourgeois society when referring to a member of the Jewish community in much the same way as the term *Hebrew* was used for this purpose in polite English-speaking society at this time. The founding of Vienna's Israelitische Kultusgemeinde Wien, the body that officially represents the city's Jews, took place in 1852, three years after Francis Joseph recognized the existence of the "Hebrew Community of Vienna."

[33] Billroth, *Lehren und Lernen*, 148–49; *The Medical Sciences in the German University*, 106–7. Billroth minces no words in describing these students as "empty-headed strivers, with their purblind eyes, hands like lead, and brains like clay, with a dictionary knowledge and a pathetic incompetence."

often fairly modest means, were members of the educated class.[34] In Vienna, by contrast, students of this background were mostly to be found only among "the great majority of the German students, the students from the quintessentially German [urdeutsch] old Imperial lands." He draws particular attention to Bohemia and to the many "Germanized Czechs" who had made great contributions to medicine. To make the distinction clear, he concludes, "In the interest of truth I have repeatedly pointed out that the undesirable elements are not German, but Galician and Hungarian Jewish elements, who, as stated before, can flourish only at Vienna."[35]

Billroth must have known all this would raise eyebrows. But if he sought to deflect criticism in the lengthy footnote that follows, he only succeeded in making matters worse.[36] After disavowing any association with what he calls "the modern Jew baiters who are now so popular" and acknowledging that he knew many Jews who were talented for the natural sciences and the medical profession and who possessed the general intellectual aptitude, energy, and capacity for hard work necessary to become good physicians, he goes on to maintain that many of the Jewish students in Vienna—by implication he is still referring only to the Hungarian and Galician Jews—were poor candidates for medicine because of their inadequate economic circumstances and uncultured social background.[37] Moreover, he even acknowledges thinking that many Eastern Jews had become "sharply degenerate through perpetual intermarriages and early marriages," approaching in some regions "a certain physical and intellectual squalidness."[38]

What generated the most heated response was the conclusion of the footnote, which requires quotation in full:

[34] Here Billroth is, in effect, describing the social milieu in which he had been reared and schooled.

[35] Billroth, *Lehren und Lernen*, 150–52; *The Medical Sciences in the German University*, 108–10.

[36] Billroth, *Lehren und Lernen*, 152–54n; this footnote was omitted from the English edition.

[37] On the differences in socioeconomic background between the Hungarian and Galician Jewish immigrants to Vienna, on the one hand, and those from Bohemia and Moravia, on the other, see Rozenblit, "Jewish Assimilation in Vienna," 230–32. It is notable that Billroth does not censure the many Jewish students from the crown lands of Bohemian, Moravia, and Silesia.

[38] Billroth, *Lehren und Lernen*, 153n. This passage calls to mind nothing so much as the similar derogatory comments once commonly expressed in the United States about inbreeding among the poor rural populations of Appalachia.

It is a rather common error to speak of the Jews as if speaking of Germans, or Hungarians, or Frenchmen who just happen to have a different religion from most of the other inhabitants of Germany, Hungary, or France. Quite often it is forgotten that the Jews are a sharply defined nation, and that a Jew can no more become a German than a Persian, Frenchman, New Zealander, or African can. Those who are called Jewish Germans are simply those who happen to speak German, happen to have been brought up in Germany, even if they poetize and philosophize [*dichten und denken*] in the German language more beautifully and better than do many of the purest Germans. They lose their national tradition as little as the Germans lose their German type where they are scattered among other nations, as in Transylvania, America. It therefore can neither be expected nor desired that the Jews become German-national in the sense that during national struggles they are able to feel the way the Germans themselves do. What they lack for that is, above all, that upon which our German sensibilities, more than we want to admit, are based, namely the entire period of medieval romanticism. The Jews have no reason to ponder with special pleasure the German Middle Ages, while this, along with Classical Antiquity (which in general is rather far removed from the Jew) completely pervades German youth and even the German intelligentsia. It is clear that significant persons of every time and every nation will always approach the great universal human questions with goodwill, but it is just as clear to me that, despite all reflection and individual sympathy, I feel the gulf between pure German blood and pure Jewish blood as deeply today as a Teuton may have felt the gulf between himself and a Phoenician.[39]

With rhetoric of this kind, it is no wonder that Brahms wryly characterized the book as "dangerous."[40]

[39] Ibid., 153–54n.

[40] Although Brahms made no annotations in his copy of the book, he did leave a bookmark (fashioned from an old piece of newspaper from the period) between pages 150 and 151, which would have made it easy for him to find the passage in question. I am grateful to Otto Biba, of the Gesellschaft der Musikfreunde, for sharing this information with me.

From Arndt to Wagner to Hanslick

A few weeks after it appeared, *Lehren und Lernen* was the subject of an unsigned two-part review in Vienna's liberal flagship, the *Neue Freie Presse*.[41] Like Billroth, this anonymous reviewer assumes German cultural superiority and, with that, the comparatively low "cultural development" (*Culturgrade*) of Billroth's targets. (It is not possible to know whether the reviewer was a gentile or Germanized Jew, but it makes no difference: the claim of cultural superiority vis-à-vis the Eastern Jews would have been the same.)[42] But then—implicitly criticizing the Prussian Billroth for his evident insensitivity to a key tenet of traditional Austrian liberalism—the reviewer goes on to note with pride that it was "a mission of German scholarship to make the sons of those lands familiar with the blessings of German scholarship."[43] He admonishes Billroth not for seeing difference in the Eastern Jewish students but for his evident unwillingness to do his patriotic duty as a German liberal living in Austria to help them overcome that difference by adopting German culture and so also, what is no less important, rejecting the blandishments of non-German nationalist movements. Indeed, he writes:

> We have every reason to be happy that [these students] avoid... the high pressure of Hungarian and Polish national agitation and seek their education in Vienna, and the personal sacrifice they bring to this goal only makes their effort all the more worthy. It is self-evident that the heterogeneity of the students' preparation offers the teacher greater difficulty here. Nevertheless, for public, cultural considerations, as well as for public health concerns in the eastern lands, we have every reason to be nothing but satisfied by the pouring in of students from those regions.

It especially disturbs the reviewer that Billroth sees the Jews as a separate and well-defined nation, and he sneers at the value Billroth places on "medieval romanticism" in the formation of German sensibilities, since that period had been characterized by "feudal authority, serfdom, an all-powerful church,

---

41 "Billroth über das medicinische Studium," *Neue Freie Presse, Abendblatt*, November 11 and 18, 1875.

42 For a useful introduction, see Malacai Haim Hacohen, *Karl Popper, The Formative Years, 1902–1945: Politics and Philosophy in Interwar Vienna* (Cambridge: Cambridge University Press, 2000), 25–34. See also Aschheim, *Brothers and Strangers*.

43 "Billroth über das medicinische Studium" (II), 4, from which I have taken the quotations in the next several paragraphs.

Aquinian state theory, robber barons, and torture," all of which was anathema to contemporary liberals. He even likens Billroth to a "race politician," who, as he imagines, must be miserable to be surrounded by thirty-four Jewish colleagues in the medical school, and he concludes:

> Billroth's "Jewry in Medicine," like Richard Wagner's "Jewry in Music," will remain an isolated voice,...merely the "personal opinion" of a celebrated surgeon. It is not granted to everyone to be born on Ur-German soil, to call himself a fellow countryman of Ernst Moriz [*sic*] Arndt and to be able to tie his childhood memories to the homeland of the cult of Herta [the Teutonic fertility goddess]. Millions of Germans and Austrians do not feel this "blood cleavage"; they measure their fellow citizens in accordance with their character and activity, patriotic love, and freethinking.

For now, let us pass over Wagner's screed on the Jews—which, as we know, scarcely remained merely the personal opinion of a celebrated composer—and consider instead this reviewer's reference to the old liberal nationalist Ernst Moritz Arndt (1769–1860). Billroth's rhetoric clearly does recall Arndt's claim that the German community was based on a common descent and, indeed, a shared historical memory of the Teutonic Middle Ages. Yet, as Brian Vick has argued, Arndt's position on the Jews does not, as is often suggested, foreshadow the racialist antisemitism of the later decades of the nineteenth century; indeed, he included the ancient Hebrews among "the progressive world-historical peoples feeding into modern culture and civilization."[44] It is Arndt's fierce anti-French rhetoric—his iconic anthem "Was ist des Deutschen Vaterland" ("What is the German's Fatherland," 1813) includes one strophe that describes "every Frenchie" (*Franzmann*) as the German's enemy—that is most relevant to Billroth's German nationalism, not Arndt's occasional outbursts against Jews. This merits a brief digression, not least because German nationalism and antisemitism during the later nineteenth century are so frequently seen as two sides of the same coin.

Like other North German youth of the *Vormärz*, the young Billroth—and this was no doubt true as well for the young Brahms—had been reared on tales of the deprivations his elders had endured during the Napoleonic occupation, thereby developing a youthful hatred for the French inculcated

---

[44] Brian Vick, "Arndt and German Ideas of Race: Between Kant and Social Darwinism," in *Ernst Moritz Arndt (1769–1860): Deutscher Nationalismus—Europa—Transatlantische Perspektiven*, ed. Walter Erhart and Arne Koch (Tübingen: Max Niemeyer, 2007), 76.

at least in part through "Arndt's songs and the soldiers' songs from the year of 1813" that were sung at every family gathering.[45] The outbreak of war between France and Prussia in August 1870 reawakened these boyhood memories. Brahms could only watch from the sidelines, and in a letter to his father of August 5, 1870, he expressed his disappointment that he could not "join in the shooting."[46] By contrast, Billroth volunteered for two months of military hospital service at the beginning of the Prussian campaign against the French. Although he did so primarily because of the opportunity this presented to develop improved techniques in wartime surgery, his patriotic motives in deciding to go to war cannot be discounted.[47] The experience proved to be cathartic. This comes through clearly in a letter to the Swiss anatomist Wilhelm His written shortly after the formal conclusion of hostilities in May 1871. Here the surgeon recounts the rush of emotion that overcame him several months earlier when the war broke out:

> The *furor teutonicus* raged within me. All of us in Germany felt the moment had come when it would be decided whether Germany was doomed to eternal political impotence or was strong enough to be an independent state. It was a struggle for existence. The primeval German [*deutscher Urmensch*], who distrusts every other nation, and above all hates the Gauls [*Wälschen*], came out everywhere. There is something almost intoxicating about feeling, at least in the imagination, like a strong beast. The Germans' sense of being equal to other nations in culture and spirit and yet of receiving only a patronizing recognition from the rest of Europe, as the government bestows it on a capable civil servant, had reached an unbearable crescendo. The duration and nature of the war was rightly lamented, and it was thought that racial hatred would be unforgiving. That may be so on the French side. In Germany racial hatred used to exist; now it is gone.[48]

---

[45] Letter of June 24, 1871, from Billroth to Wilhelm Lübke, in *Briefe*, 5th ed., 141. Notably, Billroth's paternal grandfather, in whose home he lived following the early death of his father, had been a schoolboy friend of Arndt.

[46] *Johannes Brahms: Life and Letters*, ed. Styra Avins, trans. Josef Eisinger and Styra Avins (Oxford and New York: Oxford University Press, 1997), 414.

[47] Theodor Billroth, *Chirurgische Briefe aus den Kriegs-Lazarethen in Weissenburg und Mannheim, 1870* (Berlin: August Hirschwald, 1872).

[48] Letter of May 21, 1871, in *Briefe*, 5th ed., 138–41. Brahms's own *furor teutonicus* can seen in his comment to his father of August 5, 1870, that he was "eagerly [waiting] for the French to get a good thrashing" (Avins, *Johannes Brahms: Life and Letters*, 414).

After experiencing the heady moment of Germany's awakening as a nation-state, Billroth seemed all the more dispirited by the prospect of living and working again in multinational Austria. Already in April 1870 Francis Joseph had dismissed the Bürger Ministry after only three years, and for the next twenty months the government was placed in the successive hands of more conservative and federalist cabinets headed by Count Adam Potocki and Count Carl von Hohenwart. The latter's efforts to accommodate the Czechs' demand for an arrangement similar to the Austro-Hungarian *Ausgleich* of 1867—a fearful prospect for bourgeois Germans living in Bohemia and Moravia—came to nothing, however, and by the end of 1871 the emperor was forced to turn once more to the German liberals to form a new cabinet headed by Adolf von Auersperg. But Billroth could not have foreseen the liberals' return to power when, on March 2, 1871, he reported pessimistically to a friend in Berlin that "we Germans here are only tolerated; the state is becoming more and more Slavic and Hungarian. It is a matter of life and death...that we at least maintain our scientific connection with the German Reich."[49] Seen in this light, Billroth's uncompromising defense of the Humboldtian reforms at the Vienna Medical School finds a broader political context in which to be understood.[50]

At precisely this time a division was taking place within the liberal ranks in Austria, more in response to evident Slavic gains within Austria than to anything else, between the moderate, centralist *Alten* (the Old) and the progressive, more nationally conscious *Jungen* (the Young). Despite the nomenclature, this divide was less generational than it was ideological. As the historian Richard Charmatz put it, those who were "old" placed their "Austrianism above Germanism," while those who felt they "had come into the world as German[s]" were "young."[51] It is not surprising Billroth lent

---

[49] *Briefe*, 5th ed., 141.

[50] Here, too, we may draw a parallel with Brahms. Obviously referring to his newly completed *Triumphlied*, which celebrated the German triumphs of 1870, the composer wrote thus to Joseph Joachim in October 1871 by way of announcing his intention to travel from Vienna to Berlin for an extended stay that winter: "I can hardly sing to the Bohemian Ministers in Vienna a song I have written acclaiming Bismarck" (Avins, *Johannes Brahms: Life and Letters*, 427). On the *Triumphlied*, see Daniel Beller-McKenna, *Brahms and the German Spirit* (Cambridge, MA, and London: Harvard University Press, 2004), 98–132.

[51] On the ideological differences between the *Jungen* and *Alten*, see Judson, *Exclusive Revolutionaries*, 167–74. Also useful is Carl E. Schorske, "Generational Tension and Cultural Change," in his *Thinking with History: Explorations in the Passage to Modernism* (Princeton: Princeton University Press, 1998), 141–56. I have quoted Charmatz from ibid., 142. For the original discussion, see Richard Charmatz, *Deutsch-Österreichische*

his support at this time to a pair of new initiatives in Vienna that were very much in line with the nationalist sensibilities of the *Jungen*. In December 1871 he became a founding faculty member of the Reading Society of Vienna's German Students, the same student group that would later come to his defense during the Billroth Affair.[52] In the same month, the *Deutsche Zeitung* was established in Vienna as the self-proclaimed "organ of the German party." Billroth not only bought stock in the new enterprise but also accepted appointment to its political advisory board, serving in this capacity alongside the former liberal cabinet ministers Carl Auersperg and Karl Rechbauer.

The inaugural issue of this newspaper appeared on December 17, 1871, and included an essay by Ludwig Speidel, the new organ's first feuilleton editor, entitled "Der Gott im deutschen Lager" ("The God in the German Camp").[53] Speidel begins this piece by celebrating Germany's triumphs in the "great world-historic year of 1870" but soon turns more reflective. After briefly touching upon the outpouring of thanksgiving to the biblical god that the founding of the German *Kaiserreich* had engendered, Speidel takes up his main purpose by describing a second god who was "in the German camp," one more in keeping with his own liberal sensibilities. This god was no divine being but rather the secular work ethic of the Germans themselves, "a deeply moral spirit of work, an anonymous god, who rules throughout German history." This second god had enabled the Germans to transcend poverty and rise to great accomplishment, and it was not only in the camp of the new Reich Germans, Speidel adds, but also in the Austrian camp. It had already caused the land to be cleared, the fields to be tilled, the cities to be founded, and the workshops to be filled. Now its cause—here Speidel

---

Politik: Studien über den Liberalismus und über die Auswärtige Politik Österreichs (Leipzig: Duncker & Humblot, 1907), 72–73. In a sense, this split between the *Alten* and *Jungen* anticipated the divide between the Austrian and German factions in the debate at the Vienna Medical School a few years later over the Humboldtian reform of the curriculum.

[52] Billroth served on the group's board until announcing his resignation on November 26, 1875, probably in an attempt to distance himself from his more vocal supporters at the beginning of the "Billroth Affair." He was subsequently listed as an honorary member in the group's annual report for 1875–76. See *Jahresbericht des Lesevereins der deutschen Studenten Wien's über das V. Vereinsjahr 1875–76* (Vienna: Selbstverlag des Lesevereins der deutschen Studenten, 1876), 9, 15, cited in Petra Zudrell, *Der Kulturkritiker und Schriftsteller Max Nordau: Zwischen Zionismus, Deutschtum und Judentum* (Würzburg: Königshausen & Neumann, 2003), 105n.

[53] L. Sp. [Ludwig Speidel], "Der Gott in der deutschen Lager," *Deutsche Zeitung*, December 17, 1871, from which all the quotations in this paragraph are taken.

sounds the old liberal imperative—was to deliver "civilization and *Bildung* to the *Ostmark*."[54] Speidel then concludes in the spirit of the new paper itself: "And this heroic and victorious god will be in the camp of the Germans of Austria and will battle for their cause, as long as they remain true to him in their sincere beliefs."

We can easily imagine that the liberal nationalist Billroth would have agreed wholeheartedly with Speidel's idea of a secular god of hard work who would battle for the Germans' cause, in *Deutschösterreich* as well as in the newly founded *Kaiserreich*. Matters were different several days later, however, when Speidel published an essay by the German composer and writer Peter Cornelius entitled "Deutsche Kunst und Richard Wagner" ("German Art and Richard Wagner"). In an editorial footnote, Speidel, no Wagnerian himself, declared: "[Wagner's] cause can no longer be separated from the German cause."[55] After explaining what Speidel had done in a letter of December 31, 1871, to his Stuttgart friend Wilhelm Lübke, a noted art historian, Billroth opened up with his outraged feelings about it:

> You cannot conceive of my anger over [Speidel's] remark. I could not do anything publicly, because I am a shareholder in the newspaper, but I have written a letter to the editorial board that was not bad either. Today I explained to the president of the political advisory board that I have resigned, since I could no longer stand with an editorial staff which may soon declare that the cause of Messrs Liszt (at whose Christus oratorio everything stops) or Mosenthal (see his latest opus Madeleine Morel) or [Wagner's favorite painter] Makart et al. can no longer be separated from the German cause.... Leaving music aside, what is "Wagner's cause" in the pens of Cornelius, Nohl and others...? But now Wagner's Götterdämmerung! Should that no longer be separated from the German cause?... Well, this is clearly the devil speaking![56]

---

[54] *Ostmark* is derived from the Latin *marcha Orientalis,* the term by which the southeastern frontier march of the Holy Roman Empire was identified. For a discussion of the historical context of its use in the period under question here, see Markus Erwin Haider, *Im Streit um die österreichische Nation: Nationale Leitwörter in Österreich 1866–1938* (Vienna, Cologne, and Weimar: Böhlau, 1998), 95–108 (esp. at 97–98). As suggested by Speidel's comment, the term *Ostmark* was closely associated at this time with the notion of a German civilizing mission in the East. This would later change, as we shall see.

[55] Peter Cornelius, "Deutsche Kunst und Richard Wagner," *Deutsche Zeitung*, December 29 and 31, 1871. Speidel's footnote appeared in the first installment.

[56] Billroth, *Briefe,* 4th ed., 155–56. In the published edition, the letter is mistakenly dated December 31, 1872; the correct date can be ascertained by its contents.

Billroth loathed the Wagnerian musical project; there is no question about that. But when it came to the Jews, was Wagner's cause also Billroth's cause? The anonymous reviewer of *Lehren und Lernen* for the *Neue Freie Presse* implied as much. And because of Billroth's positing of an essential unbridgeable gulf between Germans and Jews, it is easy to understand why. Beginning with Moses Mendelssohn in the later eighteenth century, Jews in German Central Europe had adopted the Enlightenment ideology of *Bildung* as the cultural and social matrix for shaping a modern identity as members of an essentially ahistorical *Kulturnation*. But here, by positing a *Volksnation* that was a matter not of culture but of shared ethnicity, myth, and historical memory, Billroth risked being seen to deny all Jews, even the most cultured, the possibility of becoming Germans.[57]

Yet for Billroth the existence of a historical *Volksnation* clearly did not preclude the existence of a modern *Kulturnation* to which ambitious, upwardly mobile Jews could belong.[58] For one thing, he did not (*pace* the reviewer from the *Neue Freie Presse*) question the *Deutschtum* of Seegen and his many other Jewish colleagues at the medical school. Indeed, it is evident from the section in *Lehren und Lernen* in which Billroth discusses "the composition of the various German peoples in the teaching staff" that his tallies include all the Jewish professors from Cisleithania among the Germans.[59] Moreover, if pure bloodlines were decisive for Billroth, how can we account for those "Germanized Czechs" whom he praised for their distinction in medicine?[60]

---

[57] For a trenchant discussion of the tensions between these two conceptions of the German nation, see Paul Mendes-Flohr, *German Jews: A Dual Identity* (New Haven and London: Yale University Press, 1999).

[58] Billroth probably would not have disagreed in principle with what Marsha Rozenblit has described as the tripartite nature of identity available to Jews during the late Habsburg period: Austrian, in terms of political allegiance; German, in terms of culture; and Jewish, in terms of ethnicity. See Marsha Rozenblit, *Reconstructing a National Identity: The Jews of Habsburg Austria During the First World War* (Oxford: Oxford University Press, 2001), 14–38.

[59] Billroth, *Lehren und Lernen*, 275–76; *The Medical Sciences in the German University*, 178.

[60] Billroth's expression "Germanized Czechs" is misleading. As we saw in Chapter 1, German and Czech ethnic groups emerged only gradually in the Czech crown lands from a wider "Bohemian" population that before 1848 (and even later in many cases) showed little in the way of articulated ethnic loyalties. What Billroth probably has in mind in this instance, then, are those educated *Bohemians* of whatever confession who, during the third quarter of the nineteenth century, chose to identify as Germans rather than as Czechs, not *Czechs* who had become Germans. At all events, the important point to be made is that Billroth acknowledged the possibility of Germanization along cultural lines. We thus have no reason to think that when Billroth praised those "well bred and cultured" medical students at Vienna who came from the *"urdeutsch* old

That Billroth's list of "nations"—and nation, not race, is the term he uses throughout—includes the motley likes of Persia (a cultural entity of long historical standing), France (a modern nation-state), New Zealand (a well-established British colony), and Africa (a large and diverse land mass of countless tribal societies that was in the midst of being colonized by more than one European power) ought to tell us that we are not dealing here with any theory of race in the modern sense of the word.

Billroth's discourse, then, is nationalist but not racialist as we now think of that term. When he speaks of racial hatred between the Germans and the French and of a gulf between those of pure German blood and those of pure Jewish blood, he is invoking these ideas "naïvely," which is to say, without the pernicious implications that would eventually adhere to these concepts in German Central Europe. They are the means of denoting the connections that bind individuals to the nation as a historical community of descent.[61] And though Billroth does not speak of a "motherland" or "fatherland," he was getting at the same idea when, while writing about the *furor teutonicus* that had overcome him at the outbreak of war between Prussia and France in 1870, he recalled the anti-French patriotic songs of 1813 that were sung at every family gathering. The idea of the nation was passed along from one generation to the next. Finally, Billroth does not assert that Jews could not become Germans.[62] His claim was that they could not become "German national" during times of "national struggle" that often had roots in a premodern history that, as even Victor Adler acknowledged, the Jews did not share.

The point of departure for Billroth's unfortunate remark about a "blood cleavage" between Germans and Jews surely was not, as the anonymous reviewer for the *Neue Freie Presse* had suggested, Wagner's *Jewry in Music*. It may instead have been a claim made by his close friend (and fellow anti-Wagnerian) Hanslick in the feuilleton from 1866 on Vienna's famous Jewish cantor Salomon Sulzer that we considered earlier in connection with *Die Königin von Saba*. This essay was republished four years later in

Imperial lands" he was excluding the likes of Adler (born in Prague) and Freud (born in the Moravian town of Freiberg), along with other German Jewish medical students of similar middle-class backgrounds.

[61] I take this notion of a "naïve" use of the category of race or blood from Alberto Mario Banti, "Deep Images in Nineteenth-Century Nationalist Narratives," *Historein* 8 (2008): 2.

[62] As Vick notes, even for the "racist" Arndt, it was possible for Jews who converted to Christianity to be accepted as members of the German nation; see Vick, "Arndt and German Ideas of Race," 76.

Aus dem Concertsaal, an anthology of Hanslick's reviews from the years 1848 to 1868 that Billroth enthusiastically recommended to his friend Lübke.[63] For Hanslick, as we have seen, Sulzer's compositions displayed "a particularly Oriental-Jewish imprint." This was in keeping with his disputation of Ambros's claim that modern synagogue music in Germany, Spain, and Poland had, through assimilation, taken on the characteristics of the music of the host nations in which it was created. Particularly notable is the way in which Hanslick's counterclaim that "stubborn adherence to national customs and traditions" runs even more strongly among Jews than "the lineament of assimilation" looks ahead to Billroth's claim that the Jews, even those who can "poetize and philosophize" in the German language, never quite "lose their national tradition." In the overall context of an admiring essay—notably, one written before Wagner had charged the critic with hiding his Jewish heritage—Hanslick's comments evidently did not strike anyone as showing an aggressive attitude toward the Jews. When echoed by Billroth in the context of his discussion of the "dark side" of the Viennese situation, they came off differently.

Let us make no mistake: it was the idea of *racial* (not cultural or religious) difference that was the basis of antisemitism, when that term emerged in 1879 to distinguish a disturbing new form of anti-Judaic sentiment from which there was no escaping. Those who argue that Billroth was an antisemite in this sense must rest their case on a single footnote that does not yield its meaning as easily as they want to believe. At all events, we would do well to remember that Billroth's exclusionary rhetoric had far more to do with the traditional liberal criteria of conviction and achievement—markers of social class—than it ever did with race or ethnicity.[64]

The Immediate Aftermath and Beyond

If *Lehren und Lernen* leaves any doubt on that question, evidence from the last twenty years of Billroth's life should remove it. We shall consider some of this evidence in Chapter 6, in which the music-loving Billroth will play

[63] Letter from Billroth to Lübke of January 30, 1870, in Theodor Billroth, *Briefe von Theodor Billroth*, 2nd ed., ed. Georg Fischer (Hannover and Leipzig: Hannchen, 1896), 117.

[64] This point is made implicitly in John W. Boyer, *Political Radicalism in Late Habsburg Vienna: Origins of the Christian Social Movement, 1848–1897* (Chicago and London: University of Chicago Press, 1981), 455–56n.

a key role in our examination of Goldmark's career at the height of his fame in the 1880s and 1890s. Other evidence from these later years that speaks to the question of Billroth's elitist but fundamentally nonracialist attitudes is better considered here, however, by way of concluding our discussion of the Billroth Affair. In a letter to His of January 2, 1881, that has nothing to do with the Jewish Question, Billroth emphasized the importance to anyone's upbringing of coming "from a good home" (*aus gutem Hause*) and states his conviction that admission to the university should be restricted to "only the most talented schoolboys."[65] And when he went on in this letter to claim superiority for the Germans in science, medicine, and surgery, he was certainly not excluding from this scientific elite his former student and assistant Anton Wölfler, a Bohemian-born Jew with whom, a few weeks later, he would perform the world's first successful gastric resection.[66]

Five years later, in an extended postscript to *Lehren und Lernen*, Billroth upped the ante on upbringing by claiming that it was more important for a physician to come from "a good home" than to possess "a gymnasium diploma and doctoral degree *summa cum laude*."[67] Once bitten twice shy, Billroth was careful this time not to single out any group of students for reproach. Yet

---

[65] Billroth, *Briefe*, 5th ed., 255. On attempts by the Austrian Ministry of Education and even Francis Joseph himself to encourage some students from disadvantaged backgrounds to seek vocational training rather than professional education, see Cohen, "Ideals and Reality in the Austrian Universities," 84–85.

[66] Billroth, *Briefe*, 5th ed., 256. Two years later, in a letter of July 3, 1883, to Vincenz Czerny, Billroth praised Wölfler's great skill as a surgeon, as well as his admirable human qualities, and he lamented that it could only be his protégé's "crooked nose" (*krumme Nase*) that was standing in the way of his receiving a proper academic appointment in Germany; Theodor Billroth, *Briefe von Theodor Billroth*, 7th ed., ed. Georg Fischer (Hannover and Leipzig: Hannchen, 1906), 304. Wölfler eventually became professor of surgery at Graz (1886) and later at Prague (1895); his *Die chirurgische Behandlung des Kropfes* (1887) was dedicated to Billroth. For Billroth's delighted letter in response, see Billroth, *Briefe*, 5th ed., 387–89. Much additional evidence could be adduced to dispute any notion that Billroth questioned the ability of *German* Jews to excel in medicine at the highest levels. For example, he chose to complete his doctorate at Berlin with the great Jewish experimental pathologist Ludwig Traube. Moreover, he chose Josef Breuer, whose father had taught religion in Vienna's Jewish community (and who later attended Brahms in his final illness), as his family internist, and later attempted, albeit unsuccessfully, to induce Breuer to accept a position in the medical faculty at Vienna.

[67] Theodor Billroth, *Aphorismen zum "Lehren und Lernen der medicinischen Wissenschaften"* (Vienna: Carl Gerold's Sohn, 1886), 53. For an English translation of this follow-up volume to *Lehren und Lernen*, see Absolon, *The Study of the Medical Sciences*, 39–83.

Deborah R. Coen, rehearsing a familiar theme, has recently construed this remark as evidence of "thinly veiled anti-Semitism."[68] To counter that claim, however, we need only to recall that Billroth did not hesitate to censure poor upbringing wherever he saw it. In a remarkable letter to Hanslick of April 22, 1892, he even criticized his very dear friend Brahms, along with Beethoven and Wagner, Germans by birth all three, for "crude behavior" that he attributed to a "lack of good breeding," precisely to their having not come, again, "from a good home."[69]

And then there are these comments, appearing in a letter to Josef and Hermine Seegen of May 14, 1889, about a young lawyer named Otto Gottlieb, who had become engaged to be married to Billroth's daughter Martha. Otto and his brother Rudi stood out from among Martha's other friends, Billroth writes, for their "good manners and free, natural, endearing ways," and he notes approvingly that they "had enjoyed a good upbringing and came from a good home." Only later in the letter, and almost incidentally, he adds: "The family is Israelite; with his parents' approval, Otto will be baptized as a Protestant, which will also be better for his career. *That is not important to me*, as long as the children who may be born are baptized as

---

[68] Deborah R. Coen, *Vienna in the Age of Uncertainty: Science, Liberalism & Private Life* (Chicago and London: University of Chicago Press, 2007), 165. It seems possible that Coen is confusing the *Aphorismen* with the earlier *Lehren und Lernen*, a book that she does not mention. Moreover, there is nothing inherently antisemitic to Billroth's unheeded proposal in the *Aphorismen* to limit enrollment to those students who had obtained an Austrian gymnasium diploma (*Maturitätszeugnis*). Were such a *numerus clausus* to have gone into effect, it would have for all intents and purposes barred admission to all students from Hungary (including non-Jews), and it would have done nothing to bar admission to Jewish students from Galicia and Bukowina, nor, of course, Bohemia and Moravia.

[69] Wyklicky, *Unbekanntes von Theodor Billroth*, 25. Quite by accident, Hanslick shared this letter with Brahms. Although Brahms, who took great pride in his parents and the upbringing they had provided him, made light of Hanslick's innocent mistake, he never really forgave Billroth. The latter died two years later without knowing the source of Brahms's changed feelings toward him, in full display during an unfortunate dinner party in Billroth's home on November 16, 1892, in which Brahms, Hanslick, Max Kalbeck, and Adolf Exner were in attendance. Billroth provided a detailed account in a letter written late that night to his daughter Else, quoted in ibid., 25–27. This letter is also quoted in part in *Billroth und Brahms im Briefwechsel*, 148–51, which provides a good account of the entire imbroglio. See also Eduard Hanslick, "Johannes Brahms: The Last Days, Memories and Letters," in *Brahms and His World*, rev. ed., 331; and Styra Avins, "Brahms the Godfather," ibid., 52.

Christians."[70] Five years later, in a deathbed letter to his wife, Christel, Billroth made sure to include "a thousand thanks to our dear...Otto, who has become like my own son! I do not doubt that he will be a true son to you and a supportive brother to Martha's sisters!"[71] Here we are about as far as we can be from any perception of an unbridgeable gulf between pure German blood and pure Jewish blood.

It is not surprising, therefore, to learn that Billroth was among the founding members of the Viennese branch of the Verein zum Abwehr des Antisemitismus (Society for the Defense Against Antisemitism) when this was founded in 1891 by a handful of gentile notables in protest of the political antisemitism that was becoming a growing fact of life in fin-de-siècle Vienna.[72] Notley and others have seen Billroth's membership as evidence that he had finally "cured himself of anti-Semitism."[73] Yet Billroth's attitude toward the Eastern Jews had probably not changed very much at all—not that that had ever really been a sign, as I have argued, of antisemitism as this was understood in his day. We might find a fair representation of the same attitude in Brahms's well-known observation about the burgeoning Viennese antisemitic movement, told to Richard Heuberger in November 1890: "I'd be in favor of hindering the never-ending supply of Galician Jews to Vienna, but all the rest is a dirty trick!"[74] Brahms's

---

[70] Billroth, *Der intime Theodor Billroth*, 229; *The Intimate Billroth*, 157 (emphasis added). Although Rudolf Gottlieb is not mentioned by name in this letter, we can discern his identity from Billroth's letter to Hermine Seegen of August 2, 1892. There Billroth couples his announcement of Rudi's engagement to the daughter of a colleague in Heidelberg with expression of regret that Rudi, whom he describes as "an able, very likeable *Mensch*," had not chosen to marry his own daughter Helene instead. See Billroth, *Der intime Theodor Billroth*, 267; *The Intimate Billroth*, 157.

[71] Letter of February 3, 1894, in *Unbekanntes von Theodor Billroth*, 143. Otto Gottlieb-Billroth eventually took on a hyphenated form of his family name in honor of his father-in-law (who had no male heirs). He published his edition of the correspondence between Billroth and Brahms shortly before his own death in 1935.

[72] Jacques Kornberg, "Vienna, the 1890s: Jews in the Eyes of Their Defenders (Der Verein zur Abwehr des Antisemitismus)," *Central European History* 28 (1995): 153–73; and idem, "Vienna in the 1890s: The Austrian Opposition to Antisemitism, the Verein zur Abwehr des Antisemitismus," *Leo Baeck Institute Year Book* 41 (1996): 161–96.

[73] Notley, *Lateness and Brahms*, 206–207. Notley cites an obituary for the surgeon that was published in the society's newspaper in which the deceased was said to have "completely freed himself" from his former "erroneous views"; see *Freies Blatt* (February 11, 1894): 3.

[74] Quoted in Richard Heuberger, *Erinnerungen an Johannes Brahms*, rev. ed., ed. Kurt Hofmann (Tutzing: Hans Schneider, 1976), 45). A somewhat different translation is given in Notley, *Lateness and Brahms*, 205.

suspicion of and distaste for the *Ostjuden* was shared not only with Billroth but with virtually all liberals of his generation, Jew and gentile alike, since the cultural difference embodied by the Jews newly arriving from the east was so at odds with the German liberal project.

It was cultural difference of this kind to which Hanslick and Speidel had alluded in their disapproving references to the putative "Jewish-Oriental" aspects of Goldmark's music. Both critics recognized the composer's accomplishments, but, as committed assimilationists, they seemed disturbed by what they perceived as his failure in works such as *Sakuntala* and *Die Königin von Saba* to fully embrace the ideology of liberal nationalism by letting go of his Jewish heritage.[75] One might say that, for Hanslick and Speidel, Goldmark had met the liberal criterion of achievement but perhaps not that of conviction. The case of Billroth's exclusionary rhetoric is, of course, a matter of a different kind, in that it pertains to public policy governing medical education in the German nation, not the creative work of a solitary artist. Moreover, it is clear that he doubted whether the impoverished students from the Eastern provinces, given what he perceived to be the limitations of their family and economic background, could be expected to meet either criterion. But at bottom, as I have argued, Billroth was no more a racist than was Hanslick or Speidel. For all three men, it was culture, not blood, that was the decisive factor in determining who could be counted among the Germans.

Although Billroth's excursus on the student body in the Vienna Medical School in 1875 is remembered today primarily on account of his controversial claims about the Eastern Jewish students, his passing remark about the many "Germanized Czechs" who excelled at medicine is worth bearing in mind as we continue our narrative in the chapter that follows. For as we shall discover there, the notion of Germanized Czechs lay at the heart of Hanslick's discourse on the music of Dvořák and Smetana when that first began to emerge in the Viennese public sphere a few years later.

---

[75] It does not seem to have occurred to either critic that Goldmark, as a Germanized Jew, might have been engaged in an orientalist project, a possibility suggested at the beginning of the previous chapter and one we will consider at greater length in Chapter 8.

Eduard Hanslick (1825–1904).

Ludwig Speidel (1830–1904)

Carl Goldmark (1830–1915)

Theodor Billroth (1829–1894)

Theodor Helm (1843–1920)

Antonín Dvořák (1841–1904)

PART TWO

From the Iron Ring to the *Fin de siècle*

| Language Ordinances,
Nationalbesitzstand, and Dvořák's
Reception in the Taaffe Era

We are convinced—and it won't be too long in coming—that the covetous Germans
will be writing about our highly gifted Dvořák: "unser Dworzak"!!
—V. J. Novotný (?), Dalibor (1880)

What good should a German expect from a modern Czech rhapsody?
—Max Kalbeck, review of Dvořák's Slavonic Rhapsody No. 2 (1882)

ANTONÍN DVOŘÁK FIRST came to widespread notice in Vienna at precisely the moment of tense political transition when, following the Reichsrat elections of 1879, the German liberals lost their traditional hold on political power in Cisleithania to Count Eduard von Taaffe and his conservative, pro-Slavic Iron Ring. The Czech composer had already gained the quiet support of Hanslick and Brahms, key players in the city's music scene and fixtures among its liberal intellectual and artistic elite, through their service on the Austrian state commission that awarded him five annual grants between 1874 and 1878.[1] Consisting largely of pieces composed in

---

[1] Hanslick served on the selection committee in each of these years; Brahms joined only in 1875. David Beveridge has provided the most thorough and

a Germanic style—including such works as the Serenade for Strings in E, the Symphony in F, the Piano Trio in G Minor, the String Quartet in E, and the *Stabat mater*—little of what Dvořák submitted with his application each year would have impressed the adjudicators as sounding especially Czech or Slavic. Yet Brahms showed a preference for a work that stood somewhat apart from many of the others, the *Moravské dvojzpěvy* (*Moravian Duets*), for soprano, alto, and piano accompaniment.[2] Admiring these pieces for their artistic worth but also sensing their commercial appeal, Brahms was only too happy to recommend them to his Berlin publisher, Fritz Simrock. Knowing the marketplace as well as anyone, Simrock not only agreed to publish the *Moravian Duets* but in early 1878 commissioned Dvořák to write a set of *Slavonic Dances* for four-hand piano as a kind of sequel to Brahms's enormously successful *Hungarian Dances* for the same medium.[3]

thought-provoking account of Dvořák's relationship with the latter; see his "Dvořák and Brahms: A Chronicle, an Interpretation," in *Dvořák and His World*, ed. Michael Beckerman (Princeton: Princeton University Press, 1993), 56–91. On the composer's relationship with both Viennese figures, see also John Clapham, "Dvořák's Relations with Brahms and Hanslick," *Musical Quarterly* 57 (1971): 241–54. On his record of winning the state stipend, see Dvořák, *Korespondence a dokumenty*, vol. 9: *Dokumenty: Kapitoly I–IX* [Documents: Sections I–IX] (2004): 131–228; and Milan Kuna, "Umělecká stipendia Antonína Dvořáka," *Hudební veda* n.s., 4 (1992): 293–315. Also useful is John Clapham, "Dvořáks Aufstieg zum Komponisten von internationalem Rang: Einige neue Entdeckungen," *Die Musikforschung* 30 (1977): 47–55.

[2] Not that these pieces were written in a musical language that was more natural and authentic for the composer than that used in the others. As Michael Beckerman has noted, Czech-speaking Moravia was very much an exotic locale to Dvořák, a Bohemian Czech, who in fact knew little about Moravian culture, and who did not base his settings on the original folk songs but rather set the words to his own, not very Moravian-sounding, melodies. See Michael Beckerman, "The Master's Little Joke: Antonín Dvořák and the Mask of Nation," in *Dvořák and His World*, 134–54.

[3] Brahms endorsed the duets in an undated letter to Simrock of December 1877, in *Johannes Brahms Briefwechsel* (hereafter *Briefwechsel*), 19 vols. to date (consisting of 16 orig. vols., rev. eds., Berlin, 1912–22; repr. Tutzing: Hans Schneider, 1974; and a *Neue Folge* consisting of 3 vols. to date, Tutzing: Hans Schneider, 1991–), vol. 10: *Johannes Brahms: Briefe an P. J. Simrock und Fritz Simrock* (1917): 60. Brahms's attraction was based on the musical settings alone, since the scores submitted in Dvořák's grant application in 1877 gave the texts in Czech only; these were replaced by German texts at the time of publication. Simrock entitled the print *Klänge aus Mähren* ("Sounds from Moravia"), thereby heightening the sense of the work's exoticism. As with the *Moravian Duets*, so with the *Slavonic Dances* Dvořák eschewed the use of authentic melodies in his settings. Instead he turned to the work of Brahms, whose *Hungarian Dances* he used as "an exemplary model for [his] corresponding 'Slavonic' ones." *Korespondence*

In the meantime, however, Dvořák had begun the year by composing the Serenade for Winds, a work, like most of his others to date, largely unmarked by any Slavicisms. Significantly, it was only after receiving Simrock's commission for the *Slavonic Dances*—in short, only in response to an anticipated demand in the German marketplace—that the composer entered an unusually intense Slavonic period, whereupon he produced a steady stream of works in which Slavic elements for the first time come to the fore. In addition to the *Slavonic Dances* (in four-hand and orchestral versions), these included the three *Slavonic Rhapsodies* and the *Czech Suite*, both for orchestra, the *Furiants* for piano, as well as the Sextet in A and String Quartet in E flat, with their specifically Czech and broader Slavic references (including movements headed "Furiant" and "Dumka").[4] In November 1878 Louis Ehlert wrote favorably in the Berlin *National-Zeitung* about the recently published *Moravian Duets* and *Slavonic Dances*, setting off a rush on the music shops by Germans in search of an exoticism that could be brought home into their parlors.[5] The *Slavonic Dances* and *Slavonic Rhapsodies*, in particular, quickly began to make the rounds, earning Dvořák international acclaim as an "overnight sensation"

---

a dokumenty, vol. 1: *Korespondence odeslaná 1871–1884 {Correspondence Dispatched 1871–1884]* (1987): 140.

[4] Beckerman has argued that "the notion of any monolithic style, whether Czech, Slavic, American, or Habsburg, [was] entirely alien to Dvořák ("The Master's Little Joke," 150). That is not to deny, as Beckerman acknowledges, "that Dvořák's sense of identity was bound up with the idea of the Czech nation." It is to suggest, however, that, as a composer, first and foremost, Dvořák "understood things pretty much in terms of how they interacted with his compositional imagination and affected his career"; that, for him, national styles (including the Czech or Slavic) were *constructed*; and that he chose which style to follow at any given instance on the basis of whatever practical considerations might have arisen, ranging from the fundamental need to find inspiration to the understandable desire to succeed in the marketplace. I should add that my own concern hereafter is with the Viennese reception of the composer's works, not with Dvořák's compositional intentions or with any clues contained in his works to his social or artistic identity or political sensibilities.

[5] *National-Zeitung*, November 15, 1878. This article (which seems self-consciously to evoke "Neue Bahnen," Schumann's earlier encomium to the young Brahms) is reprinted in Klaus Döge, *Antonín Dvořák: Leben, Werke, Dokumente*, 2nd ed. (Zurich and Mainz: Atlantis Musikbuch-Verlag, 1997), 182–85; for an English translation, see *Antonín Dvořák, Letters and Reminiscences*, ed. Otakar Šourek, trans. Roberta Finlayson Samsour (Prague: Artia, 1954), 46–48. Ehlert told of the effect his piece had had on the German public in a letter to Dvořák of November 27, 1878; see *Korespondence a dokumenty* 5: 113–14; transl. in *Letters and Reminiscences*, 48.

in Berlin, Budapest, London, and New York, as well as in a number of smaller cities and provincial towns in Germany.

Yet in Vienna the musical exoticism that had played so well elsewhere ran head on into the political crisis engendered by the liberals' recent loss of power. To be sure, none of that seemed at first to bother the city's musicians. In October 1879, for example, the Philharmonic players decided to include not one but two of Dvořák's latest orchestral compositions in their new season, the Serenade for Winds and the Slavonic Rhapsody No. 3.[6] Moreover, after leading the orchestra in a performance of the latter in the season's first concert, on November 16, the conductor Hans Richter was so taken that he commissioned Dvořák to write a new symphony for the orchestra to introduce in the following season.

Dvořák's eyewitness account of his Viennese debut, found in a letter of November 23 to his friend Alois Göbl, is likewise telling of good fortunes:

> I set out last Friday and was present at the performance of my Third Rhapsody, which was liked very much, and I had to show myself to the audience. I sat next to Brahms by the organ in the orchestra, and Richter drew me out. I had to appear. I must tell you I immediately won the sympathy of the whole orchestra and out of all the new works they tried over, and Richter said there were sixty of them, they liked my Rhapsody best of all. Richter kissed me on the spot and told me he was very glad to know me and promised the Rhapsody will be repeated at a special concert in the Opera House.
>
> I promised to go for the performance of the Serenade and had to tell the Philharmonic I would send them a new symphony for the next season. On the day after the concert Richter gave a banquet at his house to honor me in some way and invited all the Czech members of

---

[6] In October 1879 Brahms wrote Dvořák to tell him that "through rehearsals of your newer works that have taken place you have won the sympathy of the musicians here to a quite extraordinary degree." *Korespondence a dokumenty* 5: 210. Although Brahms named only the Hellmesberger Quartet, which was learning the Sextet and String Quartet in E flat, he was undoubtedly referring also to the rest of the musicians of the Vienna Philharmonic. In a letter to Simrock of October 8, 1879, he reported the Philharmonic players had scheduled the "Slavonic Dances and a rhapsody" on its *Novitäten-Probe* for that day and that Hellmesberger would also be trying out the Sextet. Brahms was not in attendance at the Philharmonic's read-through, however, and it is seems likely that it was not the *Slavonic Dances* but rather the Wind Serenade that was performed that day along with the Slavonic Rhapsody No 3. See Brahms, *Briefwechsel* 10: 131–32.

the orchestra. It was a splendid evening I shall not easily forget for the rest of my life.[7]

It cannot escape notice that Dvořák focuses almost entirely in this report on the favorable reaction to the piece among the musicians. (Richter and the orchestra's Czech members are especially singled out; he has next to nothing to say about the public's reaction.) Indeed, his description appears to move directly from a recounting of events having to do with the dress rehearsal—how else can we explain the presence of the composer (and Brahms) on stage during the performance?—to another having to do with the banquet given by Richter on the day following the concert.[8] The composer does report that he had to present himself to the public, to be sure, but the Philharmonic's dress rehearsals were to some degree open to the public, and it was probably this audience, not one made up of the orchestra's regular subscribers, about which he was writing.

However that may be, the work's reception at the subscription concert was anything but enthusiastic. "The rhapsody was respectfully but not warmly received," as Hanslick explained. "I had expected it to make a livelier effect after the impression of the dress rehearsal."[9] The Viennese correspondent for the Leipzig *Neue Zeitschrift für Musik* reported that "[t]he talented composer has raised great expectations but this rhapsody has failed to meet them." He continued:

> The audience behaved with decided coolness, and the composer, who was in attendance, was not called [to the stage]. Dvořák adheres to the

[7] *Korespondence a dokumenty* 1: 187–88. The translation of this passage given here and the continuation of it quoted below have been adapted from John Clapham, *Dvořák: Musician and Craftsman* (New York: St. Martin's Press, 1966), 131, with revisions kindly suggested by David Beveridge. The composer provided Simrock with substantially the same account; see his letter to the publisher of November 20, 1879, in *Korespondence a dokumenty* 1: 185–86. Two days later Simrock replied: "I am very pleased by your beautiful success in Vienna and hope Hanslick will write favorably in the N{eue} f{reie} Presse. He is the only one in any case whose evaluation is important." *Korespondence a dokumenty* 5: 211.

[8] Clapham, "Dvořáks Aufstieg zum Komponisten von internationalem Rang," 50, notes that the approbation seems to have been limited to Richter and the orchestra's Czech members but does not suggest that Dvořák's account refers to the dress rehearsal rather than to the subscription concert.

[9] Ed. H. [Eduard Hanslick], "Concerte," *Neue Freie Presse*, November 23, 1879; rpt., idem, *Concerte, Componisten und Virtuosen der letzten fünfzehn Jahre, 1870–1885* (Berlin: Allgemeiner Verein für Deutsche Literatur, 1886), 245–50 (at 249).

form of Liszt's Hungarian Rhapsodies, and formally as well as with respect to instrumentation the work succeeded, but it lacks Liszt's spirit. We hope the Serenade for Winds that will be performed in one of the coming concerts will give rise to an opinion about him that is more favorable.[10]

Theodor Helm, the Viennese correspondent for the *Musikalisches Wochenblatt*, another Leipzig weekly, provided a similar assessment, expressed by means of a snide remark concerning the composer's sudden ascent to prominence:

> The first two Philharmonic matinées of the season brought...as [the only] new work...the third of the Slavic Rhapsodies, frequently mentioned in these pages, by A. Dvořák, the Czech national composer who has been introduced to German concerts as a newly discovered genius, as a modern classic. This A-flat Rhapsody did not fully win us over on a first hearing, or the public, in spite of its ingenious details and truly gorgeous instrumentation. We were unable to gain the poetic image such as Liszt's Hungarian Rhapsodies involuntarily conjure up in our souls.[11]

The critical notices in Vienna's daily press were at best only mixed.[12] Josef Königstein wrote favorably of the unknown composer, singling out his compositional skill, good taste, and smooth musical diction—all of which augured a bright future for this "born musician." Yet he complained that the "national coloring" provided only a superficial binding of the whole and was no substitute for genuine "artistic unity."[13] With other liberal critics, the "national" dimension took on a more pointed meaning. Writing in the *Fremden-Blatt*, Speidel showed, with Königstein, a certain respect for the unknown composer, but he was more forthcoming in acknowledging the political realities of the time:

[10] L. Steiger, *Neue Zeitschrift für Musik* 75 (November 21, 1879): 493.

[11] Theodor Helm, *Musikalisches Wochenblatt* 11 (February 27, 1880): 119.

[12] The composer acknowledged this in his letter of November 23 to Göbl: "The reviews in the Viennese papers were good except for a few. I've kept them for you. Dr. Hanslick has not written yet, but I went to see him and he told me he liked the work very much and was also at the dress rehearsal with the score, so it must have interested him greatly. He plans to write a rather long article about me, because he wrote to Prague for some biographical facts." *Korespondence a dokumenty* 1: 188.

[13] k.st. [Joseph Königstein], "Konzerte," *Illustrirtes Wiener Extrablatt*, November 18, 1879.

We are told that Dvořák is a child of Prague, reared in the German school, yet also, in a way of course that involves good breeding, enlivened by Slavic tendencies. Next to Liszt's Hungarian rhapsodies he places his Slavic ones. We do not object to such an effort since music is given fresh blood when it takes in folk melodies; yet in our opinion it was not really proper to introduce the city of Vienna to the new composer from this national side. The Slavic folk school is not loved in Vienna; in the face of it the Viennese feels himself to be decidedly German. A rhapsody that is written by a Czech and proclaims itself Slavic will encounter a quiet opposition in Vienna.[14]

Less diplomatic were Wilhelm Frey's remarks, appearing in the *Neues Wiener Tagblatt*:

[T]hen came the "Slavonic Rhapsody," about which more noise was heard from the first rehearsals than was produced by the rhapsody itself. And that is no small thing to say. It is not good to mix music with politics, and in this space, which is devoted to technical discussions of artistic compositions, all political references and parallels will for that reason be eschewed.[15]

But Frey cannot help himself, and the space that he seems intent on inoculating from politics is the public sphere of the Philharmonic concerts:

Since Magyardom has its rhapsodies, so may this spontaneously inspired form not be begrudged to Slavdom. The score and the arrangement for two and four hands—these are the realms in which the autonomy of the nationalities can and may freely evolve, as long as the hands do not become so many fists. . . . Herr Dvořák has taken a series of Slavic melancholies, some in their native guise, some as arranged for salon use, set them one after another in the most superficial form, and called this potpourri a rhapsody. Already Herr Eduard Strauß has claimed this work for one of the next Promenade Concerts, and without demeaning these Promenade Concerts, which after all have their Mendelssohn, Schubert, and Wagner evenings, it can be concluded from this circumstance that the Slavic Rhapsody No. 3 is not suited for the realm of the Philharmonic Concerts, and that it was

[14] sp. [Ludwig Speidel], "Konzerte," *Fremden-blatt*, November 18, 1879.
[15] This and the following quotation are taken from Wilhelm Frey, "Konzert und Oper," *Neues Wiener Tagblatt*, November 19, 1879.

a mistake to offer this potpourri of suffering before the Philharmonic's public. Although the audience passed over this error with good will to the day's program, the chill brought to the hall through the musical pan-Slavism carried over into the Passacaglia by J. S. Bach; only Schumann's D-minor Symphony once again restored some warmth. As usual, the Philharmonic players performed superbly under Hans Richter's direction, yet this time they had no particular success.

Reviews of this kind must have been disheartening, but Dvořák could at least take pleasure from Hanslick's rather more encouraging report in the *Neue Freie Presse*.[16] Responding as much to his fellow liberal critics as to the music, Hanslick began by introducing the still unfamiliar composer by way of a biographical sketch and then rehearsed the favorable notices that Dvořák had already earned in Germany for his recently published *Slavonic Dances*. "Thus they are German authorities who have drawn Dvořák from his native obscurity," continued Hanslick,

> and greeted him as a man of unusual talent. I emphasize this fact because it refutes the ridiculous suspicion that Dvořák's reputation is the work of the Czech National Party.... Truly, there has been no propaganda coming from Prague made on Dvořák's behalf, and if there had been such an effort—how far in any case does Czech backing go in the world of art? The national antipathy and political enmity that is palpable in some of the Viennese evaluations of Dvořák's Rhapsody is lacking justification here, even if such a point of view were ever allowable in purely artistic matters.[17]

Then turning to those matters artistic, Hanslick again set himself pointedly apart from the other critics. Whereas Königstein, Speidel, and Frey had stressed the rhapsody's Slavic provenance—Speidel, for example, claimed that "Dvořák has constructed his rhapsody from Slavic songs and dance motives" and recounted how "[a]n old inhabitant of the Steppes, who sat close to us, immediately detected a Ukrainian song"—Hanslick suggested a model for the piece that was more emblematic of the Austrian capital: "In its popular

---

[16] "During my last stay in Vienna," he explained to his friend Ludevít Procházka, "I had to swallow many bitter pills from some of the critics; but Hanslick answered them well. His critique was very flattering." Letter of January 15, 1880, in *Korespondence a dokumenty* 1:197. I am grateful to Alan Houtchens for his English translation of this passage.

[17] Hanslick, *Concerte, Componisten und Virtuosen der letzten fünfzehn Jahre*, 248–49.

character and sensual charms, even in the easygoing breadth of its somewhat deliquescent, loosely bound form, it recalls Schubert." Moreover, he added, "the themes...are not national melodies but rather the free invention of the composer."[18]

These lines read like a case study in traditional liberal rhetoric. In the earliest example of what would become a leitmotif in his work, Hanslick seeks to distance Dvořák from the cause of Czech nationalism by implying that the composer was, in effect, "one of us"—a German.[19] But given the appointment in Austria at precisely this time of a "reactionary" cabinet formed with decisive Czech support, Hanslick's palliative could only go so far. Whereas the *Moravian Duets* and *Slavonic Dances* had, only a few months earlier, brought an exotic thrill to the self-assured Bürger of the German Reich, in Habsburg Austria, at a time when German liberal hegemony was suddenly under threat, Slavic otherness could easily provoke a less happy reaction.

The (Musical) Politics of Language

In Speidel's view, it would have been wiser for the Philharmonic players to introduce the Czech composer to the Viennese audience with something less politically charged than a work carrying the word *Slavonic* in its title. Looking ahead to the announced performance of the Wind Serenade, he noted: "Other works by Dvořák are available, which aim to be nothing but music pure and simple—thus, for example, a serenade for orchestra. Only then might one have come with the Slavonic rhapsodies. [To lead with the rhapsody] was no sin but it was a gaucherie."[20]

---

[18] Speidel, in *Fremden-blatt*, November 18, 1879. Hanslick, *Concerte, Componisten und Virtuosen der letzten fünfzehn Jahre*, 249. I am aware of no modern scholarship that has linked the themes of the rhapsody to sources in Slavic popular or folk music. Although the report of Speidel's unnamed informant, who heard reference to one Ukrainian song, is tantalizing, the composer seems never to have undertaken a careful study of Ukrainian music; see Milan Kuna, "Dvořák's Slavic Spirit, and His Relation to Tchaikovsky and Russia," in *Rethinking Dvořák: Views from Five Countries*, ed. David R. Beveridge (Oxford: Clarendon Press, 1996), 147. Nevertheless, it is worth noting that at some point Dvořák did obtain a copy of the collection *Slavia*, edited by Procházka, which included songs from Ukraine.

[19] Familiar from his service on the state commission with Dvořák's extensive portfolio of accomplished chamber and orchestral works written in a Germanic style, Hanslick had a better idea than most of where the composer's musical experience lay.

[20] Speidel, in *Fremden-blatt*, November 18, 1879. Comments such as this (and those quoted earlier) give reason to doubt Otto Biba's suggestion that the unfavorable

In spite of this encouragement, the orchestra did not follow through with its scheduled performance of the Wind Serenade, evidently unsettled by all the noise that had surrounded the performance of the Rhapsody. From Hanslick's review of the season's final concert, given on April 4, 1880, we can determine that the serenade, along with Goldmark's new overture *Penthesilea*, had originally been announced for this program but were both set aside at the last moment "for no acceptable reason." Hanslick goes on to register a similar complaint about the substitution of Liszt's *Les préludes* for the performance of the Third Slavonic Rhapsody that, as we know from Dvořák's letter to Göbl from the previous November, Richter had promised to include in a concert at the Court Opera.[21] Hanslick did not hesitate to let on how much these cancellations infuriated him, and he concluded in a scolding tone: "If on top of everything else it is a matter of new works by reputable, accredited composers, then let them answer quietly for their work, for their reputation itself. The judge [*Richter*] of the value of such compositions is not always the one whose name is Richter."[22] Hanslick knew it was not the orchestra's conductor but rather the autonomous players themselves who had determined that Dvořák's works were not to be performed.

The Philharmonic players likewise avoided programming the music of Dvořák's older Czech colleague, Bedřich Smetana. Unlike Dvořák, Smetana had done little to promote his works outside Bohemia; indeed, by concentrating on Czech opera for several years after returning home to Prague in 1861, following an extended stay in Sweden, he neglected the instrumental

---

Viennese reaction to the rhapsody "could not in the slightest have national reasons"; see Otto Biba, "Antonín Dvořák im Wiener Musikleben seiner Zeit," *Colloquium "Dvořák, Janáček, Their Time" Brno 1984*, ed. Rudolf Pečman (Brno: Česká hudební společnost, 1985), 52.

[21] From Hanslick's report we can determine that both John Clapham and Jarmil Burghauser were incorrect in claiming that the rhapsody was, in fact, repeated in concert at the Court Opera; see John Clapham, *Dvořák* (New York: Norton, 1979), 44 (where the date of the concert is given as March 29, 1880); and Jarmil Burghauser, *Antonín Dvořák: Thematic Catalogue* (Prague: Bärenreiter, 1996), 582 (where the dates of two performances are given as February 29 and March 29, 1880). Wilhelm Beetz, *Das Wiener Opernhaus 1869 bis 1945* (Zurich: Central European Times Verlag, 1949), which offers what is described as a complete listing of all performances of every kind in the building from the time of its opening through the end of the Second World War, establishes the date of this concert as March 28, 1880, and shows that *Les préludes* but not the Slavonic Rhapsody No. 2 was included.

[22] Ed.H. [Eduard Hanslick], "Musik," *Neue Freie Presse*, April 14, 1880. We have no reason to think Hanslick would have thought any differently about the Hellmesberger Quartet's decision not to perform the composer's Sextet for Strings and the String Quartet in E flat that season, despite having rehearsed both in October 1879.

genres that might more easily have found a place in the concert programs of Hanslick's Vienna. With the publication in 1880 of the Piano Trio in G minor, the First String Quartet *Z mého života* (*From My Life*), and the orchestral cycle *Má vlast* (*My Fatherland*), however, potential backers in the Austrian capital were given something to work with, and in that very year a Czech cellist in the orchestra of the Burgtheater by the name of Theobald Kretschmann (Krečmann) brought the first two movements of *Má vlast* (*Vyšehrad* and *Vltava*) to the attention of the Vienna Philharmonic.[23]

In light of recent political developments, it is not surprising that Kretschmann's efforts went nowhere. Indeed, were it not for the string quartet that Kretschmann had founded in Vienna in May 1879, little or no Czech music would have been heard in the Austrian capital during the first years of Taaffe's ministry.[24] On January 17, 1880, Kretschmann's group introduced Dvořák's E flat Quartet, op. 51, and followed this with a performance on December 12 of that year of Smetana's *From My Life* Quartet.[25] Hanslick does not seem to have been present at the first of these concerts, but he attended the second and used that opportunity to take note of Smetana's music for the first time in print. "A free night at the theater," the critic wrote, "permitted us to attend the quartet concert given by Herrn Radnitzky, Siebert, Stecher and Kretschmann." He continued:

A string quartet in E minor with the inscription "From My Life" made us familiar for the first time with Friedrich Smetana, the Bohemian composer who is much celebrated in Prague. Herr Smetana has reached his fifty-sixth year with an indefatigable output of numerous compositions. Yet his name has not penetrated beyond the narrow confines of exclusive Czechdom. We are not familiar with his operas; for all their reputed excellence they will disappear if they are not helped along right away with a German translation. But to judge from his E minor Quartet, Smetana is deserving of wider attention in any case. It is a serious, independent work, full of character, which awakens not only

[23] Theobald Kretschmann, *Tempi passati: Aus den Erinnerungen eines Musikanten*, 2 vols. (Vienna: K. Prochaska, 1910–13), 1: 94.

[24] This group was generally known as the Radnitzky Quartet, after the name of the first violinist, Franz Radnitzky. Rounding out the ensemble were the second violinist August Siebert, the violist Anton Stecher, and Kretschmann as the cellist. All but Kretschmann were members of the Court Opera Orchestra at the time of the group's founding; Kretschmann himself was made a member of that orchestra in 1881. In later years Hans Kreuzinger replaced Radnitzky as the quartet's first violinist.

[25] Kretschmann, *Tempi passati*, 1:122; 2: 243.

respect but also sincere sympathy. Smetana's invention seems to us less spontaneous and original than that of his younger countryman Antonín Dvořák, which our concert and quartet societies unjustifiably ignore; on the other hand, his style is more even, his work more steady. The national element in this quartet is negligible; it is thus comforting to note that in Czech music German is, as ever, the "language customary in the land" [*landesübliche Sprache*]. Beethoven and, to a lesser extent, Mendelssohn are his models.[26]

These remarks tell us more about Hanslick, a Bohemian-born critic who had embraced the ideology of German liberalism, than they do about Smetana, a Bohemian-born composer who had assumed the mantle of a Czech nationalist. Hanslick not only revels in a German identity that is given meaning by the assumed superiority of German culture, but seems to believe (or at least wants his readers to believe) that Smetana did so too. (It is not insignificant that Hanslick chose to refer to the composer by his given name in German, Friedrich.) Thus he could pay Smetana no higher compliment than to link his work to models found in Beethoven and Mendelssohn—nor, in his mind, do him any greater service than to call for translations of his operas into German, whereby these works (and their composer) might escape from Czech obscurity into the light of a broader world in which German (and German music) served as the lingua franca.

This review is, in fact, shot through with the rhetoric of traditional liberal nationalism. Prior to the signal events of 1866–1871, from Prussia's military defeat of the Austrians to the establishment of the German Empire, bourgeois German speakers in Austria had considered themselves to be members of a single German *Kulturnation*. But unlike their brothers in the more homogeneous *Kaiserreich*, they also, as we have seen, carried a self-imposed mission to "civilize"—to make Germans of—the non-German peoples within the multinational Habsburg state. We have already noted how one early liberal leader had argued that the Germans should "carry culture to the east, transmit the propaganda of German intellection, German science, German humanism." And we might as well now add German music to the list. Indeed, simply by substituting "Hanslick" for "German nationalist," and "music" for "language" and "nation," in Pieter M. Judson's succinct description of traditional liberal ideology, we can produce a fine outline of the critic's assumptions:

---

[26] Ed. H. [Eduard Hanslick], "Concerte," *Neue Freie Presse*, December 14, 1880; repr. in idem, *Concerte, Componisten, und Virtuosen der letzten fünfzehn Jahre*, 284–85.

German nationalists in Habsburg Central Europe [Hanslick] had traditionally conceived of their [his] own nation [German music] in universal, non-territorial, and largely cultural terms. To them [him], the German nation [German music] represented a positive force for the progressive transformation of all the region's inhabitants, a universal culture of education that offered opportunities for social and economic advancement. German liberal nationalists [Hanslick] had rarely given much thought to questions of local language use [non-German music] precisely because they [he] presumed that all ambitious Austrians [Austrian composers] would want to learn the German language [German music] in order to achieve upward social mobility. Similarly, they [he] rarely thought of their nation [German music] in specifically territorial terms because of its universal cultural significance.[27]

The liberals' assumptions about language were critical. The second paragraph of Article 19 of the Fundamental Law Concerning the General Rights of Citizens provided for the "equality of all languages customary in the land in schools, public offices, and public life."[28] Nevertheless, the constitution did not define what gave a language used in any given region status as a "language customary in the land" or specify under what specific conditions its use should be guaranteed.[29] The framers of the constitution had taken a narrow view; they meant to convey basic civil rights to individuals, but they had no intention of giving legal standing to any nationality, and it never occurred to them that serious public discourse would be conducted in any language other than German. The ideal liberal culture they were attempting to build in Austria was (at least theoretically) to be open to all people, but German identity was the price of admission.

Hanslick's music-critical discourse is replete with examples of this basic ideological principle. Moreover, perhaps because of his own family background, when it came to Czech composers Hanslick was especially inclined to assume their embrace of cosmopolitan German culture.[30] By arguing that Smetana chose to "speak German" in his string quartet, Hanslick makes an old-fashioned claim. And if the framers of the December Constitution failed

---

[27] Pieter M. Judson, *Guardians of the Nation: Activists on the Language Frontiers of Imperial Austria* (Cambridge, MA, and London: Harvard University Press, 2006), 15.

[28] See Gerald Stourzh, *Die Gleichberechtigugn der Nationalitäten in der Verfassung und Verwaltung Österreichs 1848–1918* (Vienna: Verlag der Österreichischen Akademie der Wissenschaften, 1985), 53–56.

[29] The following discussion is largely based on Judson, *Guardians of the Nation*, 11–18.

[30] As David S. Luft has argued, because of Bohemia's longstanding special relationship to Austria and to German culture, dating back to the early history of the Holy Roman

to give a precise definition of "language customary in the land," the critic for the *Neue Freie Presse* would make no mistake about that when it came to Czech music: it would always be German.

An Ill-fated Symphony

Although Smetana's music would not be heard again in Vienna for a number of years, Dvořák slowly made his way in the years that followed. It was not always easy, even with the strong backing of Hanslick and Richter. The composer made good on Richter's commission of a new symphony—his Sixth, in D major—but when he presented it for the 1880–81 season the players at first demurred and then finally refused to perform it altogether. As work on the symphony neared its completion in September 1880, the composer made plans to travel to Vienna later in the year to give Brahms a preview of the score before passing it on to Richter.[31] Writing from Vienna on November 23, Dvořák reported to Alois Göbl that Richter "likes the symphony immensely" and was planning to give the first performance on December 26.[32] Indeed, Richter wasted no time in bringing the work to the attention of the Comité. The minutes of its meeting of November 26, 1880, report that "the composer Herr Dvořák has provided a symphony and requests that it be played through in one of the next Philharmonic rehearsals."[33] This proposal went nowhere, however, and Dvořák had no further communication from Richter until several weeks later:

> Forgive me for letting you hear from me only so late. My plans to perform your symphony already in our 4th concert (December 26) unfortunately came to nothing, since our orchestra was so overburdened

Empire, "Bohemia was a part of Austria politically, culturally, and intellectually in ways that Hungary and other areas of the Habsburg monarchy were not." David S. Luft, "Austrian Intellectual History and Bohemia," *Austrian History Yearbook* 38 (2007): 117.

[31] Letter to Simrock of September 24, 1880, in *Korespondence a dokumenty* 1: 229. Dvořák's progress on completing the piece can be followed in his letters to Richter of September 28 and October 26, 1880 (ibid., 230, 233–34).

[32] Ibid., 235; transl. adapted fromRosa Newmarch, "The Letters of Dvořák [*sic*] to Hans Richter," *Musical Times* 73 (1932): 606.

[33] "Herrn theilt der Vorsitzende mit, daß der Componist, Herr Dvorak eine Symphonie zur Verfügung gestellt hat und beantragt daß dieselbe in einer nächsten philharmonischen Proben durchgespielt werden soll." Minutes of the Comité meeting of November 26, 1880 (dated December 15, 1880), Historisches Archiv der Wiener

lately that, in order to spare rehearsals, I had to select only familiar pieces, with the exception of Brahms's easy overture [*Tragic* Overture, op. 81]. I have now scheduled your beautiful work for the 6th concert (beginning of March), where we will have enough time to prepare your symphony in a worthy manner. I have also already incorporated it into my London program. If it is possible for you, then entrust us with the *first* performance of your excellent work. I also think that it is better for you if this piece goes forth into the world for the *first time* in the Vienna Philharmonic concerts with our excellent orchestra.[34]

Dvořák's gracious reply concludes: "As I said, I will also be most grateful to the gentlemen if they accommodate the symphony later and emphasize again that I lay the greatest weight on the *first* performance [being] in Vienna under *your* incomparable direction."[35]

Richter's next dispatch brought no satisfaction. The conductor began by reporting how he had been greatly distracted and worried of late owing to the sudden illness of both his mother and two of his children, who had contracted diphtheria, thereby explaining how he had fallen behind in his work. He continued:

Since the rehearsals in the theater piled up, I wasn't able to prepare your beautiful symphony for March 6. But I ask you most urgently to allow me to keep your score and parts until the middle of next week; I hope certainly to perform your work in the 7th concert, which would come in the last week of March. So allow me to have your work for just a few days; then I will report back to you *immediately*.

A postscript to this letter includes a last attempt at reassurance: "Be convinced that I will do everything to bring about a performance yet this season, since I hold it to be an honor to be the first to give a public performance of your beautiful work."[36]

Philharmoniker (hereafter HA/WP), G[eschäfts]-Z[ahl] 393; partially quoted in Hellsberg, *Demokratie der Könige*, 236.

[34] *Korespondence a dokumenty* 5: 267; this letter is undated but seems to have been sent around New Year's Day. Richter was dissembling somewhat here. Not only did the orchestra perform Brahms's *Tragic* Overture, but they also performed Goldmark's new *Penthesilea* Overture, which, along with Dvořák's Wind Serenade, had been canceled the year before.

[35] *Korespondence a dokumenty* 1: 241; this letter, which carries only the date 1881, must have been written in early January.

[36] *Korespondence a dokumenty* 5: 285. This letter is undated but must have been written in early March (although not necessarily before the 6th, as suggested by the editors of

Dvořák began his reply by expressing his concern and sympathy for the conductor in his personal troubles but then pressed on more urgently with regard to the symphony: "I would beg you, if you would be so kind, to play through it once on the next opportunity. In this way the Philharmonic players might be induced to play it sooner."[37] The orchestra did give the work a quick reading in early March but ultimately decided to put the performance off until the following season.[38] On March 13, 1881, having learned all this from Richter in what seems to have been a franker report than before—unfortunately, the conductor's letter has not been preserved—Dvořák replied: "So it turned out as I imagined! Well, I must not lose courage on that account, for your final words fill me with endless comfort and at the same time give me fresh courage for further creative work."[39] Giving up on his hope for a Viennese première, Dvořák requested return of the score and parts, and the symphony was given its first performance a few weeks later, in Prague, on a Slavonic Concert led by Adolf Čech.[40]

The unhappy fate of Dvořák's symphony in Vienna seems to have been determined by events and attitudes shaped by one of the most pressing issues in Austrian politics in the Taaffe era and beyond. Would the German language retain its traditional privileged status throughout Cisleithania? Or would Czech and other local languages gain comparable status under certain conditions pertaining to regional ethnic makeup?[41] As suggested

the critical edition of the correspondence); it might well have been written after the concert on March 6.

[37] Ibid., 1: 243; this undated letter certainly dates from prior to March 13.

[38] See Brahms's letters to Simrock of March 8 and 22, 1881, in *Briefwechsel* 10: 168–69, 170. In the second report Brahms wrote: "Following a hasty rehearsal the symphony by Dvořák was put aside until next year. One mustn't speak too badly of the people; they really are overstressed."

[39] *Korespondence a dokumenty* 1: 244. Clearly, Dvořák placed no blame for this turn of events on Richter; to his earlier salutation in the recent correspondence ("Mein lieber Herr Hofkapellmeister!"), this time he adds a second, more personal one ("Teuerster Freund!").

[40] Simrock saw to the symphony's publication (with a dedication to Richter), and the work made the rounds during the 1882–83 season. Richter first conducted it in London in May 1882, a few weeks after the English première, given by Manns at the Crystal Palace on April 22.

[41] John Clapham and Klaus Döge have both suggested that "strong anti-Czech feeling" in Vienna played a part in the postponements, yet neither offers much in the way of an explanation. Clapham asserts that the composer had discovered "rooted objections to performing two works by a new Czech composer in successive seasons" (*Dvořák*, 53) but cites no source for this information; see also Clapham, "Dvořák's Aufstieg zum

above, the framers of the constitution assumed that German would serve as the de facto language of state and serious public discourse. From the moment the constitution was ratified, however, every non-German nationalist movement in Austria set its sights on achieving linguistic parity with the Germans. It was in this crucial area that Taaffe's government first began to affect state policy in ways inimical to the interests of the German bourgeoisie.[42] April 1880 saw the enactment of the so-called Stremayr Ordinances, which mandated Czech, alongside German, as an "external" administrative language in Bohemia and Moravia, that is, as a language in which the public there could conduct business with the bureaucracy. (German, however, would remain the sole "internal" administrative language by which the bureaucrats communicated among themselves.) Since far more Czechs than Germans were bilingual, the new arrangement placed the latter group at an unaccustomed disadvantage in competition for coveted bureaucratic positions. For that reason alone, the Germans saw the Czechs' insistence on their point as being based not in practical need but in political assertiveness. Indeed, all parties could see that any threat to the traditional privileged status of the German language represented a serious threat to continued German hegemony in the multinational state.[43] Although the overheated response in the *Neue Freie Presse* that the language ordinances deprived two million Germans of rights they had possessed in

Komponisten von internationalem Rang," 50, where the reservations are attributed to "some Austrian members" of the orchestra (by which he presumably meant "some German members"). Döge (*Dvořák*, 194), citing Clapham, holds essentially the same position. Unfortunately, the Philharmonic's archive contains no evidence bearing on the matter. Because Clemens Hellsberg bases his invaluable history of the orchestra primarily on what can be found in the extant archival record, there we read simply that Dvořák's "offer [of the symphony] was accepted, but the rehearsal . . . postponed many times, so that the première took place in Prague"; Hellsberg, *Demokratie der Könige*, 236.

[42] Jenks, *Austria under the Iron Ring*, passim; Okey, *The Habsburg Monarchy c. 1765–1918*, 268–76.

[43] For a cogent analysis of the German versus Czech question, see R. J. W. Evans, "Language and State Building: The Case of the Habsburg Monarchy," *Austrian History Yearbook* 35 (2004): 1–24 (especially 13–16). See also Robert A. Kann, *A History of the Habsburg Empire, 1526–1918* (Berkeley and Los Angeles: University of California Press, 1974), 439–40; and idem, *The Multi-National Empire: Nationalism and National Reform in the Habsburg Monarchy 1848–1918*, 2 vols. (New York: Columbia University Press, 1950; rpt. ed., New York: Octagon Books, 1964), 1: 196–200.

Bohemia for centuries was exaggerated, it accurately reflected the anxieties experienced among German liberals.[44]

Similarly unsettling were the figures produced in the imperial census of 1880, which for the first time counted persons in accordance with their "language of daily use" (German: *Umgangssprache;* Czech: *obcovací řeč*). Although these statistics did not produce an accurate linguistic picture of the multinational state—respondents were permitted to choose only a single language, even if, as was often the case, they were bilingual—every nationalist group used them as though they did in fact measure mother tongue or nationality.[45] For German speakers, the picture was not pretty: the census showed clearly that they composed a smaller percentage of the overall population than expected, and that their numbers were declining. No longer able to assume their interests coincided with those of the Austrian state, liberals slowly began to redefine political identities and social conflicts in terms of a nationalist discourse that understood German identity as a matter of ethnicity rather than of liberal bourgeois cultural values.

At a liberal party conference held in November 1880, Heinrich Friedjung, a former member of the Reading Society of Vienna's German Students, proposed the creation of a German People's Party that would redirect Austrian liberalism away from its traditional loyalty to the state toward a new loyalty to the nation.[46] This call from the nationalist left gained little support, however, and the various liberal factions eventually came together to combat the rightward drift of the Iron Ring one last time in the following year under the banner of the United Left. Thereafter Friedjung joined with two other former members of the Reading Society, Victor Adler and Engelbert Pernerstorfer, along with Georg von Schönerer, the group's one-time advocate in the Reichsrat, to go about building a truly *deutschnational* progressive movement outside the sphere of traditional politics. (Friedjung and Adler were Jews, but Schönerer had not yet fully voiced the antisemitism that would divide these forces within a few years.) This movement remained largely on the fringe; its Linz Program of 1882, for example, which combined calls for a range of progressive social legislation with what amounted to subversive German nationalism, essentially went nowhere. Yet the inflammatory, high-pitched

---

[44] *Neue Freie Presse*, April 27, 1880. On this linguistic decree, see Jenks, *Austria Under the Iron Ring*, 51–70. On the German liberals' "counterattack," which sought unsuccessfully to establish German as the *Staatssprache*, see ibid., 90–103.

[45] Judson, *Guardians of the Nation*, 14; Cohen, *The Politics of Ethnic Survival*, 66–68.

[46] The following discussion is based largely on Judson, *Exclusive Revolutionaries*, 199–208; and McGrath, *Dionysian Art and Populist Politics*, 165–81.

rhetorical style associated with these activists, known as the "sharper key" (*schärfere Tonart*), would eventually color a strand of fin-de-siècle music reception in Vienna.[47] Far more significant for our purposes here, however, was the development of an explicitly German-nationalist consciousness among those who remained in the mainstream liberal fold. Placed in a disadvantageous position under the Taaffe regime, middle-class Germans would increasingly have reasons to set about defending their *Nationalbesitzstand*.

One of the first initiatives in this direction was the German School Association, a voluntary, self-help association that was founded in the spring of 1880 with the goal of ensuring continued German cultural hegemony throughout Austria by raising monies to fund German schools in ethnically mixed regions of Bohemia, Moravia, Carniola, and Tyrol where the size of the German population did not warrant establishment of a public school.[48] To be sure, this was the brainchild of the same *deutschnational* activists who would later promulgate the radical Linz Program, but in this case the group's initiative won widespread support within the broader liberal community as well. Among the eminently respectable School Association's first supporters, for example, was Brahms, who signed the initial membership appeal that appeared on the first page of the *Deutsche Zeitung* on June 26, 1880.[49] On February 20, 1881, the Vienna Academic Wagner Society (whose German-nationalist sympathies were a matter of course) sponsored the Philharmonic in a gala benefit concert for the fledgling organization. Notable for Hans von Bülow's participation as conductor, pianist, and composer, the concert ended with a well-received performance of Bruckner's Fourth Symphony.[50]

---

[47] On the Linz Program, see McGrath, *Dionysian Art and Populist Politics,* 165–81. When Schönerer subsequently agitated for the addition of an "Aryan paragraph" to the Linz Program, Friedjung, Adler, and Pernersdorfer broke off all ties with him. On the "sharper key," see ibid., 201–5.

[48] On the German School Association, see Judson, *Exclusive Revolutionaries*, 207–15; and idem, *Guardians of the Nation, passim.* See also Norbert Prohaska, *Der Schulverein: Beiträge zum 120. Gründungstag* (Vienna: Österreichische Landsmannschaft, 2000).

[49] The national-liberal ideological orientation of the *Deutsche Zeitung* made this newspaper an obvious choice for the announcement.

[50] The date of this concert is incorrectly given as March 20, 1881 in Andrea Harrandt, "Students and Friends as 'Prophets' and 'Promoters': The Reception of Bruckner's Works in the *Wiener Akademische Wagner-Verein*," in *Perspectives on Anton Bruckner*, ed. Crawford Howie, Paul Hawkshaw, and Timothy Jackson (Aldershot: Ashgate, 2001), 319. The correct date is given in idem, "Bruckner in Vienna," in *The Cambridge Companion to Bruckner*, ed. John Williamson (Cambridge: Cambridge University Press,

In view of the orchestra's involvement in a concert intended to raise funds for the cause of continued German hegemony in the border regions— Wilhelm Frey described the event as having "partly a political, partly a social-ethical character"—it seems telling that Richter had reason, only a few weeks later, finally to acknowledge to a disappointed Dvořák that his own new symphony would not also be played that season.[51] Dvořák must have taken this rejection especially hard, since he seems to have consciously designed the symphony in accordance with the cultural biases of its intended German audience. Indeed, apart from the third movement— an undisguised furiant—the Sixth reflects not only a primarily German tradition but indeed a specifically *Viennese* one, and through its many patent allusions to Brahms and Beethoven, it goes out of its way to suggest an orientation toward what the Viennese elite would have understood as the center, not the periphery.[52]

As numerous scholars have noted, the model of Brahms's Second Symphony (his *"Wiener Sinfonie,"* as Ludwig Speidel dubbed it) seems especially close at hand.[53] To cite only the most obvious parallels, both are written in the key of

2004), 32. I am grateful to Benjamin Korstvedt (private communication) for informing me that the Philharmonic players had read through Bruckner's symphony in a *Novitäten-Probe* in November 1880 but did not vote to include it in the season's subscription programs. Korstvedt suggests that the idea to perform the work in the benefit concert three months later was Richter's doing.

[51] Frey's description of the benefit concert appears in his review of the event ("Musikalischer Aufnahmsfall," *Neues Wiener Tagblatt*, February 22, 1881). Richter was undoubtedly sincere in his commitment to the Sixth, yet his attributing the postponements to the orchestra's heavy workload and to his own personal distractions seems disingenuous, especially in light of the orchestra's ability to tackle Bruckner's larger and more challenging new score for an important benefit concert. Moreover, comparison of the subscription programs for the 1880–81 season with those of the surrounding years uncovers nothing to suggest that the orchestra was under unusually heavy pressure during the season in question to learn new or otherwise challenging works.

[52] The noted Czech linguist Josef Zubatý followed precisely this strategy in his early biography of his friend when he noted that, "[a]s in all his later works, so also [in the Sixth Symphony] does Dvořák adhere strictly to the forms brought to the highest degree of perfection by Beethoven; one can hardly claim to see an important departure in the fact that an idealized Czech dance ['Furiant'] takes the place of the scherzo." Josef Zubatý, *Anton Dvořák: Eine biographische Skizze* (Leipzig: Verlag von Gebrüder Hug, 1886), 6.

[53] sp. [Ludwig Speidel], "Konzerte," *Fremden-blatt*, January 3, 1878. Among other studies that relate Dvořák's Sixth to Brahms's Second, see David Beveridge, "Romantic Ideas in a Classical Frame: The Sonata Forms of Dvořák" (Ph.D. diss., University of California, Berkeley, 1980), 268–71; Jarmila Gabrielová, "Antonín Dvořák und

D major, begin with a moderate Allegro in triple meter, and conclude with a spirited finale that sets out quietly with note-against-note counterpoint. Comparison of the two first movements is especially telling (ex. 5.1). Both give prominent display to the sound of the horns. Just as Brahms's opening theme sets out from the tonic and then by way of the submediant (B minor) comes round to a varied continuation beginning on the supertonic (E minor), so does Dvořák's opening theme move from the tonic through a B-major chord (V/ii) to a varied continuation of its own beginning on the same second scale degree.

Dvořák likewise emulates a number of distinctive aspects of Brahms's secondary theme (ex. 5.2). Both feature melodies played in the baritone range, harmonized in thirds and sixths connected by "horn fifths," and accompanied in the outer voices by a pattern consisting of pizzicato bass notes and a violin figure carried over from the transition. The two themes even share a similar tonal conceit, in that they begin either *in* or *on* F-sharp only quickly to revert to the tonic, D, before finally confirming the second key. A prominent dactylic motive heard in Dvořák's setting not only figures strongly in Brahms's movement (e.g., mm. 127–28), but also constitutes one of several allusions made to Beethoven's "Eroica" Symphony (a significant touchstone in Brahms's work as well), involving such distinctive gestures as dissonant pedal-point syncopation, a "chromatic wedge," and a sweeping melodic descent propelled by the very same dactylic motive (exx. 5.3–5.5). And to drive home the point, a voice straight out of Vienna is heard front and center: Dvořák's main theme alludes directly to the so-called *Grossvater-Tanz*, which traditionally served as the closing dance at Viennese balls (ex. 5.6).[54]

If, as I have suggested, the manifest cause of the social tension between Germans and Czechs at the time when the Philharmonic players decided to forgo a performance of the Sixth had to do with threats to the privileged status of the German language, it is surely ironic that here Dvořák in fact

Johannes Brahms: Bemerkungen zur Kompositionsproblematik der Symphonie Nr. 6 D-Dur, Op. 60," in *Colloquium: Die Instrumentalmusik (Struktur—Funktion—Ästhetik) Brno 1991*, Ethnonationale Wechselbeziehungen in der mitteleuropäischen Musik mit besonderer Berücksichtigung der Situation in den böhmischen Ländern (Brno: Masarykova Univerzita, 1994); and Lukas Haselböck, "Dvořáks 6. Sinfonie: Ein 'intertextueller' Kommentar zu Brahms' 2. Sinfonie?" *Hudební veda* 41 (2004): 341–54.

[54] Kurt Honolka has noted that Dvořák's main theme recalls the finale of Schumann's *Papillons* (in the same key of D major) but does not relate the theme of the latter to its source in the *Großvater-Tanz* or to any Viennese context; see his *Dvořák*, trans. Anne Wyburd (London: Haus, 2004), 49. Tchaikovsky would later quote the *Großvater-Tanz* in *The Nutcracker* as an unmistakable means of evoking the Habsburg capital.

"speaks German" with an unusual degree of clarity. It was not enough. In a period when many middle-class Germans in Austria were beginning to identify in terms of ethnicity, nationality trumped culture. What mattered most about the piece in a time of crisis within Viennese liberalism proved not to be that it sounded like the work of a German but rather that a Czech composed it.

Beginning of a Breakthrough

The Philharmonic's failure to program Dvořák's new symphony did not go unnoticed. On January 16, 1882, Theodor Billroth wrote to Brahms, who was away in Hamburg at the time, with news about the previous day's Philharmonic concert, at which the new *Scandinavian* Symphony by the young English composer Frederic Hymen Cowen had been heard: "It would have been more enjoyable if

EXAMPLE 5.1b Dvořák, Symphony No. 6, op. 60, I, mm. 1–23
(reduction): beginning of first group

EXAMPLE 5.2a Brahms, Symphony No. 2, op. 73, I, mm. 82–89
(reduction): beginning of second group

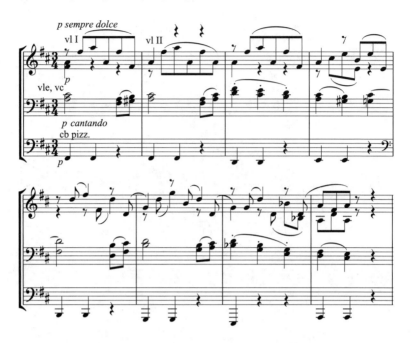

EXAMPLE 5.2b Dvořák, Symphony No. 6, op. 60, I, mm. 108–111
(reduction): beginning of second group

EXAMPLE 5.3a Beethoven, Symphony No. 3, op. 55, I, mm. 29–37 (outer voices): dissonant pedal-point syncopation

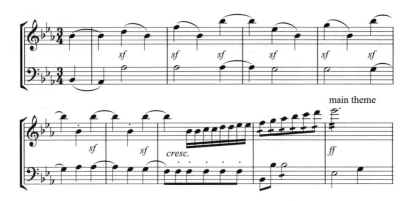

EXAMPLE 5.3b Dvořák, Symphony No. 6, op. 60, I, mm. 38–49 (outer voices): dissonant pedal-point syncopation

the new symphony by Dvořák, which has won such favor with Hanslick, had been performed. But since a rhapsody by Dvořák failed splendidly in the second Gesellschaft concert, Richter has probably lost all courage."[55]

The work in question here was the Slavonic Rhapsody No. 2, which was introduced to Vienna by Wilhelm Gericke on November 27, 1881. The response by the public and critics alike was much the same as that of two years earlier, when the Vienna Philharmonic introduced the Slavonic Rhapsody No. 3.

[55] *Billroth und Brahms im Briefwechsel*, 323.

EXAMPLE 5.4a Beethoven, Symphony No. 3, op. 55, I, mm. 57–62
(reduction): chromatic wedge

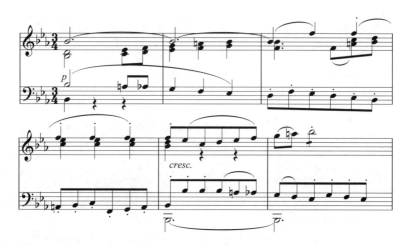

EXAMPLE 5.4b Dvořák, Symphony No. 6, op. 60, I, mm. 90–94
(reduction): chromatic wedge

EXAMPLE 5.5a Beethoven, Symphony No. 3, op. 55, I, mm. 65–68
(reduction): melodic descent with dactylic motive

EXAMPLE 5.5b Dvořák, Symphony No. 6, op. 60, I, mm. 102–4
(reduction): melodic descent with dactylic motive

EXAMPLE 5.6a *Großvater-Tanz* (beginning)

EXAMPLE 5.6b Dvořák, Symphony No. 6, op. 60, I, mm. 7–10: first theme with allusion to *Großvater-Tanz*

Eduard Schelle reported the audience's chilly response, asking how it could have been otherwise since the work, which was "welded together out of folk melodies," showed "no trace of symphonic character and true concentration of expression" and relied for its effect solely on its brilliant orchestration.[56] Max Kalbeck suggested that the rhapsody's unfortunate failure with the public could be blamed on the inclusion of the word "Slavic."[57] Even Hanslick was noticeably brief in his remarks about the piece.[58]

Nevertheless, in the face of this renewed Viennese resistance to Dvořák's music, Richter continued to give the composer hope for a performance of the symphony. Thus on January 30, 1882, Dvořák reported to Simrock he had learned from Hanslick that Richter had promised to perform the work later that season.[59] Yet the 1881–82 season came to end, not only without a performance of the symphony by the Philharmonic players, but also with Richter's resignation, evidently out of a failure to agree with the players over the makeup of their programs.

Hanslick was not pleased with any of this, and in his feuilleton of April 23, 1882, written three weeks after the season's end, he once again let the orchestra know it. Indeed, Hanslick attributed Richter's decision to resign to "loudly growing resentments" among the members of the orchestra themselves:

---

[56] E[duard] Schelle, "Musik," *Die Presse*, December 1, 1881.
[57] Max Kalbeck, "Concerte," *Wiener Allgemeine Zeitung*, November 29, 1881, quoted in the second epigraph of this chapter.
[58] Ed. H. [Eduard Hanslick], "Musik," *Neue Freie Presse*, November 29, 1881.
[59] *Korespondence a Dokumenty* 5: 285. See also Brahms's letter to Simrock of March 22, 1881 (quoted on p. 00).

In this association of artists there are well-known restless and frothing members of excessive self-esteem who sometimes make life miserable for the direction of the Court Opera as well as that of the Philharmonic concerts. They opposed Herr Richter in matters of the program (most recently because of the Brahms symphony [the First Symphony was heard for the second time in the Philharmonic's concerts on March 26]), and even encouraged the idea that in the future not the conductor but rather the many-headed "Comité" of the Philharmonic concerts should design or at least give approval to the program. Such a measure would turn the natural order on its head: the conductor would simply perform what the orchestra dictates, instead of the orchestra performing what the conductor dictates. The choice of pieces to be performed must lie in one person's hand, that of the conductor, who cannot in this acquiesce to the trusteeship of his violists and trumpeters. Certainly everyone would find it ridiculous if rather than the director of a theater, you wanted the troupe of actors to determine which pieces to perform or even only to approve them. We are convinced such a proposal would not have won the insightful majority of the orchestra members, but can easily imagine that the mere impertinence would be apt to awaken thoughts of abdication in a director of Richter's position. However, we do not want to give up the hope of seeing Herr Hanns Richter next winter, free from all doubts, at the head once more of the Philharmonic concerts.[60]

Despite Hanslick's tirade about the orchestra's behavior and his strong show of support for their conductor, Richter followed through with his resignation and was subsequently replaced for the following season by Wilhelm Jahn, one of his fellow conductors at the Court Opera. Jahn's tenure at the head of the orchestra proved to be an interregnum of only one year, however. By the time the next season rolled around, Richter had returned to the helm, now with greater influence on the players, it appears, in the matter of programming new works.[61]

---

[60] Ed. H. [Eduard Hanslick], "Letzte Concerte," *Neue Freie Presse*, April 23, 1882.

[61] In 1892 Richter claimed "it would be erroneous to believe that, during the seventeen years in which I have had the honor to be the director of the Philharmonic concerts, works by Brahms, Bruckner, Dvořák, Fuchs, Goldmark were rejected by voting, because I have generally not put works by these masters to the vote." HA/WPh, Br-R-16–024, quoted in Hellsberg, *Demokratie der Könige*, 256. As Hellsberg notes, Richter is somewhat overstating the case, in that works by some of these masters were indeed rejected by the players during the conductor's first tenure as the orchestra's director.

Meanwhile, in June 1882, Hanslick encouraged Dvořák to settle in Vienna, if only for a few years, suggesting that the proposed resettlement "need not make you a turncoat" while insisting that "after such great early successes, your art needs a wider horizon, a German setting, a larger, non-Czech public."[62] The composer had no intention of acting on this suggestion, but he must have known he could continue to count on Hanslick's advocacy of his cause in Vienna. Indeed, whether it was Hanslick's doing or not, Dvořák's music finally returned to the Philharmonic's programs under Jahn's baton during the 1882–83 season following an absence of two years. Meeting on September 16, 1882, the Comité agreed to include a "new work" by the Czech composer but did not name the piece. It seems doubtful that any serious thought had been given to performing the Sixth Symphony; this work, after all, was closely associated with Richter. Instead, on November 13 the players settled on a more modest composition, selecting for the concert of November 26 three movements from the orchestral version of *Legends*, evidently without first testing them in a *Novitäten-Probe*.[63] Since Hanslick was the dedicatee of this work, we may be justified in assuming the Philharmonic players chose it for performance as a way of mending fences with a disgruntled critic whom it was better not to cross. Indeed, it eventually became an open belief among the city's more "progressive" critics that the orchestra had come to favor Dvořák at the expense, say, of Bruckner solely because of Hanslick's influence.

In his comments about *Legends*, Hanslick departed from the strategy he had adopted in his earlier review of the Third Rhapsody. No longer did he

---

[62] *Korespondence a documenty* 5: 388. In his review of a string quartet by Karel Šebor, recently performed in Vienna by the Radnitzky Quartet, Hanslick noted that, of all the Czech composers, only Dvořák had obtained much of a reputation outside Prague, attributing this to Dvořák's singular decision to publish his scores with German publishers under German titles; see Ed. H. [Eduard Hanslick], "Concerte," *Neue Freie Presse*, January 24, 1882.

[63] Minutes of the Comité meeting of September 16, 1882, dated September 20, 1882 (HA/WPh, G.Z. 644); Minutes of the Comité meeting of November 13, 1882, dated November 20, 1882 (HA/WPh, G.Z. 703). The reports of that year's two *Novitäten-Proben*, held on September 26 and October 6, are contained in HA/WPh, G.Z. 648 and 655. The Andante and Scherzo of Bruckner's Sixth Symphony were tried out on October 6, along with Schubert's early Symphony No. 5, Moritz Käßmayer's *Drei kleine Stücke für Streichorchester*, and a few others. The works by Schubert and Käßmayer received the most votes (62), followed by the symphonic movements by Bruckner (51); all three compositions were included in the season's programs. That Käßmayer was a first violinist in the orchestra and a member of the Comité, to boot, suggests something of the cronyism that could often be found at work in these decisions.

disclaim any significant relationship between the composer's ethnic and musical heritages; instead, he ostensibly embraced popular assumptions about such a relationship, only to co-opt those to further his own take on the composer as an acculturated German:

> Dvořák, who has always lived among the Slavs, a son of the people, among the people, has become so imbued with the spirit of Slavic national melodies, that one had to worry lest [the composer] should become captive to this charming but one-sided attraction. His *Legends* show that Dvořák has no need of national reminiscences in order to create his own thing of beauty; he speaks here in the language of Schumann and Brahms.[64]

Here the critic plays on popular assumptions as a means by which to subvert them.[65]

Later that season the Sixth Symphony was finally heard in Vienna, not in the Philharmonic series, but in one of the concerts of the Gesellschaft der Musikfreunde, where Gericke directed it on February 18, 1883. Although Wagner's death five days earlier drew the lion's share of critical attention that week, Hanslick did not fail to call attention to the work's belated performance. He began his review by noting that the work "is dedicated to Hanns Richter, who had performed it repeatedly with great success in London and had also previously booked it for the Philharmonic concerts." But then came a pointed complaint:

> Unfortunately our Philharmonic players no more troubled themselves with it than they had with Dvořák's beautiful Serenade for Winds. We are all the more grateful to Herr Gericke for making us acquainted with the new symphony, which certainly belongs to the most accomplished and best of the last thirty years.[66]

---

[64] Ed. H. [Eduard Hanslick], "Concerte," *Neue Freie Presse*, November 28, 1882, rpt. in idem, *Concerte, Componisten und Virtuosen der letzten fünfzehn Jahre*, 338–40.

[65] Hanslick's earlier review of the Sextet in A, introduced by the Hellmesberger Quartet on March 31, 1881, follows a similar strategy. See David Brodbeck, "Dvořák's Reception in Liberal Vienna: Language Ordinances, National Property, and the Rhetoric of *Deutschum*," *Journal of the American Musicological Society* 60 (2007): 71–131 (at 98–99).

[66] "Ed. H. [Eduard Hanslick], "Musik," *Neue Freie Presse*, February 20, 1883. These opening sentences were dropped when the review was reprinted in *Concerte, Componisten und Virtuosen der letzten fünfzehn Jahre*, 370–71.

This was high praise, inasmuch as Hanslick was setting the new work alongside the very best symphonies written since Mendelssohn and Schumann. In fact, it seemed to epitomize everything that Hanslick valued in music. "It is thoroughly healthy music," he writes:

> untormented and original, that Dvořák offers us in this symphony. To the delightful freshness and naturalness of his earlier works is now brought an enjoyable mastery of form. The theme of the first movement is a true stroke of luck: a genuine symphonic theme, simple, powerful, as if cast of ore. With complete joy we follow the consummate yet in no way dry working out of this theme, with its ancillary ideas; the composer remains the victorious lord of his material until the end.[67]

At the same time, to say that Dvořák had "mastered" the symphonic style, had "grown into the highest forms of instrumental music," is, for Hanslick, tantamount to saying that he had joined the great German liberal nation by adopting the genre of the grand symphony as his own. Moreover, the critic seems to set Dvořák pointedly apart in this sense from the New Germans: "In our time of reflection, poor in production, we are pleased to encounter a naturally feeling, happily productive talent such as Dvořák, who has grown into the highest forms of instrumental music and has remained faithful with pronounced singularity to the ideals of our classical period."[68]

Although the characterization of "our time of reflection" is susceptible to more than one interpretation, it clearly carries a negative edge. And given what we know about Hanslick's aesthetics, it appears that for him program music in the manner of Liszt's symphonic poems, through its dependence on an extramusical text, stands in the same inferior relation to "pure music" (*reine Musik*) that, say, the moon (which can only reflect light) stands in relation to the sun (which generates light).[69] This is not to suggest that Hanslick opposed all forms of program music. Rather it underscores the low esteem in which he held music meant to be understood solely in terms of a program. What is relevant here, however, in the context of the review of the Sixth Symphony is the suggestion that those who can produce a "sun" (read: Dvořák) are original and productive in a way that those who can only produce a "moon" (read: the New German composers) cannot be.[70]

---

[67] Hanslick, *Concerte, Componisten, und Virtuosen der letzten fünfzehn Jahre*, 370–71.

[68] Ibid.

[69] For a recent discussion, see Nicole Grimes, "German Humanism, Liberalism, and Elegy in Hanslick's Writings on Brahms," in *Rethinking Hanslick*, 173–76.

[70] Whatever his intention, Hanslick was pleased with this formulation and made use of similar locutions, as we shall see, in his reviews of the Seventh and Eighth symphonies.

"Bohemian schools in Vienna"

Like Hanslick, Max Kalbeck scolded the Philharmonic for rejecting the Sixth
Symphony while praising Gericke for filling the breach by scheduling it in
the Gesellschaft concerts. But whereas Hanslick only implicitly linked the
work and its composer to the German tradition, Kalbeck was rather more
explicit in making the same point, noting how "the 'Bohemian Schubert,'
encountered so often in Dvořák's chamber music, has in the symphony
grown into the Bohemian Beethoven."[71] What follows is a convoluted anal-
ogy wherein Beethoven is the Angel of God with whom Dvořák, cast as the
biblical Jacob, must wrestle before crossing the Jordan and entering Canaan.
Although it is clear Kalbeck does not consider the work at hand to be a grand
symphony in the style of Beethoven, he does make mention of the opening
Allegro's many allusions to the *Eroica*. Moreover, in his admiring description of the development of this movement, one he claims is marked by an
"astonishing wealth of healthy life, thorough know-how, and serious work,"
we find characterizations that very clearly recall Hanslick's coded language
for Germanness in music. By identifying the scherzo as a furiant, to be sure,
Kalbeck implicitly acknowledges the Czech background of that movement,
but even here he makes room for the German element: "Beethoven beats the
time, but Dvořák sets it to music" (*Beethoven schlägt der Tact, aber Dvorzak
musicirt dazu*). And in the finale, too, he writes, we find the "musical fraternization of the Czechs and Germans."

There was no such happy fraternization at this moment in Vienna as
a whole, however. Only a week after the belated performance of the Sixth
Symphony, Brahms reported to Simrock on the generally discouraging conditions, as he found them, in his adopted homeland:

> In a city and a country where everything is going, no, falling down-
> hill, you may not expect things to get better with music. It really is a
> very great pity, not merely with regard to music, but with regard to
> the entire beautiful country and the lovely, fine people. I think that
> we will yet experience the catastrophe—but in the meantime, we are
> founding Bohemian schools in Vienna.[72]

---

[71] Max Kalbeck, "Concerte," *Wiener Allgemeine Zeitung*, February 20, 1883, from which
the other quotations in this paragraph are taken.

[72] Brahms, *Briefwechsel*, vol. 11: *Briefe an Fritz Simrock*, ed. Max Kalbeck (1919): 17.

This passage not only registers Brahms's general loathing of—his despondency over—the conservative-clerical drift of the policies of the Taaffe regime; it also highlights a rankling instance of the ongoing language conflict that was just then hitting close to home.[73] Since its founding in Vienna in 1872, the Comenius School Association, a voluntary bourgeois association whose goals anticipated those of the more recently founded German School Association from the other side of the language divide, had been attempting to gain permission to open a private Czech-language school in the city's Tenth District, where the majority of Vienna's rapidly growing Czech immigrant population lived.[74] When, in November 1882, Taaffe's Ministry of Education declared that there was no legal impediment to this plan, the outcry from the city's liberal establishment was fierce. By the next summer, the controversy was coming to a head in a series of notable developments. On June 20, 1883, the *Neue Freie Presse* published a report of the School Commission of the Lower Austrian Diet that laid out the German objections to the proposed Czech school in terms of Article 19 of the constitution. Since German, as the report claimed, was the only *landesübliche Sprache* in Lower Austria and especially "in the German city of Vienna," there could be no legal basis for the founding of a Czech school; moreover, the establishment of such a school would cause "an obvious erosion" of German's status as the one and only language customary in the land, since the proposed new Czech school would replace a German one.[75]

In a debate that took place the following day in the Lower Austrian Diet, Friedrich Maaßen, the recently named rector of the University of Vienna, spoke to the matter at some length. As a clerical-conservative—he was a professor of Roman and canon law in the theology faculty—and a politically

---

[73] Brahms followed the language controversy with great interest—and considerable chagrin—and it may have been at around this time that he acquired his copy of a pamphlet entitled *Die Nationalitäten—, das ist: Sprachenfrage in Oesterreich. Ein Vorschlag zu ihrer Lösung von einem Deutsch-Oesterreicher* (Vienna: Verlag von L. Rosner, 1881); see Kurt Hofmann, *Die Bibliothek von Johannes Brahms: Bücher- und Musikalienverzeichnis* (Hamburg: Karl Dieter Wagner, 1974), 42.

[74] By 1880, immigrants from the Bohemian crown lands of Bohemia and Moravia made up nearly 27 percent of Vienna's residents; see Michael John, "'We Do Not Even Possess Our Selves': On Identity and Ethnicity in Austria, 1880–1937," *Austria History Yearbook* 30 (1999): 21–24. See also Monika Glettler, "Minority Culture in a Capital City: The Czechs in Vienna at the Turn of the Century," in *Decadence & Innovation: Austro-Hungarian Life and Arts at the Turn of the Century*, ed. Robert Pynsent (London: Weidenfeld and Nicolson, 1989), 49–60.

[75] "Die czechische Schule in Wien," *Neue Freie Presse*, June 20, 1883; the story carries the date "June 19."

active federalist, Maaßen was no friend of the liberals, and in his speech he championed the Czech cause in a way that seemed to be calling the entire liberal nationalist project into question:

> Do you think that in a state in which these nationalities upon which you want to force the superiority of the German language can avail themselves of the free press and free speech, where the freedom of association and freedom of the press exists, do you think it will be possible to force the other nationalities to recognize the German language as the official state language? I don't think so, and if it were possible, I would not wish it to be so. Does the German *Volk* exist merely in language, not also in attitude, and does equitableness not also belong to that attitude? Equitableness bestows honor to a people; national imperiousness and national arrogance are great sins. If I were not convinced that equitableness is also a German property, I would not give a tinker's dam for *Deutschthum*.[76]

Maaßen acknowledged he was speaking as an individual and not in the name of the university, but the faculty were incensed, and on the day following the speech a number of the leading full professors in the three secular faculties, including both Hanslick and Billroth, presented the rector with a brief address, diplomatic but unequivocal in meaning, in which they made clear that they "did not share the political and national opinions expressed in [Maaßen's] speech."[77] Although Brahms was in Wiesbaden, hard at work

---

[76] *Neue Freie Presse*, June 21, 1883. Although the position Maaßen is taking here—that to make German the official state language would be to act inequitably toward the non-German peoples of multinational Austria—may appear liberal by the standards of contemporary American political discourse, it by no means represented liberal ideology during the period under question. The liberals of Hanslick's and Billroth's generation were nothing if not "imperious" and "arrogant" with respect to German language, science, and culture, although it should also be remembered they did recognize the possibility of German acculturation by upward-striving Jews, Czechs, and members of other social groups and in this sense probably viewed themselves as showing the "equitableness" that Maaßen finds lacking in them. For a reading that differs from mine, see Notley *Lateness and Brahms*, 18–19.

[77] "Von der Universität," *Neue Freie Presse*, June 24, 1883. Maaßen's speech also precipitated a strong response among the Viennese student body that fell out along a predictable German-Czech faultline, recalling in this sense the controversy that Billroth's remarks about the Eastern Jewish students had set off eight years earlier. See "Demonstration auf der Universität," *Neue Freie Presse, Abendblatt*, June 23, 1883; and "Von der Universität," *Neue Freie Presse*, June 24, 1883. Although Notley characterizes the protesters as "radically pro-German students" (*Lateness and Brahms*, 18), this overstates the case; the attitudes expressed here were not far from those of the liberal mainstream.

on his Third Symphony, he did what he could to keep abreast of events and in letters to Billroth and Hanslick thanked both heartily for speaking up in the matter at hand. As he put it to Hanslick: "One must be as much an Austrian as I am, love the Austrians as much as I do, to feel sad every day when reading the newspaper, and then suddenly, as now, to feel such deep pleasure!"[78]

To Max Kalbeck, Brahms's act of composing his new symphony within sight of the Rhine, steeped not only in nationalistic lore but also in rich memories of the composer's Romantic youth, seemed momentous. Here, as he put it, "all the circumstances were to fall into place to foster the planned work and to give it the content by which to justify his artistic existence."[79] Among these circumstances, Kalbeck placed special weight on those having to do with Brahms's German identity. In particular, he suggested that one of the key reasons the composer decided to summer in Germany that year, after having passed the previous five summers in Austria, was his desire to work in the midst of the Niederwald Denkmal, the monument topped by a large statue of Germania that was going up along the Rhine near Rüdesheim in honor of the foundation of the Wilhelmine Empire. Implicitly suggesting that Brahms's German pride had more to do with the concept of nation than of state, he notes how "the liberal German in Brahms was up in arms against Austria's escalating Czech-Clerical special-interest politics."[80] By explicitly linking the Czech nationalists with the Clerical conservatives, Kalbeck demonstrates how readily Austrian German liberals, including Brahms, continued to associate bourgeois Czech nationalism with the unenlightened forces of reaction. But whereas Brahms did remain in the Rhineland long enough to witness the dedication of the monument on September 28 from the Rüdesheim wine garden of his friends Rudolf and Laura von Beckerath, this probably had a less profound effect on him than Kalbeck imagined, in

---

[78] Undated letter from Brahms to Hanslick from late June 1883, in Eduard Hanslick, "Johannes Brahms: The Last Days; Memories and Letters," trans. Susie Gillespie, Andrew Homan, and Caroline Homan, in *Brahms and His World*, rev. ed., 327. See also Brahms's letter of June 27, 1883, to Billroth, in *Billroth und Brahms in Briefwechsel*, 348–49.

[79] Kalbeck, *Johannes Brahms*, 3: 379–80. For a recent study, see David Brodbeck, "Brahms, the Third Symphony, and the New German School," in *Brahms and His World*, rev. ed., 95–116.

[80] Kalbeck, *Johannes Brahms*, 3: 381, 382n.

an especially poetic telling, and by then, at any rate, Brahms had completed the symphony.[81]

Around this time the *Allgemeine Deutsche Musikzeitung* reported the rumor that Brahms "has moved his residence from Vienna to Wiesbaden."[82] Responding to this bit of gossip, as well as perhaps to the recent news that Serbo-Croatian had been introduced as an external language in Dalmatia, alongside German, the composer's friend Elisabeth von Herzogenberg made light of the Austrian situation in a letter of October 1, 1883: "I can't believe—until I hear it from your own lips—that your enthusiasm for the Niederwald monument is leading you to settle in Wiesbaden for good....Do you fear the great Croatian monarchy, with its supportive tendencies toward Dvořák rather than you?"[83]

If, as Kalbeck claimed, Brahms thus "had reason to sulk about the Viennese," none of this clouded his personal relationship with Dvořák.[84] On the contrary, only a few days after receiving Elisabeth's letter, Brahms was visited by the Czech composer, who subsequently reported to Simrock that he had spent "[q]uite lovely days with Dr. Brahms, who just arrived from Wiesbaden. I have never seen him in such a cheerful mood. We were together every noon and evening, chatting about many things."[85] Here Dvořák heard parts of Brahms's new symphony for the first time, performed by the composer at the piano. Two months later, Brahms's Third Symphony would be coupled with Dvořák's Violin Concerto in a Philharmonic concert. The critical reception of the latter work tracks a faultline that was growing more pronounced in bourgeois politics and would resurface repeatedly in music-critical discourse in the years to come.

[81] Kalbeck, *Johannes Brahms*, 3: 384–85, 400; but cf. Beller-McKenna, *Brahms and the German Spirit*, 146–47, and Kurt Stephenson, *Johannes Brahms und die Familie Beckerath* (Hamburg: Christians, 1979), 25. The first of the composer's friends to see the new work probably was Franz Wüllner, who visited Brahms in Wiesbaden in late August and won from him a promise to come to the German capital to conduct the symphony with the Berlin Philharmonic (as reported in the *Allgemeine Deutsche Musikzeitung* 10, 1883: 378).

[82] "Johannes Brahms hat seinen Wohnsitz von Wien nach Wiesbaden verlegt." *Allgemeine Deutsche Musikzeitung* 10 (1883): 350.

[83] Brahms, *Briefwechsel*, vol. 2: *Johannes Brahms im Briefwechsel mit Heinrich und Elisabeth von Herzogenberg,* ed. Max Kalbeck (1921), 8. As Elisabeth knew, Brahms had witnessed the dedication of the Niederwald Denkmal.

[84] Kalbeck, *Johannes Brahms*, 3: 401.

[85] Letter of October 10, 1883, in *Korespondence a documenty* 1: 366–67.

Two Critics in Counterpoint

Although Hanslick remained without question the most dominating and influential voice in Viennese music criticism of his day, by the mid-1880s he was to come under challenge from a younger figure, Theodor Helm, the long-time Viennese correspondent for the *Musikalisches Wochenblatt*.[86] As a *Wagnerianer*, admirer of Liszt, and recent convert to Bruckner's cause, Helm occupied a place that was to some degree opposite Hanslick's in the contemporary aesthetic divide. Equally significant, however, is the gulf that separated the two critics in terms of political ideology. This became especially meaningful after January 1884, when, from a large pool of some forty applicants, Helm was appointed music critic for the *Deutsche Zeitung* following the death of its long-serving critic, Franz Gehring.[87] As we have seen, this paper was founded thirteen years earlier by self-described *Jungen*, liberal activists whose German-nationalist consciousness had developed in part in opposition to early Czech demands for a political arrangement comparable to what the Hungarians had achieved in the *Ausgleich* of 1867.[88] In many respects, this "organ of the German party" staked out a position to the nationalist left of the *Neue Freie Presse*, the established organ of the centralist *Alten*.[89] Not surprisingly, Helm's criticism reflected liberalism's new politics

---

[86] Helm's work also appeared in other German music periodicals, as well as in the *Pester Lloyd*, among other newspapers.

[87] Among the unsuccessful applicants was Guido Adler, a founding member of the Vienna Academic Wagner Society and a former student of Hanslick at the University of Vienna. See Adler's correspondence with the philosopher Alexius Meinong from early 1884 in *Alexius Meinong und Guido Adler: Eine Freundschaft in Briefen*, ed. Gabriele Johanna Eder (Amsterdam and Atlanta: Rudopi, 1995), 79–82.

[88] The emergence of the *Jungen* of the early 1870s represents an early step toward favoring German-national interest over centralist state interest; see Judson, *Exclusive Revolutionaries*, 201.

[89] As we have seen, the Czechs' position was briefly strengthened in 1870–71, when Francis Joseph dismissed the Bürger Ministry and installed, in succession, more conservative and federalist-minded cabinets headed by Count Adam Potocki and Count Carl von Hohenwart; only in late 1871 did the emperor turn back to the liberals to form a cabinet. On the political orientation of the *Deutsche Zeitung*, see Edith Walter, *Österreichische Tageszeitungen der Jahrhundertwende: Ideologischer Anspruch und ökonomische Erfordernisse* (Vienna, Cologne, and Weimar: Böhlau Verlag, 1994), 68–74. Quoted there (at 74) is the following passage from the memoirs of Sigmund Mayer (published in 1911): "The success against Hohenwart emboldened the 'Young Germans.' The *Neue Freie Presse* was not sufficiently anti-Hohenwart, so they founded the *Deutsche Zeitung*." Kurt Paupié characterized the *Deutsche Zeitung* as *nationalliberal*; the *Neue Freie Presse*, as *deutschliberal*; see his *Handbuch der österreichischen Pressegeschichte 1848–1959*, 2 vols.

of German nationhood in Cisleithania in a way that Hanslick's work did not. More than that, as we shall discover, throughout his writings on Dvořák the younger critic seemed very much aware of acting the part of national liberal counterbalance to the more traditional German liberal Hanslick.[90] As he later explained to Heinrich Friedjung, "Outside of my main calling in music and music history I was always extraordinarily interested in everything political."[91]

Helm clearly was proud of his appointment to the staff of the leading German-nationalist daily, and he drew pointed attention to it in the regular column he continued to write for the *Musikalisches Wochenblatt*: "Since the continuation of this music letter was delayed as a result of my accepting a new position as critic for one of Vienna's major political organs, I must first of all catch up on what there is still to report from the Philharmonic concerts."[92] What follows, however, is a lengthy reproach of Hanslick for his failure to appreciate any living composer other than Brahms and Dvořák, coupled with assurances of his own respect for both men's work: "I wholeheartedly acknowledge myself to be one of the most sincere admirers of Brahms's genius and of his phenomenal mastery and am certainly not blind

(Vienna: Wilhelm Braumüller, 1960) 1: 134. The *Deutsche Zeitung* thus was the natural choice in which to announce the establishment of the German School Association in 1880, as noted earlier.

[90] Helm and Hanslick had once been on friendly terms, and in early 1871, at the latter's request, Helm had even substituted as the music critic for the *Neue Freie Presse* during one of Hanslick's extended absences from Vienna. (Helm signed those feuilletons as "–m.") By 1883, however, the two had grown estranged. Michael Krebs has attributed this primarily to disagreements over musical politics (which is to say, over the merits of composers such as Wagner, Liszt, and Bruckner); yet, as we shall see, the two critics' differing views of Dvořák may suggest that contrasting *deutschliberal* and *national-alliberal* perspectives were at play, too. See Krebs, "Theodor Helm (1843–1920): Ein Musikschriftsteller im Umkreis von Anton Bruckner," part 1: 87–88, 99–101 (with quotations from the critics' correspondence with one another). Not surprisingly, shortly after assuming his position at the *Deutsche Zeitung* Helm decided no longer to contribute reviews to the *Pester Lloyd*; see the letter of December 1884 to Helm from Max Falk (the Budapest newspaper's editor), quoted in ibid., part 1: 106. In later years Helm would resume his work for the *Pester Lloyd*, often basing his reviews on those he had written for the *Deutsche Zeitung*, but now with a muting of the German-nationalist sentiment.

[91] Unpublished letter of February 10, 1908 (Wiener Stadt- und Landesbibliothek H.I.N. 163.348), quoted in ibid., 8.

[92] Theodor Helm, *Musikalisches Wochenblatt* 15 (February 7, 1884): 88. Helm's first review for the *Deutsche Zeitung* was published on January 11, 1884.

to Dvořák's native talent and compositional technique." With statements of this sort, Helm has earned a reputation among scholars as one of the most fair-minded and balanced Viennese critics in a period of highly charged, partisan music reception. But when Helm undercut his praise of Dvořák's talent and technique by going on to regret his "hypernational trend," that was something altogether different.[93]

In this regard, it is instructive to compare the reviews by Hanslick and Helm of Dvořák's Violin Concerto, performed by the noted Czech virtuoso František Ondříček in the Philharmonic's concert of December 2, 1883.[94] Hanslick's evaluations of the first movement and Adagio are unremarkable, but his commentary on the last movement spoke to his readers in openly political terms:

> The Finale . . . pleases through its fresh, naïve festiveness; there is about it something of a Bohemian country fair. Dvořák unites Slavic national reminiscences, happily enough, with eminent German art. His music is the best kind of "politics of reconciliation" [Versöhnungs-Politik]; Germans and Czechs accept it without hesitation with the same pleasure.[95]

Helm's account of the same movement suggests that Hanslick may have indulged in some wishful thinking:

> The clearest, most lucid and effective movement of the work is the finale, which is unmistakably modeled on that of Beethoven's Violin Concerto. Like Beethoven, Dvořák attempts a studied popular tone;

---

[93] Helm, *Musikalisches Wochenblatt* 15 (February 7, 1884): 89.

[94] This concert also included the first performance of Brahms's Third Symphony. Kalbeck implies that Dvořák attended the concert and then traveled with Brahms a few days later to Budapest to attend a performance of his Sixth Symphony (Kalbeck, *Johannes Brahms*, 3: 413). Yet, as David Beveridge as suggested (private communication), this seems highly unlikely, inasmuch as Dvořák was ill at this time, had just canceled a trip to Hamburg for this very reason, and quite likely did not travel to Budapest to the hear the Sixth Symphony on December 5. Moreover, as Beveridge notes, the composer's letter to Simrock of January 1, 1884, regarding a forthcoming performance of Brahms's Third Symphony in Berlin strongly suggests he had not previously heard the work in concert. All this can be inferred from Dvořák's letters to Max Schütz in Budapest (November 24, 1883), to Julius von Bernuth in Hamburg (on December 1, 1883) and to Fritz Simrock in Berlin (January 1, 1884); *Korespondence a dokumenty* 1: 373, 374, and 381.

[95] Ed. H. [Eduard Hanslick], "Concerte," *Neue Freie Presse*, December 5, 1883.

like that immortal master he has the solo violin strike up the tune, as it were, to which the choir of instruments responds in confirmation. But here we see the harsh difference between talent and genius. Dvořák, in his pronounced popular character, is at times decidedly trivial, whereas Beethoven gives us a musical setting of country life in the poetic scene. At the same time even the unpretentious German folk tune is vastly more pleasant to German ears and hearts than the Czech idiom that Dvořák smuggles into the classical sonata form. In the event, Ondříček's truly surpassing interpretation of Dvořák's concerto was extolled, but the composition was rejected with telling silence.[96]

Hanslick, citing a catchword from contemporary political discourse in a period of acute tension between Bohemia's two main groups of inhabitants, saw common ground for a reconciliation between German high culture and Slavic otherness: in his view the composer was, musically speaking, an acculturated German—a "Germanized Czech," to recall Billroth's locution—and in that case no harm could come from enlivening the sonata style with local color.[97] Helm imagined things very differently. Genius versus talent; poetry versus triviality; an unpretentious German folk tune versus a Czech idiom that has presumably despoiled the classical form into which it has insinuated itself—these binary opposites suggest not only his claim for German cultural superiority but also his emphasis on essentializing difference, rooted in ethnicity, hierarchically organized, and effectively unbridgeable. The "German ears and hearts" of Helm's readers could never appreciate the "Slavic national reminiscences" produced by Hanslick's protégé. A comparative reading of the two critics' rhetoric, in short, provides concrete evidence of how, under the sway

[96] Helm, *Musikalisches Wochenblatt* 15 (1884): 43. Since Helm's position with the *Deutsche Zeitung* did not begin until a few weeks after this concert, he did not contribute a review of the piece to that paper; nevertheless, the outlook revealed here is fully consonant with that which would come to mark his criticism for his new employer. Note the sharp difference between this rhetoric and that displayed in Helm's review of the Sextet three years before, wherein he wrote approvingly of how the composer "gives us the most delightful Slavic-national melodies,... introduced with admirable skill into the realm of classical chamber music." Helm, *Musikalisches Wochenblatt* 12 (1881): 300. Particularly instructive is how something akin to the erstwhile "delightful melodies" is now characterized as an unpleasant Czech *idiom*.

[97] Ironically, this is not how Hanslick had conceived things with respect to Goldmark's *Die Königin von Saba*. As I have suggested, he seems to some degree to have heard Goldmark's use of local color in that work as an expression of the composer's essential self.

of a younger generation, German liberalism was becoming less liberal and more German, with Germanness itself becoming more ethnic and less cultural.[98]

Dvořák knew enough by now to react cautiously when he learned that the Philharmonic players had programmed the Slavonic Rhapsody No. 2 for the following season. In a letter of October 20, 1884, he thanked Richter for continuing to take interest in his music but added:

> I have some misgivings about the choice of the "Slavonic Rhapsody" (forgive my frankness), for the reason that the Viennese public has from the beginning shown a prejudice against compositions that have a Slavic flavor and it will not on that account be successful, as it might be in other circumstances.[99]

Dvořák proposed a number of other works as worthy substitutes, including the Sixth Symphony and the newly published *Husitská* Overture (which, under the circumstances, he suggested should be billed as simply a "Dramatic" Overture). That he remained eager for the Philharmonic to perform the symphony is understandable enough; that he sought a performance in Vienna of the overture seems less explicable, given its patent nationalist symbolism, which no change of title could hide. In any event, Richter was not dissuaded from his original plans, and the Philharmonic performed the rhapsody as scheduled on March 1, 1885.[100]

---

[98] King, *Budweisers into Czechs and Germans*, 75–76.

[99] *Korespondence a dokumenty* 1: 442.

[100] The overture dates from 1883, when it was written on a commission from František Adolf Šubert, director of the Czech National Theater, who was planning to write a dramatic trilogy in commemoration of the Hussite period. Although Dvořák completed the overture in short order, Šubert never got beyond finishing the first play of the set. Brahms, for one, did not care for this work, at least in part on nationalist grounds, and he was chagrined to learn that Simrock had agreed to publish it. Thus in a postscript to a letter to the publisher of August 18–19, 1884, he wrote: "If they are not understood or enjoyed, I at least hope my bad jokes won't be misunderstood! Dvořák would probably not stand for it, if you wanted to be his publisher *and* critic, and rightly so. So if you want to be Royal-Bohemian National-Publisher, then the most I can do is to be sorry that even worse things by Dvořák have contributed to that. You know and believe that I only wish Dvořák would always give you good things, as he can. (Unfortunately, the Overture is bragging, insolent, and bad.) But you are concerned with business matters, and I know enough to say nothing to you." Letter of August 18–19, 1884, in *Briefwechsel* 11: 67 (emphasis added). A portion of this passage is also translated in Beveridge, "Dvořák and Brahms," 83–84, but Brahms's humorous description of Simrock is erroneously given there as "Royal Bohemian National-Composer." We shall return to this work in Chapter 7.

With Dvořák's having already established his German credentials in Vienna by now with both a symphony and concerto, Hanslick seems perfectly willing this time to grant the composer's "national material" its due without feeling the need to engage in special pleading of any kind:

> The designation "Rhapsody" seems to me fitting and important: the composer does not offer a form that is strictly symmetrical in accordance with Classical traditions, but rather a fantastic rambling one that has its own somewhat freer logic. It is the logic of the rhapsodist, who, inspired by national material, seizes the strings, follows the poetic impulse, and here and there departs episodically, but nevertheless is not untrue to the basic mood.[101]

Helm was less generous. In his brief notice for the *Deutsche Zeitung*, he did allow that the Rhapsody "is not entirely lacking in individual beautiful combinations or in orchestral brilliance and effective buildups," but he regretted missing "that elementary power which in Liszt's Hungarian Rhapsodies involuntarily sweeps the listener away. How very differently did Liszt's Rhapsody in F, heard in the Gesellschaft concert before last, ignite!" Moreover, whereas Hanslick failed to mention the audience's response, Helm made certain his readers knew that the work "was not entirely successful; the sparse applause applied only to the magnificent performance."[102]

A Night at the Opera

The years in which these early Viennese performances of Dvořák's music took place witnessed increasing erosion of German prerogatives in the Czech crown lands. In 1880, as we have seen, Czech was introduced as a second language, alongside German, in which the public in Bohemia and Moravia was permitted to communicate with the governmental bureaucracy. In 1882 the University of Prague was divided into separate German and Czech divisions. In the same year, Taaffe extended voting rights to lower-middle-class men in a move that he correctly anticipated would cause the German liberals to lose control of the Bohemian Diet in the elections of June 1883 to the conservative nobility and Czech nationalists.[103] And in the Reichsrat elections of June 1885,

---

[101] Ed. H. [Eduard Hanslick], "Concerte," *Neue Freie Presse*, March 5, 1885.

[102] h——m [Theodor Helm], "Concerte," *Deutsche Zeitung*, March 6, 1885.

[103] These hotly contested elections were probably what stimulated the remark by Kalbeck quoted above about Brahms's dismay at the deleterious effect of Czech-Clerical

the first to be held since Taaffe widened the suffrage, the United Left suffered the loss of fifteen seats. Four years earlier, the perceived need to stand together for German interests against Taaffe had brought liberals and progressives together under the umbrella of the United Left. But by September 1885 this coalition had split into separate parliamentary clubs over how far to push the national question. When the more moderate majority reconstituted the United Left as the German Austrian Club, the restive minority of German nationalists immediately bolted and formed a new German Club.[104]

It was in this context that the Vienna Philharmonic planned its 1885–86 subscription season. Meeting on October 12, 1885, the Comité decided for the fourth year in a row to include a work by Dvořák, this time choosing the *Scherzo capriccio*. One committee member, a Czech violist named Alois Buchta, was absent from the meeting but had sent a written statement to be read aloud to his colleagues in which he nominated Smetana's *Vltava* (*The Moldau*) for performance. Although the parties agreed, evidently for the first time, to include a work by this recently deceased Czech composer, no decision was made on what that might be.[105] Three days later, the Comité reconvened, this time with Buchta in attendance, and settled on the overture to Smetana's comic opera *Die verkaufte Braut* (*The Bartered Bride*).[106] Yet the 1885–86 subscription concerts would in fact include no work at all by a Czech composer, as both Dvořák's

politics on the course of events in Austria. Here, of course, Kalbeck was speaking not only for Brahms but also for himself and other like-minded German liberals.

[104] Cohen, *Politics of Ethnic Survival*, 105–14; Judson, *Exclusive Revolutionaries*, 241–43.

[105] The minutes of the meeting of October 12, 1885 (HA/WPh, G.Z. 1047) list all the works chosen for performance, arranged alphabetically by composer. This includes the following notation: "Smetana?" An explanation follows: "Regarding [the work by] Smetana, a statement by Herrn Buchta is read in which the symphonic poem 'Vltava,' is recommended. It is determined that a work by this composer is to be performed, but the selection remains open" (Bezüglich Smetana's gelangt ein Schreiben des Hrn. Buchta zur Verlesung in welchem die symph[onische] Dichtung 'Vltava' anempfo[h]len wird. Es wird beschlossen, daß ein Werk dieses Componisten aufgeführt wird, nur bleibt die Wahl noch offen). Among the works chosen that day were Bruckner's Symphony No. 7—this would be the first symphony by the composer to be played in its entirety in the subscription concerts—as well as an as-yet undetermined symphony by Brahms.

[106] Meeting of October 15, 1885 (HA/WPh, G.Z. 1050). At this same meeting, the Comité determined that the symphony by Brahms to be played would be his new Fourth Symphony. The players' uncertainty on this selection at its meeting of October 12 may be related to the somewhat cool reception the symphony had received when Brahms and Ignaz Brüll performed the two-piano version before a small group of friends in Friedrich Ehrbar's piano salon on October 8.

scherzo and Smetana's overture were eventually dropped from the programs. These cancellations undoubtedly reflected, at least in part, the prevailing political tensions. But events that took place in the Court Opera that season may suggest a more proximate cause.

It was there, in fact, that Dvořák's worst fears about the fate of his music in Vienna would be realized. In 1880 Franz von Jauner, director of the Court Opera from 1875–1880, had set into motion tentative plans to stage a Viennese performance of Dvořák's *Vanda*, but these fell through, probably for reasons similar to those that led the Philharmonic players to drop the Wind Serenade and Sixth Symphony from its programs at around the same time.[107] Jauner subsequently sought to induce his successor, Wilhelm Jahn, to stage *Der Bauer ein Schelm*—that is, *Šelma sedlák* (*The Cunning Peasant*) in Emanuel Züngel's German translation—but he finally had to report to Dvořák that the new director had rejected the work on account of its poor libretto.[108] Following on the heels of earlier letdowns, this news must have disappointed. Nevertheless, the composer would, in fact, come to regret that Jahn subsequently reconsidered his decision, for when *Der Bauer ein Schelm* finally was introduced at the Court Opera, on November 19, 1885, it closed after only two highly controversial performances.[109]

Hanslick, to be sure, made no mention of the work's reception in his review for the *Neue Freie Presse*, which focused on the opera itself. He wrote at length and, as we might expect, quite favorably about the musical setting but, echoing Jahn, complained about the "childish libretto." Particularly

---

[107] The opera's plot, which involves Polish resistance against German-speaking peoples, could not have eased its way. On the aborted performance of *Vanda*, see Alan Houtchens, "From the Vistula to the Danube by Way of the Vltava: Dvořák's *Vanda* in Vienna," *Rethinking Dvořák*, 73–80. Houtchens notes the Slavic leanings of Taaffe's government but does not, as seems likely, connect liberal resentment at this turn of affairs to the institutional backlash against Dvořák.

[108] As Jauner diplomatically stated it, "The music is very beautiful, but the libretto does not recommend itself." Letter from Jauner to Dvořák of February 13, 1882, in *Korespondence a dokumenty* 5: 358. At the same time, Jauner and Hanslick did what they could to induce Dvořák to compose an original German opera for Vienna, but neither did anything come of that; see Clapham, "Dvořák's Relations with Brahms and Hanslick," 247–52.

[109] Eduard Mouček, writing in the Czech newspaper *Dalibor*, placed much of the blame for this failure on "the mad passion of blind fanatics against everything Czech," exempting only the reliable Hanslick in this regard. Eduard Mouček, "Dvořáků Šelma sedlák ve Vidni," *Dalibor* 7 (1885): 434; quoted in Reittererová and Reitterer, *Vier Dutzend rothe Strümpfe*, 79–80.

annoying in Hanslick's view was the decision to convert the opera's setting from Bohemia (as in Josef Otakar Veselý's original libretto) to Upper Austria: "The character of the music is…Slavic.…A composer who wished to portray Upper Austria with these melodies belongs in the observation room of the lunatic asylum."[110] Yet despite this change in the story line—and even though, as Hanslick wryly notes, the Bohemian dialect used in Züngel's version had been standardized for the Viennese performance—the performance drew noisy opposition.[111]

"The new comic opera *Der Bauer ein Schelm* by the Czech national-composer Anton Dvořák created quite a fiasco at today's first performance," reported the *Deutsche Zeitung*, continuing:

> Apart from the convulsive applause of the members of the Czech voluntary associations, every one of whom seemed to be in the house, which was answered each time by opposition, and a few signs of approval that had to do more with the performers, not a hand was lifted during the entire performance.[112]

It is clear from this and nearly every other review that Jahn and Hanslick were not alone in their skeptical assessment of the libretto, which relied heavily on *The Marriage of Figaro* by way, perhaps, of Smetana's *Bartered Bride*:

> The new work…suffers above all from an unbelievably foolish libretto worked out in a tasteless manner from a very old idea. In the music is found, in addition to many trivialities that please only a Slavic-national ear, many pretty melodies and a number of pure orchestral effects as well.…His national friends were unable to force a curtain call by the composer.

---

110 Ed. H. [Eduard Hanslick], "Hofoperntheater," *Neue Freie Presse*, November 21, 1885. The critic reprinted this piece many years later in Eduard Hanslick, *Am Ende des Jahrhunderts {1895–1899}* (Berlin: Allgemeiner Verein für Deutsche Litteratur, 1899), 132–40, from which I have quoted here (at 135–36). In the original version of the review, Hanslick specified the observation room of Theodor Hermann Meynert, director of the psychiatric clinic at the Vienna Medical School.

111 "The libretto, published by Simrock in Berlin, names a certain Herr Züngel as the German translator; our Court Opera Singer Mayerhofer has taken the trouble to rework this from the Bohemian-German dialect into [standard] German. Something was won by that—the singers no longer have to twist the tongue [*die Zunge*] on Züngel—but unfortunately the story line nevertheless remained unchanged" (ibid., 135).

112 "Hofoperntheater," *Deutsche Zeitung*, November 20, 1885, from which the following two quotations likewise are taken.

But, as we read on, suspicion mounts that something more was at work in producing the uproar:

> We have heard that the most stringent police precautions were taken in order to prevent the multiple demonstrations that were expected. In fact a number of persons who had allowed themselves to hiss were arrested in the gallery. At bottom, the utter dramatic worthlessness of the Dvořák-Veselý opus is not worth partisanship for or against.

This review is anonymous, but it betrays Helm's hand in its supposition that only a "Slavic-national ear" could perceive beauty in the work's "many trivialities" (as well as in the somewhat backhanded praise of the "pretty melodies" and "pure orchestral effects"). Nor is it difficult to see through this account's veneer of political disinterestedness: although the author may have wanted to leave the impression his objection was based in the work's weaknesses alone, he missed no opportunity to stress the otherness of both the "Czech national-composer" and those "national friends" in the theater who, despite their enthusiasm, were unable to rouse the larger German share of the audience to demand a curtain call.

A more detailed and colorful account of the event is found in Josef Königstein's review for the *Illustrirtes Wiener Extrablatt*, published under the title "*Der Bauer ein Schelm*, oder: Ein Scandal in der Hofoper":

> A performance with a police contingent and arrests—that is something the public in attendance at yesterday's premiere of Anton Dvořák's two-act opera "Der Bauer ein Schelm," produced in honor of the Empress' name-day, scarcely expected. Already after the Overture, which was based on Slavic tunes, the applause coming from part of the second parquet and the standing room was answered with whistles from the gallery. After the first ensemble the gallery reacted again to the applause from below, only this time with hisses. During the rest of the evening the applause was not objected to, the whistlers and hissers were quiet—that is, they had been detained by the police, removed from the gallery, and after releasing their personal data again let go. It was a band of 12–15 students who had responded in the form of a counter-claque to the invitation distributed on yellow slips of paper "to prevent Czech music from appearing in Vienna." The police were informed of the scheme and about thirty detectives...were assigned to the gallery and the police brigade at the sentry post in the Giselastraße had been increased considerably in order to nip every outbreaking scandal

in the bud. The result of these cautionary measures was reported at the outset.[113]

Accounts appearing in the *Neue Freie Presse* and the *Das Vaterland* differ in the details but not in the substance.[114] According to the reporter for the *Neue Freie Presse*, at least some of the protesters came from *Teutonia*, one of Austria's most powerful and influential student fraternities.[115] The politicization of Viennese operatic life along national lines upon which this group insisted is made clear in Helm's recollection that:

> Just as the enormous success [in January 1886] of [Viktor Nessler's] *Trompeter von Säkkingen* (which the German *Burschenschaft* in Vienna tried from the outset to propagandize through urgent communications to the main newspapers, above all Heinrich Reschauer's *Deutsche Zeitung*, which at the time set the tone in matters of domestic politics) was understood as a victory of the German-nationalist cause in Vienna, it appeared doubly glorious in comparison to the outright fiasco suffered two and a half months earlier by a Czech national opera, Anton Dvořák's *Der Bauer ein Schelm*. At the first performance of this textually unsatisfying though musically charming work, the noisy applause of Czech students was completely hissed down by German students, while the regular audience behaved toward the new work quite indifferently. Already at the first (and only) repetition Dvořák's opera played before empty seats.[116]

---

[113] This and the excerpt quoted below are taken from *Illustrirtes Wiener Extrablatt*, November 20, 1885.

[114] "Demonstration in der Hofoper," *Neue Freie Presse*, November 20, 1885; "Verhaftungen in der Hofoper," *Das Vaterland*, November 20, 1885.

[115] On the political activism of Austria's nationalist fraternities, seePaul Molisch, *Geschichte der deutschen Hochschulen in Österreich von 1848 bis 1918*, 2nd ed. (Vienna and Leipzig: Wilhelm Braumüller, 1939), 80–137.As Molisch notes (ibid., 109), in 1888 the Austrian Educational Ministry determined that, of the Monarchy's 235 student groups, 121 pursued political goals, including 81 *deutschnational* groups and 36 groups identified as "ultra-Slavic" (*extrem slawisch*). For the background of many German-nationalist politicians in the *deutschnational* student groups, seeLothar Höbelt, *Kornblume und Kaiseradler: Die deutschfreiheitlichen Parteien Altösterreichs 1882–1918* (Vienna: Verlag für Geschichte und Politik; Munich: R. Oldenbourg Verlag, 1993), 72–79.

[116] Theodor Helm, *Fünfzig Jahre Wiener Musikleben (1866–1916): Erinnerungen eines Musikkritikers*, ed. Max Schönherr (Vienna: Im Verlag des Herausgebers, 1977), 188. Helm's account originally appeared in serialized form between 1915 and 1920 in the Viennese periodical *Der Merker*. This "living history" of fifty years of Viennese musical life, which is based on Helm's own concert reviews, reflects the

As suggested here, objection to Dvořák in the more readily accessible realm of the Court Opera came not from members of the elite social groups that had access to the eight annual Philharmonic concerts—there polite silence was more likely to greet a work than whistles and hissing—but from German-nationalist university students who were well versed in the "sharper key" discourse that was beginning to characterize a new era of populist politics in Austria. These *deutschnational* activists were roused to action not by the opera's story (now set in Upper Austria, after all) or even its musical setting, but by its composer's ethnicity.[117] If Helm, a more mainstream German nationalist, turned a blind eye toward the students' tactics, a traditional liberal such as Königstein deplored their very motivation:

> The demonstration of the young people against the work of an Austrian composer who is much better known and more frequently performed in Germany and England than in his homeland cannot be condemned enough. What is to become of art, if one begins to measure its creations according to national standards! What is beautiful remains beautiful whether it was created by a Russian or a German, an Italian or a Czech.

Although Dvořák must have known that *völkisch* pan-Germanism was little more than a marginal movement, that would scarcely have been much comfort as he witnessed the spectacle at first hand in the theater. It is no wonder, then, that when a few days later he completed the first part of the oratorio *St. Ludmilla*, the composer bitterly inscribed the manuscript: "Completed

---

unusual historiographical approach first seen in the various volumes of Hanslick's *Die Moderne Oper* series (several of which I have quoted in this book); even in this culmination of a life's work, then, Helm's self-conscious "rewriting" of Hanslick seems apparent. On Hanslick's project, see Karnes, *Music, Criticism, and the Challenge of History*, 48–75.

[117] Jeremy King offers a succinct description of the newly emerging *völkisch* parties in Bohemia that serves well to describe a similar development in Vienna: "Radical, contradictory, simultaneously innovative and backward-looking, leaders of these new parties tended to have more diverse social origins than the Constitutionalist notables [i.e., the traditional liberals] they battled, and to court support less through appeals to reason and to the public good than to emotion and to self-interest. *Völkisch* leaders were more emphatically national than Constitutionalist ones, and also much more emphatically ethnic. Language defined the 'nation' for them much more than did citizenship, enfranchisement, and achievement more generally. So did religious origin; the German National parties soon began excluding Jews, even baptized ones." King, *Budweisers into Czechs and Germans*, 71. In much recent musicological writing on fin-de-siècle Vienna, the radical German nationalists tend to be characterized as

in the days when *The Cunning Peasant* was murdered in Vienna."[118] For his part, Jahn never again risked staging one of Dvořák's operas.

Má vlast *in Vienna*

In 1883 the enterprising Theobald Kretschmann—the Czech cellist who had, without effect, brought the first two movements of Smetana's *Má vlast* to Richter's attention in 1880—initiated a series of six concerts for small orchestra held in the intimate Ehrbar Hall on Sundays beginning at 4:30 in the afternoon. After much negotiation, the Comité of the Philharmonic agreed to allow Kretschmann, by then a member of the orchestra's cello section, to use sixteen colleagues, mostly string players, in his little orchestra, provided that he programmed no works that were scheduled to be heard in the Philharmonic's own series. Pickup musicians filled out the rest of the band.[119] Given the exclusive nature of the Philharmonic's subscription series and the concerts of the Gesellschaft der Musikfreunde, whose tickets were always spoken for in advance by the same well-to-do patrons, Kretschmann could be seen to be stepping into the breach here, and even Hanslick later had to acknowledge it was good that the many music lovers who were shut out from the offerings of the two established institutions were hereby provided a "more modest and less expensive feast for the ears."[120]

For Hanslick, however, the initial promise of Kretschmann's series was left unfulfilled. The performances were too often underrehearsed, and what had begun with a desirable programming mix of lesser-known orchestral works with interesting new ones soon gave way to an increasing diet of mediocre compositions that were heard, in Hanslick's opinion, not because they deserved to be performed but solely for "purely personal considerations."[121]

occupying a place in the right wing. But as King notes, they really cannot easily be placed to the right or left of the political spectrum; rather they belonged to "a new political dimension altogether" (ibid.).

[118] "Dokončeno ve dnech popravy 'Šelma sedláka' ve Vídni."; see Burghauser, *Antonín Dvořák: Thematic Catalogue*, 251.

[119] Kretschmann, *Tempi passati*, 2: 54–63. The day of the week and the odd starting time were probably decided with an eye toward the availability of the Philharmonic players, who were tied up earlier on Sundays by the 12:30 p.m. starting time of the Philharmonic's concerts and during the rest of the week with performances at the Court Opera.

[120] For a good discussion of slightly later efforts to provide more widely accessible symphonic concerts in Vienna, see Notley, "'*Volkskonzerte*' in Vienna."

[121] Ed. H. [Eduard Hanslick], "Concerte," *Neue Freie Presse*, November 11, 1886.

In view of the inclusion of music by the likes of Vojtěch Hřímalý (1842–1908) and Karel Šebor (1843–1903), we might suppose those considerations involved Kretschmann's continuing advocacy for new music by the widest possible range of Czech composers.[122]

This series came to an abrupt end after only three years, when Kretschmann's request to perform Wagner's *Siegfried Idyll* in the small hall of the Musikverein led to a falling out with the Comité and a subsequent ban on his use of any Philharmonic players in his little orchestra. Undeterred, Kretschmann made a scouting trip through a number of Bohemian cities in the summer of 1886 to recruit players for a new, somewhat larger ensemble, and in the fall, in what seemed to many to be a quixotic quest, he announced a new series to be held in the Bösendorfer Hall of "30 Orchestral Evenings produced by Theobald Kretschmann on Wednesdays (exceptionally also on Saturdays)."[123] A number of critics turned out to review the first concert, given on November 3, 1886, but few paid much attention to the series thereafter.[124] The only Viennese critic to give it any sustained attention was Hugo Wolf, who covered no fewer than seven of the thirty concerts in the *Wiener Salonblatt*.[125]

One of these was the concert of November 13, the third in the series, on which Kretschmann finally saw to it that Smetana's *Vltava* and *Vyšehrad* were given a hearing in Vienna.[126] Wolf was mightily taken by the "spirit and musico-poetic feeling" of Smetana's music, by its "mastery of form" and instrumentation that was worthy of Berlioz. Although he could scarcely believe

---

[122] A list of the new works performed in the two series is given in Kretschmann, *Tempi passati*, 2: 59–61. We can be certain that, whatever Hanslick might have thought about the music of Hřímalý and Šebor, he would have applauded Kretschmann's decision to perform Dvořák's String and Wind serenades.

[123] The billing read: "30 Orchester-Abende veranstaltet von Theobald Kretschmann an Mittwochen (ausnahmsweise auch an einigen Samstagen)."

[124] Hanslick, in *Neue Freie Presse*, November 11, 1886; dr. h. p. [Hans Paumgartner], "Concerte," *Wiener Abendpost*, November 16, 1886; Max Kalbeck, "Concerte," *Die Presse*, November 18, 1886. Hanslick and Paumgartner both include a brief discussion of the first concert; Paumgartner's comments about the quality of performance, especially on the part of the winds, are especially scathing. Kalbeck discusses no music in his piece and probably had not even attended any of the three concerts given by the time his feuilleton appeared.

[125] Wolf's reviews of these concerts appeared in the *Wiener Salonblatt* between November 7, 1886, and February 27, 1887, and are reproduced in *Hugo Wolfs Kritiken im Wiener Salonblatt*, 2 vols. (Vienna: Musikwissenschaftlicher Verlag, 2002), 1: 170–93 *passim*.

[126] The date of this concert is incorrectly given as November 16, 1886, in Kretschmann, *Tempi passati*, 1: 94.

the Philharmonic had previously held back from performing this outstanding music, he thought he knew, making a tacit nod toward Hanslick, where to place the blame for that circumstance:

> [T]hese are two masterpieces; but that is enough to deter the Philharmonic from involving itself with works of such rank, and since Dvořák and Brahms provide fuel in the amplest manner, very many more burnt offerings in honor of the Philharmonic's public will have to be given up before the nasty smoke that under the prevailing circumstances threatens every artistic breath with suffocation will have cleared away.[127]

Notably, although Wolf made a brief reference to the Slavic tunes that he mistakenly assumed Smetana had used in both pieces, he barely touched on the work's "national" element. Instead, sounding a theme that would be taken up by other critics many times in later years, he stressed Smetana's credentials as a musical progressive and describes a situation whereby this Czech composer's works stood no chance at the Philharmonic in the face of the championing by Hanslick of Brahms and Dvořák, evidently assuming (incorrectly, as we shall see) that Hanslick would find little to like in Smetana's orchestral works.

The national element stood front and center, by contrast, when *Vltava* gained a second hearing in Vienna six months later. This performance took place during a festive all-Slavic concert given on May 3, 1887, in celebration of the twenty-fifth anniversary of the founding of the Slavischer Gesangverein (Slavic Choral Society).[128] In a brief notice in the *Neue Freie Presse*, Hanslick made a point to emphasize that the audience included not only many Slavs but also a large contingent of Germans who had come to enjoy a program that offered something different from the usual Viennese fare. Hanslick himself had mixed feelings about the selection of choral and orchestral works, which included "very pleasing numbers" along with others that did not do justice to "this musically most talented people."[129] He complains about the

---

[127] Hugo Wolf, "Concerte," *Wiener Salonblatt*, November 28, 1886, in *Hugo Wolfs Kritiken im Wiener Salonblatt*, 1: 171.

[128] The concert program is reproduced in Hellsberg, *Democratie der Könige*, 271.

[129] h. [Eduard Hanslick], "Concerte," *Neue Freie Presse*, May 5, 1887, from which the remaining quotations in this discussion are taken. Although Hanslick signed his feuilletons "Ed. H." and in later years used "e.h." to sign other, shorter notices such as the one at hand, I am confident in my assertion that "h" was in this case also Hanslick. Compare the brief report on the performance of Bruckner's Symphony No. 2, given in a concert by the Gesellschaft der Musikfreunde, on February 20, 1876 (h., "Concert," *Neue Freie Presse*, February 22, 1876), and the letter from Hanslick to an unnamed

length of the concert as well as the overabundance of "Slavic melancholy" and toward the end explains why he departed before the performance of the final three choral pieces: "even the most sincere interest must lag before the completely insufferable ardency that ruled in this thundery evening." Hanslick made certain, however, not to leave before hearing *Vltava*. His verdict on the work was mixed: "There is a pleasing national element in this tone poem [*Tondichtung*], which unfortunately does without a unified development of its motives and as a result only makes the impression of a potpourri." Here again we see evidence that Hanslick's mind was not closed to program music, not even to Czech-national program music. Where this work fell short for the critic was in the matter of form, not content.

What is most notable about Hanslick's report, however, comes at the very end:

> [T]his festive concert, which was given exclusively by Slavs and for Slavs, avoided every demonstrative streak, and was not disturbed by the slightest discord. Neither in the hall nor at the entrance could you see a Czech, Polish, Croatian banner or emblem, and even the giant laurel wreath that [the soloist] Frau Essipoff received bore black-yellow stripes with the German inscription: "Der großen Meisterin" [To the great maestra]. For that reason you could pick out from the stormy applause almost as many "Bravos" as "Slavas."

For the readers of the *Neue Freie Presse*, it would have meant a good deal to learn about this affirmation, within a decidedly pan-Slavic context, of the presumed universality of the German language and of the supremacy of the supranational state, symbolized by the black and yellow colors of the Habsburg flag. That is a sentiment with which we can be sure Hanslick, who had only recently finished his essay on Viennese music for the *Kronprinzenwerk*, would have agreed.

The "Czech Brahms"

During the same season in which Kretschmann introduced *Vltava* and *Vyšehrad* in his new series, the Philharmonic players, seemingly illustrating Wolf's claim about burnt offerings, scheduled two new works by Dvořák in close succession, the *Scherzo capriccioso* (December 5, 1886) and the Seventh Symphony (January 16, 1887). Concerning the latter, Hanslick virtually quoted his earlier review of the Sixth Symphony: "If we have already described the joy, in our time of reflection and poor production, of encountering such an original, natural, and happily creating talent, we are strengthened in that feeling of late by this symphony."[130] As we might expect, Helm duly reported the "lukewarm" (*lau*) reception the work had received and was less than enthusiastic. Clearly looking for signs of Dvořák's national difference, he finds them at last toward the end: "The green banks of the Moldau are allowed to break in mostly in the finale, whose second theme bears that Slavic-national tint that Dvořák likes so much to introduce into the classical sonata and symphonic form."[131]

Next, on the subscription concert of December 4, 1887, came the *Symphonic Variations*, recently published but dating from ten years earlier. Dvořák was in attendance, and this time for once he was pleased by the Viennese reception. To Simrock he reported: "As Brahms says—and he knows the Viennese public very well: never before has a composition had as great a success as the 'Variations.' [They] were played splendidly and the public offered loud applause." Brahms himself confirmed much of this assessment a few days later in his own letter to the publisher, to whom he reported: "Dvořák's Variations impressed and were received with uncommon interest here, far more than any of his other works."[132]

Yet Helm was singularly unimpressed, and even Hanslick began his review with something less than a ringing endorsement:

> In truth, [this work] will be of interest mostly to the musician who listens through all twenty-seven of the many-sided variations, following the rhythmic and harmonic ups and downs with close interest. A large public will probably have to rely upon striking details and have no special liking for the theme. This is taken from a Czech chorus with which I was not very familiar, "Já jsem guslar" ["I am a minstrel"], a singularly constrained, creeping, dry melody in C major, seven bars long. If we are surprised already in the second bar of the theme by

correspondent of February 17, 1876, that is quoted in Höslinger, "Eduard Hanslick in seinen Briefen," 134, which was clearly written to obtain information to be used in the notice of that forthcoming performance.

130 Ed. H. [Eduard Hanslick], "Concerte," *Neue Freie Presse*, January 25, 1887.

131 Theodor Helm, "Concerte," *Deutsche Zeitung*, January 21, 1887.

132 Letter of December 6, 1887, in *Korespondence a dokumenty*, vol. 2: *Korespondence odeslaná 1885–1889* [Correspondence Dispatched 1885–1889] (1988), 288. Brahms's report to Simrock also gives evidence of Brahms's thoughts about his friend's social identity: "The hours spent with [Dvořák] were very agreeable and nice, and I am happy that he isn't a fanatical Czech as I've sometimes feared" (letter of December 9, 1887, in *Briefwechsel* 11: 167–68). See also Brahms's letter to Simrock of November 7, 1887 (ibid., 165): "Everything you wrote about Dvořák pleases me very much. I had really always thought and feared he was a very fanatical Czech!" Elitist remarks such

the strongly incisive F sharp, so does the first variation smuggle into the C-major harmony a rather bad-sounding B flat and A flat. Similar harmonic harshness, cross-relations, and awkward doublings appear frequently thereafter through the course of the work.[133]

But before long Hanslick struck a tone familiar from earlier, more positive evaluations, rehearsing praise for qualities such as originality, inspiration, and guilelessness, combined with seriousness of purpose, all of which, again, he found lacking in most other contemporary fare:

> Nevertheless a great serious streak runs through the whole, a rich and characteristic creative fantasy, as occurs extremely rarely in music composed nowadays, consisting in part of the Music of the Future and in part of kapellmeister music. Dvořák is not merely an illustrious, but also a genuine, original, naïve talent. Primitive and natural, like few others, he shows an ingenious inspiration even in his weaker compositions.

Hanslick even went so far as to place the composer in the company of Brahms:

> Next to Brahms, in my estimation, Dvořák is today's most gifted instrumental composer. Artistic perfection does not appertain to his works, nor does the cohesive power and cogent imperative of Brahms's music; [his works] are more sensuous, more innocent, gentler, more diffuse. No longer a young man in years, in his music Dvořák remains as much even still; Brahms grows ever more powerful, compact, able.

If in this comparison Brahms would seem to have all the mature qualities and Dvořák all the youthful (less mature) ones, it is nonetheless clear from the context of the entire review that Hanslick has not altered his basic belief that it is precisely through his combination of qualities from both sides of the

---

as these can be interpreted as a token of Brahms's characteristic belief that Czech nationalism—and the devout Roman Catholicism he knew Dvořák practiced—could not be reconciled with the German liberal project. Early on, in a letter to Simrock of December 10, 1877, Brahms had written: "Dvořák seems to me to be a typical Czech" (*Briefwechsel* 10: 62).

133 Ed. H. [Eduard Hanslick], "Concerte," *Neue Freie Presse*, December 6, 1887, from which the following two quotations also are taken; reprinted in Eduard Hanslick, *Aus dem Tagebuche eines Musikers (Der "Modernen Oper" VI. Theil.)* Berlin: Allgemeiner Verein für Deutsche Litteratur, 1892), 237–38.

ledger that Dvořák had achieved preeminence in contemporary music that rivaled Brahms's own.[134]

In response, Helm began his critique by emphasizing the only point on which, in his view, Brahms and Dvořák could be treated as equals: here, by way of complaining about the Philharmonic's conservative programming, Helm scoffed that both were "protégés of the *Neue Freie Presse*" (and were therefore, by implication, accorded special favor by the players). Thereafter he distinguished the German and Czech composers from one another, and again in such a way as to favor the former without exception:

> In the first of the latest concerts [November 13, 1887] we heard Brahms's beautiful Haydn Variations; in the third, new *Symphonic Variations* by Dvořák. It was immediately clear that the latter had been inspired by the former. But what a difference between the original and the imitation! Already in the selection of the theme: in Brahms's case, as is well known, the simple yet rich, immediately memorable Chorale St. Anthonii; in Dvořák's case, a laboriously creeping Czech folk melody. And from such resounding nothingness the composer brings forth twenty-seven variations: a hard test of patience for the listener who desires more than contrapuntal vignettes and orchestral piquancy, who also craves something to enliven the heart. In his Opus 56 Brahms makes do with eight variations (or, properly, nine, if we count the finale), but each is a character piece of the highest rank. How purely the seventh variation smiles through its tears! In Dvořák's work many sound surprising, yet most [sound] stilted, some even trivial! The work is probably best characterized this way, that the composer leaps from amidst a pretentious fugue into an unadulterated Czech popular tone, which strikes a German listener as anything but appealing. This is a first impression, unaided by looking at the score; nevertheless, we have no desire to hear another performance. When absolute music is so lacking in poetry, when the working out is so noticeable

---

[134] One month later, on January 12, 1888, Hanslick submitted letters of recommendation in support of Brahms's nomination to the Knighthood of the Order of Leopold and Dvořák's nomination to receive the Order of the Iron Cross, Third Class. The former is reproduced in Lorenz Mikoletzky, "Johannes Brahms und die Politik seiner Zeit," in *Brahms-Kongress Wien 1983: Kongressbericht*, ed. Susanne Antonicek and Otto Biba (Tutzing: Hans Schneider, 1988), 394–95; the latter, in *Korespondence a dokumenty* 9: 275. In his letter for Dvořák, Hanslick described the composer as "one of the most accomplished and original composers of the present day; after Brahms one may name him the first." Both composers received their honors from the emperor that summer.

and triviality dons a learned mask, for that we have to thank "sound-ing forms in motion." In the last Philharmonic concert Dvořák's new work was respectfully dismissed.[135]

Here the dichotomies are, if anything, even more heavily weighted against Dvořák than before: whereas Brahms transforms his simple yet rich and memorable theme into a series of character pieces of the highest order, Dvořák is able to derive from his unpleasant "Czech" melody little more than trivial and stilted variations, which makes the learned tone of the fugal passage seem all the more insincere. When Helm privileges the "German listener," we can be certain that the distinction is as much national as it is cultural. Thus if Hanslick's message was that "Dvořák is one of us," then Helm would seem to be replying, "No, he is not." By stressing difference, in other words, Helm's discourse suggests a desire to cordon off and to protect what he views as German *Nationalbesitzstand* from outside encroachment. As we resume our consideration of Goldmark's career now in the same decade of the 1880s, we shall see how in his case the debate over who could and could not count as "one of us"—a German—took on a particularly urgent tone.

---

[135] *Musikalisches Wochenblatt* 19 (1887): 5–6. Helm makes two errors here. Although only recently published, the *Symphonic Variations* had been composed in 1877 (as Hanslick had noted). Moreover, the theme is not a folk melody but rather an original tune by Dvořák ("Huslař"), taken from the Choral Songs for Male Voices, B. 66, no. 3; it seems evident that Helm was misled by Hanslick's reference without attribution to "Já jsem guslar." Note how Helm enhances Hanslick's own negative characterization of the theme as "creeping" (*schleichend*) by describing it as "laboriously creeping" (*mühsam schleichend*) The penultimate sentence contains another clear jab at Hanslick, of course.

CHAPTER SIX	Liberal Accreditation and
	Antisemitic Attack
	Goldmark's Reception Revisited

Many things would speak in Goldmark's favor, for instance, his lovely earnestness
and his hearty goodwill in such matters. I also think his name is so well respected
that the Ministry can overlook the Judaism!

— Johannes Brahms, letter to Eduard Hanslick (ca. 1879)

I N EARLY MARCH 1875, Goldmark passed the evening before the dress
rehearsal of *Die Königin von Saba* sitting in a café with his friends Brahms
and Billroth.[1] During this time, as we now know, the latter was at work on
Lehren und Lernen, with its disapproving comments about the Jewish medical

---

[1] Goldmark, *Erinnerungen*, 130; *Notes from the Life*, 234. Neither Brahms nor Billroth
was entirely unfamiliar at this point with Goldmark's setting, as both had been in
attendance at the gala benefit concert held at the Musikverein on January 11, 1874,
that included the first performance of the Queen's Entrance March from Act I of
Goldmark's still-unheard opera. Like Goldmark, Brahms had been asked to contribute
a new composition for this occasion, but having nothing suitable at hand, he appeared
only in his role as the conductor of the Singverein in choral pieces by J. S. Bach and
Mendelssohn. Billroth's attendance is suggested by his letter of December 29, 1873,
to Wilhelm Lübke; see Billroth, *Briefe*, 5th ed., 166.

students from Hungary and Galicia. That Goldmark's brother Joseph, who studied at the Vienna Medical School in the 1840s, had come from the same background as did the students whom Billroth now criticized for their lack of good breeding and a proper gymnasium education lends a certain irony to this situation. Although we have no direct evidence of what Goldmark thought of Billroth's harsh observations when they came to light later the same year, it does not appear that the two men's friendship suffered on account of them. Indeed, the publication of *Lehren und Lernen* seems to have caused no serious rupture in the surgeon's social circles. As Billroth put it in a letter of October 3, 1876, to Wilhelm His, "My affair from the previous winter is as good as forgotten, and it must be said of my many Jewish friends and admirers of both sexes that they have forgotten the inconsiderate manner that—whether rightly or not—I felt necessary to use and bear me no enmity."[2]

Notably, Billroth did not hesitate to include Goldmark a few months later in the intimate "little midday circle" of cultural elites who were invited to dine in his home following the first Viennese performance of Brahms's First Symphony on December 17, 1876.[3] A few weeks later, on January 5, 1877, he hosted a musical evening at which Brahms and Goldmark each conducted some of his own choral works.[4] And in April 1878, Goldmark joined Brahms and Billroth for the first part of their month-long tour of Italy, traveling with the two of them to Florence, Perugia, Assisi, and as far as Rome.[5] Later that year, Billroth closed himself off from his circle of friends as he worked to complete his massive new *Chirurgische Klinik, Wien*

---

[2] Letter of October 3, 1876, quoted in Wyklicky, *Unbekanntes von Theodor Billroth*, 77–78.

[3] Letter of December 15, 1876, from Billroth to Brahms, in *Billroth und Brahms im Briefwechsel*, 227–28.

[4] Richard Heuberger, "My Early Acquaintance with Brahms," in *Brahms and His World*, rev. ed., 342; this memoir was originally published as "Aus der ersten Zeit meiner Bekanntschaft mit Brahms," *Die Musik* 5 (1902): 223–29. See also idem, *Erinnerungen an Johannes Brahms*, 11.

[5] See Billroth's letter to Brahms of May 7, 1878, in *Billroth und Brahms im Briefwechsel*, 264. Goldmark returned to Rome in April 1881 for the belated first Roman performance of *Die Königin von Saba*, and while there bumped into Billroth and Brahms, this time traveling together with Gustav Nottebohm. See the discussion in *Billroth und Brahms im Briefwechsel*, 505–510. Goldmark seems to have conflated these experiences from 1878 and 1881 in *Erinnerungen*, 138–44; *Notes from the Life*, 251–63. I have quoted from Goldmark's recollection of his meeting with Brahms and Billroth in Rome in 1881 in the second epigraph of Chapter 4.

1871–1876.[6] In a humorous note to Hanslick of November 22, 1878, Brahms attributed Billroth's uncharacteristic self-imposed isolation to "his famous fat book."[7] Six days later Billroth followed up with Hanslick about both his isolation and his new book in a letter that, by contrast, seems deadly serious:

> It's really too bad that one sees so little. The older I become, I find that the number of those with whom I like to chat, in earnest and in jest, grows ever smaller. The greatest part of life lies behind us, and we don't have a lot more time to lose. Why, then, don't we see each other more often? For me it's the same with Brahms.
>
> Eight days ago I completed my largest and, I hope, improved surgical work. I shall now draw a line and never again write anything serious on surgery. Whatever I still have to say can be said through my many talented students, who flourish so powerfully on the dung of my ideas and publications that they're already too much for me. Something powerful is taking place within me. So with this decision to conclude my literary career I have once again become a free man. The blood in my brain again circulates more easily, I will dedicate myself now solely to humanitarian activity and keep better company with my friends; not, to be sure, in the manner of the local boring salon life, but rather free, in the way that it makes me happy.
>
> Today I had the following idea. We must come together somewhere every two weeks, without our wives, we men alone. You, Brahms, and I, perhaps also Goldmark, who is such a dear fellow, will form the regulars, the trio or quartet. We alone will decide who else to include in our society, at most twelve altogether, at the very most twenty. We will be aristocratically artistic and keep boring society at arm's length. We will invite others only after common agreement and will be very rigorous and ruthless against the attempts of interlopers. The thing does not require a broader form. But we must commit ourselves to keep coming. If you are not keen on this proposal, simply say it doesn't suit you, and I'll let it go too.[8]

[6] Theodor Billroth, *Chirurgische Klinik, Wien 1871–1876: nebst einem Gesammt-Bericht über die chirurgischen Kliniken in Zürich und Wien während der Jahre 1860–1876: Erfahrungen auf dem Gebiet der practischen Chirurgie* (Berlin: Hirschwald, 1879).

[7] Christiane Wiesenfeldt, "Johannes Brahms im Briefwechsel mit Eduard Hanslick," in *Musik und Musikforschung: Johannes Brahms im Dialog mit Geschichte*, ed. Wolfgang Sandberger and Christiane Wiesenfeldt (Kässel, Basel, London, New York, and Prague: Bärenreiter, 2007), 292.

[8] Billroth, *Briefe*, 5th ed., 224–25.

Billroth's idea seems to have gone nowhere, and in any case the surgeon went on to publish a number of medical papers in the years to come. What is most significant in view of his allegedly racist views, however, is his determination that Goldmark, a Jew, deserved an honored place in his proposed fraternity of "artistic aristocrats," right alongside Brahms and Hanslick.

Indeed, by the later 1870s Goldmark had assumed a respected place in the very center of the city's rich cultural life. This can be seen not only in the considerable attention paid to his compositions but also in his invitations to act in various official capacities. Between 1877 and 1883, for example, Goldmark served as a juror for the Beethoven Prize in composition that was established by the Gesellschaft der Musikfreunde for recent graduates of its conservatory.[9] When Hanslick sought Brahms's advice in 1879 on who might join them as the third panelist in selecting the winner of the stipends that were given annually by the Ministry of Religion and Public Education to "young, needy, talented composers" in Cisleithania, it was Goldmark whom Brahms recommended.[10] Later Goldmark served a term as president of the Vienna Composers' Society, founded in 1885 as a kind of counterweight to the Vienna Academic Wagner Society, and with Brahms as its president.[11] And in the following year, he was made an honorary member of the Gesellschaft der Musikfreunde.[12]

Yet both Hanslick and Speidel continued to struggle to accept Goldmark's credentials as a fully German composer. Consider the critics' responses to

[9] Johannes Behr, "Brahms als Gutachter und Preisrichter," in *Bruckner—Brahms: Urbanes Milieu als kompositorische Lebenswelt im Wien der Gründerzeit*, ed. Hans-Joachim Hinrichsen and Laurenz Lütteken (Kassel: Bärenreiter, 2006), 145–53.

[10] The undated letter from Brahms to Hanslick that is quoted as the epigraph to this chapter probably relates to this appointment, which indicates a date of ca. 1879. Christiane Wiesenfeldt has suggested a date instead of 1874 or 1875, based on her assumption that it is related instead to Goldmark's possible appointment as Johann Herbeck's successor as *Hofkapellmeister*; see Wiesenfeldt, "Johannes Brahms im Briefwechsel mit Eduard Hanslick," 285–86. This seems improbable, however, not only because of Goldmark's lack of appropriate experience, but precisely because his religion could not possibly have been overlooked for such a court position. For Brahms's report to Goldmark and Hanslick on the applicants for a state stipend during the fall of 1879, see Wiesenfeldt, "Johannes Brahms im Briefwechsel mit Eduard Hanslick," 294–95.

[11] On the Vienna Composers' Society, see U[we] H[arten], "Wiener Tonkünstler-Verein," *Oesterreichisches Musiklexikon*, 5 vols. (Vienna: Verlag der Österreichischen Akademie der Wissenschaften, 2006), 5: 268–69.

[12] The date of Goldmark's honorary membership has frequently been given erroneously as 1866; I am grateful to Otto Biba for confirming the correct date of 1886.

the Overture to Heinrich von Kleist's *Penthesilea*. The composer's powerful musical setting, introduced by the Vienna Philharmonic to its subscribers on December 5, 1880, follows Kleist's play closely in depicting the frenzied passion between Penthesilea, the Amazon queen, and Achilles, the most handsome of the Greek heroes assembled against Troy.[13] The tumultuous opening allegro, in E minor, depicts the battle outside the Trojan gates that is precipitated when the female warriors surprise the unsuspecting Greeks in an ambush (ex. 6.1). This eventually leads to a love scene between Penthesilea and Achilles at the "Festival of Roses," a gentle andante in E major with oboe accompanied by syncopated chords in the strings. With the return of the allegro theme, ever more agitated, love gives way once again to hate and battle; Achilles is killed and a hollow funereal march conveys the story of the death of Penthesilea in despair over her fatal deed.

Goldmark was pleasantly surprised by the audience's favorable reception of the work at its première.[14] But, again, he must have been disappointed by Hanslick's and Speidel's reviews. Hanslick began with an anecdote in which he recalled his experience of playing through the new work at the piano ahead of time with Billroth:

> At the first two chords [see ex. 6.1] we felt as though we had fallen off the bench. In our long experience with dissonances, which are increasing in number by every year, we never imagined that anyone would blurt out such a thing. It sounds like a sharp whiplash along with the victim's scream; Wagner's Valkyries gallop in more considerately than these Amazons of Goldmark.[15]

---

[13] The published score carries the notation: "For the sake of understanding, it is recommended that at performances the following remark be inserted into the concert program: Penthesilea und Achilles—Das Rosenfest—Kampf und Tod."

[14] In an unpublished letter to his brother Leo, written shortly after the performance, Goldmark implicitly made reference to the Philharmonic's decision, as we have seen, not to perform the overture during the previous season: "For almost two years a poor opinion of the work has prevailed here, put about by the orchestra and not shaken off by the piano score; the profound effect [made at the première] was therefore all the more surprising"; unpublished letter of December 10, 1880, GFC-LBI, Series I, Folder 4 (Carl Goldmark [composer]).

[15] Ed. H. [Eduard Hanslick], "Hofoperntheater. Concerte," *Neue Freie Presse*, December 7, 1880; rpt. in Hanslick, *Concerte, Componisten und Virtuosen der letzten fünfzehn Jahre 1870–1885* (Berlin: Allgemeiner Verein für Deutsche Litteratur, 1886), 282–84 (at 282); trans. adapted from Paul A. Bertagnolli, *Prometheus in Music: Representations of the Myth in the Romantic Era* (Aldershot, Hampshire: Ashgate, 2007), 324.

EXAMPLE 6.1 Goldmark, *Penthesilea*, op. 31, mm. 1–5

EXAMPLE 6.1 Continued

If this overture thus offers immediate proof of what Hanslick understood as Goldmark's abiding love of dissonance, its "piercing" (*grell*) tone, as the critic had to acknowledge, was at least true to the drama. As he explains:

> The poetry of the horrific—that is certainly what a composer wants to bring and should bring to the task of making a musical setting of Kleist's famous tragedy....In truth, a composer of a *Penthesilea* Overture must gather together all the hideous things that can be forced from music—that "cheerful art," as it was known in the Middle Ages—if he wants to at least approximate the frightful impression of Kleist's drama.[16]

Although Hanslick obviously had his doubts about using "the cheerful art" toward an unbeautiful end, he grants that Goldmark—"this most deadly serious of composers"—had done so out of his own inner necessity, citing "the hot-bloodedness, the passion, his decisive characteristics, which dominates his feelings, sometimes at the expense of beauty, but never at the expense of truth, or of that which seems true to him."[17] Given the overture's Hellenic subject matter, perhaps it would have been dubious for Hanslick to suggest that Goldmark's music was "Jewish-Oriental" (albeit no more so than for Speidel to hear ghetto strains in *Ländliche Hochzeit*). Yet it is not hard to read into his description of the composer's artistic personality something of the same essentializing view. In any case, unbridled passion was not the kind of quality Hanslick associated with *Bildung*. And inasmuch as the work "is conceived and structured more poetically than musically," *Penthesilea* falls short in Hanslick's estimate on another count, as the critic looks in vain for what Beethoven had achieved in his *Egmont* and *Coriolan* overtures, which, even with their "most pregnant dramatic characteristics, flow, universally understandable, unified, and in an uninterrupted musical stream."[18]

Speidel held back his thoughts about *Penthesilea* for more than three weeks, by which time Brahms's new *Tragic Overture* had been heard in the Vienna Philharmonic's subscription concert of December 26, 1880.[19] This allowed the inevitable comparison to be made between the two composers, one that did not work to Goldmark's advantage. Recalling one of Hanslick's objections to *Penthesilea*, Speidel notes that Goldmark had imposed a form

---

[16] Hanslick, *Concerte, Componisten und Virtuosen der letzten fünfzehn Jahre*, 282–83.

[17] Ibid., 283.

[18] Ibid., 284.

[19] sp. [Ludwig Speidel], "Konzerte," *Fremden-Blatt*, December 30, 1880.

on the work from the outside, so to speak, on the basis of the dramatic program, and he contrasts this unfavorably with Brahms's approach in the *Tragic Overture*, in which Speidel found the same "genuine" and "expansive" musical form that Beethoven had created. Thus the *Tragic Overture* not only unfolds more strictly, more seriously than *Penthesilea*, in Speidel's view, but indeed constitutes "one of the more successful attempts to reawaken the spirit of Beethoven's overtures."[20]

Speidel also shared Hanslick's dislike for the overwrought nature of Goldmark's overture, but he seemed even less generous than his fellow critic in accounting for it. After noting that Goldmark sought to "force the ear to see," Speidel seeks to dismiss that attempt as folly by quoting several lines from Christoph Martin Wieland's "Wettstreit der Malerei und Musik" (1781), in which the god of the Muses reminds Music that "all your enchantments are only sweet tumult and beautiful enigma if the other Muses do not lend you their support."[21] With Wieland's admonishment in mind, Speidel finds fault in the "new school" of composers, in which he includes Goldmark, which aims to make music "surpass the word in understandability, the image in clarity."[22] Speidel acknowledges that Goldmark's colorful instrumentation is effective and that his musical setting seems to match the unfolding of events in the poem. "But this provides little pleasure," he writes, and the critic is only too glad to "leave this hide-and-seek-playing west-eastern decorative music behind and turn to [Kleist's] poem, in which the color arises from the passion, from the passion that retreats before no consequence, which is genuinely German."[23]

Speidel, who recalls here a striking locution borrowed from Goethe that he had first used several years earlier in connection with *Sakuntala*, is more explicit than Hanslick had been in expressing continuing doubt about Goldmark's German credentials and in hearing "the East" in music that ostensibly has to do with Classical Antiquity.[24] Goldmark may have been

---

[20] Ibid.

[21] In the Wieland's original the verses read: "... Ein andermal, mein Kind / Vergiß nicht, spricht der Gott der Musen, / Daß selbst der Götter Ohren—blind / Und alle deine Zaubererein / Nur lieblicher Tumult und dunkle Räthsel sind /Wenn andre Musen dir nicht ihre Sprache leihen." In quoting the poem in his review, Speidel omits "spricht der Gott der Musen" from the second line and gives "schöne Räthsel" for "dunkle Räthsel" and "ihren Beistand" for "ihre Sprache" in the fifth and sixth lines.

[22] Speidel, in *Fremden-Blatt*, December 30, 1880.

[23] Ibid.

[24] Wilhelm Frey included *Penthesilea* among those works by Goldmark, along with *Die Königin von Saba*, *Sakuntala*, and some of the chamber music, that are indicative of "an

riding a wave of celebrity by now, but he must have wondered just what he had to do to satisfy Speidel and Hanslick that he was a real German composer. As it turns out, composing an expansive "Wagnerian" work would prove decisive in this regard. And so, too, would the emergence in Vienna of a form of anti-Judaic sentiment that called into question certain fundamental beliefs that these older, traditional liberal nationalists held dear.

An "Explosion" of Antisemitism

The first incursions of antisemitism into Vienna's urban political culture came by way of two politically marginal groups. Among the city's artisans, the Jews became a convenient scapegoat for the severe economic downturn that came in the wake of the devastating stock market crash of 1873. By the end of that decade, as we have seen, university students in Vienna and elsewhere had begun to embrace racial antisemitism as a component of their Wagner-influenced, radical nationalist ideology. I have already suggested that the publication in 1878 of Wagner's essay "What is German?" was a factor in the initial exclusion around this time of the "alien" Jews from the "German" *Burschenschaften*. Each of the new "regeneration essays" of Wagner's later years—"Modern," "Publikum und Popularität" ("Public and Popularity"), and "Das Publikum in Zeit und Raum" ("The Public in Time and Space") in 1878; "Wollen wir hoffen?" ("Shall We Hope?") in 1879; "Religion und Kunst" ("Religion and Art") in 1880; and "Was nützt diese Erkenntniß" ("What Boots this Knowledge?"), "Erkenne dich selbst" ("Know Thyself"), and "Heldenthum und Christenthum" ("Hero-dom and Christendom") in 1881—was marked by a similar claim that Jewish-bourgeois materialism was responsible for the supposed contemporary decay in German civilization.[25] It was Georg von Schönerer who brought these two strains of economic and cultural anti-Judaic sentiment together and then introduced them into the wider political spotlight. To be sure, for the first ten years of his public career Schönerer, elected as a progressive-liberal representative to the Reichsrat in 1873, had worked to improve the economic plight of the rural and urban petty producers. But by 1882 this concern with social well-being

exotic world of ideas that is not for a long time exhausted with the all too limiting concept of the oriental"; see W[ilhelm] F[rey], "Merlin," *Neues Wiener Tagblatt*, November 20, 1886.

[25] James Treadwell, *Interpreting Wagner* (New Haven: Yale University Press, 2003), 211–12.

and economic fairness was becoming secondary in his program to the radical German nationalist and antisemitic ideology that he seems to have picked up from the various student corporations with which he had been associated since the late 1870s.

In the spring of 1882, an "explosion" of anti-Judaic sentiment was suddenly felt throughout Austria.[26] The liberal press at first treated *Antisemitismus*—this neologism, imported from Germany, had only recently begun to appear in Viennese political discourse—as a reactionary legacy of the old Jew hatred under a new name, an unfortunate regressive tendency that could be overcome through progressive education.[27] That this was a naïve hope was perhaps best revealed in the infamous Wagner *Commers* held at the University of Vienna on March 5, 1883, as a memorial to the recently deceased composer. This "masterpiece of revolutionary political agitation," as it has been called, in which Schönerer played a leading, climactic role, at once marked the Reichsrat deputy as an irredentist subversive and solidified his growing reputation as a racial antisemite.[28] The new ideology of racial antisemitism that grew up around this charismatic figure proved to be an effective political strategy in the years to come, and even within more mainstream bourgeois political culture, the tide of politics was now beginning to move away from traditional liberal concerns in economic and social policy and in the direction not only of nationalism (as noted) but also of populism and antisemitism.

Judson's elegant summary of the differences in their conception of *Deutschtum* between traditional liberal ideology and the newer ideology of racial antisemitism also suggests one of the reasons racial antisemitism could at one time be understood as a progressive ideology, in the sense of being

[26] Whiteside, *Socialism of Fools*, 88.

[27] Judson, *Exclusive Revolutionaries*, 227. See, for example, the leading articles in the *Neue Freie Presse*, April 6, 1882, and *Die Presse*, April 8, 1882. Although Jew hatred had a long history among the Austrians, it had relatively little effect in the public sphere during the liberal heyday of the 1860s and 1870s. "Jew aversion," to recall the locution Hanslick coined, was a rather different thing and, as I have suggested, can be detected in both Hanslick's and Speidel's reviews of *Sakuntala* and *Die Königin von Saba*.

[28] For an account of this *Commers* and its immediate aftermath, see Whiteside, *Socialism of Fools*, 94. See also James Deaville, "'Die Wacht an der Donau'?!? The Wiener akademischer Wagner-Verein, Wiener Moderne and Pan-Germanism," in *Wien 1897: Kulturgeschichtliches Profil eines Epochenjahres*, ed. Christian Glanz (Frankfurt am Main: Peter Lang, 1999), 49–84.

more "democratic" and concerned with the economic well-being of the lower social strata. His account is worthy of quotation at length:

> Since 1848 the liberals had repeatedly justified their political hegemony using a theory of meritocracy that imagined a fundamental equality among all males. The liberals institutionalized this equality in a civic order that guaranteed the vote to men whose talents and abilities had gained for them property and education. Their achievement of property guaranteed their commitment to the health and security of the community. Their education enabled them to see beyond narrow self or corporate interest, to perceive what was good for the entire community. These male property owners would rule until the fledgling liberal school system had educated the rest of society in its political responsibilities and until the self-help institutions had helped the lower classes to achieve economic and moral independence. Other national groups, like the lower classes, could attain a higher political and social status by adopting the culture of the Germans.
>
> For racial anti-Semites, membership and participation within the political community depended on racial identity rather than on education or property, or indeed on greater political ability. The liberal values of education, experience (demonstrated mostly by financial success or social status), or even dedication to the community paled before the real issue of racial identity. If liberals clothed their political exclusivity in a language of merit and community service, anti-Semites defined politics as an all-out struggle among different races for mastery of the state. Anti-Semitism also conveyed a social equalitarianism with revolutionary overtones: all racial Germans were equal and had a right, based only on their racial heritage, to participate actively in community affairs. Germans as an embattled national group should have more rights than other so-called nations or races.[29]

During their first years in opposition after 1879, liberals had sought to maintain their traditional political and social hegemony by gradually adopting a nationalist rhetoric that, prior to the onset of the Taaffe era, they had not needed to employ. But with this new emphasis on the nation came contesting notions of the German community itself. Traditionally liberals had defined Germanness as a matter of cultural and economic achievement. Was this defining feature of the old liberal community, with its deference to class and education, now simply to be treated as the defining feature of the new

[29] Judson, *Exclusive Revolutionaries*, 228.

national community? Or was national identity to be based instead on racial considerations that transcended the old criteria of "conviction and achievement"? Obviously, although Jews could be members of the German community under the first scenario, under the second they decidedly could not.

These questions soon divided both the German School Association and the newly formed German Club. In April 1886 Schönerer resigned from the former when it refused to bar membership by Jews, and in July of that year he led the establishment of an explicitly antisemitic rival organization, the German National School Association.[30] Around the same time, the national and social activist Otto Steinwender attempted to force the resignation of the Jewish German nationalist Heinrich Friedjung as editor of the *Deutsche Zeitung*, the influential post to which Friedjung had been appointed when, on June 13, 1886, this newspaper became the short-lived official organ of the German Club.[31] After failing in this effort, Steinwender and a number of other members of the German Club, mostly from the Alpine regions, bolted from the party and founded the more radical German National Union on a populist platform of anticapitalism and antisemitism (somewhat moderated, to be sure, from Schönererian standards).[32] Meanwhile, in yet another fissure within the liberal ranks, the Viennese liberal-democrat Karl Lueger was beginning to use Catholic social rather than German nationalist ideology to build his own political movement around economic populism and antisemitism.[33]

Eschewing antisemitism, the rump German Club eventually rejoined the moderates in the German Austrian Club from whom they had split only a few years earlier to form the United German Left. The inclusion of the word *German* in the party's name is telling. This new coalition, though still adhering to more or less traditional liberal social and economic policy positions, was far more nationally conscious than had been the case with earlier mainstream liberal alignments. Indeed, in 1886, Ernst Plener, the party's leader, led the United German Left in a boycott of the Bohemian Diet, thereby

---

[30] Whiteside, *Socialism of Fools*, 124–25. Notley notes that Brahms later made at least one modest financial contribution to the German School Association, in 1893, suggesting that this was intended to support the older, nonracist group at a time of financial need; see Notley, *Lateness and Brahms*, 214.

[31] Heinrich Friedjung, *Ein Stück Zeitungsgeschichte* (Vienna: Genossenschafts-Buchdruckerei, 1887).

[32] Although the *Deutsche Zeitung* eventually adopted antisemitism, this did not fully take place until 1894, when Theodor Wähner acquired the newspaper. See Walter, *Österreichische Tageszeitungen der Jahrhundertwend*, 73.

[33] Boyer, *Political Radicalism in Late Imperial Vienna*, 184–246.

emulating the strategy taken in the Reichsrat during the pre-Taaffe era by the Czech National Party.[34]

Critical Breakthrough

It is important to bear all these political developments in mind as we take up Goldmark's reception in Vienna during this same tumultuous period. On November 19, 1886, the composer's second opera, *Merlin*, set to a libretto based on Arthurian legend by Mahler's friend Siegfried Lipiner, was given its première at the Vienna Court Opera. Although it failed to achieve the enduring widespread popular success of *Die Königin von Saba*, *Merlin* was produced fairly often both in Central Europe and abroad during the composer's lifetime. Moreover, it fared well with many who had been left cold by Goldmark's first opera. Describing *Merlin* as a "good deed" (*rechte Tat*), Brahms shared his enthusiasm about the work with Richard Heuberger after playing through the newly published piano score in advance of the première: "You have to have respect for a chap like Goldmark; it's a joy . . . to see how the whole thing will work, how everything has its place. And there's nothing in it that sounds Jewish at all [*es jüdelt gar nicht*], not a single 'triplet.' "[35]

Brahms's use of a pejorative expression to characterize what, in his opinion, the music does *not* do (viz., speak with characteristically "Yiddish" inflections) only emphasizes the pleasure he takes in what he thinks it *does* do (viz., speak in "pure German").[36] At the same time, the implicit criticism of *Die Königin von Saba*, with its orientalizing melodic style, is obvious. Billroth shared Brahms's enthusiasm for *Merlin*—we can guess for the same reason—and on the night of the opera's première he even hosted a banquet in honor of

---

[34] Judson, *Exclusive Revolutionaries*, 242–45.

[35] "Vor so einem fixen Kerl wie Goldmark muß man Respekt haben; es ist eine Freude . . . zu sehen, wie das alles wirken wird, wie alles an seinem Platze steht. Und dabei jüdelt es gar nicht, gar keine 'Triole'" (Heuberger, *Erinnerungen an Johannes Brahms*, 155).

[36] S.v. "jüdeln" in *Deutsches Wörterbuch von Jakob Grimm und Wilhelm Grimm*, http://woerterbuchnetz.de/DWB/?sigle=DWB&mode=Vernetzung&hitlist=&patternlist=&lemid=GJ01101. Although this verb, used for centuries to describe stereotypical "Jewish speech," carried negative connotations, it did not have the far-reaching ugly associations intended by *verjüdeln*, an antisemitic fighting word of more recent coinage that we shall later encounter in certain strands of Viennese music-critical discourse.

Goldmark and Lipiner in which he, a notorious night owl, kept both men up until three o'clock in the morning to discuss their new work.[37]

In more than one passage in his memoirs, Goldmark indicated that he viewed Brahms as the *spiritus rector* behind many of Hanslick's judgments. If he thus, whether rightly or not, blamed Brahms for inspiring Hanslick's "miserable review" of *Die Königin von Saba* in 1875, he also had to attribute to Brahms's influence the critic's rather more favorable notice of the new opera in 1886.[38] Yet it seems clear that Hanslick would have come by his opinion about this work on his own, if only because here for once was a new opera that avoided every trace of a popular style for which he had little sympathy.

This was a topic about which Hanslick had recently vented his spleen in his review of Sigismund Bachrich's music for the ballet *Sakuntala*, performed by the ballet corps of the Vienna Court Opera in October 1884. "To orientalize in music," he writes, "no longer causes embarrassment to the theatrical composer."[39] Hanslick acknowledges the "moderate" and effective use of Arabian and Indian local color, respectively, in Weber's *Oberon* and Spohr's *Jessonda* but is clearly troubled by the tendency among recent composers to evoke the East in more "strongly colored" works. Hanslick's list here of newer operas and their referents is extensive and includes Rubinstein's *Feramors* and Felicién David's *Lalla Rookh* (the Persian); Auber's *Le premier jour de Bonheur*, Meyerbeer's *L'Africaine*, and Delibes's *Lakmé* (the Indian); Goldmark's *Die Königin von Saba* and Rubinstein's *Die Maccabäer* (the Hebraic); Gounod's *Le tribut de Zamora* (the Moorish); and Verdi's *Aida* (the Egyptian). "This

[37] Brahms was in attendance at Billroth's home that evening but seems to have left before the night's late close; see his postcard to Billroth of November 20, 1886, in *Billroth und Brahms im Briefwechsel*, 414. Goldmark tells in his memoirs of a very favorable letter received from the surgeon about the work, unfortunately now lost (Goldmark, *Erinnerungen*, 89; *Notes from the Life*, 162).

[38] The composer evidently wrote very favorably to Hanslick about *Merlin* around the same time he praised the work to Heuberger. See Goldmark, *Erinnerungen*, 90, 122; *Notes from the Life*, 162, 219. The claim that Brahms was responsible for the negative tone of Hanslick's review of *Die Königin von Saba* was made in a conversation between Goldmark and Heuberger that took place on November 28, 1893, in connection with Goldmark's overture *Sappho*. On this occasion Goldmark described Brahms as his "weather vane," adding, "When I see and speak to him, I know how Hanslick will write." Heuberger, *Erinnerungen an Johannes Brahms*, 164.

[39] Ed. H. [Eduard Hanslick], "Hofoperntheater," *Neue Freie Presse*, October 7, 1884; rpt. in *Musikalisches Skizzenbuch (Der "modernen Oper" IV. Theil): Neue Kritiken und Schilderungen* (Berlin: Allgemeiner Verein für Deutsche Literatur, 1888), 89–91, from which the quotations in this and the following paragraph are taken.

trend toward strongly national characteristics," he continues, "has reached a dangerous height in the most recent operas; *Aida* and *Die Königin von Saba* seem to me to be the limit in orientalizing music beyond which one cannot proceed without doing harm to the musical beauty." Then, using descriptive language with which we are already familiar from Hanslick's review of *Die Königin von Saba*, he adds: "We have had just about enough monotonous oriental minor tunes in the most recent operatic literature, with their whining, by turns passionately piercing, by turns quietistic seesawing singsong. For our taste, the composer can easily go overboard in the virtue of national, especially oriental, exactness."

Particularly notable is the claim that follows: "To the modern composer, the ethnographically sharp differences among Indian, Persian, Egyptian, Hebraic must in any case nearly dissolve into a general idea: oriental music." This observation, which seems obvious enough, runs counter in certain respects to Hanslick's earlier claim that the "Jewish-Oriental" style came naturally to Goldmark by way of his Jewishness. Was Hanslick now claiming, if only implicitly, that Goldmark's evocation of ancient Palestine in *Die Königin von Saba* had been a strategic choice made by a (German) composer bent on orientalizing rather than an inscription of his Jewish essence into music?

This critic's review of *Merlin* suggests that he was not yet willing to take that step.[40] With its absence of anything that sounds Jewish, it is no wonder that Hanslick hailed the composer's new opera as a "decided advance in Goldmark's progress." And though the critic "once again recognizes the composer of *Die Königin von Saba*," he now "finds him, to his advantage, grown and clarified." That Hanslick wants to have things both ways comes through especially clearly in what follows:

> With sincere pleasure I miss in *Merlin* a distinctive trait of *Die Königin von Saba*: the Jewish-Oriental melodies, whose sickly moaning spoiled for us the undeniable beauties of the opera. The subject matter certainly justified the Jewish local color in the music as well, but did not make it any more pleasing. Will *Die Königin von Saba*, precisely because of this striking national character, be judged more original, more "Goldmarkian" than *Merlin*? That may be the case and would not exactly be unfounded. The Oriental, with its passion and colorful display, but also with its unrest, intensity, and exalted solemnity, does

---

[40] Ed. H. [Eduard Hanslick], "Merlin," *Neue Freie Presse*, November 21, 1886; rpt. in *Musikalisches Skizzenbuch*, 76–85, from which the next several quotations are taken.

not lie merely within the subject matter of *Die Königin von Saba*, but within our composer himself, who grew up under a doubly Oriental influence, the Jewish and the Hungarian. The subject of his first opera met this lineage halfway; it permitted Goldmark to give full expression to a notable characteristic of his talent, for which *Merlin* presented no point of contact.

Hanslick's essentializing claim that the music of Goldmark's first opera reflected the composer's *Gemüt* in a way that the second did not scarcely requires further comment.

Where *Merlin* and *Die Königin von Saba* do share common ground, in Hanslick's estimation, is in showing the influence of Meyerbeer and especially early Wagner. It is Goldmark's relation to the latter, of course, that draws the bulk of Hanslick's attention:

> People inquire nowadays of each composer how he stands with respect to Richard Wagner. It strikes us most pleasantly—with how little must we rejoice!—that Goldmark calls his *Merlin* an opera [not a *Musikdrama* or *Handlung*].... Not only in its title, but also in its essence, *Merlin* inclines toward pre-Wagnerian or rather pre-*Tristan* operatic music.

To be sure, he adds, *Merlin* shows that "Goldmark has inhaled the Wagnerism that has been in the air these thirty years," as evidenced, for example, "by the sharp relief of the dramatic element, by the modulations that flush restlessly through all the fissures of chromaticism and enharmonicism, by the perpetually characterizing, [tone] painting orchestral accompaniment." But Goldmark comes in for praise nonetheless for having rejected the "compositional method" of *Tristan* and the *Ring*:

> Song melody prevails in Goldmark's work (although it does not flow too richly); it does not fade away into stammering declamation, swaying to and fro upon the endless melody of the orchestra. Where emotion gathers in lyric points of rest, Goldmark casts it in those architectonic forms that before Wagner supplied the jewel of every opera: he brings forth broad symmetrical ensembles, choruses of knights, of elves, and of women, even strophic songs, marches, and finely structured ballet music. Of leitmotifs he makes very moderate usage.

Later, however, when discussing the long duet in Act II between Merlin and Vivien, Hanslick rehearses one of his own leitmotifs. Here he expresses displeasure at Goldmark's overwrought style, aligning it this to time with the excesses of musical modernism:

> The one thing we regret in this love scene (as in similar ones by R. Wagner) lies in the musical spirit of our times: the holding onto the most strained affect for all too long, the relentless storm of excitedness, which overtaxes the nerves of the listener, as well as the voices of the singers.

Theodor Helm was rather more enthusiastic than Hanslick about the work's basis in Wagnerian opera. Indeed, much of his very favorable review of the work was given over to enumerating the many allusions he found in it, not only to Wagner's early operas but also to his later music dramas.[41] Still, Helm shared Hanslick's perception that *Die Königin von Saba* was a more "authentic" work:

> In the case of *Die Königin von Saba*, we get the impression that Goldmark had to write this work, that he composed it from within, from personal experience, from the national-religious memories of his youth. *Merlin* came to the composer from the outside; he composed the subject objectively, more purposefully, than from an inner need. The more characteristic, personalized atmosphere of Goldmark's first opera, the more original local coloring, which of course was unsympathetic to some listeners just by its distinctive oriental manner, can be denied by no one. By contrast, *Merlin* shows major technical advances, notably in relation to the often admirably worked-out orchestration.

In closing his review, Helm reported that the triumphant success of the first performance was marred only by the "strenuous efforts of an unfortunately insistent claque." Although the critic fails to identify this noisy party, it is easy enough to guess that he was alluding to antisemitic audience members, probably drawn from the same *völkisch* student groups that had in the previous season disrupted the first performance of Dvořák's *Der Bauer ein Schelm* and before that had participated in the Wagner *Commers*.

The most telling review of Goldmark's opera, however, may be that of Ludwig Speidel. This critic was known best for his work as the Court Theater critic and feuilleton editor for the *Neue Freie Presse*, not for his music reviews in the *Fremden-Blatt*, our concern with him up to now. Not surprisingly,

---

[41] Theodor Helm, "Hofoperntheater," *Deutsche Zeitung*, November 21, 1886, from which the two quotations that follow are taken.

Speidel's critical writings for both publications evince a consistent set of cultural attitudes. The one body of work can shed light on the other. Consider the case of two related feuilletons that appeared in the *Neue Freie Presse* in the months leading up to the première of Goldmark's opera. In an essay of January 6, 1886, written in commemoration of the centenary of the death of Moses Mendelssohn, Speidel extols his subject as the person who had led German Jewry "out of the spiritual-intellectual ghetto" (*aus dem geistigen Ghetto*). By translating the Jewish Bible into German, Speidel writes, Mendelssohn had done the great service of bringing his fellow Jews to the German language, through which they had even learned "to think and feel German."[42] Five months later, in an essay of May 18, 1886, marking the centenary of the birth of the great *Vormärz* political writer and satirist Ludwig Börne, Speidel hit on several of the same themes. He describes how Börne, a child of the Frankfurt ghetto whose given name was Juda Loew Baruch, followed the path of Moses Mendelssohn, not only learning German, indeed obtaining a rare mastery of the language, but, again, learning to think and feel German. Indeed, Speidel offers Börne's life story as a case study of the process, "denied by many, doubted by a lot," whereby "a German is made from the Jew."[43]

Of course, this is nothing other than a perfect realization of the old quid pro quo.[44] Notably, Speidel recognized something of the same thing later that year in *Merlin*. In this opera, he writes, Goldmark had subjected "his entire artistic being to a clarification." This "clarification" could scarcely have been more significant, for not only has "the exotic... been drained from [Goldmark's] music," as Speidel put it, but the music itself "has been elevated to a unified German character."[45] This was obviously quite a change

---

[42] Ludwig Speidel, "Moses Mendelssohn," *Neue Freie Presse*, January 6, 1886.

[43] "Der Vorgang, dessen Möglichkeit von Vielen geleugnet, von Manchen bezweifelt wird: wie nämlich aus dem Jude ein Deutscher wird, dieser Vorgang kann an Börne als einem classischen Beispiele wahrgenommen werden." L. Sp. [Ludwig Speidel], "Ludwig Börne (Zu seinem hundertsten Geburtstag)," *Neue Freie Presse,* May 18, 1886.

[44] As we have seen, Wagner, when discussing Börne's case in *Jewry in Music*, could not quite bring himself to make a comparable full-throated assertion of the writer's Germanness.

[45] sp. [Ludwig Speidel], "Hof-Operntheater," *Fremden-Blatt*, November 21, 1886. This review was by no means entirely favorable: Speidel coupled praise for the composer's instrumentation and use of orchestral color, for example, with reservations about what he heard as Wagnerian echoes to a degree that called the composer's own originality into question. Like Hanslick, however, Speidel does note with approval that Goldmark seemed to have rejected Wagnerian formal advances in favor of more traditional vocal forms.

in Speidel's perception of Goldmark, and hereafter he would be fully in the composer's corner. It had been one thing for a traditional liberal nationalist to make glib assertions about the "non-German" aspects of Goldmark's music during the relatively *judenfreundlich* 1860s and 1870s; it was something altogether different to continue to do so during the increasingly *judenfeindlich* 1880s and 1890s.

The difference in tone between the critic's earlier review of Goldmark's first symphony, *Ländliche Hochzeit*, for example, and that of his Second Symphony, played by the Vienna Philharmonic on February 26, 1888, is remarkable. Indeed, the latter reads as though Speidel had found a work that is unblemished in every respect:

> Karl Goldmark has the dazzling success of two operas behind him. The entire world imagined him at work in his dearest Vienna or his even more beloved Gmunden on new projects aimed once again at exciting the public from the stage. Ill-advised! As a genuine *Tonkünstler* he has been seized by a longing for the forms of pure music, which, unlike the rather more limited operatic profession, grant the musician freedom to express his innermost feeling without restraint. It is not an opera, no, but a symphony that Goldmark has carried back from his summer holidays....
>
> One has the feeling that this symphony was written by a man who has just thrown a great weight off his shoulders: so freely and daringly it steps out, a fundamental consciousness of boundless power and profound pleasure holds sway throughout its four movements. The audacious modulatory procession of the whole, the harsh ricocheting back and forth of the unusual counter-themes, the bold strokes of instrumentation—everything announces an artistic power intent on enjoying itself, whether the world scolds or applauds with approval. In this sense of freedom, [Goldmark] has spurned the yoke of a poetic program, which held together the divergent movements of his first symphony (*Ländliche Hochzeit*). In general, in his newest work he reminds us neither of himself nor of others, even if once a stray cloud from his *Sakuntala* Overture rushes by or a thunderbolt of Beethoven's spirit reminds us that the *Eroica* is in E flat, too. Goldmark's symphony also bears a praiseworthy witness to an energetic self-liberation by the composer.[46]

---

[46] sp. [Ludwig Speidel], "Konzerte," *Fremden-Blatt*, March 2, 1888, from which the next several quotations are taken.

For Speidel, it appears, this "self-liberation" had enabled Goldmark to leave the figurative ghetto once and for all, and for that he is deserving of praise for having earned his German stripes. Speidel goes on to recall a striking locution first used in his review of *Die Königin von Saba* (and then borrowed by Hanslick, as we have seen, in his review of *Merlin*): "With Goldmark the East is doubly present: by birth and heritage; he is Israelite and Hungarian, Jew and gypsy." As he continues, he explains how Goldmark's earlier music had been marked by "melancholic, anxious, strangely crimped melodies that stemmed from the synagogue or [the composer's] own strained disposition [*Gemüt*]." But then comes the same satisfaction we noted already in connection with *Merlin*, as Speidel reports that "in his last opera and even more decisively in his symphony, this inclination to the East is completely done away with," with not even so much as "a trace of dialect" left behind.

There could be no denying, by contrast, that the symphony does include one prominent passage in the slow movement that looks toward the other side of Goldmark's Eastern roots, the Hungarian (ex. 6.2). Music of this sort was wholly different from that which Speidel associated with Goldmark's Jewish heritage. After all, as the critic points out, German composers such as Haydn, Beethoven, and Schubert had long ago incorporated the gypsy style "as an interesting province into the empire of German music."[47] But what is most remarkable about this part of the review comes next. After acknowledging the proven appeal of this style, Speidel notes how "it will be a comfort to many that the gypsies are 'Aryan'," while quickly adding, "And Goldmark's music has maintained this gypsy quality."[48]

With this striking reference, Speidel flaunts the late nineteenth century's "modern" biologically conceived theorizing of race by equating the use of the gypsy style by Goldmark (a "Semite") with those of the "Aryan" masters Haydn, Beethoven, and Schubert.[49] Indeed, with that "anti-antisemitic" point subtly

[47] Here Speidel recalls Hanslick's description of Viennese music in his *Kronprinzenwerk* essay in terms of empire.

[48] Theodor Helm suggested as much, too, but he maintains a position that Speidel seemingly no longer holds. In the Andante, he claims, "Goldmark wrote from his inner self; here wails and grumbles the national composer of *Die Königin von Saba*." And he places the fate of the new symphony on the degree to which the public has tolerance for this kind of "melancholic orientalism." Theodor Helm, "Concerte," *Deutsche Zeitung*, March 9, 1888. In other words, whereas Speidel now sees the style of the Andante as a strategic choice made by a German composer, Helm continues to view this style in essentializing terms.

[49] According to late-nineteenth-century racial theory, the gypsies (i.e., the Romani people) were classified as Aryan; this was an inconvenient truth for the later National

made, the old liberal nationalist critic turns from the subject of the composer's eastern heritage to his firm embrace of German culture:

> [The symphony] is German in its invention and certainly German in its aesthetic rendering. The first movement is in both respects the

EXAMPLE 6.2 Goldmark, Symphony No. 2, op. 35, II, mm. 14–35 (reduction): Hungarian style

most outstanding, with a peacefully and nobly performed main idea, in which the capacity for development and advancement is distinctly marked. Only with the development, however, is it shown what a devil of a theme this had been in the first place. The composer reduces it with passionate energy into its constituents, and as if from a witch's cauldron it rises again to its initial beauty.

Notably, the end of this passage almost reads like an account of a Beethovenian sonata form, with its description of the symphonic main theme as something to be broken down in the development into its component parts and then triumphantly recombined at the outset of the recapitulation. Thus, as striking as Speidel's comments about Oriental inclinations and musical imperialism may be, what seems really at stake for him is to establish Goldmark's *German* credentials. The Jew has been assimilated; the gypsy, colonized; the German, celebrated.

Goldmark was clearly proud of this long-awaited accreditation by Speidel of his *Deutschtum*, and he took the step of sending Speidel a profuse note in which he expressed his gratitude (and showed off his *Bildung*), hereby initiating a friendly correspondence between the two that would be carried on for a number of years to come:

> Honored, Herr Doktor. I would have liked to have thanked you personally...and cordially grasped your hand for the warm recognition, for the joy, that today's review brought me. Dessoff once told me: A word of praise from Speidel would be worth more than that from all others combined. In fact, whoever has experienced this can well imagine what Goethe [*recte*: Schiller] meant when he wrote: "The man who has gained the approval of the best of his time, has lived for all times"—how refreshing, how inspiring is the approval of able, significant people.[50]

At the Summit

By the turn of the 1890s, Goldmark had reached the peak of his importance within the mainstream cultural life of Vienna. Nearly every season, for example, saw the inclusion of at least one (and often more) of his works on the programs

Socialists but, as the liberal nationalist Speidel impishly suggests, presumably a "comfort" to those racists of his own day who would not wish to do without their Hungarian Rhapsodies and the like.

[50] I am grateful to Thomas Aigner for providing me with a transcription of Goldmark's thank-you note (Wiener Stadt- und Landesbibliothek H.I.N. 113.091).

of the Vienna Philharmonic. These included three new overtures—*Im Frühling* (*In Spring*), *Ouvertüre zum gefesselten Prometheus von Aeschylos* (*Prometheus Bound*), and *Sappho*—and a new Scherzo, op. 45, as well as the older overtures *Sakuntala* and *Penthesilea*, the *Ländliche Hochzeit* Symphony, and the Violin Concerto. Goldmark's music was no less ubiquitous in other venues. Thus in February 1891 Wilhelm Frey could note with satisfaction that Vienna had been enjoying a "Goldmark cycle" that winter, with performances by the Philharmonic players of *Im Frühling* and *Ländliche Hochzeit* sandwiched around a performance of the *Frühlingshymne* in the concerts of the Gesellschaft der Musikfreunde.[51] Goldmark's music could be heard frequently as well in the chamber music concerts of the resident Hellmesberger and Rosé quartets. And at the Court Opera, *Die Königin von Saba* was performed at least once (and often several times) in nearly every season, while *Merlin* too was heard with considerable frequency before being eclipsed by the composer's third opera, *Das Heimchen am Herd* (*The Cricket on the Hearth*), following its première on March 21, 1896.[52]

By and large, Goldmark's new works received good notices in the establishment press, not only by the likes of Hanslick and Speidel but also by Helm and younger critics as well, such as Max Kalbeck and Robert Hirschfeld. To illustrate, let us turn to a sampling of reviews of the composer's three new overtures. First to be heard was *Im Frühling*, performed by the Philharmonic players on December 1, 1889 (and given another hearing in the following season on December 7, 1890). Perhaps recalling his experience of *Penthesilea*, Hanslick originally approached the work with a degree of wariness and puzzlement. What, after all, was he to expect from music by a composer of Goldmark's temperament that carried the title *In the Spring*?

> The inscription put us in a hopeful and yet at the same time somewhat anxious mood.... Will Goldmark, the powerful King of Dissonances, take leave of his most piercing chords for the sake of May? Will he glorify spring without at the same time making opposition to it? Will he not bring us poison-flaming flowers from the Orient and nightingales from Bayreuth? These were the concerns that were spoken under the breath. Goldmark has subdued them in a most delightful manner.[53]

---

[51] W[ilhelm] Fr[ey], "Konzerte," *Neues Wiener Tagblatt*, February 24, 1891.

[52] For statistical information concerning these performances, see Beetz, *Das Wiener Opernhaus*, 172–73 (on *Die Königin von Saba* and *Merlin*), 168–69 (on *Das Heimchen am Herd*).

[53] Ed.H. [Eduard Hanslick], "Concerte," *Neue Freie Presse*, December 8, 1889; repr. in Hanslick, *Aus dem Tagebuche eines Musikers (der 'Modernen Oper' VI. Theil)* (Berlin: Allgemeiner Verein für Deutsche Litteratur, 1892), 270–71 (at 270).

With its clear allusion in the main theme to the beginning of Mendelssohn's sunny *Italian* Symphony, this charming evocation of spring certainly had nothing "oriental" about it (ex. 6.3).[54] And though it was easy enough to hear echoes of the Forest Bird scene from *Siegfried* in "the songs of finches and skylarks" that inhabit the development, this seems not to have disturbed Hanslick one bit. Yet Goldmark is unable to leave well enough alone (as we might imagine Hanslick thinking) and soon pays a less welcome "visit to 'Wahnfried'." This occasions some of the critic's finest purple prose:

> Wagnerian harmonies, at first diffident and scattered, later plunge downward from the mountaintops like a wild chase; syncopated chromatic sixth chords in the strings and woodwinds against which the basses and trombones invoke a gruesome procession of rising diminished seventh chords. This is not the obligatory spring weather we had counted on but rather a little preliminary run-through of Armageddon, in which rivers, forests, mountains tumble about and all the bowels of the globe threaten to rupture.[55]

One wonders just how seriously to take all this. In any case, the Wagnerian outburst is over soon enough, and the "delightful bird concert" returns to bring the work to an exultant close. "So warmly felt and so freshly painted," this music—a fine display of "the cheerful art"—tugged at Hanslick's heartstrings in a way that perhaps none of the composer's earlier works had managed to do.

Speidel's response was, if anything, even more enthusiastic.[56] He notes approvingly that Goldmark, by turning to the depiction of spring, was following the healthy lead of Mendelssohn, in whose work (along with that of Ferdinand Hiller and others in the Mendelssohn School) could be found many similar examples. Speidel considered Goldmark's musical illustration to be well nigh perfect; his command of form, sovereign. What is most notable, however, comes at the end: "Goldmark has achieved a fresh nature [*Gemüt*], as much by what life has given him as by what life has denied him."[57] This, of

---

[54] This obvious allusion, which Hanslick did not mention but surely recognized, is noted in favorable reviews by Theodor Helm, "Concerte," *Deutsche Zeitung*, December 14, 1889, and Max Kalbeck, "Concerte," *Die Presse*, December 14, 1889.

[55] Hanslick, *Aus dem Tagebuche eines Musikers*, 270, from which the quotations in the remainder of this paragraph are also taken.

[56] sp. [Ludwig Speidel], "Konzerte," *Fremden-Blatt*, December 13, 1889.

[57] Ibid. Goldmark thanked the critic for this new sign of his "approval and appreciation" in an unpublished letter of December 13, 1889 (Wiener Stadt- und Landesbibliothek SB 93.857).

course, only underscores Speidel's conviction expressed earlier in his reviews of *Merlin* and the Second Symphony that Goldmark had left the musical ghetto once and for all.[58]

EXAMPLE 6.3a Goldmark, *Im Frühling*, op. 36, mm. 1–12

---

[58] In his memoirs, Goldmark provides an anecdote about an occasion with Brahms when the latter had become furious after reading a favorable review Speidel had written of a new work by Goldmark. Although Goldmark connected this anecdote with the review quoted

EXAMPLE 6.3a Continued

above of the Second Symphony (see Goldmark, *Erinnerungen*, 87–88; *Notes from the Life*, 157–58), it is more likely that it was Speidel's review of *Im Frühling* from the following year that aggravated Brahms, for in it the critic, in the midst of his discussion of how Goldmark had followed in the path of Mendelssohn and his school, snidely remarked that Brahms would never have found his way as a composer if Mendelssohn and Schumann had not given him the direction to follow (Speidel, in *Fremden-blatt*, December 13, 1889).

The *Prometheus Bound* Overture, heard on March 23, 1890, went over equally well with Vienna's mainstream critics. Once again, Hanslick approached the work with a degree of wariness, notwithstanding his recent pleasant experience of *Im Frühling*. After all, the Prometheus myth offered nothing in the way of the easily understandable musical allusions such as was afforded, for example, by the subject of spring: "Would the loathsome

EXAMPLE 6.3b Mendelssohn, Symphony No. 4, op. 90, I, mm. 1–10

EXAMPLE 6.3b Continued

vulture that pecks at Prometheus's liver not also simultaneously bite at our ears? Instead of the hero, would not his brother Epimetheus appear, causing everything to emanate from Pandora's box?" Yet, to Hanslick's delight, there was "virtually nothing repulsive or ugly" in the music, despite the "incisive tragedy of the composition, glowing red-hot in the fire of the most vigorous orchestra."[59] And whereas in the similarly tragic *Penthesilea* Goldmark had been faulted for placing the poetic element before the musical, this time he is praised for turning matters around: in *Prometheus Bound* the "burning energy of expression" is coupled with "musical content and lucid form."[60]

This is the key element for Hanslick, who has no tolerance for music that aims to be understood as "a dramatic copying" (*eine dramatische Nachmalerei*) of a literary work, and so serves as nothing more than a "brilliantly illustrated marginal notation."[61] Thus he writes:

> The Overture begins likes a solemn quiet sea with an Adagio in C minor; this gradually builds into more vigorous motion, which comes into full flow in the Allegro (likewise in C minor). Following the defiant, sharply marked main theme is a second theme in C major of a noticeably gentle, almost idyllic expression [ex. 6.4]....Some will take umbrage at the peaceful tone of this second theme. Whether it signifies the recollection of earlier happiness or the hope for salvation I will leave to the masters of exegesis [*Auslegekünstlern*] to decide. It seems to me, however, to be a credit to the composer that he interrupts and pacifies the agonies of torment of the bound Prometheus, that he allows him and us to catch our breath. This contrast was musically necessary; in an orchestral piece we first want music and only then tragedy, insofar as it can be explained in the former.[62]

Here Hanslick applauds Goldmark's decision to put musical considerations first in composing his C-major theme, and he makes no attempt to hide his contempt for anyone who would seek to explain the music in terms of a detailed

<hr>

[59] Ed. H. [Eduard Hanslick], "Concerte," *Neue Freie Presse*, November 28, 1890; rpt. in Hanslick, *Aus dem Tagebuche eines Musikers*, 298–300 (at 299); trans. adapted from Bertagnolli, *Prometheus in Music*, 325

[60] Hanslick, *Aus dem Tagebuche eines Musikers*, 298.

[61] The first quotation is from Hanslick, *Aus dem Tagebuche eines Musikers*, 298; the second, from Hanslick, "Liszt's Symphonic Poems," 46.

[62] Hanslick, *Aus dem Tagebuche eines Musikers*, 298–99.

EXAMPLE 6.4 Goldmark, Ouverture zum "Gefesselten Prometheus" des Aeschylos, mm. 117–24: second theme, beginning

program. That same contempt is evident at the end of the review as well; in a passage in which Goldmark is praised for steering clear of the dangers of strict program music, Hanslick pointedly turns a disparaging eye toward a composer who, in his view, had shown none of Goldmark's good judgment:

> Goldmark's merit is that he does not lose himself in pedantic depic-
> tive details, but instead has always kept his eye on the larger whole
> and created a musical artwork from his dangerous material. In order
> to properly understand what is meant by these words, one needed
> only to stay on a bit at the Philharmonic concert after Goldmark's over-
> ture and have a listen to Liszt's *Dante* Symphony.[63]

Speidel takes a somewhat different approach. He notes that by including Aeschylos's name in his title, Goldmark gives the listener an "absolutely fixed pro-gram" and from that a clear dramatic cue to follow.[64] But whereas ten years earlier, in his review of *Penthesilea*, he had complained that Goldmark wanted to make music "surpass the word in understandability, the image in clarity," writing now about *Prometheus Bound*, Speidel reverses that criticism entirely: "[Goldmark's] overture is [thus] music and image at the same time," he writes, "tone and mean-ing are looped intimately together; by hearing we believe we are also seeing." The critic then goes on to share with his readers a précis of what he both hears and sees in the various sections of the piece. Of particular note is his account of the second theme, whose "lagging triplets" (*nachhinkende Triole*)—a feature that Hanslick left unremarked—remind him of a motive from *Sakuntala* and here are associated with the "laments and pleadings" of the Oceanides, who attend the bound Titan at the rock (see ex. 6.4). Earlier this music might well have caused

[63] Ibid., 300.
[64] L[udwig] Sp[eidel], "Konzerte," *Fremden-Blatt*, April 2, 1890, from which the remain-ing quotations in the paragraph are taken.

Speidel to doubt Goldmark's German credentials, as had been the case in his reviews of *Sakuntala* and *Die Königin von Saba*. But nothing of the kind occurs on this occasion, and there is no suggestion that Speidel heard any orientalisms at all in a work that he, like Hanslick, called one of Goldmark's best. For Speidel there evidently was no turning back once Goldmark had established his German credentials to his satisfaction in *Merlin* and the Second Symphony.[65]

Unlike Speidel and Hanslick, who had virtually nothing (and nothing at all good) to say about the *Dante* Symphony, Helm weighted his review of the concert overwhelmingly toward Liszt's still-controversial work. This he extols, by way of quoting from Wagner's essay "The Public in Space and Time," as "one of the most astounding deeds in music," in which "the soul of Dante's poem is shewn in purest radiance."[66] Goldmark's more modestly scaled *Prometheus Bound* does come in for its own share of praise, however. In a notable departure from Hanslick's dramatically open-ended reading of the "idyllic" second theme (see ex. 6.4), Helm (like Speidel) specifies Goldmark's intent here as to be a depiction of the Oceanides; but in that case, Helm writes, it is not clear why the composer "had these daughters of the sea sing in such an open oriental manner," even echoing a passage from *Sakuntala*.[67] But here again there is no suggestion, such as we saw in certain earlier reviews by Hanslick and Speidel, that these triplets ought to be read as markers of Goldmark's supposed Eastern self. And Helm concludes by describing the work as well written, colorfully orchestrated, and dramatically effective and notes that it proved anew how Goldmark remained in "unabated vogue" among the Philharmonic's regular audience.

After the wholly positive experience of the *Spring* and *Prometheus Bound* overtures in 1889 and 1890, Hanslick was clearly let down by Goldmark's *Ouvertüre zu Sappho*, performed by the Vienna Philharmonic on November 26, 1893. His description of the work as "genuine Goldmark, Goldmark in monumental size; a fiery sea of passion, a primeval forest of dissonances; more intellectually stimulating than beautiful, more shocking than enjoyable, altogether 'frightfully interesting,' as the Berliners say," is not meant to be complementary.[68] And even less so is his suggestion that Goldmark

---

[65] Once again Goldmark thanked the critic for his review in an unpublished letter of April 11, 1890 (Wiener Stadt- und Landesbibliothek SB 113.089).

[66] Theodor Helm, "Concerte," *Deutsche Zeitung*, April 1, 1890. "The Public in Time and Space," in Richard Wagner, *Religion and Art*, trans. William Ashton Ellis (Lincoln and London: University of Nebraska Press, 1994): 84–94 (at 93).

[67] Helm, in *Deutsche Zeitung*, April 1, 1890.

[68] Ed. H. [Eduard Hanslick], "Concerte," *Neue Freie Presse*, November 28, 1893; rpt. in Hanslick, *Fünf Jahre Musik {1891–1895} (der "Moderne Oper" VII. Teil)* (Berlin: Allgemeiner Verein für Deutsche Litteratur, 1896), 231–33 (at 231–32).

had sketched the love's grief of the protagonist with such an intensity that what he produced would be sufficient to depict "three Sapphos with enough left over for a Medea or an abandoned Ariadne."[69] As with *Prometheus Bound*, Hanslick fears Goldmark's choice of dramatic subject will only give license to the "exegetes" to practice their dubious art:

> Once an instrumental work is inscribed "Sappho," it is not hard to make out Phaon, Melitta, Sappho's jealously, and her plunge from the Leukadian Cliffs. The acumen of the exegete and hermeneutician [*Aus- und Unterleger*] operates easily with a fixed itinerary. I have often fought against these interpretive feats, which are based on the false assumption that pure instrumental music is capable of precise expression.[70]

Like Smetana's symphonic poem *Vyšehrad*, which the Philharmonic players had performed two weeks earlier (and to which we shall return), Goldmark's *Sappho* Overture—presumably composed with Grillparzer's tragedy from 1818 in mind—sets out with a harp solo that evokes an ancient bardic quality appropriate to its poetic content (ex. 6.5).[71] Taking note of the similarity between the two recently heard works, Hanslick complains that, whereas "Smetana's grey harpist, despite his sadness, begins with a pure E-flat major triad," Goldmark, composing in the dark key of E-flat minor, opens with a dissonant chord that, in effect, superimposes the triads of G-flat major and E-flat minor. This was not only a surprising decision, Hanslick writes, but a questionable one as well, "something like beginning a lyrical poem with the word 'nevertheless'."[72]

This bon mot was followed by a peculiar account of the new lyrical theme in the oboe that soon enters above a repetition of the harp's opening music (ex. 6.6). Hanslick detects in this passage two familiar, well-defined Eastern locales: "Judging by the lamenting triplet figures, augmented fourths, and diminished sixths, the Greek poetess might have been a niece of 'Sakuntala' and frequently in Palestine as well."[73] We are familiar with the critic's linking

---

[69] Hanslick, *Fünf Jahre Musik*, 233.

[70] Hanslick, in *Neue Freie Presse*, November 28, 1893; Hanslick, *Fünf Jahre Musik*, 233 (where the last sentence is dropped).

[71] We know Hanslick assumed that Goldmark's source was Grillparzer since it was the Austrian dramatist who had invented the character of Melitta, Sappho's slave.

[72] Hanslick, *Fünf Jahre Musik*, 232.

[73] Ibid.

EXAMPLE 6.5a Goldmark, *Sappho Overture*, op. 44, mm. 1–4

EXAMPLE 6.5b Smetana, *Vyšehrad*, mm. 1–2

of augmented fourths and diminished sixths to "Jewish-Oriental music," of course, but the theme in question contains neither. Nor does Hanslick's characterization of "lamenting triplets" seem quite right in the case at hand, since, with the exception of one quintuplet, the music flows freely and evenly in eighth notes in compound duple meter. It is as though Hanslick has simply recycled a set of locutions that had originally been used to describe, say, the sultry theme played by the English horn and bass clarinet in the Entrance March from *Die Königin von Saba* (see the last nine bars of ex. 3.11) or, for that matter, the sung unison melody heard at the beginning of the third act of Rubinstein's *Die Makkabäer* (see ex. 3.10). By hearing Eastern-tinged harmonic intervals and "Jewish triplets" where none seem to exist, Hanslick reverts to an essentializing mode with respect to the Jewish composer that even now—when Goldmark was as much a part of the Viennese cultural establishment as Brahms and Hanslick himself—questions his status as a fully acculturated German composer.

Writing two days after the publication of Hanslick's review, Robert Hirschfeld, a one-time student of Hanslick at the University of Vienna, clearly took issue with his former teacher's criticism.[74] For Hirschfeld, all the suffering of the noble poetess is poured out in the opening dissonant

---

[74] Rob[ert] Hirschfeld, "Concerte," *Die Presse*, November 30, 1893.

chord in the harp that so troubled Hanslick. And whereas the older critic had called into question the appropriateness of beginning a work in such a manner, Hirschfeld finds a precedent in the dissonant beginning of two notable works by Beethoven, the First Symphony and the composer's own *Prometheus* Overture. Nor is Hirschfeld, the son of a Moravian rabbi, troubled by the seemingly Eastern exoticism of the ensuing elegiac oboe theme:

> Just as everything that King Midas touched turned to gold, so does everything that Goldmark touches [become] oriental triplets. Today no one knows how to imitate the melodies of the Greeks. And so Goldmark has Sappho sing as he himself tends to sing. But if you seriously wanted to criticize the composer for the oriental tint of the Sappho melody, then he would be able to counter with reference to Lesbos, Sappho's homeland, with reference to the lesbian school, which surely showed a more oriental than Hellenic character. As France rules our literature, as Italian influences are unmistakeable with our classics, so did the Orient give impetus, direction, and color to Hellenic art.[75]

Here, even as he acknowledges his opinion that Goldmark, a fellow Jew, was given to an exotic manner of musical expression, Hirschfeld troubles himself to justify the nature of Sappho's music by grounding it historically as a reflection of the orientalizing period in Greek art that was in full flourish at the time of Sappho's birth in the seventh century B.C.E.[76] In other words, the overture's Eastern tint is here justified as something that properly belongs to Goldmark's musical depiction of a "Western" subject, not as an inappropriate intrusion of the composer's "Eastern" *Gemüt*.

---

[75] Ibid. Helm was the only other critic to make reference to Sappho's presumed sexual orientation (see Theodor Helm, "Concerte," *Deutsche Zeitung*, December 5, 1893). Notably, however, Brahms had used this subject to needle the composer at a dinner party held in the home of their mutual friend Johann Strauss on the day before the Philharmonic's performance of the work. According to Richard Heuberger, Brahms teased his friend on this occasion by referring to him as "Sappherich." Since the suffix "-erich" is a common way in German of converting a female noun into a male noun (e.g., die Taube, der Täuberich), Brahms was in effect teasing Goldmark by attributing to him Sappho's same-sex orientation. Goldmark took this ribbing with a good nature, replying "Tomorrow I'll have my failure, but today let me eat my soup in peace!" By the time of the 1837 edition of the *Brockhaus Bilder-Conversations-Lexikon*, the term "Sapphic love" was firmly associated with female same-sex eroticism. The anecdote about the dinner party is told in Heuberger, *Erinnerungen an Johannes Brahms*, 63.

[76] For a recent study, see Ann C. Gunter, *Greek Art and the Orient* (Cambridge: Cambridge University Press, 2012).

EXAMPLE 6.6 Goldmark, *Sappho Overture*, op. 44, mm. 29–37

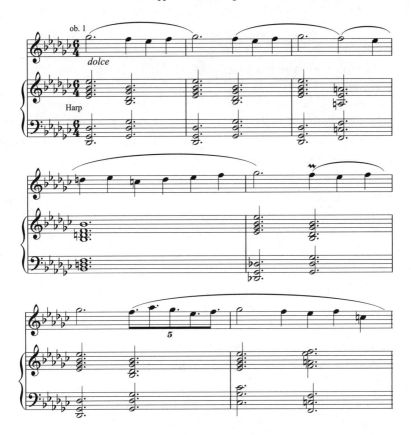

Speidel and Helm joined Hanslick in taking note of the work's high degree of dissonance, and yet both also acknowledged that Goldmark's good standing with his audience gained him quite a bit of leeway to push further in this direction than a less beloved figure might dare to do.[77] Speidel stands apart from Hanslick, however, in his response to the oboe's introductory melody, which he simply describes as an "exotically lamenting song" without further comment and with no implication that he thought the melody might somehow represent Goldmark's essential self. And he concludes his review by quoting approvingly an unnamed member of the audience overhead saying, "I don't agree with Goldmark, but I admire his work." We could scarcely wish for a clearer statement of the esteem in which Goldmark was now held in Viennese high culture.

---

[77] See sp. [Ludwig Speidel], "Konzerte," *Fremden-Blatt*, December 3, 1893 (from which the quotations in this paragraph are taken); and Helm, in *Deutsche Zeitung*, December 5, 1893.

Yet this did nothing to spare the composer from attack by younger critics of a different breed whose work appeared in Vienna's rising antisemitic press.

The Jewish Question Redefined

Speidel never wavered from his conviction that assimilation was the desirable course for the Jews of Central Europe—even in the face of growing evidence of resistance to this idea. Consider an exchange from 1895 with his friend Theodor Herzl, the future leader of the Zionist movement but at that time the Paris correspondent for the assimilationist *Neue Freie Presse*. In an early entry from his diary, Herzl recounts a conversation with Speidel concerning the Jewish Question. Here, reminding us of a position Hanslick had taken in 1848, Herzl explained that the Jews remained a foreign body among the nations as a result of the "socially pernicious characteristics" (*gesellschaftswidriger Eigenschaften*) developed, by historical fate and through no fault of their own, in the ghetto. Being forced into usury by the Church, he suggested, had damaged the Jews' character. And even now, after the emancipation, he continued, they remained "ghetto Jews." To be sure, they may have left the world of money and entered the liberal professions, but that only served to threaten the earning power of—and to draw a predictable response from— the middle classes of the host cultures.

Yet, remarkably, Herzl concluded that antisemitism might not be such a bad thing after all, if it were to spur the Jews to overcome their difference by forcing them to adapt to their host cultures through a kind of "Darwinian mimicry." To this, Speidel responded: "That is a world-historical view" (*Das ist eine welthistorische Auffassung*). It is difficult to know exactly what Speidel meant to convey by this laconic remark, but it is safe to say he was happy that Herzl, too, remained committed to the assimilationist project. That would soon change. Shortly after leaving Speidel's home, Herzl endured an ugly antisemitic taunt from two young men as his carriage passed by. It suddenly dawned on him that this taunt was directed not at his person but at the Jews as a race, and in the face of that reality, as he confided to his diary, "the world historical is useless."[78]

---

[78] See Theodor Herzl, *Briefe und Tagebücher*, 7 vols., ed. Alex Bein et al. (Frankfurt am Main: Ullstein; Berlin: Propyläen, 1983–c. 1996), 2: 48–51; Eng. trans., *The Complete Diaries of Theodor Herzl*, ed. Raphael Patai, trans. Harry Zohn, 3 vols. (New York and London: Herzl Press and Thomas Yoseloff, 1960), 1: 9–11. For a succinct account, see Beller, *Herzl*, 24–25.

This pessimistic insight concerning the prospects of assimilation lies at the heart of a powerful play that Herzl wrote several weeks later. Entitled *Das Neue Ghetto* (pub. 1898), this tragic work concerns a Viennese Jewish lawyer named Jakob Samuel who loses his close friendship with a gentile to political expediency, is implicated through his wife's family in shady financial dealings, and ultimately loses his life in a duel with a nobleman that his honor, especially as a Jew, does not allow him to refuse. Ironically, *Das Neue Ghetto* drew a rave review from that arch-assimilationist, Ludwig Speidel. Clearly taking a position that is at odds with Herzl's basic message that the Jews, even the well-to-do Jews who feature in the play, would never be permitted to be integrated into European society, Speidel writes thus of the ill-fated protagonist: "It is [Samuel's] most pressing task to cast aside everything that estranges him from his fellow human beings. That is the second, real emancipation of the Jew, without which the first emancipation remains a formality."[79]

As Speidel knew all too well, these years saw the emergence in the margins of certain music critics who, for racial reasons, would forever consign Goldmark to this "new ghetto." Already in the opening paragraph of Theodor Helm's review of *Im Frühling* from December 1889, we can see something of the crosscurrents of broad popular appeal and implacable racist opposition that were beginning to characterize Goldmark's Viennese reception:

> A grand overture by Goldmark entitled *Im Frühling* ... won roaring applause. Paying tribute to the author of *Merlin* and *Die Königin von Saba* is not risky; at most it threatens a new outburst from the anti-semites. For obvious reasons, the majority of the Philharmonic's regular subscribers need not worry much about those.[80]

It was no secret that Jews were disproportionately represented among the Philharmonic's elite subscription base, and Helm knew as well as anybody that the more marginal student groups that had embraced racial antisemitism over the previous decade, and that made their presence known from time to time at the Court Opera and elsewhere, thus far had little access to the exclusive Philharmonic series. Indeed, most people in Vienna at this time "experienced" orchestral music only vicariously, by keeping up with the city's music critics. And at precisely this time two new organs came into being that

---

[79] L. Sp. [Ludwig Speidel], "Carl Theater," *Neue Freie Presse*, January 18, 1898; translation adapted from Beller, *Vienna and The Jews*, 133–34; see also idem, *Herzl* (London: Peter Halban, 1991), 26–29.

[80] Theodor Helm, "Concerte," *Deutsche Zeitung*, December 14, 1889.

for the first time gave a platform to younger critics who were associated with the radical *deutschnational* movement and the ideology of racial antisemitism. First to appear, in January 1889, was the *Deutsches Volksblatt*, a new daily newspaper that promised its readers to be neither *verjudet* nor *verpfafft* (i.e., neither "Judaized" nor "clericized"), although it quickly aligned itself with the ascendant Christian Socials of Karl Lueger.[81] Soon to follow, in April 1890, was the *Ostdeutsche Rundschau*, which, reflecting its more Schönererian, *alldeutsche* point of view, was especially fanatical in its praise of all things Teutonic. Here we find a new music-critical discourse that was centered on the "progressive" music of Wagner, Liszt, and Bruckner while flouting the conservative, "Jewish" musical establishment through the use of sharper-key rhetoric.[82]

A case in point is provided by the review of Goldmark's *Im Frühling* by the Bruckner disciple August Göllerich. This appeared in the *Deutsches Volksblatt* on December 5, 1889:

> The Philharmonic finally offered so-called "new works," namely a freshening up of a Handel oboe concerto by Herr Bachrich and . . . compositions by J[ean] L[ouis] Nicodé [a set of orchestral variations], who, based on the name, may be an accentuating bedfellow of [the concert-master] Herr Rosé (in the use of the accent "aigu" or "fermé") and C. Goldmark.
>
> In a touching manner today's "most distinguished" representatives of so-called "absolute" music—nothing seems less absolute to the perceptive person than music—lurch back and forth between programs and good breeding, ever since their lord and master Johannes Brahms—the only one among them of importance—produced a rather "tragic" overture. This time Goldmark dutifully hides his program lust, which in *Merlin* he freely indulged in wailing chromaticism, in accordance with the aforementioned example [i.e., the *Tragic Overture*]

---

[81] Boyer, *Political Radicalism in Late Imperial Vienna*, 226.

[82] For a discussion of Bruckner and Brahms in this context, see Notley, *Lateness and Brahms*, 27–32. Of the two newspapers, the broadsheet *Deutsches Volksblatt* had far and away the larger circulation, no doubt in part because of its sensationalist and frequently crude tone. The *Ostdeutsche Rundschau* had a much smaller circulation and struggled financially; nevertheless, it was marked by writing of much higher quality despite its tabloid format. For a brief discussion, see Bruce F. Pauley, *From Prejudice to Persecution: A History of Austrian Anti-Semitism* (Chapel Hill: University of North Carolina, 1992), 47–48.

behind two words and shows thereby, as a consummate absolutist, how absolutely nothing can occur to you "in spring" . . .

All our "absolute" musicians, the kind we coddle, are no poets after all, but mere music-makers [*Musikanten*], who find their delight in an empty play with form and measure out their music by the cubic meter. Must their idioms that sweet-talk the workaday life not seem boring to the deeper mind of poets, did R. Wagner, when one happily had made Brahms into a temporary "second Beethoven," not have to exclaim: I cannot be a musician in times like these?!

"Go ahead, applaud gaily the catchphrase of the day—we know what will happen!" you want to call out to the Goldmark-seeking subscription base of the Philharmonic concerts . . . .

Last Sunday [Nicodé's variations], because they contain much that is more significant than Goldmark's triplet activity, which alights all too simply and openly on the most exploited commonplaces of spring, was much less applauded than the overture, after which the composer was called forth by his tribe in a lively manner.[83]

Here we have a multicount indictment—of the Jewish concertmaster, Arnold Rosé (who shares nothing more with the Prussian composer Nicodé than the French diacritical mark in the spelling of his name); of Brahms and empty, boring absolute music; of the superficial, largely Jewish audience; and, of course, of the Jewish composer Goldmark himself (and his trivial triplets).[84]

Three months later, the Vienna Academic Wagner Society, which had always included Jewish members, split over the question of antisemitism, with Schönerer and his followers forming a separate, explicitly antisemitic New Richard Wagner Society. The founding meeting of the splinter group took place in a beer hall just outside the Ringstrasse on March 20, 1890. Among other attendees at this celebratory event were official delegations from several of Vienna's student fraternities, the very groups in which, as we have seen, racial antisemitism had first begun to take hold in Vienna some ten years earlier. Bruckner was named an honorary member of the new organization, and Göllerich, whom the *Deutsches Volksblatt* described as the

---

[83] A[ugust] Göllerich, "Aus den Concert-Sälen," *Deutsches Volksblatt*, December 5, 1889.

[84] Several months earlier, Göllerich had disparaged Brahms's use of "Jewish-temple triplets" in the Andante of his Third Symphony. Göllerich's review of Brahms's Third Symphony, which appeared in the *Deutsches Volksblatt* on March 28, 1889, is quoted in Notley, *Lateness and Brahms*, 33.

"intellectual-spiritual creator" (*geistiger Schöpfer*) of the breakaway group, was named its honorary chairman.[85] Not only Göllerich but also several other members of the new organization, including Joseph Stolzing, August Püringer, Hans Puchstein, and Camillo Horn, were active as music critics.

It was a simple matter for these young radicals to use Wagner's call for a regeneration of German civilization in the face of the ruinous effect of Jewish-bourgeois materialism as a weapon to wield against Vienna's "debased" musical culture, in which Jews seemed to play an outsized role. This can be seen in the inaugural issue of the *Ostdeutsche Rundschau*, which appeared on April 6, 1890, and included a brief report on a concert produced by the newly founded society that included piano performances of three symphonic poems by Liszt, as well as Hans Sachs's final number from *Die Meistersinger* and a handful of shorter vocal pieces. After proudly mentioning the large number of bedfellows who had already come together in the "most fervent cultivation of national music," the anonymous author of this notice extended an enthusiastic invitation to all "art-understanding and art-enthused comrades" to join the new society, which aimed to deliver "an astonishing, joyful, and audaciously liberating act of excommunication of a non-German power that is hostile, in art and life as well as in music, to the Germanic-idealistic worldview."[86]

This same issue of the *Ostdeutsche Rundschau* also included Göllerich's review of the recent concert in which the Philharmonic players had paired Goldmark's *Prometheus Bound* Overture with Liszt's *Dante* Symphony.[87] Like Helm, Göllerich made tacit reference to Wagner's "The Public in Time and Space," but instead of doing so merely to praise Liszt's work, as Helm had done, he also sought to use Wagnerian thought to attack Goldmark and his many champions among the Philharmonic's subscribers. In this essay Wagner was concerned to explain "the tragedy of the fate of any creative spirit in its submission to the conditions imposed upon its activity by time and space."[88] Using this as his cue, Göllerich reports his regret, presumably on the late Liszt's behalf, about the fast tempos that were taken seemingly only in order to ensure that there would be time and space enough left in the concert to

[85] "Neuer Richard Wagner-Verein zu Wien," *Deutsches Volksblatt*, March 27, 1890. For discussion, see Notley, "Bruckner and Viennese Wagnerism," 66–67.

[86] "Neuer Richard Wagner-Verein," *Ostdeutsche Rundschau*, April 6, 1890.

[87] Aug[ust] Göllerich, "Musikalische Wiener Ostern," *Ostdeutsche Rundschau*, April 6, 1890, from which the quotations in this and the following paragraph are taken.

[88] Here I use the translation from "The Public in Time and Space" given in Raymond Furness, *Wagner and Literature* (Manchester: Manchester University Press, 1982), 10.

perform the *Dante* Symphony—"an eternal work," as Wagner had called it—"after Goldmark's truly rather 'bound' *Prometheus*."[89] This leads to a snide remark that in the overture at hand Goldmark "exploits the never-ending improvements of [Prometheus's] chronic liver distress" only to gain time and space, as it were, "for the most modern and dubious salon-yodeling."

With that Göllerich turns his attack from the composer onto the orchestra's regular subscribers, whose taste he likens to that of the shallow public that had recently been drawn to see the sensationalist Viennese performances by a traveling American mind reader named Anna Eva Fay:

> Even though the progress of our Philharmonic public, which takes almost as much interest in Goldmark's shackles as it does in the mesmerizings of the mentalist Miss Fay, has throve so widely that a cry for help like the well-known "Ei, Herr Jesus" of a Leipzig performance was squelched in the opportune varnishing of all unfeigned feelings, the Philharmonic's pageant in the Musikvereinssaal agreed that this performance of the Dante Symphony had been too funny for words. Soon we would have to join in this laughter in a different sense, in that we could hear some leading and sniffing souls distinctly complain that they absolutely must not find those places in the score in which heaven begins and with it salvation.

In Wagnerian fashion, Göllerich makes a convoluted connection in this passage between the title of Goldmark's overture (*Der gefesselte Prometheus*) and "Goldmark's *Fesselungen*...and those of...Miss Fay." (*Fesselungen* translates as both "shackles" and "mesmerizings.") And in a final allusion to "The Public in Time and Space," he recalls for his readers Wagner's cutting remark about the the dazed and bewildered response by the public to a performance in Leipzig of the *Dante* Symphony.[90]

Like his earlier review of *Im Frühling*, this one, too, attacks several targets at once. Here "salon-yodeling" suggests an inauthentic (because Jewish) appropriation of rural Alpine yodeling (implying what is "genuinely" German in the *völkisch* sense). Göllerich mocks the audience for covering up its genuine,

---

[89] "Die Eile erstreckte sich hiebei sogar auf die Zeitmaße der in wenig ergötzlichem Kunterbunt durchgespeitschten Werke und ließ namentlich Liszt's Dante-Symphonie, die als "ewiges" Werk—wie sie Wagner nannte—ohnedies schlecht in den Rahmen eines modernen Abonnements taugt, in ganz absonderlicher Umgebund erscheinen: nach einem thatsächlichrecht 'gefesselten' 'Prometheus' von Goldmark."

[90] Wagner, *Religion and Art*, 93n.

obviously negative reaction to Liszt's symphony in a tight-lipped display of its good upbringing. And to top it off, there is the sneering reference at the end presumably to Hanslick, one of those "sniffing souls" who simply refused to come to grips with Liszt's music.

The Music-critical Discourse of Antisemitism

The chief music critic for the *Ostdeutsche Rundschau* during its first years of existence was not Göllerich but another charter member of the New Richard Wagner Society, the civil servant Joseph Czerny, who published under the eminently Wagnerian nom de plume Joseph Stolzing.[91] (Göllerich was a resident of Linz, not Vienna, and so he was unable to review Viennese concerts on any regular basis.) Czerny's preview of the 1890–91 Viennese concert season is typically coarse in tone. He notes that Goldmark and Brahms are "the right composers for the predominantly Jewish audience of the midday [Philharmonic] concerts" and then continues:

> We are very curious about the Philharmonic's repertoire, which will be assembled, as ever, from the frequently heard symphonies of Beethoven, Schubert, and Schumann, along with the most recent Jewish works. What a pleasing spectacle awaits us when Hanslick, Hirschfeld, Königstein, and Kalbeck will again bestow the palm to their great (?) fellow-clansmen Goldmark, Goldschmidt, Brahms, et al., and lead them into the temple of immortality. Long live the music-making and music-loving Jewry! Strange! In the realm of politics Jewry is liberal, in that of music, conservative.[92]

It is not that Czerny or anyone else seriously thought the composer Brahms or the critic Kalbeck were Jews by birth.[93] It was enough to warrant

[91] In later years, after moving to Munich, Josef Stolzing-Czerny became a National Socialist and served as the music critic for the Nazi Party's official newspaper, *Völkischer Beobachter*. He had a hand in editing Hitler's *Mein Kampf* prior to its publication. See also Winfried Schüler, *Der Bayreuther Kreis von seiner Entstehung bis zum Ausgang der Wilhelminischen Ära* (Münster: Aschendorff, 1971), 85, 127.

[92] Translation from Notley, "Brahms the Liberal," 122 (slightly adapted).

[93] As noted in the Introduction, it has sometimes been falsely said that Kalbeck's original family name was Karpeles, a surname carried by many Jews. We can be certain that if any antisemitic critic at the fin de siècle had heard such a story, he would not have hesitated to reveal that name to his reading public.

contempt that they were Jews by association and attitude. As Wagner's son-in-law Houston Stewart Chamberlain would explain a few years later in his *Grundlagen des neunzehnten Jahrhunderts* (*Foundations of the Nineteenth Century*):

> One does not need to have the authentic Hittite nose to be a Jew; the word indicates rather a special kind of feeling and thinking; a person may very rapidly become a Jew without being an Israelite; some need only to associate actively with Jews, read Jewish newspapers and become accustomed to the Jewish conception of life, literature and art.... We must agree with Paul, the apostle, when he says, "For he is not a Jew who is one outwardly in the flesh, but he is a Jew who is one inwardly."[94]

For the likes of Göllerich and Czerny, mainstream Viennese music culture at the fin de siècle was marked Jewish—and anything but German national.

This can be seen particularly clearly in the writing of August Püringer, yet another critic whose work appeared in the *Ostdeutsche Rundschau*. Some of Püringer's articles, like those of Czerny, were published under a Wagnerian nom de plume, in this case Hagen; others were signed with either the author's full name or in the abbreviated form "A. Prgr."[95] Writing as Hagen in a feuilleton of August 6, 1893, Püringer bemoans what he calls *Kunstjudenthum* (Art-Jewry) and in particular what he describes as the lamentable *Verjudung* (Judaization or Jewification) of Vienna's musical culture.[96] In a passage that

---

[94] Houston Stewart Chamberlain, *Die Grundlagen des neunzehnten Jahrhunderts*, 2 vols. (Munich: F. Bruckmann, 1906), 1: 544–45, 574. The Pauline passage is found in Romans ii: 28–29. I have taken my translation from Steven E. Aschheim, "'The Jew Within: The Myth of 'Judaization' in Germany,'" in his *Culture and Catastrophe: German and Jewish Confrontations with National Socialism and Other Crises* (Houndmills, Basingstoke, Hampshire, and London: Macmillan, 1996), 58.

[95] Püringer, whom Schüler describes as a "credulous-reckless fanatic" (*leichtgläubig-unbekümmert Fanatiker*), was born in Vienna in 1874 but settled in Germany after the turn of the century. See Schüler, *Der Bayreuther Kreis*, 161–62. The first of his many articles for the *Bayreuther Blätter* appeared in 1904; the last, in 1935. It is not known when he died. See Annette Hein, *"Es ist viel 'Hitler' in Wagner": Rassismus und antisemitische Deutschtumsideologie in den "Bayreuther Blätter" (1878–1938)* (Tübingen: Max Niemeyer, 1996), 82, 92, 130–32, 147, 177, 333, 356, 370, 372, 438, 455, 459, and 470.

[96] Hagen [August Püringer], "Kunstjudenthum," *Ostdeutsche Rundschau*, August 6, 1893, from which the following two quotations are taken. For a thoughtful critique of the notion of *Verjudung*, see Aschheim, "'The Jew Within': The Myth of 'Judaization' in Germany."

might as well have been penned by Wagner himself, he begins by recycling key themes from *Jewry in Music*:

> If we now consider the universally known materialistically oriented, virtually ideal-negating spirit of Jewry, its innate business sense, which makes the highest of things seem useless and worthless to it, finally the inability that, as a general rule, springs from such a spirit to create in the ideal realm, what is more, in the midst of the Aryan peoples, to whom it is alien and unsympathetic in its tenacious racial constancy (about which Wagner's *Jewry in Music* may offer closer insight to those who are eager to learn more)—then we would be confronted with the insoluble riddle of how there should be found among the Jews so much interest in art (and especially in the most ideal of them, music), were we not to recall the virtuoso cunning that Jewry knows so well how to use to achieve its international power that it should have to overcome a strong instinctive distrust among all the peoples, and that it could never overcome this completely if it did not participate—if also only externally for appearance—in the life of the soul, that is, in the artistic creations of the people under consideration.[97]

Püringer follows this with an extensive quotation from *Jewry in Music* itself before turning his focus onto the current musical situation in Vienna. To retain something of the Wagnerian character of the passage, I translate here quite literally:

> That it is now finally time to counteract the modern Judaization of our artistic conditions, especially in the breeding grounds of the same, the conservatories, schools that deserve no longer their beautiful name, that they lovingly preserve for us what the true artistic spirit has built in increasing development, and which, with its heavily Jewish staff, which has been interested in the exclusive cultivation of the most empty salon music, with its jewified administrative board, rents out its concert halls as Jewish synagogues (!), which can be called downright factories of the falsification of the purely artistic life of the soul, factories for the production of the international Jewish virtuosity,

---

[97] As Pamela Potter has argued, Wagner, in *Jewry in Music*, does not describes the Jews as a distinct race, and it was left to his followers to make that distinction and to develop systematic correlations between race and music, as Püringer does here. See Pamela M. Potter, "Race in German Musical Discourse," in *Western Music and Race*, ed. Julie Brown (Cambridge: Cambridge University Press, 2007), 50–51.

that it should be high time to [go about] such work is shown to us nowhere more clearly than by taking a glance at today's concert hall and opera house; in the one we observe illuminated under cold electric lights a virtuosity divested of any warm inwardness, whose most adored representatives are the Jews Brüll, Grünfeld, Rubinstein, and the Rosé Quartet, who are extolled as "musical gods"; in the other prevail Mascagni, Goldmark, and Massenet, with their supersaturated instrumentation, the almost ape-like seeking after crass harmonies, the base and repugnant coquetting with the public's depraved whims of taste (while the true artist cannot comport himself ruggedly enough for modern society!)—and finally Mascagni and consorts with the Jewish-nervous pursuit of a "naturalistic opera," which can be called the downright negation of the true essence of music (passionate naïveté). Without Music-Jewry we would scarcely, according to what Wagner preached to us, have had to catalogue such adverse folly; only a mind that is alien and closed to the German spirit can put up with misunderstood Wagner-aping and the most strained "tone painting" and venture to douse it with the most frivolous stories of circus clowns and courtesans.

But even our orchestras are quite "black," and the most tender German female personages, like an Elsa, a Freija are portrayed by racially pure Jewesses and are dragged shamelessly onto the forestage to the thunderous applause of a public already completely blinded, made uncritical, and patronized by Hanslick and Frey.[98]

In the face of this situation, Püringer argues, "a true German national party will have to struggle tirelessly for the purification of the German life of art and the mind." And while the critic acknowledges that the artist may well choose to stand above any party, he insists the German national party is no party in the ordinary sense but rather a "community of the people." With that in mind, he concludes with a thoroughly *völkisch* call to arms:

---

[98] With his reference to "Wagner aping," Püringer is very likely alluding to Nietzsche's cutting words in the second postscript to his essay "The Case of Wagner" (1888): "I waste no words on the clever apes of Wagner, Goldmark, for example: with *The Queen of Sheba* one belongs in the zoo—one can make an exhibit of oneself" (Friedrich Nietzsche, *The Birth of Tragedy and The Case of Wagner*, trans. with commentary by Walter Kaufmann, New York: Random House, 1967, 1888). On the trope of the Jews as black, see Sander Gilman, *The Jew's Body* (New York and London: Routledge, 1991), 171–77.

The artist is rooted in the life of the people and receives his artistic power from it. When this people is endangered, then so too is endangered the purity of art...—and woe to the artist who does not step into the breach in such times of the toughest adversity and danger like the hero for his fatherland![99]

Three months later, Püringer revisited this feuilleton in his review of the Philharmonic's concert of November 26, 1893, which, as we have seen, included the première of Goldmark's *Sappho* Overture. Before turning to the music, however, the critic provided his readers with a detailed résumé of his recent account of the "Judaization" of Vienna's musical life, and he reminded them of how he had concluded on that occasion by extending an invitation to all genuine artists not to assume an indifferent position in the question of "Art-Jewry," but rather to take up the struggle against it after the model of Wagner.[100] Püringer was thus bitterly disappointed, as he reported, that Hans Richter, who, as an immensely talented conductor and a former student and intimate of Wagner no less, had the potential to play an unrivaled role in the serious musical life of Vienna, yet had instead failed to answer the call. This was demonstrated, in Püringer's opinion, above all in the repertorial selection of the Philharmonic concerts, which, he argued, should be a showcase of symphonic masterpieces for all the world to see, but in which Richter had chosen to program instead "Jewish junk" (*jüdische Trödelwaare*) such as Goldmark's *Sappho*, "a piece of rubbish from beginning to end"—a decision that could only be judged "outrageous":

How every musician longs to hear the Prelude to *Parsifal*, not performed for more than three years.... [T]hrough the performance of such works, Herr Doktor, you fulfill your artistic calling, ennoble the taste, the spirit of the deformed masses, while by performing such babble as the above-named overture...you commit a crime against misguided humanity!...Woe to him who does not make the most of his talents. Richter ought to be, in accordance with his ability, a staunch outpost

---

[99] Püringer, in *Ostdeutsche Rundschau*, August 6, 1893.

[100] August Püringer, "Drittes philharmonisches Konzert," *Ostdeutsche Rundschau*, November 30, 1893, from which the following quotations are also taken. It is on the basis of this review, in which the critic seems to take writing credit for "Art-Jewry," that I identify Hagen as Püringer. Reittererová and Reitterer's identification of Hagen as Max Vancsa, a noted historian, seems highly doubtful, not only in light of the review at hand but also because the positions taken in Vancsa's signed work for the *Die musikalische Presse* and other organs give little evidence of Hagen's radical politics; see Reittererová and Reitterer, *Vier Dutzend rothe Strümpfe*, 435–36.

against the "plastic demon of the degeneration of humanity," which may never be permitted to destroy our artistic world! May the future be better!

In this passage Püringer quotes one of Wagner's ugliest epithets for the Jews, from "Know Thyself" (1881). In this late regeneration essay, Wagner summed up his views on the Jewish Question more than thirty years following the original publication of "Jewry in Music" (1850). Püringer's quotation is taken, in the words of Alex Bein, from

> the ominous sentence which...no work of anti-Semitic "philosophy" failed to notice: "A wonderful, incomparable phenomenon: the plastic demon of the degeneration of humanity in triumphant safety and as a German citizen of the Mosaic faith to boot, the darling of our liberal princes and the guarantor of the unity of our Reich!"[101]

Here Wagner has not only reiterated the old idea that the Jews were "plastic" in the sense of being pliable and thus ostensibly being able to adapt to German culture even though they could never be a part of that culture or truly understand it. He now also described the Jews as "demons," evil spirits lurking in the Germans' midst. The essay as a whole was essentially a charge to the Germans to develop a greater racial consciousness, made necessary now that the German state, in what Wagner considered an act of utter folly, had given the Jews to think of themselves as Germans by making them citizens with full equal rights. For, as Wagner writes, "Only when the demon...is no longer able to find among us any where or when for his salvaging [*Wo oder Wann zu seiner Bergung*] will there be no longer among us—any Jews."[102] This, of course, is the truly ominous sentence in the work at hand. Whether or

---

[101] Bein, *The Jewish Question*, 606–7 (translation of the quotation from Wagner slightly modified). For the German text in question, see Wagner, *Gesammelte Schriften und Dichtungen*, 10: 272. It is notable that Houston Stewart Chamberlain quoted this very passage in a lecture entitled "Richard Wagner's Regeneration Theory," delivered to the New Richard Wagner Society just a few months earlier on May 17, 1893. Chamberlain's lecture was subsequently published in the *Bayreuther Blätter* 18 (1895): 181. Püringer was likely in attendance at this lecture. For Püringer's own "regeneration essay," which even includes the admonition in the plural "Erkennet Euch selbst!" ("Know Yourselves!"), see August Püringer, *Künstler- und Publicums-Unarten: Ein Warn- und Mahnruf* (Bad habits by artists and the public: a warning and exhortation; Vienna: Friedrich Schalk, 1895), quoted at 8.

[102] This sentence from "Know Thyself" is quoted in Bein, *The Jewish Question*, 607, but I have provided my own translation.

not Goldmark knew Wagner's essay, the message that lay behind Püringer's quotation from it in his review of *Sappho*—which Goldmark very likely did know—could not have escaped him. He made no attempt as yet to counter this kind of racist diatribe in public. As we shall see, however, there would eventually come a time when even this most mild-mannered of composers could hold himself back no longer.

CHAPTER SEVEN

"Politics Makes Strange
Bedfellows"; or, Smetana's
Reception in the 1890s

With Smetana, though he betrays the Wagnerian school, we encounter a strictly
national composer whose works we must respect unconditionally and without
partisanship.

—Alarich v. d. Germanen (*Ostdeutsche Rundschau*, 1894)

THE RECEPTION OF Czech music in the imperial capital at the end of the
century continued to reflect the larger issue of German-Czech relations in
Bohemia. In January 1890, Taaffe persuaded the Old Czechs, together with the
German liberals, who were still pursuing the boycott of the Bohemian Diet
they had begun four years earlier, to come to Vienna to attempt to settle their
major differences once and for all. (The more radical Young Czechs, from the
one side, and the *völkisch* parties, from the other, were pointedly excluded.)[1]

---

[1] Old Czech and Young Czech factions had begun to emerge within the Czech National
Party already in the 1860s, and in 1874 the party formally split into two. The Old
Czechs, led by František Rieger, retained the name "National Party"; the Young Czechs
adopted the name "National Liberal Party." There were several points of disagree-
ment. In general the Young Czechs were more vigorous in defense of civil liberties and
evinced a more pronounced anticlericalism; they were less comfortable in cooperating

Resulting from these much-watched negotiations were the *Wiener Punktationen*, a series of draft agreements affecting the courts, the chambers of commerce and industry, and the school boards, that were designed to divide the crown land into two separate administrative zones, a German-speaking borderland, where German would be the sole external and internal administrative language, and a bilingual interior region including Prague, where Czech would be the external language but German remain the internal one.[2] Most German Bohemians favored the proposed arrangement, and it was only the most radical among them who saw any strategic advantage in holding out against it. But to the Young Czechs, this *Böhmischer Ausgleich* (Bohemian Compromise) constituted an unacceptable infringement on Bohemian state right, which asserted the territorial integrity of the crown land as well as its essential Czech character. In March 1891 German-Czech relations took a decided turn away from potential accommodation toward greater confrontation when the Young Czechs, led by outspoken radicals such as Julius and Eduard Grégr and Jan Vašaty, took nearly all the Czech seats in the elections to the Reichsrat on a platform of outright opposition to Taaffe's proposed Compromise. In April 1892, the increasingly irrelevant Old Czechs acknowledged the direction in which the winds were blowing by withdrawing their support of the very agreement with the German liberals they had helped to negotiate.

All this was very much in the air when, on February 21, 1892, in the annual Nicolai Concert given to benefit the orchestra's pension fund, the Philharmonic players introduced Dvořák's *Husitská* Overture. This was a striking choice of repertoire, inasmuch as the overture is one of the few works by Dvořák to convey any real sense of Czech-nationalist meaning. Quoting two chorale melodies, *Svatý Václave* ("St. Wenceslas") and the battle hymn *Ktož jsú bože bojovníce* ("All ye warriors of God"), this overture evokes the Hussite Crusades (1418–1437), whereby Czech patriots fought off the attempts made by the German rulers of the Holy Roman Empire to restore Catholicism in those parts of Bohemia that had adopted the "heretical" teaching of Jan Hus, a reformist priest burned at the stake in 1415. What made the fifteenth-century martyr an especially meaningful figure in the later nineteenth century was not anything having to do

---

with the "feudal-conservatives"; and, as we shall discover, they were unwilling to cede much of anything on the question of Bohemian state rights.

[2] See Jenks, *Austria Under the Iron Ring*, 239–74; Bruce M. Garver, *The Young Czech Party 1874–1901 and the Emergence of a Multi-Party System* (New Haven: Yale University Press, 1978), 146–53; Höbelt, *Kornblume und Kaiseradler*, 52–65; and King, *Budweisers into Czechs and Germans*, 81–83.

with his religious significance, however, but rather his insistence on using the vernacular in the liturgy and his work in codifying the Czech written language. Hus was, in short, a natural rallying figure in the contemporary political debates about language rights and, by extension, Bohemian state right.[3]

In his review of the Philharmonic's performance, Helm acknowledged Hus's present-day relevance in a backhanded way by referring scornfully to the Young Czechs' firebrands in the Reichsrat. The overture's "martial (or, more correctly, fanatical) sounds may well have swollen the hearts of those who are of a like mind to Messrs. Grégr and Vašaty," he wrote, adding "the noisy applause for the piece that came from some of the seats sounded decidedly like a demonstration and for that reason...had to arouse opposition. One cannot possibly expect German listeners to be crazy about a musical glorification of the Hussites."[4] Surely Helm's readers in the *Deutsche Zeitung* would have been pleased to learn that the Germans in the audience had staged a counterdemonstration.

The readers of the *Neue Freie Presse*, by contrast, would have gotten a very different picture from Hanslick, who used especially vivid language in his depiction of the work's "powerful, almost uncannily urgent energy":

> From the slow introduction, whose theme is taken from an old Bohemian hymn, we meet in embodied form the melancholy devotion of the Hussites; from the Allegro, their utter wildness and pugnacity. The piece sounds as fanatical as though it were orchestrated in places with hatchets, scythes, and cudgels.[5]

If Hanslick describes, in effect, the "martial (or more correctly, fanatical) sounds of the Hussites"—again, one has the feeling Helm was responding as much to cues given by Hanslick as to the music itself—he reports no uproar in the hall and puts the best light on things in any case by persisting with his

---

[3] See Cynthia Paces and Nancy C. Wingfield, "The Sacred and the Profane: Religion and Nationalism in the Bohemian Lands, 1880–1920," in *Constructing Nationalities in East Central Europe*, 117; and František Šmahel, "The Hussite Movement: An Anomaly of European History?" in *Bohemia in History*, ed. Mikuláš Teich (Cambridge: Cambridge University Press, 1998), 81.

[4] h – m [Theodor Helm], "Nicolai-Concert der Philharmoniker," *Deutsche Zeitung*, February 25, 1892.

[5] Ed. H. [Eduard Hanslick], "Musik," *Neue Freie Presse*, February 23, 1892; reprinted in Hanslick, *Fünf Jahre Musik*, 189–90, from which the following quotation is also taken.

claim, even with regard to what can only be described as an essay in Czech nationalism, that Dvořák was an acculturated German:

> The Hussite Overture will do no harm in Vienna, although we might not have struck up music before a gathering of people on Žižka's Mountain. In spite of all its excess and noise, examined from the purely musical standpoint the composition betrays an ingenious talent and great technical mastery. Dvořák does not fall back on the formlessness and searching after false contrasts that repulses us in the "dramatic" symphonies of so many New German composers. More profoundly than many Germans, this Slav knows his Beethoven, whose Coriolan and Egmont overtures are not completely without impact on the "Husitska."

To be sure, Hanslick conceded something with his reference to the *Ziskaberg*, the popular name for the hill overlooking Prague from which Jan Žižka, the Hussite military leader, had, to the strains of "All ye warriors of God," defeated the first German-led crusade in July 1420. But this historical allusion rankled Hanslick far less than it did Helm, who concluded his review by using the allusion to that defeat to make an unfavorable comparison between Dvořák's overture and the final piece on the program, Liszt's *Hungarian Rhapsody No. 2*:

> The concert, which began on a defiantly Czech note, closed in an unadulterated Hungarian manner. With the difference, however, that in Liszt's rhapsody the fiery Magyarism seems to take pleasure rather harmlessly in its own existence, while Dvořák's Hussites obviously want to threaten the lives of us Germans, if only musically for the time being. Therefore it won't be taken amiss that we preferred the piece of national music that was played at the end of the Nicolai Concert to that which was heard at the beginning.[6]

Helm undoubtedly would have preferred Liszt to Dvořák on stylistic grounds alone: as we have seen in earlier reviews of the latter's Slavonic Rhapsodies, he never placed those works in the same league as the former's Hungarian ones. But here that tells only part of the story. Seen through the eyes of the *Deutsche Zeitung*, artistic assertions of Czech nationhood touched on real and timely political concerns in a way that evocations of gypsies simply did not.

[6] Helm, in *Deutsche Zeitung*, February 25, 1892.

Smetana Breaks Through

It was during this same turbulent period that parts of Smetana's *Má vlast* (*My Fatherland*)—a set of six symphonic poems that has been termed a "monument of *českost*" (Czechness)—were finally introduced to the Philharmonic's subscribers.[7] First to be heard, on March 2, 1890, was *Vltava*. This was followed in short order by *Z českých luhů a hájů* (*From Bohemia's Woods and Fields*), *Vyšehrad*, and *Šárka* (heard on January 29, 1893, November 12, 1893, and November 11, 1894, respectively).[8] Hanslick found something to like in each of these pieces, and in his review of *Šárka* he even urged the Philharmonic to proceed apace in programming the remaining two movements of Smetana's patriotic cycle (*Tábor* and *Blaník*). His reason was simple: "In our days of sometimes feeble, sometimes fussy music-making, we greet with joy every creation which stems from a genuine, strong talent."[9] For Hanslick, "seriousness," "genuineness," and "strength" were healthy attributes (neither fussy nor feeble) of the liberality that remained, for him at least, a cornerstone of German identity (and cultural superiority). He had already identified some of these traits a decade earlier in the *From My Life* Quartet, and he must have been gratified to find more of the same in *Má vlast*.

This only raises interest, of course, in the *českost* of Smetana's symphonic poems. As Michael Beckerman has argued, Czechness does not spring directly from musical style per se, but rather "comes about [only] when, in the minds of composers and audiences, the Czech *nation*...becomes a subtextual program for musical works,...which [in turn] animates the musical style, allowing us to make connections between the narrow confines of a given piece and a larger, dynamic context."[10]

---

[7] The characterization of *Má vlast* is taken from Richard Taruskin, *The Oxford History of Western Music*, vol. 3: *The Nineteenth Century* (Oxford and New York: Oxford University Press, 2005), 451–52.

[8] Hanslick's reviews of the four works appeared in the *Neue Freie Presse*, respectively on March 4, 1890; February 7, 1893; November 28, 1893; and November 13, 1894. For a brief discussion of Hanslick's reception of *Má vlast*, see Jaroslav Střítecký, "Eduard Hanslick und die tschechische Musik," in *Festival Česká hudba / Musica bohemica: Problémy a metody hudební historiografie*, ed. Rudolf Pečman (Brno, 1974), 90–93. In the meanwhile, the players also performed the Overture to *Prodaná nevěsta* (Overture to *The Bartered Bride* but billed simply as a *Lustspiel-Ouvertüre*) on March 15, 1891.

[9] Ed. H. [Eduard Hanslick], "Concerte," *Neue Freie Presse*, November 13, 1894.

[10] Michael Beckermann, "In Search of Czechness in Music," *19th-Century Music* 10 (1986–87): 73.

But where does that leave a listener like Hanslick? Although *Má vlast* is indubitably the product of a self-consciously Czech composer, would that have made any difference to the way in which this music was heard by Hanslick, for whom any programmatic work about Bohemia, especially one entitled *My Fatherland*, was bound to have had a personal resonance? Bohemia was his fatherland too, after all. These questions are perhaps most pertinent with regard to *Vyšehrad* and *Vltava*, the two movements of Smetana's programmatic cycle that are tied most closely to the critic's hometown, Prague.

In his review of *Vltava*, Hanslick took up his support of Smetana from where he had left off a decade earlier in his review of the *From My Life* Quartet. He begins, however, with a complaint—not about the music but that the work had been announced to the public using a Czech title:

> A great effect was made by a new work, Smetana's symphonic poem *Vltava*. This is how the work was identified in the placards. I thought we still spoke German in Vienna, and that no one here was obligated to know that "Vltava" means the Moldau. Apparently Hof-Kapellmeister Richter, as well as many of his listeners, thought "Vltava" was the name of some great unknown hero of the Czech nation. The fault lies in the first place with the music publisher, who has supplemented the title of the entire work [i.e., *Má vlast*] and even all the performance markings with a German translation, but not "Vltava," which is decisive for understanding. And yet the Czechs want to disseminate Smetana's works throughout Germany. Why, therefore, conceal on the title page the name "Moldau," which is known by as many millions of people as the hundreds who know the word "Vltava"? The Czech publishers have harmed their musical heroes with such "patriotic" nonsense more than they know. [11]

None of this got in the way of Hanslick's appreciation of the music, however. "The composition itself," he wrote, "is the work of a genuine and illustrious talent" and is "much more unified and more naturally developed" than any of Liszt's symphonic poems.[12] A detailed account follows of how Smetana

---

[11] Ed. H. [Eduard Hanslick], "Concerte," *Neue Freie Presse*, March 4, 1890; rpt. in Hanslick, *Aus dem Tagebuche eines Musikers*, 300–304. When the Philharmonic players performed *Vltava* for the subscription concerts for the second time, under Gustav Mahler's direction on December 2, 1900, Hanslick raised the same objection; see Ed. H. [Eduard Hanslick], "Concerte," *Neue Freie Presse*, December 4, 1900.

[12] It may have been the comparison made here with Liszt's symphonic poems that explains at least in part Hanslick's more favorable comments about the form of

portrays the various scenes of the Bohemian landscape, as the river winds its way from its twin sources toward Prague, with Vyšehrad towering above:

> Smetana's "Moldau" is a beautifully designed, unified piece, worked out without any monotony, that reveals an original talent and, with regard to instrumentation, one of the most eminent students of Liszt and Berlioz. It makes no pretense to deep musical content, to polyphony and contrapuntal art in the working out of motives; it works through song-like (not "endless") melody, through clear, symmetrical form and delightful sound. As nature painting, Smetana's "Moldau" has the advantage of conjuring up in the imagination completely typical images that require nothing in the way of a detailed program, and nowhere compels the composer to tasteless overstepping of boundaries.

With his pointed reference to "unendliche Melodie," of course, Hanslick manages to add to his earlier reproach of Liszt by getting in some additional digs at Wagner: the critic was only too happy to distinguish Smetana from association with the New German School. At the same time, while he clearly admires Smetana's abilities as a musical landscape painter, he sees nothing in the composer's canvas that might have to do with Czechness. Nor, however, does he hear the work in terms of otherness or exoticism: Hanslick took pleasure, after all, in how Smetana had portrayed the Moldau, not the Vltava.[13] Although Richard Taruskin is probably correct in suggesting that it is only the conventions of historiography that have caused the composer to be seen almost exclusively as a leading nationalist rather than as a leading progressive as well, it is worth noting that Hanslick does not deport himself in accord with either reading of history.[14] He sees neither a Czech nationalist nor a *Zukunftsmusiker*, but only an unmarked (which is to say "German") composer, a worthy companion to the likes of Brahms (and Dvořák).

In a manner that recalls his first published notice on Dvořák, Hanslick follows his discussion of the music with a brief sketch of the composer's biography and then enters into an extended discussion of the relative merits of his work in the instrumental and operatic spheres. Hanslick leaves no doubt he prefers the former to the latter, and he holds the same thing true with respect

---

Vltava than in his earlier brief notice after hearing the work performed during the twenty-fifth-anniversary concert of the Slavischer Gesangverein three years earlier.

[13] Notably, Hanslick stood alone among Viennese reviewers in referring to the piece as *Die Moldau*; every other Viennese critic respected the Czech title under which the piece had been billed.

[14] Taruskin, *Oxford History of Western Music*, 3: 447.

to Dvořák's oeuvre. To be sure, he acknowledges the freshness and vitality of Smetana's early comic operas, *Der Kuss* (*The Kiss*) and *Die verkaufte Braut* (*The Bartered Bride*), but he hastens to suggest—wrongly, as events would turn out—that neither could be expected to have any more success outside Prague than Dvořák's *Der Bauer als Schelm* (*The Cunning Peasant*) and *Die Dickschädel* (*The Pig-Headed Peasants*).[15] For Hanslick, however, the real problem lay in Smetana's decision to adopt a late Wagnerian style for his tragic opera *Libussa*, which Hanslick had heard already in Prague. Acknowledging his linguistic limitations, he implied that only a listener who was intimate with the Czech language could appreciate the work's "famous dramatic and declamatory details." As for the music, this opera, like "all emulations of Wagner," had left him with "the impression of unhealthiness, broodiness, and distressing tedium." Although Hanslick makes it known he is no more pleased with Dvořák's own tragic operas, he does not allow this judgment to cloud his general delight in the instrumental and chamber works of both composers.

But that only made the Czech billing of *Vltava* all the more irritating, and so Hanslick concludes in the spirit in which he had begun:

> Our Philharmonic players might draw from Smetana and Dvořák many other very effective and interesting works for their repertoire. But with regard to the title, we wish to be treated no worse than the provincial judges in Prague, who, according to the most recent compromise, need understand nothing more than Czech.

Since the Bohemian Compromise stipulated the continued use of German as the sole internal administrative language throughout the whole of Bohemia, Hanslick was clearly mistaken in this last complaint. Yet by insisting that the Austrian capital was in effect a "German city," what he really seems to be registering is indignation over the tacit declaration made in Taaffe's proposed compromise that the Bohemian capital had by now for all practical purposes become a "Czech city." To a traditional liberal nationalist like Hanslick, especially one who hailed from Prague, this was not at all how the liberal Germanizing project was supposed to have turned out.

Hanslick was not alone in his warm embrace of *Vltava*. In decided contrast to virtually every work by Dvořák heard thus far in Vienna, Smetana's

---

[15] As we have seen, *The Cunning Peasant* failed miserably during its short run at the Court Opera in 1885. *The Pig-Headed Peasants,* by contrast, has never been performed in Vienna.

symphonic poem met with universal critical acclaim. This may seem surprising at first in view of the composer's reputation as a Czech nationalist, especially with respect to the city's German-nationalist critics. Yet Helm, writing in the *Deutsche Zeitung*, and even Hans Puchstein, the music critic for the upstart *Deutsches Volksblatt*, had nothing but good things to say about the composer and his work.

Herein lies a perfect example of how politics makes strange bedfellows.[16] For all their opposing goals, Austria's radical German nationalists had much in common ideologically with the Young Czechs: both groups espoused strong anticlericalism, left-liberal politics, and antisemitism (directed, in the case of the Young Czechs, against Bohemia's Germanophile Jews).[17] The Young Czechs championed the music of Smetana while criticizing that of Dvořák for being too beholden to German liberal interests in Vienna and too keen on putting international success ahead of national consciousness.[18] This last consideration is worthy of note. As we shall explore in greater detail below, Vienna's German-nationalist critics saw Smetana not as a threat but as a salutary model for German composers to emulate in advancing their own cause. But the German nationalists' preference for Smetana also had to do with the composer's affinities for Wagner's music dramas and the symphonic poems of Liszt. (Like Taruskin, these critics recognized Smetana for the musical progressive that he was in no less a measure than he was a musical nationalist.) Dvořák could only suffer by comparison on account of his close association with Brahms and—what was worse—from his status as a protégé of the "conservative" (and "Jewish") critic Hanslick. In other words, it worked to Smetana's advantage with this critical faction that he could be linked, in a way that Dvořák could not at this stage of his career, to the New Germans.

[16] For a somewhat complementary argument that in Prague in the years around 1900 sharply articulated nationalist divisions between Germans and Czechs in the political sphere were by no means always observed in the cultural sphere, see Gary B. Cohen, "Cultural Crossings in Prague, 1900: Scenes from Late Imperial Austria," *Austrian History Yearbook* 45 (2014): 1–30.

[17] On Czech antisemitism in the 1890s, see Hillel J. Kieval, *The Making of Czech Jewry: National Conflict and Jewish Society in Bohemia, 1870–1910* (New York and Oxford: Oxford University Press, 1988), 64–77; and Christoph Stölzl, *Kafkas böses Böhmen: Zur Sozialgeschichte eines Prager Juden* (Munich: Hans Pribil, 1975), 44–107 passim.

[18] For a useful discussion of the contrasting reception of the two Czech composers along these lines, albeit in a later historical period, see Brian S. Locke, *Opera and Ideology in Prague* (Rochester: University of Rochester Press, 2006), 54–58.

What most mattered for Puchstein, for example, was that Smetana's "love for his fatherland (*engeres Vaterland*) and his enthusiasm for his nation" had not prevented him from embracing the "masters of the New German School" and modeling his operas on those of Wagner and his symphonic poems on those of Liszt.[19] Thus Puchstein gleefully contrasts the audience's warm embrace of *Vltava* with the cold shoulder it later turned to Brahms's First Symphony, the concert's closing number:

> Vltava was acclaimed and the symphony was—nixed. No wonder the public, deeply moved by the inwardness, the deep feeling, the warmth that inspire all the works of our great classical masters and the modern musical trio of Wagner, Liszt, and Bruckner, accustomed to the wealth of melodies that sound forth from all their compositions, is able to develop no taste for Brahms, who certainly understands the outwardness, the purely technical side of his art, but lacks inwardness.[20]

And for his part, Helm lamented that "the Czech national composer . . . has been treated very shabbily by the conservative critics vis-à-vis their protégé Anton Dvořák, perhaps because of his leanings toward Wagner and Liszt."[21] Somewhat unusually, Helm did not wait until after Hanslick had weighed in on the music to publish his review of this concert. (Both critics' notices appeared on the same day.) It must have come as something of an unpleasant surprise, therefore, when Helm discovered that Hanslick was scarcely any less enthusiastic about *Vltava* than he was. Politics makes strange bedfellows indeed.

---

[19] H.P. [Hans Puchstein], "Musik," *Deutsches Volksblatt*, March 8, 1890. Puchstein's use of the phrase "zu seinem engeren Vaterlande" is notable, in that he is making the point that Smetana's fatherland was Bohemia, not Austria or the Austro-Hungarian Monarchy. As Kirsten Belgum has noted, the expression "aus dem engeren Vaterland" was frequently used in nationalist discourse in Germany at this time as a way of stressing regional patriotism within the larger state. See Kirsten Belgum, *Popularizing the Nation: Audience, Representation, and the Production of Identity in Die Gartenlaube* (Lincoln and London: University of Nebraska Press, 2008), 207n. See also Haider, *Im Streit um die österreichische Nation*, 280–81. As we have already seen with respect to *Die Königin von Saba* and will see yet again in connection with Czech composers, more centralist-minded critics sometimes used the adjectival "vaterländisch" (patriotic) in reference to works by Austrian composers in the broader sense.

[20] Puchstein, in *Deutsches Volksblatt*, March 8, 1890.

[21] Theodor Helm, "Concerte. Noch etwas über Graf Laurenstein," *Deutsche Zeitung*, March 4, 1890.

Helm undoubtedly had *Vltava* in mind the following year, when the Philharmonic gave its first performance of Dvořák's Eighth Symphony in a subscription concert of January 4, 1891, that also included Edvard Grieg's *Peer Gynt* and a symphony by Haydn. The critic judged Dvořák's Adagio to be the best of the symphony's four movements because its style, which was "more dramatic than symphonic," seemed in his opinion better suited to the composer's strengths. After describing this movement as "program music whose program had been withheld," he asks:

> Why this halfway-ness? Herr Dvořák should screw up the courage and, like his more ingenious fellow countryman Smetana, who died too early, write genuine, openly avowed "symphonic poems." [This is a] field in which he might win more and more long-lasting laurels than in that of the grand symphony, which his in and of itself highly creditable talent seems to us insufficient to realize with completely new and at the same time truly significant content.[22]

In his discussion of Dvořák's finale, Helm had both Smetana and national politics in mind. There he writes: "The characteristic interval succession of [the main] theme is also found in a passage from the famous *Rákóczy March*. Did the most talented living musical representative of Czechia [*Tschechovien*] hereby want to make a friendly neighborly call on Budapest?" The implication of Helm's reference to the symphony's composer, of course, is that the living Dvořák was not as talented as the late and lamented Smetana. The intent of Helm's reference to the *Rákóczy March*, revered as the Hungarian national anthem, is likewise clear, but his use of the name *Tschechovien* may be less so. As Helm would have known, within radical German-nationalist discourse this was the name used to identify what would be the Czech territory, separate from *Deutschösterreich* (and not including the German-speaking regions of Bohemia), if the monarchy were ever to be divided along national lines.[23]

---

[22] Theodor Helm, "Concerte," *Deutsche Zeitung*, January 9, 1891, from which the next quotation is also taken. The reference to Smetana as a "more ingenious" (*genialer*) composer is pointed, since, as we have seen, *genial* is one of Hanslick's favorite descriptors of Dvořák.

[23] This same term had been used among Czech nationalists as early as 1848, when František Palacký proposed a federalist division of the empire according to language groups that would include, among others *Deutschösterreich* and *Tschechovien*. See "Deutsch-böhmische Briefe," *Grenzboten* 47/2 (1887): 303. Nowadays "Česko"

As we might expect, Hanslick's evaluation steered clear of this kind of political rhetoric. Rather, in his review of the Eighth Symphony we encounter themes that we have come to know from their appearance in his earlier discussion of the Sixth and Seventh Symphonies. Although these undoubtedly betray a sense of a cultural superiority also seen before, they nevertheless embody genuine admiration:

> Dvořák is a serious artist who has learned much and yet has not for all his learning lost his innocence and freshness. An original personality speaks from his works, and from this personality blows the refreshing breath of the inexhaustible and spontaneous. Here [the works] spring up with abundance, there less so, here higher, there lower, but spring up and develop do they all. And this natural, blooming growth is what in our time of prevailing reflection wins us quickly and holds us willingly.[24]

Yet even Hanslick went so far in this instance as to make an unflattering nod toward the composer's Czechness: "Instead of ending [the third movement with the repetition of the scherzo] the composer tumbles head over heels—"Der Wenzel kommt!"—into an uncouth, polka-like village dance. Dvořák would have done well to suppress this superfluous coda, which is more Bohemian than beautiful."[25]

By referring in this way to the title of a well known folk song of the type commonly used at the time to denigrate Vienna's poor Czech

(Czechia) is sometimes used informally for what is formally known as the "Česká republica" (Czech Republic).

[24] Ed. H. [Eduard Hanslick], "Concerte," *Neue Freie Presse*, January 6, 1891; reprinted in idem, *Aus dem Tagebuche eines Musikers*, 340–41. My translation of the final sentence of this excerpt is taken from Notley, *Lateness and Brahms*, 33.

[25] Hanslick, *Aus dem Tagebuch eines Musikers*, 341. This ending clearly did not fall in line with Hanslick's assessment from only six weeks earlier of the composer's new Piano Quintet, op. 81, introduced by the Hellmesberger Quartet on November 13, 1890: "[Dvořák] has long since divorced himself from the wild passion and sudden glaring contrasts of his Slavonic Rhapsodies, as well as from the exaggerated foregrounding of the Slavic character." After noting the quintet's "truly international style," the critic continued: "Dvořák's compositions are unquestionably more universally understandable and affective than those of his Russian and Norwegian colleagues. . . . The German School, of which they all are products, he denies the least. . . . Beethoven, Schubert, Brahms are his only models." Ed. H. [Eduard Hanslick], "Concerte," *Neue Freie Presse*, November 18, 1890, rpt. as "Neue Quintette von Brahms und Dvořák (1890)," in *Aus dem Tagebuch eines Musikers*, 316–20 (at 319).

immigrants—Wenzel is a diminutive of Wenceslaus, the German name of Bohemia's patron saint and, in its Czech form (Václav), a common given name among Czechs—Hanslick is guilty of stereotyping, more along class than ethnic lines, that seems especially jarring in the context of what was an overwhelmingly favorable review.[26]

True to form, Helm seized on this opportunity as a point of departure for his slightly later critique of the work for the *Musikalisches Wochenblatt*, this time clearly slighting Dvořák and Hanslick at one fell swoop. While acknowledging that Dvořák's "addiction to Slavic national composition...affects certain passages not at all unpleasantly," he quickly adds that

> elsewhere (above all in the trivial polka-like conclusion of the third movement and perhaps also in much of the finale) [it does so] all the more disgustingly....If only the trivial ending [of the third movement] weren't there! Even the critic of the "Neue Fr[eie] Presse," who is fanatically taken by Dvořák, has to concede that this ending sounds more Bohemian than beautiful.[27]

Yet then comes the coup de grâce. Tacitly directing his attention to Hanslick's Prague origins, Helm observed that this critic "has only words of praise for the bawdiness of the finale, which he hears and enjoys as perhaps only a native Bohemian can: Chacun à son goût." This last line not only casts doubt on the inherent sensibilities of an entire non-German people, but also calls Hanslick's own German credentials into question.

Helm's jab, however, pales in comparison to the over-the-top rhetoric seen in Camillo Horn's review for the *Ostdeutsche Rundschau*, published under the title "How You Write 'Criticism'." Whereas *Peer Gynt*—a Nordic work through and through—comes in for high praise, the Eighth Symphony earns only condemnation:

> Everyone who attended the last Philharmonic concert, in which Grieg's uncommonly absorbing, singular music to "Peer Gynt" was performed,...will with great joy recall the noble work, performed with such distinction, perhaps regretting at the same time not having immediately left the concert hall with this delightful feeling. To be sure, Herr Beckmesser-Hanslick does not hold to this view— although in other instances he loves to flee the concert hall before

[26] On "Der Wenzel kommt!" and other such derogatory folk songs, see Reittererová and Reitterer, *Vier Dutzend rothe Strümpfe*, 289n.

[27] *Musikalisches Wochenblatt* 22 (1891): 47, from which the next quotation is also taken.

the last number, and yet reports nevertheless on the same—for there was to be performed a work by his darling Dvořák (say, if you are able, Dworschak). No doubt this time the Hofrat must have "gorged" rather heartily beforehand in order to be able to remain at the concert so long. . . . To every impartial person . . . it is clear Grieg was the hero of the day. . . . But the Hofrat is not, indeed cannot be, of such an opinion, since he is not to be numbered among the impartial.[28]

Horn continues at this point with a gloss on Hanslick's review of the same performance (a portion of which was quoted earlier), interweaving passages adapted from that account with his own sarcastic commentary. To illustrate the references, here I provide Hanslick's text and Horn's parody in columns (emphasis added in both):

Hanslick	Horn
Placed, as the final number, in the most dangerous position, it has triumphed nonetheless with the most genuine means.	"*Placed, as the final number, in the most dangerous position,*—(this place of honor belongs otherwise to the best number)—"*it has nonetheless triumphed with the most genuine (!) means.*" Well, that is what I call in unadulterated fashion—Jewish, a work rejected by the public, therefore to be "rooted out." "*The work unmistakably Dvořák from beginning to end*" (unfortunately! Even the French, badly versed in geography, would have guessed his homeland, Tschechovien); further: "*It (the symphony) sounds clearer, more popular*"— perhaps too popular;———"*which results in a richness of ideas*" (unfortunately of the paltry kind!)———
The work, unmistakably Dvořák from beginning to end, can be distinguished in a fundamental way from his first two symphonies, [which are] already known in Vienna.	
It sounds friendlier, clearer, more popular than the first, pathetic [one] in D major, and the second, wildly romantic [one] in D minor. . . . Dvořák loves to work with many motives, *which results in a richness of ideas* but	

---

[28] C[amillo] H[orn], "Wie man 'Kritiken' macht," *Ostdeutsche Rundschau*, January 17, 1891. The reference near the end of this passage is to Hanslick's practice of making early departures from performances of Bruckner's symphonies, presumably in order to dine at his usual hour.

frequently also a characteristic unrest in his pieces. The first as well as the second movement of his new symphony flows in a path without any change in meter or tempo, *yet through the succession of diverse moods has about it something of the rhapsodic.* . . . Dvořák is a serious artist who has learned much and yet has not for all his learning lost his innocence and freshness. An original personality speaks from his works, and from this personality blows the refreshing breath of the unspent and spontaneous. Here [the works] spring up with abundance, there less so, here higher, there lower, but spring up and develop do they all. *And this natural, blooming growth is what, in our time of prevailing reflection, wins us quickly and holds us willingly.*

"yet through the succession of diverse moods has about it something of the rhapsodic." Something?! Good Lord, how mildly you judge!

Many points of Hanslick's review, which as always surrounds itself with the halo of impartiality, remain to be disputed but I will mention only the final sentence: *"And this natural, blooming growth (!) is what in our time of prevailing reflection"* (Herr Hanslick's racial comrades may thank him) *"wins us quickly and holds us willingly."* And what does Herr Brahms, the "embodied reflection," say to that?[29]

Having finished with parody, Horn takes wider aim at Hanslick as a "foreign" representative of the despised supranational monarchy and its traditional liberal nationalist elite:

As in everything else so also unfortunately in the essence of art do we see the striving of the state and of the Germans, or, to put it better, of those who want to be numbered among them, to rear the Slavs and

---

[29] Notley, *Lateness and Brahms*, 33, considers this review in the context of discussing the radical German nationalists' targeting of Hanslick as a Jew and linking of Brahms to the Jews as well. As it happens, we know what Brahms thought about his friend's new symphony. In a conversation with Richard Heuberger of January 6, 1891, he said: "Too much that's fragmentary, incidental, loiters about in the piece. Everything fine, musically captivating and beautiful—but no main points! Especially in the first movement, the result is not proper. But a charming musician! When one says of Dvořák that he fails to achieve anything great and comprehensive with his pure, individual ideas, this is correct. Not so with Bruckner, all the same he offers so little!" Heuberger, *Erinnerungen an Johannes Brahms*, 47; transl. in Beveridge, "Dvořák and Brahms," 82.

Jews to the detriment of their own people. Thus...Dvořák received a State Stipend long before Bruckner; but what is Dvořák next to a Bruckner?

What we find here is something very different from what Speidel had in mind in 1871, when he invoked "the God in the German camp" whose mission it was to spread "civilization and *Bildung* to the *Ostmark*." Such a liberal nationalist mission clearly was not a concern with which Horn had any sympathy. Indeed, it is fair to assume that Horn's conception of the *Ostmark* would have aligned with that Schönerer, in whose *deutschnational* rhetoric it was used instead as a synonym for "German" Austria in the racial sense.[30] In true Wagnerian fashion, Horn, a German Bohemian who had studied at the Prague Conservatory, treats Hanslick not as a fellow German but as one "who wanted to be numbered among them" (that is, as an acculturated Jew). And this "imposter," of course, not only had sat on the state commission that awarded the Slavic composer several stipends in the 1870s, but was also largely responsible for impeding Bruckner's fortunes.[31] To a *völkisch* nationalist like Horn, then, the critic of the *Neue Freie Presse* was an almost irresistible target—as both a Jew and a powerful representative of the hated liberal elite, and as both an opponent of an unjustly neglected German composer and a champion of an unworthy Slavic one.

Just how "unworthy" becomes clear, finally, in the essay's concluding lines, in which, by likening Dvořák to Meyerbeer, Horn in effect condemns him as a Jew:

> Dvořák, who...might appropriately be called the Bohemian Meyerbeer, is only original where he is Slavic; but where he is Slavic he is for the most part vulgar. Moreover, his most recent, though fortunately still unpublished work is extremely boring and dry; we were sorry for the Philharmonic players, capable as they are of playing Grieg so beautifully, for being "condemned" thereafter "to the torments of Hell." Indeed, if [only] our artists were national, then that and much else would be better. Will this ever happen? We can only hope!

[30] On this Schönererian redefinition of *Ostmark* along racial lines, see Haider, *Im Streit um die österreichische Nation*, 101–3. During the period from 1938 to 1945, *Ostmark* was the Nazis' preferred term for the land of the former First Austrian Republic.

[31] Given Hanslick's prominence, no one could have doubted the identity of the subject of a report appearing in the *Deutsche Kunst- und Musikzeitung*: "It is an open secret in Vienna that because of a certain someone [*vor einem Jemand*] the Philharmonic players are afraid to cultivate Bruckner's compositions on their programs" (*Deutsche Kunst- und Musikzeitung* 4, 1888: 34).

Although they had hitherto been largely distinct issues, here for the first time the Jewish and Czech questions have become conflated in the rhetoric of radical German nationalism. By the end of the century, in the maelstrom that was Vienna 1897, this conflation would become the rule in the work of the *deutschnational* critics. But for another few years Smetana would continue to be spared attack from this flank in a way that Goldmark and Dvořák were not. The reasons for this anomalous treatment, already touched on in Puchstein's review of *Vltava*, may be found in the extensive coverage given to the first Viennese performances of Smetana's operas, the subject to which we now turn.

Czech Opera in Vienna

On the afternoon of May 31, 1892, a special chartered train pulled into Vienna's Franz Josef Station after making the six-hour journey from Prague. On board were the operatic personnel of the Czech Landes- und Nationaltheater, who had come to the imperial capital in order to per-form in the city's Internationale Ausstellung für Musik- und Theaterwesen (International Exhibition of Music and Theater), held in the Prater from May 7 to October 9, 1892. The Czechs, who were scheduled to appear dur-ing the first week of June, had announced an ambitious program centered on five operas by native composers: Bedřich Smetana's *Prodaná nevěsta* (*The Bartered Bride*) and *Dalibor*, Antonín Dvořák's *Dimitrij*, Karel Benda's *Lejla*, and Karel Šebor's *Nevěsta husitská* (*The Hussite Bride*). Rounding out the bill were Zdeněk Fibich's melodrama *Námluvy Pelopovy* (*The Courtship of Pelops*) and two spoken plays, including one by František Adolf Šubert, the National Theater's general director.[32]

---

[32] The most detailed source on the Czech National Theater's guest residency remains Fr[antišek] Ad[olf] Šubert, *Das Böhmische National-Theater in der ersten internation-alen Musik- und Theater-Ausstellung zu Wien im Jahre 1892* (Prague: Im Verlage des Nationaltheater-Consortiums, 1892); my description of events in this and the following paragraph is based on that account (pp. 8–14). The guest residency is discussed briefly in Reittererová and Reitterer, *Vier Dutzend rothe Strümpfe*, 54–63; Martina Nußbaumer, "Identity on Display: (Re-)Präsentationen des Eigenen und des Fremden auf der Internationalen Ausstellung für Musik- und Theaterwesen in Wien 1892," *Historische Anthropologie. Kultur, Gesellschaft, Alltag* 13 (2005): 52–55; idem, *Musikstadt Wien: Die Konstruktion eines Images* (Freiburg i. Br., Berlin, and Vienna: Rombach Verlag, 2007), 339–41; Oscar Teuber, "Das Ausstellungs-Theater und seine Thaten," in *Die inter-nationale Ausstellung für Musik- und Theaterwesen Wien 1892*, ed. Siegmund Schneider (Vienna: Perles, 1894), 305–9; and Oskar Fleischer, *Die Bedeutung der internationalen*

Šubert had been shuttling between Prague and Vienna over the previous few weeks attending to all the final preparations, and he now stood on the station platform awaiting the arrival of his company. There he was joined by Franz von Jauner, co-director of the Theater an der Wien and artistic director of the Exhibition Theater, as well as by a delegation of Czech representatives to the Reichsrat and the leaders of several Czech voluntary organizations in Vienna, all of whom had turned out to greet their Bohemian compatriots, some 270 persons altogether, including soloists, choir, orchestra, ballet, administrative personnel, and technical staff. The festivities continued the following morning, when the group assembled in the Exhibition Theater for a well-attended public rehearsal for that evening's sold-out, opening night performance of *Prodaná nevěsta*. After thanking the Exhibition Commission for its invitation, Šubert called upon Jauner to speak. Knowing Šubert was skeptical about the prospects for a favorable reception in Vienna, Jauner began by acknowledging his own admiration for the Czechs' work and then added his assurances that they would be greeted in Vienna with the same sympathy with which so many Viennese artists had been greeted in Prague in the past.[33] In response, Šubert invited his troupe—first in Czech, then in German—to hail the Exhibition Commission with a three-fold "Sláva!" (Hurrah!), whereupon he turned to his players once more and exclaimed:

> We are received by all sides in Vienna in a friendly, even cordial manner, which will certainly be an incentive to you to take up your task with joyous courage. Let us make a toast to the success of the great undertaking, which gives us the opportunity to display our national dramatic and musical products for the first time outside Prague![34]

The National Theater's appearance in Vienna, then, was a political act, and it invited a politicized response. On the one hand, performance on an international stage of compelling Czech-language theatrical works symbolized the emergence of the Czechs as a modern nation of European standard. Prague now looked not toward Vienna in a state of cultural subservience but toward Berlin and Paris

Musik- und Theater-Ausstellung in Wien für Kunst und Wissenschaft der Musik (Leipzig and New York: Internationales Verlags- und Kunstanstalt, 1894), 65–66.

[33] Šubert's doubts are reported in Guido Adler, *Wollen und Wirken. Aus dem Leben eines Musikhistorikers* (Vienna: Universal-Edition, 1935), 64. Adler was in charge of the music-historical division of the exhibition but also played a role in administering the artistic productions in the Exhibition Theater and Concert Hall.

[34] Šubert is quoted in "Die Musik- und Theater-Ausstellung," *Neue Freie Presse, Abendblatt*, June 1, 1892.

as cultural equals.[35] On the other hand, in Vienna, capital of the multinational Habsburg state, this public display of cultural independence by one of the monarchy's Slavic nationalities could only be viewed against the background of traditional assumptions of German cultural superiority.

The cultural politics that were embedded in the Czech National Theater's Viennese performances, of course, formed but a part of the broader political battleground involving ongoing tensions between the monarchy's German and Czech nationalities, tensions that were coming to a new head at that very moment, with the Bohemian Compromise on the verge of complete collapse. The *Neue Freie Presse*, the voice of Austria's traditional liberal establishment, spoke unmistakably to those tensions—and to the potential for the International Exhibition to help to ameliorate them—in its lead article for May 8, 1892, written to mark the exhibition's opening:

> For us Austrians, the word "international" has a more comprehensive meaning than for all others; for us it does not merely bind nation to nation but also nationality to nationality. Since we are not a nation, and our empire itself is made up of a collection of nationalities, every project that helps to overcome the separatist impulse of the peoples and unite them in pursuit of a common goal brings a double blessing: it unites us with the other nations and unites us with ourselves. The more deeply and painfully we feel every day how very much the latter above all is necessary for us, the more we must appreciate that the Viennese Exhibition of Music and Theater is also an international undertaking in this sense, one that creates contacts in the realm of art between peoples within our own state who often turn their backs on one another in a hostile and confrontational manner. In one respect at least they are brought closer together, an experience that will perhaps have a positive effect on many other areas of interaction.[36]

This might have seemed a naïve hope. Only a few months earlier, as we have seen, the Vienna Philharmonic's performance of Dvořák's *Hussite* Overture had sparked a minor contretemps along national lines. Yet nothing of the kind

[35] It was only fitting, therefore, that the Czechs' week in the Exhibition Theater was sandwiched between similar residencies by Berlin's Deutsches Theater and the Théâtre National de l'Odéon from Paris. See also Katherine David-Fox, "Prague–Vienna, Prague–Berlin: The Hidden Geography of Czech Modernism," *Slavic Review* 59 (2000): 735–60, and Christopher P. Storck, *Kulturnation und Nationalkunst. Strategien und Mechanismen tschechischer Nationsbildung von 1860 bis 1914* (Cologne: Wissenschaft und Politik, 2001).

[36] "Wien, 7. Mai," *Neue Freie Presse*, May 8, 1892.

seems to have occurred that June in the Exhibition Theater. Not surprisingly, Czechs and other Slavs were disproportionately represented in the audiences; prominent by their presence were the Czech and Polish members of the cabinet; large numbers of Reichsrat delegates from Bohemia, Moravia, Slovenia, and Croatia; members of the Bohemian and Moravian nobility and large land-owning classes; and representatives of Vienna's many Slavic voluntary associations, as well as, of course, members of the Czech press. Clearly, Slavic pride was in full display throughout the week. But, if only out of an initial curiosity, large numbers of bourgeois Germans attended the performances as well—and were no less won over by them. As Helm described matters this time: "Today the Czech Opera from Prague achieved complete *artistic* success. We stress the word "artistic," since the delightfully folk-like as well as finely developed work and its outstanding performance could not have failed in hospitable Vienna to have an effect even on a non-Slavic audience."[37]

In view of the Czechs' subaltern status within the Austro-Hungarian Monarchy—and nowhere was this status more evident than with respect to language and high culture—it comes as no surprise that many Viennese had read the National Theater's ambitious prospectus of works with some incredulity. Critic Max Dietz put it thus in his report for the *Allgemeine Kunst-Chronik*: "Czech opera! The thing is new and for our concertgoers hardly any less surprising than, say, an Indian flute concert."[38] Yet, as we learn from the continuation of this report, the public was quickly disabused of its preconceptions:

That the Czechs would sing German, Italian, French, even Russian operas in translation, one might have thought possible, but original works—that had to provoke curiosity. The musical talents of the Slavic-Bohemian people were already sufficiently known. The Czechs are valued everywhere as good musicians. They have not, however, been thought capable of creative achievements in the realm of art, least of all in opera. The vocal troupe of the deserving Director Šubert has set us straight.

This turnabout was owed in no small measure to the impression left by *Prodaná nevěsta* and *Dalibor*. In fact, the public response to both of Smetana's

[37] h—m [Theodor Helm], "Ausstellungs-Theater," *Deutsche Zeitung*, June 2, 1892 (emphasis in original).

[38] Max Dietz, "Die tschechische Oper," *Allgemeine Kunst-Chronik* 16 (1892): 309, from which the next quotation also is taken.

works was so favorable that the scheduled operas by Benda and Šebor were set aside to allow encore performances of each. And even those additions proved insufficient to meet the demand: in the end, the troupe stayed on for an extra day to give an unscheduled final performance of *Prodaná nevěsta*, thereby causing a one-day postponement of the opening performance by the Théâtre National de l'Odéon.[39]

Inevitably, the state of German-Czech relations figured prominently in the critical commentary, both musical and political, of the Czechs' residency in Vienna. Certainly none of this was lost on "D," the anonymous author of "Czechen in Wien," a political lead article that appeared on June 5, 1892, in the *Wiener Allgemeiner Zeitung*:

> In Vienna these days one speaks of nothing but the Czechs. But the species of the "Bohemian question" that is now the order of the day is highly welcomed. Herr Vašaty with his Russo-mania has nothing to do with it, nor Herr Grégr with his state-right theory, nor Herr Rieger with his liking for the Feudal Conservatives. Even the sea serpent of the Compromise, this red thread that moves through the history of Austria during the last twelve years, has not come to the surface.... Count Taaffe can put his reconciliation plans to bed. He has been trumped, indeed completely deposed by the Muses, who had the power to create in a single evening a mood that thoroughly destroyed many years' worth of artificially harbored, unadulterated bad blood and strife. One breathes again as it were, as though awakened from a nightmare. A brother has been won, for now in art, hopefully soon also in life.... The productions of the Czech Theater in the International Exhibition in the Prater are a deed, a great deed in the field of art that cannot remain without consequences in other areas.[40]

As the author continues, he follows a time-honored tradition by placing the blame for the current distrust and lack of amity between Austria's

---

[39] The final schedule of musical works was June 1, *The Bartered Bride*; June 2, *Dimitrij*; June 3, *The Atonement of Pelops*; June 4, *The Bartered Bride*; June 5, *Dalibor*; June 6, *The Bartered Bride* (in place of *Lejla*); June 7, *Dalibor* (in place of *The Hussite Bride*); June 8, *The Bartered Bride* (added date). All these were evening performances; the spoken dramas were given on the afternoons of June 5 and 6.

[40] Anonymous (signed "D."), "Czechen in Wien," *Wiener Allgemeine Zeitung*, June 5, 1892, from which several of the following quotations are also taken. A portion of this article is also cited (with the incorrect date of June 4, 1892) in Nußbaumer, "Identity on Display," 54; and idem, *Musikstadt Wien*, 339–40.

German and Czech peoples on fear rooted in simple ignorance. He indicts those who "obtain their power and influence through national discord" by escalating conflicts and creating new ones where none exist, by setting one side against the other, while concealing from them both "the goodness and beauty that is entwined like a heavenly gleaming ribbon around all nations." Against this backdrop of contentiousness, the author introduces a "Bohemian question" that is rather more welcomed. "Then all of a sudden"—the reference here is to the recent opening night performance of *Prodaná nevěsta*—"a man or an event comes along, and the blind are given sight." He continues:

It is said to be a miracle. But the natural process of removing the binders from the eyes explains everything in the simplest way. In the presumed enemy is seen a brother... a comrade in ability and achievement. We are astonished to have known nothing for so long of the existence of an art that aligns itself in the most worthy manner alongside the art of the great civilized nations [*Culturvölker*].

Therefore we are sincerely pleased by the triumph the Czech nation celebrates in the realm of its art. This people, the most competent, industrious, canny, and economically progressive in Austria after the Germans, has now shown itself the absolute equal to the Germans. What these two peoples could achieve for the unity of the whole, if they peacefully granted one another a respite in service of the national commonwealth!

At first blush, this appears to be a call for what nowadays would be described as multiculturalism. Yet the well-defined cultural hierarchy that had always been part and parcel of liberal ideology lies scarcely hidden beneath the surface:

Tempered with Hussite tradition, Czechdom is saturated in its historical development with free-thinking ideas, such as pervade the German bourgeoisie, and only the unceasingly stoked animosity and quarrel from time to time estranges it to some extent from liberal and progressive views and robs it of the power to shake off the reaction that clings to its coattails. That the Czechs are now excelling so greatly in the realm of art places them once more completely in the rank of the civilized nations, for cultivation [*Bildung*] that results from unbiased thinking and art that strives toward the highest are the best means of protection against backsliding into obsolete and outdated doctrines. We hereby bend down in honor of the Czech artistic achievements, which signify a gain for the culture of all humankind, and commend the merits in ability that have allowed the Czechs to experience such a triumph in Vienna.

The anonymous author applauds the Czechs for successfully transcending the reactionary forces of feudal conservatism (with its clericalism and obsolete doctrines) and choosing to acculturate to progressive German liberalism (with its free-thinking ideas and aspirations to high art). Here, in other words, the old German liberal imperative has evidently been realized.

This political commentator was no music or theater critic, however, and he does not explain why *Prodaná nevěsta* warranted the place he accords it alongside the artistic products of the "civilized nations." More than one critic found that explanation in Mozart. For example, Oscar Teuber, writing in the *Fremden-Blatt*, cites Prague's historic importance as a "Mozart city" and then argues that the composer had, long after his death, remained a living inspiration among Bohemian musicians, whether they identified as German or Czech. While Teuber conceded that *Prodaná nevěsta* was "filled with the fresh, original life of a young people, deeply rooted in the folk character, national through and through," he attributes the work's "consummate artistic countenance...to the powerful, instructive influence of the Mozart tradition, the beneficent fusion of the Slavic and German spirits, the happy fertilization of the Slavic *through* German art" (emphasis added). It is no wonder, then, that earlier in the same review Teuber had borrowed from contemporary political discourse by pointedly describing the night of the first performance as an "Ausgleichs-Abend," an evening of compromise, in which "the hostile brothers [were brought together] peacefully in the domain of music."[41]

Albert Kauders, the music critic of the *Wiener Allgemeine Zeitung*, takes this line of reasoning even further.[42] He acknowledges that the Czechs celebrate Smetana as the founder of their national music and recognizes that Smetana's operas are "intrinsically Czech-national" on account of their Czech texts, their stories based in Czech history, and their portrayal of "a certain local coloring in tone and rhythms." But, for Kauders, these features do little to explain the works' deeper importance. "In its innermost basic character,"

---

[41] Oscar Teuber, "Zwei czechische Opern im Austellungs-Theater," *Fremden-Blatt*, June 4, 1892.

[42] K. Anders [Albert Kauders], "Die böhmische Oper in Wien," *Wiener Allgemeine Zeitung*, June 3, 1892, from which the following quotation is taken. Nußbaumer, "Identity on Display," 54, erroneously cites the source of this review as the *Wiener Zeitung*; she gives the correct source in *Musikstadt Wien*, 341.

he writes, "[Smetana's] music is nevertheless—German; and even the most exaggerated national vanity will probably not be offended by this word, if it is added that I count among German art everything that confesses the Gospel of Bach, Mozart, and Beethoven and emulates their sublime teaching in deed and work." Moreover, Kauders suggests that Smetana was a German composer before he ever became a Czech one, in that "Smetana's talent suckled at the breasts of German art and, imbued with German artistic spirit, he went on to give national coloring to the products of his invention." Finally, to those who would argue for a pan-Slavic musical sensibility, he counters by writing that "Russian music is the child of a completely different spirit from [the mother of] Smetana's art. These heterogeneous productions cannot be brought under the same roof unless by force. German spirit and rancid Russian liquor! The highly subtle artist Smetana knew on which side he had to acquit himself." This is not Smetana speaking, of course, but Kauders, a Germanized Jew from Bohemia who is presumptuous enough to speak here on the late composer's behalf. But in these last lines the critic does seem to have got things at least half right: Smetana may not have been the acculturated German liberal whom Kauders describes, but neither was he a *Slavonic* composer. What gets lost here, of course, is the composer's own decided identity as a specifically *Czech* nationalist.

The importance of that identity, by contrast, was not lost on the critics who wrote for Vienna's German-nationalist newspapers. For these men, as noted above, Smetana appealed both as a model for German composers to follow in developing an explicitly German-national consciousness and because his music was steeped in the aesthetic principles of the New Germans. The latter consideration was foremost in Helm's mind. In a brief notice that appeared in the *Deutsche Zeitung* on June 2, the critic stressed the appeal of *Prodaná nevěsta* to Slavic and non-Slavic audiences alike.[43] Then in a feuilleton that appeared two days later, he built on this notion by adopting a now familiar strategy of explicitly linking Smetana to the German tradition (which he clearly associates with the "fine workmanship" to which he had alluded in his previous notice). He observed how the composer has developed the music of *Prodaná nevěsta* "from the spirit of Czech folk song," but with "pure artistic taste" and a "well-practiced, secure hand." And he marveled at the "characteristic and interesting treatment of the orchestra" and sonorous blending of the

[43] Helm, in *Deutsche Zeitung*, June 2, 1892. By contrast, as we have seen Helm frequently criticized Dvořák's music for what he described as its limited appeal, restricted to those who listened with a "Slavic-nationalist ear."

voices. "In this way," he continued: "the composer—although a Slav through and through—does not stand opposite to German music, rather one notices quite clearly that he made his studies among its Classical masters: among Mozart and Beethoven, Mendelssohn and Schumann, the charming Lortzing and the great Richard Wagner."[44] Yet it is only Wagner who warrants any further comparison, as Helm takes note of certain thematic reminiscences as well as what he calls Smetana's "spiritual kinship" with Wagner, whereby the Czech composer consciously adopts the German master's technique of thematic reminiscence.

But what appeals to the German-nationalist critics, again, are not only Smetana's progressive (i.e., New German) musical credentials but also his national consciousness. Thus the *Deutsches Volksblatt* pointed to *Prodaná nevěsta*—indeed, to the Czech National Theater's entire project—as something worthy of emulation at home. Reviewing the Czechs' opening night performance at the Exhibition Theater, this newspaper's unnamed critic reported that

> One *consistently* saw Aryans on the stage, a rare sight for our eyes. The entire production had about it something fresh, unjaded. Oh, if only the Germans of our *Ostmark* were capable of such fresh national enthusiasm. We left the [Exhibition] Theater ashamed that we are not in a position to achieve for ourselves a truly national popular theater [*Volksbühne*] that is equally free of Jewish influence.[45]

Obviously, we are at a great remove here from the liberal-nationalist rhetoric of a Kauders or a Teuber, with its assumption of Smetana's acculturation to German norms. To the anonymous author of these last-quoted lines, by contrast, the importance of Smetana's work lay precisely in its insistence on its own Czechness.

---

[44] Theodor Helm, "Tschechische Oper," *Deutsche Zeitung*, June 4, 1892.

[45] "Die erste Vorstellung des tschechischen Nationaltheaters," *Deutsches Volksblatt, Abend-Ausgabe*, June 2, 1892 (emphasis in original). See also the anonymous feuilleton "Das königlich böhmische Landes- und Nationaltheater in Prag," *Deutsches Volksblatt*, June 2, 1892: "We cannot conclude without mentioning once again the strong national consciousness shown by those in charge of the Czech National Theater. If a critic in Vienna challenges a theater that, at least according to its name, presents itself as a theater for the German people to promote French dramas of adultery a little less and instead to cultivate the German classics and popular dialect drama, then he runs the danger of being mocked."

Thus in Vienna, in the summer of 1892, *Prodaná nevěsta* was all things to all people. As the composer himself would have wished, it was a source of national pride for his fellow Czechs. But for traditional liberal nationalists the opera could be seen as a cultural product of an enduring supranational Austrian state in which German—and German music—remained the lingua franca. And for the city's *deutschnational* critics the work represented nothing less than a salutary model of national consciousness, an example of what might be accomplished by properly "German" composers in *Deutschösterreich*.[46] Each of these groups would soon be heard from again: within a year, Smetana's opera would be staged once more in Vienna—although this time under very different circumstances.

Czech Music Everywhere

Sparked by the National Theater's performances in the Prater, Viennese interest in Czech music soon reached an all-time high. In its 1892–93 subscription season, for example, the Vienna Philharmonic included performances of both Fibich's programmatic concert overture *Noc na Karlštejně* (*A Night at Karlstein Castle*), heard on November 20, 1892, and Smetana's symphonic poem *Z českých luhů a hájů* (*From Bohemia's Woods and Fields*), which followed on January 29, 1893. Meanwhile, the Bohemian String Quartet had conquered the city on January 19, 1893, in an all-Czech debut concert that featured Smetana's *From My Life* Quartet. Public enthusiasm for the visitors from Prague was such that three additional performances had to be scheduled: on January 24 (another all-Czech concert, in which the *From My Life* Quartet shared the bill with Dvořák's String Quartet in E, B57), and on February 10 and 27 (with additional performances of works by Smetana and Dvořák).[47]

---

[46] Sandra McColl has noted a similar situation with regard to Bruckner, who, depending upon the writer's ideology, could be seen in contemporary music-critical discourse as an Austrian, a German, a Catholic, or even a proletarian; see McColl, *Music Criticism in Vienna 1896–1897*, 88.

[47] The quartet's name—Böhmisches Streichquartett—can be translated as either Bohemian String Quartet or Czech String Quartet. The popularity of this ensemble in Vienna grew over several years following this, to the extent that it soon eclipsed that of the local Hellmesberger and Rosé quartets. See Elizabeth Way Sullivan, "German Nationalism and the Reception of the Czech String Quartet in Vienna," in *Nineteenth-Century Music. Selected Proceedings of the Tenth International Conference*, ed. Jim Samson

This flurry of activity in the Viennese mainstream led an unnamed critic for the *Ostdeutsche Rundschau*—here sounding very much like the anonymous critic for the *Deutsches Volksblatt* from the previous year—to couple praise for Smetana with a bitter complaint about the willingness of his fellow Viennese to countenance an egregious infringement of *Nationalbesitzstand*:

> The concerts announced on the advertising pillars would have us believe that we are in Moscow, Paris, Prague, or anywhere but a German city of music. The admiration and enthusiasm with which the Czechs stand up for Smetana as their only truly important composer should be for us Germans an example worth heeding. It is really shameful that the only true artistic successes in the Exhibition Theater were the performances by the Czech National Theater. Our Court Opera has not produced a staging of such consummate artistry as that of *The Bartered Bride* for many, many years.[48]

Šubert, in fact, had already sought to exploit the interest shown in Czech opera the previous summer by requesting permission to stage a series of guest performances in the Vienna Court Opera. The director, Wilhelm Jahn, held out against the idea of opening up his stage to any of the monarchy's national theaters, but he did at least now begin to consider introducing some of Smetana's operas himself.[49] When negotiations for an immediate German-language performance of *The Bartered Bride* at the Court Opera fell through, the work was acquired by the Theater an der Wien, the city's leading venue for operettas, where a long and successful run in Max Kalbeck's German translation opened on April 2, 1893.[50]

As with *Prodaná nevěsta* in the Exhibition Theater, so now with *Die verkaufte Braut* in the Theater an der Wien, the critical response was overwhelmingly enthusiastic.[51] Helm renewed his praise of "the innumerable

---

and Bennett Zon (Aldershot, Hants, England, and Burlington, VT: Ashgate, 2002), 296–313.

[48] Anonymous (signed "M."), *Ostdeutsche Rundschau*, January 29, 1893.

[49] In a memorandum to the management of the Court Theaters dated December 8, 1892 (quoted in Reittererová and Reitterer, *Vier Dutzend rothe Strümpfe*, 164), Jahn noted: "This request to allow the Czech National Opera residency at the Court Opera would certainly not be a one-off, since the Hungarian and Polish National Operas would surely follow suit."

[50] Reittererová and Reitterer, *Vier Dutzend rothe Strümpfe*, 66–72.

[51] Reittererová and Reitterer provide transcriptions of fifty-four reviews or other notices, but without offering any critical commentary; see ibid., 227–92 (from which I have quoted several reviews below).

beauties of the work, whose music unites the naïve freshness of the folklike-ness [*Volksthümlichkeit*] with true art."[52] Richard Heuberger, in an obvious allusion to Taaffe's still-unratified Bohemian Compromise, noted the work gave "proof that true art is not bound by national borders, and under its victorious banner brings together 'to unity and heartfelt community' all spir-its who are warmly sentient to good and beauty without compromise and demarcation of separate regions."[53] The phrase "unity and heartfelt commu-nity" (*Eintracht und herzinnigem Vereine*) is a quotation from Schiller's famous poem "Das Lied von der Glocke" (The Song of the Bell), a text widely under-stood as a symbol of German national unity. The poem's first line, "Concordia shall be its name" (*Concordia soll ihr Name sein*), carries a double meaning in Heuberger's review: the opening performance of *Die verkaufte Braut* was designed as a benefit for *Concordia*, the Viennese society of journalists and writers, whose very name in this context was suggestive of reconciliation between the nationalities.[54] In the same spirit, other critics used the occa-sion to chide Jahn for programming contemporary works by non-Austrian composers such Mascagni and Massenet at the Court Opera when a work by so fine an "Austrian" (*oesterreichisch*) or "patriotic" (*vaterländisch*) composer as Smetana might easily be staged instead.[55] And Albert Kauders picked up from where he had left off the previous year by enthusing that "Smetana's music speaks the commonly understood language of beauty and feeling so unequivocally that it overwhelms every heart whether sung in Czech or German or Botucano."[56]

For Kauders, the German-language production was all the more signifi-cant in that it refuted "all those honorable and dishonorable naysayers" who

---

[52] Theodor Helm, "Theater, Kunst und Literatur," *Deutsche Zeitung*, April 4, 1893.

[53] R. Hr. {Richard Heuberger], "Die verkaufte Braut," *Wiener Tagblatt*, April 4, 1893.

[54] The significance of Heuberger's quotation of Schiller is noted in Reitterová and Reitterer, *Vier Dutzend rothe Strümpfe*, 239n. On Concordia, see Peter Eppel, *"Concordia soll ihr Name sein..." 125 Jahre Journalisten- und Schriftstellerverein "Concordia": Eine Dokumentation zur Presse- und Zeitgeschichte Österreichs* (Vienna, Cologne, and Graz: Böhlau, 2004).

[55] These descriptions are taken, respectively, from reviews by Robert Hirschfeld, "'Die verkaufte Braut' von Fr. Smetana (Erste Aufführung in deutscher Sprache)," *Die Presse*, April 5, 1893; and –n [Albert von Hermann], "Die verkaufte Braut von Ferdinand Smetana," *Das Vaterland*, April 6, 1893. See also the report in the *Illustrirtes Wiener Extrablatt*, April 8, 1893.

[56] k.a. [Albert Kauders], "Theater an der Wien," *Wiener Allgemeine Zeitung*, April 4, 1893. Kauders makes his point by including here, together with Czech and German, an indigenous language from the Brazilian Amazon.

had doubted whether the work could survive the loss of the "national-popular dialect" of the Czech original. Indeed, Kauders praises Kalbeck—here traditional assumptions about German cultural superiority are transparent—for having elevated Karel Sabina's original libretto to "a higher level," in part by producing new verse in place of "endless text repetitions." The critic acknowledges that Kalbeck, because he did not know Czech, had been unable to reproduce the "hearty, popular" qualities of Sabina's text, but he quickly adds that "the original earthy smell is missed…only by meticulous cognoscenti of the work," and argues that an unbiased, unschooled listener will enjoy it thoroughly.[57]

The ideology of traditional German liberal nationalism is evident to an even greater degree in Eduard Hanslick's review for the *Neue Freie Presse*. Hanslick had been conspicuous by his silence during the previous summer's residency by the Czech National Theater—Albert von Hermann had provided coverage for the *Neue Freie Presse* in his place—but he now weighed in at length. Hanslick had recently written favorably about Smetana in reviews of the Vienna Philharmonic's performances of the *Overture to The Bartered Bride* and of two movements from the orchestral cycle *Má vlast*, and now, in words similar to those employed there, he hails *Die verkaufte Braut* as a model of good taste in comic opera: "Always natural, folksy and melodious, it never becomes vulgar or common, a highly unusual occurrence in this field."[58]

At the same time, however, Hanslick devotes a good part of his review to the twin projects of cautioning others not to be too easily seduced by the opera's exoticism and convincing them of the necessity of judging the work according to the "neutral" standards of the German (and Italian) styles:

> The value of this opera is unquestionable; under the impression of that charming Czech performance in the Prater it may even have become somewhat overvalued. "Mozart's 'Figaro' transformed into Czech!" it was said at the time at every turn. [Smetana's] "Bartered Bride" is far from being worthy of Mozart; but it is very Mozartean. Out of the Czech national soil there bloom here and there in Smetana's opera

---

[57] Idem, "Theater an der Wien," *Wiener Allgemeine Zeitung*, April 5, 1893. For an extended discussion of Kalbeck's adaptation, see Reittererová and Reitterer, *Vier Dutzend rothe Strümpfe*, 114–39.

[58] Ed. H. [Eduard Hanslick], "Oper und Ballet," *Neue Freie Presse*, April 5, 1893 (from which the next several quotations are taken); reprinted in Hanslick, *Fünf Jahre Musik*, 80–84.

little Italian flowers and German ones too, such as those native to Schubert's, Weber's and Lortzing's gardens. And that is a good thing for the opera. Were it so utterly Czech that it had no international connections whatever, it could never exert a powerful effect on German soil, as it is now doing in Vienna.

In Hanslick's view, Smetana stood up to this test in that, as an inheritor of Prague's Mozart tradition, he had been trained as a German musician, which enabled him to cast his national originality in strict, pure form. Nevertheless—perhaps still smarting over earlier comparisons with *Figaro*, and despite the composer's "favorable" pedigree—Hanslick found the opera to some degree wanting: "In particular, the power and fullness of the musical invention do not seem all that astonishing to me; one must test it in the purely lyrical songs, not in the dances, in which national airs pulsate and seduce us through their exotic allure."

Having made these points, Hanslick gets down at last to assessing the work, and here he passes the same favorable judgment that characterizes his reception of Smetana's orchestral music:

> What favored an objective evaluation was the fact that it was staged in German, since it was free of the alluring charm of being foreign and of other extraordinary influences that affected minds at the time of the Exhibition. This music is consistently natural, modest, unaffected, lapses neither into the pathos of grand opera nor into the triviality of burlesque, never sacrifices the voice to the orchestra, nor the musical form in a one-sided way to dramatic pretensions. Anyone who has endured years of nothing but the breast-beating of overwrought dramatic effects and the pinpricks of "ingenious" refinements, will find the music of *Die verkaufte Braut* as refreshing as a cooling bath. It leads us from the fumes and torpidity into the blessed sweetness of fresh air.

For Hanslick, then, the opera's natural, modest, and unaffected style—unlike Helm, he found nothing Wagnerian here—offered a welcome antidote to the more labored, reflective manner of the day. Yet for all the stress he laid on the importance of assessing the work as sung in the "neutral" German language, the audience in attendance at that evening's performance, the third overall, encountered something altogether different. In the first two performances, the leading role of Marie had been sung by the Viennese soprano Toni Diglas, the understudy who had substituted for Lili Lejo when the latter fell ill following the dress rehearsal. But when Diglas herself became indisposed after the second performance, on April 3, the Theater hastily replaced *Die verkaufte Braut* on the following evening's bill with Carl Zeller's operetta *Der Vogelhändler* (*The Bird Seller*), while summoning the Prague soprano Anna Veselá from the Bohemian capital to step in for Diglas. Although Veselá had sung Marie to great acclaim in the Czech National Theater's performances at the Exhibition, she knew the part only in Czech (i.e., as Mařenka), and so for four evenings (April 5–7 and 9) Smetana's opera was given in curious bilingual performances.[59]

This extraordinary situation did not go unnoticed by the press, of course. On April 6 the liberal *Illustrirtes Wiener Extrablatt* began its report with a wry rhetorical question:

> What will the Young Czech Club say to that? A daughter of Libuše has joined German artists and come to the aid of a Viennese Theater. Trust such a thing to happen just as the Bohemian Diet is being opened! The Compromise has not yet come about and already alliances between Germans and Czechs are being formed in the domain of music.[60]

Not to be outdone, the cover of the humorous Viennese newspaper *Der Floh* carried the heading "Der Ausgleich nach Noten" (The Musical Compromise) over a cartoon showing Veselá and the tenor Georg Streitmann singing to one another before a bemused audience of well-dressed Bürger. Here we learn that: "*He* sings in German and *she* sings in Czech and yet they understand one another. Ah, thou god of languages and races, if the peoples would only communicate by singing instead of speaking, how quickly they could come to terms with each other!"[61] Less humorous but more noteworthy in some respects is the report in the *Fremden-Blatt*: "Yesterday came the third act of the great musical compromise drama, and now let anyone say that the Viennese are prejudiced and 'irreconcilable.' First the joyous guest performance at the Exhibition, then Smetana at the Theater an der Wien, and now unadulterated Czech words on German soil!"[62] Readers could scarcely

[59] Diglas returned for one performance on April 8 and then, beginning on April 10, alternated with Lejo until the end of the run; see Reittererová and Reitterer, *Vier Dutzend rothe Strümpfe*, 150–51.

[60] -sch [Ludwig Lazar Basch], "Theater an der Wien," *Illustrirtes Wiener Extrablatt*, April 6, 1893.

[61] "Der Ausgleich nach Noten," *Der Floh*, April 9, 1893 (emphases in original).

[62] "Theater an der Wien," *Fremden-Blatt*, April 6, 1893. Reittererová and Reitterer, *Vier Dutzend rothe Strümpfe*, 255n, suggest that the author of this unsigned noticed was Oscar Teuber.

have missed the ironic allusion made in this last line to *Unverfälschte Deutsche Worte* (Uncorrupted German words), the radical *deutschnational* and antisemitic political organ founded ten years earlier by Georg von Schönerer, the older brother of Alexandrine von Schönerer, the owner (and co-director) of the Theater an der Wien.

As *Die verkaufte Braut* neared the end of its run at the Theater an der Wien, the artistic reconciliation to which it had contributed threatened to unravel in the Theater in der Josefstadt. There, on May 1, 1893, the Böhmische Volkstheater-Gesellschaft, directed by Ladislav Chmelenský, opened a six-week guest season of Czech plays. First to be performed was Jan Nepomuk Štěpánek's *Čech a Němec* (*The Czech and the German*), a "Romeo-and-Juliet comedy set in the *Biedermeier* period," as Peter Lotar later described it, that concerns the efforts of a young Czech man and German woman to overcome their parents' animosity toward one another and marry.[63] The play itself may have been an historical comedy from a more innocent time, but in late-nineteenth-century Vienna its subject alone (not to speak of the introduction of the Czech language in a Viennese theater) was enough to provoke a demonstration by *völkisch* students, who disrupted the performance with hissing and whistling and were eventually removed from the theater by security personnel.[64] A few days later, an anonymous pan-German critic who wrote under the pseudonym Valentin Bröckerl pointedly described the appearance of the Böhmische Volkstheater-Gesellschaft at the Theater in der Josefstadt as a "provocation" that justified such protests—even while, in an admiring nod toward the ongoing performances of *Die verkaufte Braut* at the Theater an der Wien, he added: "But it is something else again to translate a first-rate work into German and so to concede that, if you want to get on with Germans on their territory, you have to speak their language."[65] But this episode even caused the *Neue Freie Presse*—now clearly second-guessing

[63] Peter Lotar, *Eine Krähe war mit mir* (Stuttgart: Deutsche Verlags-Anstalt, 1987), 205. Dvořák's *Domov můj* (*My Homeland*), in its first Viennese performance, was heard as a prelude; the ballet music from Smetana's comic opera *Dvě vdovy* (*The Two Widows*) and one of Dvořák's Slavonic dances were presented as the entr'actes. See the announcement in "Theater," *Wiener Zeitung*, April 30, 1893. This announcement erroneously suggests that the play had originally been performed in 1786 under the title *Der Bettelstudent*; in fact, *Čech a Němec* dates from 1816.

[64] "Locales (Scandal im Theater in der Josephstadt)," *Wiener Abendblatt*, May 2, 1893. The account provided there is strikingly similar to those found in the newspaper reports quoted in Chapter 5 of an earlier disturbance by pan-German students of Dvořák's opera *The Cunning Peasant* in November 1886.

[65] Valentin Bröckerl, *Ostdeutsche Rundschau*, May 7, 1893.

the optimism it had shown a year earlier in anticipation of the residency by the Czech National Theater—to respond with indignation of its own, not to the performances themselves but to rumors that the press in Prague had urged Vienna's Czech population to return fire:

> Not without justification, it has been regarded as one of the most beautiful successes of last year's Viennese Music- and Theater Exhibition that it managed, at least in one realm, that of art, to bring the Austrian nationalities closer to one another or to have them removed from political struggles and opposition. The highly developed artistic sense of the Viennese population made the first step, and its approval, given on the basis of artistic merit wherever it was found, gave rise to a thankful echo, which began to express itself in various friendly manifestations. If this gain is again lost, then the Czech press may be proud of itself for having contributed the most to that. One will become more careful in giving approval to Czech artistic efforts, if from it one has to fear that doing so will draw derogatory conclusions as to Vienna's German character. No longer will the Czech language be heard on the Viennese stage so impartially if distrust is roused such that, not artistic, but rather national goals are pursued.[66]

Indeed, the political chasm between Germans and Czechs seemed to be growing wider by the day. In May 1893, Taaffe was forced to close the Bohemian Diet when the Young Czechs revolted against his efforts to carry out portions of the Bohemian Compromise by decree. Weeks of violent street demonstrations followed, eventually leading the government to impose a state of emergency September 12 throughout the provincial capital. Then, in October, Taaffe stunned all parties when he sought to placate the Young Czechs by agreeing to their demand for a modified franchise reform. Although this proposal appealed to a number of German factions as well, it alienated the Conservative members of the governing coalition, driving them into an unlikely alliance with the German liberals, who saw the opportunity to return to the cabinet at last, and who stood to lose in any case if the vote were extended any further to the lower social classes. His power base broken, Taaffe resigned as minister-president on November 11, 1893, after fourteen years in power.

---

[66] "Wien, 3. Mai," *Neue Freie Presse*, May 4, 1893; this editorial is erroneously dated May 9, 1893, in Reittererová and Reitterer, *Vier Dutzend rothe Strümpf*, 71.

Hanslick's Vyšehrad

In his reviews of the *From My Life* Quartet and *Vltava*, Hanslick showed himself to be very much attuned to his times, in that both were used to comment on Austria's highly charged language politics. We might expect to find a similar direct response to this ongoing controversy in his reception of Smetana's *Vyšehrad*, performed by the Vienna Philharmonic on November 12, 1893, the very day after Taaffe's resignation, and yet what we uncover is something rather more complex. By the end of the century the "high castle" had become firmly established as a Czech national shrine, central to the myths associated with Libuše, the Přemyslid dynasty, and the history of the nation. (See Fig. 7.1, which shows a contemporary romanticizing vision of the pre-Hussite castle.) In this context, it would have been difficult for Hanslick not to affirm that Smetana was a Czech, and yet, for all that, one still gets the impression that what gains the composer a good notice here is his command of a musical style marked by the same set of salutary qualities the critic had always seen as German:

> "Wyssehrad" [is] one of the twelve [*sic*] symphonic poems that Smetana has brought together in a series of patriotic-musical pictures under the overall title "Mein Vaterland." Two of these orchestral pieces, "Die Moldau" and "Aus Böhmens Hain und Flur," were previously brought to successful performance. The third, "Wyssehrad," no less brilliant on the outside, seems to me to be paltrier at its musical core. The magic of romantic atmosphere, the full display of the colors of the modern orchestra is also at work in this composition, as is as well the great strength of all Smetana's music: to be clear, clear in its main design as well as in the fine relations of its individual parts. Smetana does not lapse into secret make-believe, hide-and-seek, and brooding; freely and openly he sings of what moves his heart. The Czech composers retain a healthy naïveté; the Russians, though likewise still an unexhausted nation, seem in their modern musicians, for example, Tchaikovsky, more prone to reflection.[67]

Despite the overall favorable tone of this assessment, Hanslick's displeasure with the "musical core" of the piece cannot go unnoticed. His concern probably has less to do with Smetana's music per se than with its use in the

---

[67] Hanslick, in *Neue Freie Presse*, November 28, 1893. See the discussion in Chapter 5 of the negative shading of Hanslick's use of the word "reflection" in contexts such as this..

FIGURE 7.1 Vyšehrad. After a lithograph by A. Pokorný, late nineteenth century. Reproduced in *Prague in Picture Postcards of the Period 1886–1930*, edited by Edmund Orián (Prague: Belle Epoque, 1998). Used with permission of the editor.

service of the work's "poetic idea," one that, by comparison to those of *Vltava* and *From Bohemia's Woods and Fields* (another musical landscape painting), seems designed to rouse Czech national sentiment. This was bound to cause some consternation, not least in light of the recent street demonstrations in Prague and the ensuing collapse of the Iron Ring. It would have been especially difficult under these circumstances for Hanslick to miss how Smetana's symphonic poem might be read in terms of Czech nationalist ideology. Here, as told in the work's program, was precisely the kind of reconstructed "memory" of a once-glorious Czech-Bohemian state that conferred legitimacy on the idea of contemporary Bohemian home rule:

> At the sight of the rock, the poet's memory is carried back to the remote past by the sound of the harp of the bard Lumír. There rises the vision of the rock in its ancient splendor, its gleaming golden crown that was the proud dwelling place of the Přemysl kings and princes, the ancient dynasty of Bohemia.
>
> Here in the castle, knights would assemble at the joyous summons of trumpets and cymbals to engage in splendid tourneys; here the warriors would gather for combat, their arms clanging and glittering in the sunlight. Vyšehrad resounded with songs of praise and victory.

Yearning for the long-perished glory of Vyšehrad, the poet now beholds its ruin. The devastation of furious battle has thrown down its lofty towers; fallen are its sanctuaries; and demolished the proud abodes of its princes. Instead of songs of triumph and victory, Vyšehrad quakes at the echo of its glory. From its ruins there comes only the melancholy echo of Lumír's song, so long forgotten and unheard.

As we have seen, Hanslick knew from personal experience as a budding young composer in Prague during the *Vormärz* how the image of Vyšehrad might be used to evoke memory of ancient Czech statehood, how the citadel could be seen as a reminder of Bohemia's former greatness and, with that, as a potent symbol of the Czech nation (*národ*). Now, however, writing in response to Smetana's symphonic poem half a century later as an aging German liberal notable, he sought to undermine this notion by offering in its place an alternative vision of the Bohemian fatherland (*vlast*).

Hanslick begins by informing his readers about the work's poetic idea by means of a clearly unsympathetic gloss on Smetana's program:

The vignette on the title page [Fig. 7.2] shows us a bard who plays the harp while glancing up toward the old ducal castle with a melancholy look. Therein the poetic idea of the composition is perfectly reflected. It begins with harp arpeggios; harp chords carry the slow, rhythmically monotonous main theme alone, repeated over and over to the point of fatigue. Then trumpet fanfares displace the serious sounds of the harp; according to the preface, the bard beholds the proud past of the old citadel, with its jousting tournaments and songs of war; a national-sounding theme (C major) rises up in a shining fortissimo in the entire orchestra and then gradually sinks back into the Largo of the beginning. After the splendor—the ruin.

Beckerman has suggested how a more sympathetic listener—one interested in entering into what Taruskin calls the "nationalist compact"—might hear the same music (or its first pages, at any rate):

The opening [harp] chords [see ex. 6.5b]...are not specifically Czech [but] when Smetana juxtaposes [them] with the image of the great rock Vyšehrad, and that image is further abstracted into a symbol of the enduring quality of the Czech people, [they] become imbued with a sensibility, and the sensibility becomes tied to something concrete. Having been suffused with Czechness, the chords become Czech and

FIGURE 7.2 Smetana, *Vyšehrad*, arrangement for piano four hands, title page. Music Division, Library of Congress.

impart this quality to surrounding material, which ultimately redefines and enhances the very sensibility that produced it.[68]

Hanslick will have none of this. Not only does he disregard Smetana's invitation to collaborate in the creation of *českost*, he even offers some starkly different readings of his own:

[68] Beckerman, "In Search of Czechness," 72–73.

Just as from the same music, different images rise up before different listeners, so may the mere title of a musical work lead one to ideas that lie at a great remove from the composer's intention. The word "Wyssehrad" causes me to recall two poetic works that move me powerfully whenever I actually look upon the old rock-castle. One of the most beautiful novels by Ferdinand von Saar, *Innocens*, takes place on the Wyssehrad. There lived the model of that kindly priest whom Saar, a young lieutenant in those days in command of the citadel, befriended. And how artfully, almost imperceptibly, are the military and landscape themes bound together in the portrayal! "Thicker, shinier grass-growth covers all the trenches and slopes, and around the sunken canon-carriages sprout violets and primroses. The lawn is always decked out cheerfully, and many firing ports are hidden by a wild rose bush in full bloom, which a long-standing peace allowed to grow hard on the masonry."

It is not surprising that Hanslick was drawn to the work of Ferdinand von Saar, whose liberal readership overlapped with his own. Nearly all Saar's fiction is set in contemporary Vienna, Bohemia, or Moravia, and in it the author offers a nuanced portrait of the social structure of the age in a way that recalls the manner in which Hanslick's collected music criticism offers a "living history" of Vienna's contemporary musical life.[69] Saar's novel is set in the months before the outbreak of war in Italy in 1859 and relates an episode in the life of a young lieutenant (possibly modeled on the author himself, as Hanslick suggests) who is given watch command at the citadel. A kindly priest named Innocens befriends the officer and eventually tells of how his vows had been tested by an attraction to the quartermaster's daughter. The priest's lonely struggles take place, in the words of Hanslick's old friend Robert Zimmermann, against the backdrop of "the desolate Wischehrad [*sic*], the old ducal castle of Prague, with its fragmentary walls and entrenchments overgrown with grass," a far cry from what Smetana had in mind (Fig. 7.3).[70]

As Hanslick completes his review, he builds on this non-national image in leading his readers from the *Nachmärz* to the *Vormärz*, and to the world of Young Bohemia:

[69] On Saar, see Eda Sagarra, "Social Types and Social Reality in the Narrative Fiction of Ferdinand von Saar," in *Ferdinand von Saar: Ein Wegbereiter der literarischen Moderne*, ed. Karl Konrad Polheim (Bonn: Bourvier Verlag Herbert Grundmann, 1985), 150–57.

[70] Robert Zimmermann, Review of Ferdinand von Saar, *Innocens* and *Heinrich der Vierte*, *Wiener Zeitung*, March 21, 1867.

FIGURE 7.3 Vyšehrad. Phototype by K. Bellmann, 1897. Reproduced in *Prague in Picture Postcards of the Period 1886–1930*, edited by Edmund Orián (Prague: Belle Epoque, 1998). Used with permission of the editor.

The other poet of whom I am thinking may already be unknown to today's generation: Friedrich Bach, of Prague, who in his "Sensitiven" revealed an uncommonly lyrical talent but soon fell silent. I often accompanied the good-hearted doctor, who was completely pro-saic and unkempt in everyday life, on walks with Joseph Bayer, which ended toward [the monastery at] Emaus, with its view of the Wyssehrad. Soon after my departure from Prague, Friedrich Bach was assigned as the regional doctor in a world-forsaken country-town in the Temeser Banat, and for years was counted as lost. Then suddenly he gave a sign of life, the first and last from his exile: a poem "Ex Ponto," which appeared in a poetry album, now likewise lost, on the occasion of the wedding of our empress [*Österreichisches Frühlingsalbum* (Vienna: Braumüller, 1854)]. The longing of the poor Prague poet for the "spring roses on the rock of the Wyssehrad" has something more deeply moving about it and for me more stirring than the harp chords and tour-nament visions of Smetana. Permit me just once, by way of exception, to allow the dry prose of a concert report to end poetically! Friedrich Bach's poem (dated aus Steierdorf bei Oravitza) reads:

> Interrupted joyous dances—
>   Disappointed feeling—
>   Faded blooms—
>   Extinguished song—
> Forced abandonment—
>   And misunderstood being—

All this I can bear;
I would like but one thing:
Far above the green heights,
Far above the laughing eyes,
Far over the blue seas
I would like to look yonder;
To ride on roaring storms
Into the beautiful fatherland,
To glide on rocking waves
Towards the steep wall of mountains—
When swallows draw blissfully
High above the City on the Moldau,
And spring roses bloom
On the rocks of Wyssehrad!

Bach, whose work appeared frequently in both *Ost und West* and *Libussa*, had been a central figure in Young Bohemia. His poetic style owed as much to that of the great Czech Romantic poet Karel Hynek Mácha as it did to the German Romantics; indeed, several of his poems appeared in Czech translation in the literary journal *Květy* (Blossoms), and at least two were originally even written in Czech.[71] Bach was an accomplished musician as well as poet, and he formed a key link between Young Bohemia and the so-called *Prager Davidsbund*, to which both he and his friend Hanslick had belonged in the mid-1840s.[72]

Unable to find his footing as a physician in the Bohemian capital, Bach left the city in 1847 to sign on as a doctor with the engineering company that had been commissioned by the Austrian government to build the first railroad in the Temeser Banat (an ethnically mixed region that straddles

---

[71] Julius Reinwarth, ed., *Gedichte von Friedrich Bach* (Prague: Calve, 1900), v–xxxv.

[72] Founded by Wilhelm August Ambros and modeled after Robert Schumann's largely fictitious "League of David," the *Prager Davidsbund* directed its energies to the fight against philistinism and the cult of virtuosity. See Hanslick, *Aus meinem Leben*, 1: 41–45. For a more comprehensive account, see Bonnie Lomnäs, Erling Lomnäs, and Dietmar Strauß, *Auf der Suche nach der poetischen Zeit: Der Prager Davidsbund: Ambros, Bach, Bayer, Hampel, Hanslick, Helfert, Heller, Hock, Ulm. Zu einem vergessenen Abschnitt der Musikgeschichte des 19. Jahrhunderts*, 2 vols. (Saarbrücken: Pfau, 1999). Also helpful is Grimm, *Eduard Hanslicks Prager Zeit*, 78–89. For a charming recollection of Bach and the entire Young Bohemia movement in the early 1840s, see "Des Dichters und Doctors Medicinä Friedrich Bach erster Patient: Ein Erinnerungsblatt von A. W. Ambros," in *Wiener Zeitung*, May 9, 1872, reprinted in Lomnäs and Strauß, *Auf der Suche nach der poetischen Zeit*, 2: 204–208.

present-day Romania, Hungary, and Serbia). Writing to Joseph Bayer soon after his arrival, Bach characterized his new life as one of exile.[73] It is surely significant, then, that in his only extant poem from this period Bach alludes to Ovid's *Epistulae ex Ponto* (Letters from the Black Sea), expressions of extraordinary sadness and desolation written during the poet's exile in the barbaric Black Sea town of Tomis. If the banished Roman poet longed for the Eternal City, the displaced Bach yearned for the "City on the Moldau" and the "beautiful fatherland" that he had left behind. There is more than a little irony to be savored, therefore, in Hanslick's later quotation of "Ex Ponto" by way of ending his review of Smetana's symphonic poem. Here it is the critic (not the composer) who is the persona of the program, and Bach who is Lumír, the bard whose song tells of a better time and place (one that has nothing to do with Smetana's intention).

Implicit in Hanslick's review is a song of lament for a Prague that no longer existed; it tells of his recognition that his hometown was quickly becoming the "Czech capital for a Czech land" that nationalists such as Smetana wanted it to be.[74] What is explicit in the review—and in its rejection of Smetana's program—is a very different imaginary geography. Thus when Hanslick shares with us his gaze upon the old rock-castle, we see nothing of the fabulous royal residence of the ancient Czech Přemyslids, but only the venerable fortress of the Austrian Habsburgs, now overgrown with wild grasses and rose bushes. This is not Smetana's Vyšehrad as proud agent of national rebirth, but a Romantic space of the critic's own living memory. This is the Wyssehrad (to paraphrase the opening sentence of *Innocens*) that rose up on a rocky hill overlooking the Moldau at the south end of *Prag*, the German-speaking yet nationally indifferent city that had once been home to both Friedrich Smetana and Eduard Hanslik.

[73] Reinwarth, *Gedichte von Friedrich Bach*, xxxi.
[74] David-Fox, "Prague-Vienna, Prague-Berlin," 737.

| Goldmark's *Deutschtum* Revisited

The force of suggestion, of agitation is a new, powerful thing. "Propaganda" is only the strongest instrument of the Roman hierarchy. With his inflammatory incitements Kossuth led an entire nation into war. We see this force in socialism, in antisemitism.

—Carl Goldmark, "Über musikalischen Fortschritt: 'Eine Mahnung'" (1905)

THE EFFLORESCENCE OF Czech music in the Austrian capital during the mid-1890s coincided with what John Boyer has called "the collapse of the liberals and the antisemitic conquest of Vienna."[1] A key moment in this momentous change took place in April 1895, when Karl Lueger and his Christian Socials, running on an explicitly antisemitic platform, made a strong showing in Vienna's City Council elections, aided by the support of the lower bureaucracy and public-school teachers, voters who had tradition-ally sided with mainstream liberal candidates. On May 16, 1895, Richard Heuberger recorded Brahms's angry response to this turn of events:

[1] I have quoted from the title of the last chapter of Boyer, *Political Radicalism in Late Imperial Vienna*, 316–410.

The master was completely horrified about the fact that the anti-Semites had gotten the upper hand in the official positions of the city of Vienna and that Lueger had become vice-mayor and would soon be mayor. "Didn't I tell you already years ago that it would happen? You and all the others, too, laughed at me then. Now it's come to pass and with it the clerical economic system. If there were an "Anti-Clerical Party"— that would make sense! But anti-Semitism is insanity![2]

Brahms was right about Lueger's immediate political prospects. In the next round of elections, held in September 1895, the Christian Socials gained a clear majority in the City Council and promptly elected their leader as mayor. Francis Joseph refused at first to install an antisemite in the office, but in April 1897, after the City Council had elected Lueger for the fifth time, the emperor finally bowed to the inevitable.[3]

This triumph of political antisemitism within the municipal sphere, however, held little sway in influencing Jahn's programming decisions at the Imperial Court Opera Theater. On February 28, 1896, for example, the Viennese public heard the first performance of *Walther von Vogelweide* by Albert Kauders, the Bohemian-born Jewish composer who wrote music criticism for the *Wiener Allgemeine Zeitung*. Three weeks later, on March 21, came the première of Goldmark's *Das Heimchen am Herd*. Not surprisingly, these repertorial decisions did not sit well with August Püringer of the *Ostdeutsche Rundschau*, who concluded his scathing review of *Walther von Vogelweide* by looking ahead to the opening of *Das Heimchen am Herd* in a few weeks' time: "We want to come back to both topics, "Jewry in Music" and "Acts of our Court Opera Administration for German Art," in fourteen days, when the new opera by Goldmark has seen the light of the world."[4]

For *Das Heimchen am Herd* Goldmark turned to a libretto by Alfred Maria Willner, freely adapted from Charles Dickens's Christmas story *The Cricket on the Hearth*. A sentimental, domestic tale with an element of simple fantasy (the eponymous cricket acts as guardian angel), *Das Heimchen am Herd* obviously sits at a great remove from the high drama of both *Die Königin von Saba* and *Merlin*. Departing from the more contemporary musical styles used in those earlier operas, Goldmark now employed old-fashioned set numbers,

[2] Heuberger, *Erinnerungen an Brahms*, 82; trans. in Notley, *Lateness and Brahms*, 211.

[3] On Lueger, see Richard S. Geehr, *Karl Lueger: Mayor of Fin-de-Siècle Vienna* (Detroit: Wayne State University Press, 1990).

[4] Hagen [August Püringer], "Walther von der Volgelweide," *Ostdeutsche Rundschau*, March 3, 1896.

choruses, and dances, linked by *secco* recitative. The music is simple and at times folklike.

For Hanslick, this fairy-tale opera stood as a "renunciation" of Wagnerian music drama; the critic delighted in its many wholesome melodies that are "singable and simple" and regular in their periodical rhythm—qualities that, as we have seen, Hanslick had too often found missing in Goldmark's music. Here "the voices rule, the orchestra accompanies." Goldmark's *Cricket* thus "preaches the eternal truth"—and this is, of course, Hanslick's own sermon—"that music cannot exist without the laws of form and symmetry, lest it degenerate into a mere pathological stimulation of the senses."[5] Still, Hanslick is not unstinting in his praise. He questions the novelty and originality of the composer's melodic invention, for example, even as he lauds the "rosy-cheeked wholesomeness" of the individual numbers as a welcome contrast to the "threatening shadows of the young Goldmark." And he extols the effective orchestration but then, with his next breath, cries out: "The harsh modulations, the nesting in chromatic and enharmonic passages, especially the up and down chase of the chromatic chord progressions!" Even in this modest piece, then, Hanslick has no trouble making out the "'Court Composer to the Queen of Sheba,' the attending cricket on Goldmark's hearth, who reports *anytime* something happens, merry *or* poignant."[6]

Although the *Deutsche Zeitung* had adopted an antisemitic editorial policy two years earlier, when it was taken over by Theodor Wähner, one of Lueger's closest allies, Theodor Helm's review of *Das Heimchen am Herd* evinced no racial prejudice.[7] Like Hanslick, Helm heard little in the new work that reminded him of "the earlier Goldmark," no "Oriental melismas" or "sultry modulations." Helm was somewhat less generous than Hanslick with regard to the decidedly unmodern style that Goldmark had adopted for the work, though he recognized that it did suit the "old-fashioned, cosy subject matter." And when Helm took note of what he called literal quotations by Goldmark of two German folksongs ("So viel Sterne am Himmel steh'n" and "Wenn ich

---

5   Ed. H. [Eduard Hanslick], "Hofoperntheater," *Neue Freie Presse* March 22, 1896; repr. in Hanslick, *Am Ende des Jahrhunderts*, 9–17 (at 14–15).

6   Ibid., 16 (emphasis added).

7   Theodor Helm, "Hofoperntheater," *Deutsche Zeitung*, March 24, 1896. Knittel (*Seeing Mahler*, 12) erroneously cites the beginning of Wähner's editorship as 1882, but the change in editorial policy did not occur until 1894. As we have seen, during the late 1880s, when the newspaper briefly served as the official organ of the German Club, it was even edited by a Jew, Heinrich Friedjung, who retained his position in the face of attempts by antisemitic members of the German Club to have him removed.

ein Vöglein wär"), he saw that this, too, was in keeping with the subject matter, and it was certainly no cause for concern. We cannot say the same thing, however, about the reaction by Vienna's avowed antisemitic writers.

This brings us back to the critic for the *Ostdeutsche Rundschau* and his promise to consider *Das Heimchen am Herd* in the light of Wagner's *Jewry in Music*. Alluding to his earlier feuilleton "Art-Jewry," with its accusations of "misunderstood Wagner-aping" by Jewish composers like Goldmark, Püringer begins his review by characterizing Goldmark as a "slavish epigone" of Wagnerian instrumental music.[8] And though he does acknowledge the composer's skill in orchestral technique, he assures his readers that this was no compensation for Goldmark's lack of a fecund musical imagination, evidenced not only by the individual works themselves (which, in his opinion, had to make do with the "strained 'tone painting'" mentioned in "Art-Jewry") but also by Goldmark's comparatively small output despite his advanced age. Soon turning to the composer's two earlier stage works, Püringer describes *Merlin* as a "boring chivalric opera" that had already started to lose its hold even on the Viennese stage and then writes off the greater staying power of *Die Königin von Saba* to the special circumstances created by Vienna's large community of Jewish music-lovers: "*Die Königin von Saba*, which by its admixture of Hebraic melodies has a repugnant oriental appeal, has become a kind of Jewish national opera and thus understandably continues to have its appreciative audience." This insinuation that Goldmark had sought to inscribe himself and his "race" in his first opera could not have gone over well with the composer: Max Graf later reported that the only time he ever saw Goldmark become angry was when *Die Königin von Saba* was taken to be a "Jewish national opera."[9]

With that, Püringer turns at last to the work at hand, which he reads as an out-and-out imitation of Engelbert Humperdinck's recent fairy-tale opera *Hänsel und Gretel* (1893). Here we find all Wagner's negative associations with Jewry—imitation in place of creativity, cunning in commerce and in the marketplace, an alien culture that is in possession of its own press to further its aims at the expense of Germans:

8 Hagen [August Püringer], "Das Heimchen am Herd," *Ostdeutsche Rundschau*, March 25, 1896, from which quotations that follow are taken.
9 Max Graf, "Karl Goldmark: Zum hundertsten Geburtstag," *Der Tag*, May 18, 1930; a slightly different version of this anecdote is given in idem, *Legend of a Musical City*, 120. For his part, Graf, over the composer's objection, held to the same position taken by Goldbaum and any number of other earlier commentators in claiming that Goldmark had inscribed into his score childhood memories of his Jewish upbringing.

Now the composer seems to have felt the urgent necessity to restore his badly tarnished luster, even with his friends, and, with the speculative sense that is characteristic of his race, has very cleverly made himself the first to give allegiance to the star of Humperdinck, shining brightly in the German operatic sky, as he had once been attached to the coattails of Richard Wagner. This musical event lay in the air for eighteen months; a work as original and brilliantly crowned as "Hänsel und Gretel" had to find its imitators; the audience downright longed for it, and it was obvious that the first who succeeded in bringing this imitation onto the market could be certain of a major success. Well, Jewry, which has always been great in imitation and treating foreign inventions and discoveries as grist for the mill, was also this time the first on the mark, and so we are already seeing its racial comrades' press at work in using the Jewish forgery to push our national original masterwork off into the shadows; the audience, which swears by [the Jewish] press, will perhaps take care of furthering this work.

Püringer is harshly critical of the many instances, as he judges, in which Willner's libretto of *Das Heimchen am Herd* hews to the example set by that of *Hänsel und Gretel*, although he finds triviality, for example, in the former, where the latter is poetic. What is more, Goldmark's musical setting is even more dependent on *Hänsel and Gretel* than is Willner's story line. "It is the same style," he writes, "which, ensuing from Wagner's 'Meistersinger,' incorporates folklike elements, uses closed song forms, ... does not disdain light dance rhythms, and aptly uses the orchestra as much as possible for mood painting, in some places seeks therewith humorous effects."

Yet, in Püringer's opinion, Goldmark, in spite of his best efforts, falls short because he lacks Humperdinck's "sense for the folklike, humor, and fresh swelling invention," leading him instead to throw himself into the sentimentalities of the story with musical settings that lack "melodic invention and have no folklike effect at all." In addition to the many examples of "misunderstood Humperdinck-aping" Püringer finds in the score is at least one direct imitation of *Die Meistersinger*. But what really outrages the critic is what he takes to be Goldmark's literal quotation in the third act's ensemble of the folksong "So viel Stern am Himmel stehen" (ex. 8.1). "We could not believe our ears," he writes. "We have seldom experienced a greater tastelessness and absurdity! It shows what understanding Herr Goldmark possesses of our folksong!" Whereas Helm, in noting the same resemblance between Goldmark's ensemble and apparent folksong source, found nothing inappropriate about the allusion, for Püringer it was nothing but inappropriate for

EXAMPLE 8.1a Goldmark, *Das Heimchen am Herd*, Act III ensemble, beginning

Gu-ten Mor-gen, Herr Tac-kle-ton, gu-ten Mor-gen Herr Tac-kle-ton, habt uns ge la - den, da sind wir schon! Gar gern als Eu - re - Gä - ste zum heu-ti - gen - Hoch-zeits - fe - ste, zum Hoch-zeits - fe - - ste

EXAMPLE 8.1b "So viel Sterne am Himmel stehen" (German folk song), beginning

So viel Stern am Him mel ste - hen so viel Schäf-lein als da ge - hen in dem grü - nen grü-nen Feld, so viel Vö - gel als da flie-gen, als da hin - und wie-der flie gen so-viel mal sei du ge grüßt, so-viel mal sei du ge grüßt.

the Jewish composer to lay claim in this way to a culture of which he could never be a part. The critic goes on to observe that the opera might very well have been brought to an end with this ensemble, if only the composer and his librettist had not felt it necessary to tack on a few additional numbers that merely rehearse earlier music. Rubbing salt into the wound, Püringer concludes with utter contempt and scorn: "The composer has the mishap [*Dem Komponisten passirt dabei das Malheur*] that absolutely nothing more occurs to him."

"A word of reply"

Goldmark could not have been oblivious to these kinds of attacks, and yet his memoirs are noticeably silent on the subject of fin-de-siècle antisemitism. To be sure, the composer hints of its existence in Vienna when, in the midst of describing how he had come to Wagner's defense in the 1860s, when this was by no means a popular thing to do, he asks, rhetorically, whether this might have been why he was later "outlawed from the official Wagnerians." Since the Vienna Academic Wagner Society always included Jewish members, this seems to be a veiled reference instead to the offshoot antisemitic New Richard Wagner Society that was founded in 1890. But the book is otherwise free of any discussion of the painful subject.[10]

This is not to say, however, that Goldmark never intended to broach this topic in writing, any more than, as I have argued, he wished to hide from the public his Jewish descent. Goldmark worked on his memoirs in 1910 and 1911 but, as noted, did not live to complete them. The autograph manuscript on which the posthumously published volume of 1922 is based is therefore a fragment. This manuscript runs to 233 pages and carries the heading "Erinnerungen aus meinem Leben" (hereafter: *Erinnerungen* MS).[11] It breaks off on page 233 with the annotation: "Folgen die Einlagen auf Seite 8" (The enclosures follow on page 8). The published edition accords with this manuscript, but only up through the first sentence of page 232, which reads: "'Heimchen am Herd' wurde im Winter 1896 zum ersten Male aufgeführt" ("[The] Cricket on the Hearth" was performed for the first time in the winter of 1896). And with this simple declarative sentence, the book comes to an abrupt end.

No one other than the composer is named on the title page, but in its catalogue the Rikola Verlag, the book's publisher, identified Goldmark's daughter, Minna Hegenbarth-Goldmark, as editor. (It was Minna who eventually donated the manuscript to the Hungarian National Library along with other primary source materials from her father's legacy.)[12] Minna's most consequential editorial decision had to do with the text she suppressed. This passage—all but the first

<hr>

[10] Goldmark, *Erinnerungen*, 77; *Notes from the Life*, 138–39. It is not true, however, as is often claimed, that Goldmark ever belonged to the Vienna Academic Wagner Society.

[11] Budapest, National Széchényi Library, Shelfmark: Ms. mus. th. 131.

[12] Goldmark never married. His only daughter was born out of wedlock on July 2, 1866, to his housekeeper, Marie Benel, and given the name Wilhelmina. Minna goes unmentioned in Goldmark's memoirs, and I have seen no evidence of her in the composer's life for many years to come, apart from an entry in a pocket notebook, preserved in the National Széchényi Library, Budapest, that evidently dates from around 1885 or somewhat later: "Minnas Geburtstag 2ᵗ Juli 1866." The page in question is reproduced in István Kecskeméti, "Goldmarkiana: Unbekannte primäre Quellen in Ungarn," in *Musica Conservata: Günter Brosche zum 60. Geburtstag*, ed. Josef Gmeiner, Zsigmond Kokits, Thomas Leibnitz, and Inge Pechotsch-Feichtinger (Tutzing: Hans Schneider, 1999), 145. But it seems likely Goldmark was involved in her support from early on, especially after the early death of her mother in 1871. It is perhaps not insignificant that Minna's birth came shortly before Goldmark reestablished contact with his brother Joseph and

sentence of page 232 and the whole of page 233—had been prompted, at least in part, by the Berlin production of *Das Heimchen am Herd*, which opened on June 27, 1896. Although the new opera was well received by the public, critics reacted negatively to Willner's "clumsy" treatment of Dickens's story, as well as to the supposed lack of originality in Goldmark's setting and the general eclecticism of his score. (For Püringer, as we have seen, these very shortcomings were evidence of the composer's Jewish origins.) Goldmark tells us that one of the Berlin papers in question had given him the opportunity to reply to this criticism in print, that he accepted this offer and went about writing his defense, but finally decided not to publish it because it had grown "too large for a newspaper and the moment had passed."[13] Now several years later, seizing the opportunity presented by the memoirs he was in the process of writing, Goldmark picked up the thread of that earlier unpublished essay and began to address the criticisms leveled at both the text and the music of *Das Heimchen am Herd* at that time. After thirty-one lines in this vein, the *Erinnerungen* MS breaks off, as noted, with the instruction that the text was to continue on the eighth page of some unnamed enclosure.

It is evident from context that this annotation refers to some lost manuscript closely related to a seventy-one-page autograph preserved in the archive of the Hungarian State Opera. The extant manuscript is entitled "Gedanken über Form und Stil (Eine Abwehr)" (Thoughts about Form and Style [A Defense]), and in it Goldmark couples a defense of his work with a forthright discussion of his bitter and painful experience of racial antisemitism (hereafter: *Abwehr* MS).[14] The manuscript carries the by-line "Carl Goldmark

ask him for a loan to help cover Mosenthal's charges for writing the libretto for *Die Königin von Saba*. In any case, in 1890 Goldmark successfully appealed to the emperor for legitimization of her birth. Soon thereafter Minna married the German academic sculptor Ernst Hegenbarth, and in later years Goldmark was clearly close to her and her husband and their children; see, for example, Ludwig Karpath, *Begegnung mit dem Genius*, 2nd ed. (Vienna: Fiba-Verlag, 1934), 37. I am grateful to Thomas Aigner for sharing with me his transcription of the petition in question: "Majestätsgesuch Carl Goldmarks um Legitimierung seiner Tochter Wilhelmine vom Juli 1890," Vienna, Haus-, Hof- und Staatsarchiv (hereafter HHStA), Z 21723 / I.M. 1890 ad 3281. [1]890.

13 "'Heimchen am Herd' wurde im Winter 1896 zum ersten Male aufgeführt. Als ich im Sommer des selben Jahres die Oper in der königlichen Oper in Berlin (Kroll) aufführte, wurde sie von einigen Blättern so maßlos angegriffen, daß eines derselben, wohl das heftigste, sich veranlaßt sah, mir mitzuteilen, daß es bereit wäre, eine Entgegnung aufzunehmen. Und ich schrieb bis eine Broschüre daraus wurde, für eine Zeitung zu groß[,] und die Zeit der Aktualität war vorüber" (*Erinnerungen* MS, p. 232). On the Berlin criticism, see Heinrich Welti, "Die Zukunft der Märchenoper," *Die Nation* 13 (1896): 607–8.

14 Carl Goldmark, "Gedanken über Form und Stil (Eine Abwehr)," Ungarische Staatsoper Budapest, Archiv, Sign. 78.11.11. This text is discussed briefly in Gerhard J. Winkler,

August 1896 Bad Fusch," indicating that the text it transmits originated in the aftermath of the Vienna and Berlin productions of *Das Heimchen am Herd*, but it could not have been written out until after a performance of *Die Königin von Saba* in Wiesbaden on May 17, 1909 (to which reference is made in a crossed-over passage on the first page of the *Abwehr* MS) and probably not until 1910 or 1911. The *Abwehr* MS, therefore, though not the occasion that prompted the discussion it contains, can be placed at the time when Goldmark was working on his memoirs.[15] Not only are the two pages of text suppressed from the *Erinnerungen* MS nearly identical to passages found in the first nine pages of the *Abwehr* MS, but the remainder of the text of the latter follows logically from the break-off point in the former, more or less in accordance with Goldmark's annotation.

It is impossible to determine how much more and exactly what parts of "Thoughts about Form and Style" would have been included in the memoirs had the book been completed. What is relevant here, however, is Goldmark's decision to publish a substantial portion of the essay in holiday editions of the *Neue Freie Presse* on Easter and Pentecost 1911.[16] It was there, as I shall argue, that the composer rebutted at last the kind of antisemitic attacks under which he had suffered since the 1890s at the hands of critics such as Göllerich, Czerny, and, in particular, Püringer.[17]

"Carl Goldmark und die Antisemitismus," *Burgenländische Heimatblätter* 60 (1998), H. 3: 128–34. See also idem, " 'Multikulturalität' und 'Heilige deutsche Tonkunst'," 283–84; idem, "Carl Goldmark und die Moderne," in *"Denn in jenen Tönen lebt es": Wolfgang Marggraf zum 65. Geburtstag*, ed. Helen Geyer, Michael Berg, and Matthias Tischer (Weimar: Hochschule für Musik Franz Liszt, 1999), 229–43 (at 229, 232); and idem, "Joseph Joachim, Carl Goldmark—Zwei parallele jüdische Musikerbiographien aus dem historischen Westungarn," in *Musik der Juden im Burgenland*, ed. Gerhard J. Winkler (Eisenstadt: Amt der burgenländischen Landesregierung, 2006), 79–100 (at 98–100).

[15] On the date of the Wiesbaden performance, see Gerda Haddenhorst, *Die Wiesbadener Kaiserfestspiele* (Wiesbaden: Selbstverlag der Historischen Kommission für Nassau, 1985), 222.

[16] Karl Goldmark, "Gedanken über Form und Stil (Eine Abwehr)," *Neue Freie Presse*, April 16 and June 4, 1911. These two installments reproduce most, but not all, of the text found in the *Abwehr* MS. The *Neue Freie Presse* promised, but seems never to have published, a continuation that presumably would have covered the remaining unpublished portion of the manuscript apart from certain crossed-over passages that Goldmark probably never intended to publish.

[17] Consider the bitter allusion to Püringer's review of *Das Heimchen am Herd* found in one passage in which Goldmark sarcastically mentions the "unforgivable crime" he had committed of having "had the mishap" [*Es ist mir das Malheur passirt*] of unknowingly using two bars of a German folksong. Winkler, in "Carl Goldmark und die Antisemitismus,"

Goldmark acknowledges that the polemical tone of his essay was out of character. (The composer was widely known for his reserve.) Yet, as he writes in a passage that was toned down for the version that appeared in the *Neue Freie Presse*, there was something different and fundamentally disturbing about the nature of the criticism at hand:

> It is always suspicious when a composer, who through a series [of large] works that have long been the common property of the musically educated world, is now attacked in his mature years, [when] a new large work that repeats the full success is attacked with such vehemence, as in recent times was the case from many sides on the occasion of the performance of my *Heimchen am Herd* (and also of *Die Königin von Saba*). Certainly the greatest composers have difficult times and can write weaker [material], but then these are not very successful. If his work does have this kind of success, then it stems from a talent that has already been proven elsewhere, and cannot be compared to works of doubtful character; alone for the reason that the authors are not on equal footing with respect to their powers. One is inclined to test such an evaluation for its purity and honesty, all the more so when some of these judgments appeared in publications that are already characterized by their political orientation. It is painful and sad that an entire life full of honest artistic work…does not protect against being pelted with such filth and dirt where this has happened not merely to my works but also to me personally. In my entire long life it never occurred to me to defend against the worst attack with even a word….I respect every view that flows out of artistic conviction; [I] remain on personally friendly terms even with those who are not sympathetic toward my artistic creations….But there is a boundary where silence would be cowardice or suicide; and there may be granted to the author a word of reply.[18]

"Joseph Joachim und Carl Goldmark," and "'Multikulturalität' und 'Heilige deutsche Tonkunst,'" incorrectly identified the essay as unpublished, and he attributed the omission in the composer's memoirs of any discussion of antisemitism to the "shock" Goldmark felt when, late in life, his assumptions about the possibility of assimilation were so clearly called into question in the new antisemitic response to his music. Yet the publication of a large part of "Thoughts About Form and Style" in 1911 demonstrates that Goldmark was in fact determined to challenge his racist critics head on.

[18] "Es ist immer verdächtig, wenn ein Componist, der durch eine Reihe großer Werke, die längst Gemeingut der musical[ischen] gebildeten Welt sind, nun in reifen Jahren ein neues größeres Werk, das wiederholt vollen Erfolg hat mit solcher Vehemenz angegriffen wird, wie dies in letzter Zeit gelegentlich der Aufführung meines Heimchen am Herd (und auch der König[in] von Saba) von mehreren Seiten der Fall war. Gewiß auch die größten Componisten haben schwere Stunden und können

Although the proximate cause of Goldmark's essay was the critical reception of *Das Heimchen am Herd*, it is in particular the claim made in Püringer's review of that work that *Die Königin von Saba*, through its "admixture of Hebraic melodies," possessed a "repugnant oriental appeal" (*fremdartiger orientalischen Reiz*) that made it a kind of national opera for the Jews on which I want to focus. Lurking in the background of the entire episode is, once again, *Jewry in Music*. The keyword that appears throughout Wagner's essay is *fremdartig* (used pejoratively here and in the sense of "foreign" or "alien").[19] It appears four times: first, to describe the supposedly unattractive outer appearance of the Jews; second, to describe their supposedly shrill manner of speaking and singing; third, in a particularly convoluted reference (even for Wagner), to explain the bewildered response of the Jews to "our" music, whose true nature would always seem "alien" to *them*; and finally, as one of several negative characterizations of the music produced by Jewish composers themselves, which Wagner claims is not only "alien" but also "cold, odd, indifferent, unnatural, and contorted" (*fremdartig, kalt, sonderlich, gleichgiltig, unnatürlich und verdreht*).

In "Thoughts about Form and Style," Goldmark confronts his critics' Wagnerian assumption that the Jews, because of their essential "rootlessness,"

Schwächeres schreiben, aber dann fehlt diesen der starke Erfolg. Hat sein Werk aber diesen Erfolg, dann entstammt dieser seiner anderen Orts schon erprobten Begabung und kann nicht mit Werken zweifelhaften Charakters verglichen werden; einfach schon darum nicht, weil die Autoren in ihren Potenzen sich nicht gleichen. Man ist dann leicht geneigt ein solches Urtheil auf seine Reinheit und Ehrlichkeit zu prüfen, um so mehr, als einige dieser Urtheile in Blättern erschienen, sie schon durch ihre politische Richtung gekennzeichnet sind. Es ist schmerzlich und traurig, daß ein ganzes Leben voll ehrlicher künstlerischer Arbeit, stets nur dem Idealen zugewendeten Streben, dem auch die Zustimmung nicht fehlte, nicht schützt davor mit solchem Unflat und Schmutz beworfen zu werden, wo dies nicht blos meinen Werken sondern auch mir persönlich geschehn ist. Es fiel mir in der langen Zeit meines Lebens nicht ein, mich auch nur mit einem Worte auf die heftigsten Angriffe zur Wehr zu setzen....Ich respektiere jede aus künstlerischer Ueberzeugung fließende Ansicht; blieb auch selbst mit Personen, denen mein künstlerisches Schaffen nicht sympathisch ist[,] in persönlich-freundschaftlichem Verkehr....Aber es giebt eine Gränze, wo Schweigen Feigheit, oder Selbstmord wäre; und da mag wohl auch dem Verfasser ein Wort der Gegenrede gestattet sein"; "Gedanken über Form und Stil" (*Abwehr* MS pp. 2–4). Hanslick must surely be counted among those critics to whom Goldmark was close personally even if the two did not see eye to eye on musical matters.

[19] "Fremdartig" is not inherently pejorative. Indeed, in many of the reviews of *Die Königin von Saba* cited above, it is used in the more neutral sense as "exotic."

can never produce "authentic" German music, or music that belongs to any nation.[20] Here, again, is Wagner:

> As long as the separate art of music possessed a really organic need for life, up until the time of Mozart and Beethoven, there were no Jewish composers to be found: it was impossible for an element completely foreign [*gänzlich fremdes*] to this living organism to take any part in its growth. Only when a body's inner death is evident can outside elements gain entry, and then only to destroy it.[21]

And here is Goldmark's straightforward response: "I wrote... *German* music. That is proved by all my chamber and orchestral works, as well as by all my operas." He continues:

> Of course, how often one hears from the farthest left wings of our extreme modernists that a non-Aryan (*nous autres*) cannot comprehend the German spirit. To have been born on German soil or to have been nursed, satiated and reared solely on the sources of German culture means nothing. He who has not nursed on true Aryan milk at the so-called Aryan breast cannot understand the Aryan spirit.[22]

After stating the antisemitic argument in this way, Goldmark attempts to undermine it with what seems to him to be a self-evident argument. He lists a number of Jews who, as performers, conductors, even polemicists, were unsurpassed in their devotion to the cause of German music, from Felix Mendelssohn and his rediscovery of Bach's *St. Matthew Passion* to Gustav Mahler and his performances of *Tristan* and *The Marriage of Figaro*. "O splendid logic!" he writes. "O righteousness! None of these understood the German spirit! That's what they, one after another, are saying without thinking, and if it were only limited to that. But it is so convenient with a single work to exclude the one who is inconvenient from an entire cultural enterprise."[23]

The "inconvenient" person in question was Goldmark himself; the work, none other than *Die Königin von Saba*; the cultural enterprise, *die heilige deutsche Kunst* ("sacred German art," to use a Wagnerian locution). What

[20] For a convenient summary of the "linguistics of anti-Semitism" that underlies this trope, see Gilman, *Jewish Self-Hatred*, 209–11.

[21] Osbourne, *Richard Wagner: Stories and Essays*, 38.

[22] Goldmark, in *Neue Freie Presse*, June 4, 1911, from which the next several quotations are taken.

[23] Mentioned also are the violinist Joseph Joachim, the pianists Anton Rubinstein and Carl Tausig, and the Wagnerians Hermann Levi and Heinrich Porges.

the composer had in mind in this case was Püringer's characterization of his opera a *"fremdartige{s} Werk."* Goldmark knew, of course, that this had been intended to impugn his opera as something foreign to the German *Volksnation*—as a Jewish opera, not a German one—but he deftly turns the argument around by co-opting the term of abuse and using it as a positive descriptor of the work's exoticism (which, of course, presumes Goldmark's position within the German *Kulturnation*):

> The word was [used] not so much to describe the distinguishing char-
> acteristic of the work as to attach a blemish to it, and yet that is its
> greatest praise, since it does in any case describe its subjective charac-
> teristic. The *fremdartig* work shall no doubt be said not to belong to the
> German spirit, to German art. Really, then to what? As an artwork,
> such as it is, it has not simply fallen from Heaven, and it must have its
> ancestors with all its forms and characteristics, good and not so good,
> descended from a highly developed culture and artistic direction. This
> *"fremdartig"* [work] should reluctantly perhaps be called Oriental.

It had been bad enough for Goldmark that liberal critics such as Hanslick and Speidel had once written about *Die Königin von Saba* in a way that cast doubt on his German credentials, but neither had ever questioned that he could, in fact, *become* an acculturated German composer. Püringer saw things very differently. When he spoke of the opera as "fremdartig," this was tanta-mount to saying that, by virtue of his Jewish race the composer was himself indelibly "alien," with no rightful place in the national-cultural life of the Germans. Goldmark parries this Wagnerian rhetoric not only by insisting that his opera had descended from "a highly developed culture" but also by suggesting that things could not be otherwise for a serious composer of Jewish descent. He writes:

> To come right out and say it, a strong deep folk ethos can be found
> among the Jews, to be sure, but, as a nation, they possess no, not even
> so much as a trace of, modern art of their own. Where would it come
> from in any event? Therefore, as already noted, [is it] to be attributed
> to Oriental art? I am not familiar with [even] four measures of genu-
> inely Oriental music, which, clearly periodic in form and shape, would
> be presentable as a melody according to our concepts.[24]

---

[24] Although Ferdinand Scherber, in his preface to the composer's memoirs, reports that in his work as a music critic Goldmark maintained that "Jewish-Oriental-exotic music could exert a stimulating influence on our Western art" (*Erinnerungen*, 7; *Notes from the*

There is considerable irony—and poignancy—in the fact that it was in Püringer's review of *Das Heimchen am Herd*, with its complaint about the Jewish composer having appropriated German folksong with no proper national claim to it, that the claim is made that Goldmark's putative use of Hebraic melodies in *Die Königin von Saba* had for this reason made it a Jewish national opera. And in a telling footnote Goldmark implicitly denies that *Die Königin von Saba* could ever be characterized as nationalist art on such a basis: "To be sure, authentically Oriental folk song is also song, but not of the type that might find a place in our Western art. What one commonly designates in our art as 'Oriental' are only tints, representations."

To illustrate with one such "representation," let us briefly consider the melody heard in the Entrance March of Act I of *Die Königin von Saba*, as the Queen's light- and dark-skinned slaves present Solomon with the magnificent gifts they bear from Arabia (ex. 8.2). The composer uses the English horn here (doubled at the lower octave by the bass clarinet) for the same purpose as in later works such as Camille Saint-Saëns's *Samson et Delila* (1877) and Alexander Borodin's *In the Steppes of Central Asia* (1880), not to speak of his *Sakuntala*—as a sure-fire means of evoking the Orient. Even more emblematic of that atmosphere is the melody itself, which is based on the so-called Hungarian Gypsy scale, with a "gapped" augmented second between the third and fourth scale degrees (D flat–E flat–F flat–G natural–A flat etc.). Notably, Goldmark had discussed this scalar type in a much earlier unpublished manuscript, written in Pest in the summer of 1858. Entitled "Eine Ansicht über Fortschritt" (A View on Progress), this essay documents the young composer's attempt to show how, in the wake of Beethoven, Mendelssohn, and Schumann, music might still be advanced with respect to "the specifically musical and purely instrumental."[25] (He explicitly leaves the program music of Berlioz and Liszt out of consideration.) Goldmark begins with Mendelssohn and asserts that the source of the late composer's originality was

Life, x), he cannot be trusted on this point with regard to the Jewish element, not least because he seems to have been relying on sources he did not have at hand. Scherber's claim echoes one he made in an article published shortly after Goldmark's death: "It remains unknown that Goldmark was a writer on music. His essays, which I happened upon strewn across forgotten Viennese daily newspapers but then unfortunately lost track of, were adroitly written and cleverly arranged....I still remember one of the essays, in which he advocated the use of 'Jewish-Oriental-exotic melodies in our Western music'" (Friedrich Scherber, "Nochmals Carl Goldmark," *Signale für die musikalische Welt* 73 [1915]: 37. What Scherber is probably recalling are Goldmark's reviews of David's *Le désert* and *Lalla Roukh*, neither of which made any reference to Jewish music.

[25] "Eine Ansicht über Fortschritt," Ungarische Staatsoper Budapest, Archiv, Sign. 78.12.12. This manuscript is dated July 11, 1858.

EXAMPLE 8.2 Goldmark, *Die Königin von Saba*, op. 27, Act I, Queen's Entrance March: excerpt

his melodic structure, and in particular his signature use of the harmonic minor scale, with its interval of the augmented second between the sixth and seventh scale degrees. Since Goldmark illustrates this scale in the key of A minor, we might assume that he has in mind something like the beginning of the main theme of the last movement of the *Scottish* Symphony, with its prominent use of G sharp and F natural (ex. 8.3). He then goes on to suppose that it should be possible "to elevate the scalar characteristics of various national melodies...to the level of art." He makes a point of stressing that his interest lies not in national music per se but solely in the scales that can be derived from it. For that purpose, Italian, Spanish, and English music is of no use, he explains, since, for all its surface distinctions in melodic character and rhythmic motion, the scales on which it is based are entirely conventional. What Goldmark has in mind instead are "more oriental melodies" (*mehr orientalische Weisen*), in which deviation from the standard scales can be found in abundance.

Following the age-old practice of deriving the unfamiliar from the familiar, he offers for comparison a fragment of the harmonic minor scale in F (from notes C to G), which, as noted, he associated with Mendelssohn, with two other scalar fragments, each spanning the same interval, but with a differing location of the interval of the augmented second (ex. 8.4). The use of altered scales such as these, he argues, offers the modern composer of art music a means of creating melodies that "obtain an individuality" (*eine Eigenthümlichkeit gewinnen*) that Goldmark sees as the key to furthering musical progress. As practical evidence of the truth of this proposition, he cites large comprehensive works already successfully written in this way, including the Hungarian operas of Ferenc Erkel and Franz Doppler, the Russian operas of Anton Rubinstein, and the Russian compositions of Mikhail Glinka.

Having thus "legitimized" the use of these scales, Goldmark shares a few thoughts about the aesthetic character of melodies based upon them:

EXAMPLE 8.3 Mendelssohn, Symphony No. 3, op. 56, IV, mm. 3–10

If we turn away almost with indignation from the idea of encountering in a quartet or symphony a melody formed from a newfangled scale, then it is, on the one hand, only the unfamiliarity of the foreign, which by nature we always approach only slowly and with difficulty, on the other hand, habit contributes not a little bit always to thinking of such a melody with all the rhythmic movement, figuration, and peculiarities of a national music, in which form it would scarcely be conceivable in classical music.[26]

Indeed, even though Goldmark acknowledges that those Hungarian and Russian works cited above contain "much that is beautiful, noble, even dignified," he seems to fault them at the same time because they not only are based on the "newfangled scales" in question but also include all those other features of "national music" for which he finds no room in "classical music." But in the scales themselves—viewed as abstract entities—Goldmark finds "nothing invidious, unaesthetic" for use in the "noblest music."

If in 1858 Goldmark's concern had been theoretical and directed toward the composition of "pure instrumental music," later, with *Die Königin von Saba*, his concern was practical and directed toward the composition of an opera, one that, given the *locus dramaticus*, could benefit from the introduction of melodies based on the exotic scale in question.[27] But it is important to remember that Goldmark had originally thought about all this in far more abstract terms, and this, of course, problematizes the notion that

[26] "Wenn sich unser Gefühl fast mit Indignation von dem Gedanken abwendet, in einem Quartett oder einer Symphonie einer, aus einer neumodischen Scala gebildeten Melodie zu begegnen, so ist es einerseits nur die Ungewohntheit des Fremden, dem wir uns von jeher naturgemäß nur langsam und schwer nähern, anderseits [*sic*] trägt die Gewohnheit auch nicht wenig dazu bei, um eine solche Melodie immer mit allem rü[?]thmischen Bewegungen, Figuren und Spezialitäten einer Nationalmusik zu denken, in welcher Form sie zur klassischen Musik allerdings nicht gut denkbar ware" (ibid., p. 12).

[27] As we saw in his reviews of Anton Rubinstein's *Der Thurm zu Babel* and *Die Makkabäer*, Ludwig Speidel posited the augmented second as a musical token of Jewishness.

EXAMPLE 8.4 Exotic scales, transcribed from Carl Goldmark, "Eine Ansicht über Fortschritt," Ungarische Staatsoper Budapest, Archiv, Sign. 78.13.12

Der Mendelss[ohn] Analog

F moll

any of the opera's exotic-sounding melodies either welled up spontaneously from childhood memories of his father's singing (to describe matters in a benignly essentializing way) or else manifested the composer's inescapable "Fremdartigkeit" (to put a more sinister spin on the same essentialism).

We would do better to conceive of *Die Königin von Saba*, then, not as a Jewish national opera or even a "Jewish-Oriental" one, but as an out-and-out *Orientalist* opera.[28] And Goldmark leaves no doubt about what was Self and what was Other:

> The work in question belongs in its entire structure to German art. Did Chopin, with his musical character that sprang from his Polish homeland, not belong to German art? Just as certainly *The Queen of Sheba* belongs to German art, just as the composer, living among Germans (in Vienna) since his childhood, owes his entire artistic *Bildung* to German art—Beethoven and Bach were his teachers. The "Fremde" in the work is nothing other than the strong representation of a musical characteristic that is appropriate to the subject matter.[29]

What Goldmark calls "representations," we would call "Orientalist signifiers." As Derek Scott and others have observed, these tend to relate much more closely to one another than they do to any particular ethnic musical practice, a point made already in 1884 by Hanslick, as we have seen, in his review of Bachrich's ballet *Sakuntala*.[30] Such signifiers are surely what Hanslick was responding to in *Die Königin von Saba* when he complained about all those

[28] Notably, in his memoirs Goldmark suggests it was probably the lingering spell left on him from his reading as a young man of *One Thousand and One Nights* that eventually led to the composition of both *Sakuntala* and *Die Königin von Saba* (Goldmark, *Erinnerungen*, 96; *Notes from the Life*, 173–74). For a rare instance of a Viennese critic who recognized the Orientalist aspect of Goldmark's opera, see Dr. Robert Hirschfeld, "K.k. Hofoperntheater," *Wiener Abendpost*, October 5, 1896, quoted in Reittererová and Reitterer, *Vier Dutzend rothe Strümpf*, 312.

[29] Goldmark, in *Neue Freie Presse*, June 4, 1911.

[30] Derek Scott, "Postmodernism and Music," in *The Routledge Companion to Postmodernism*, ed. Stuart Sim, 2nd ed. (New York: Routledge, 2005), 130; idem, "Orientalism and Musical Style," *Musical Quarterly* 82 (1998): 309–35.

"lamenting, whining tunes, augmented fourths and diminished sixths"; indeed, Hanslick used almost exactly the same locutions to describe the Egyptian local color found in certain passages of Verdi's *Aida*.[31] The lack of ethnic specificity associated with Orientalist signifiers likewise helps to explain why Speidel seemed to hear the same "strangely crimped melismas" in both *Die Königin von Saba* (from the Hebrew Bible) and *Sakuntala* (from a Sanskrit play).

Perhaps precisely in response to the unwelcome tendency of critics of every stripe to characterize his music in an overly reductive manner as "Jewish-Oriental," Goldmark claims to have produced distinctly different styles for the Arabian personages of the opera's Entrance March and the Indian penitents in *Sakuntala*. Moreover, he claims he achieved a great differentiation of style throughout *Die Königin von Saba*, "even in the characterization of the Temple Ritual."[32] Consider the pseudo-liturgical setting of the scene in Solomon's Temple, the sensuous theme that introduces the Indian title character of *Sakuntala*, and the sultry melody for English horn from the Queen's Entrance March (ex. 8.5). Although they can be distinguished from one another in their scoring and in certain other respects, all three passages, with their shared ascending scalar triplet motive, were cut from the same bolt of cloth.[33] And as for the complaint that Eduard Kulke made in his review that Goldmark had chosen to set the Temple Ritual using "echoes of the synagogue" rather than a chorale in the style of Bach, the composer sidesteps that charge by pointing to the "special difficulty" he faced in setting this scene, since he "was not able to use Marian hymns or Protestant chorales and yet had to arouse in the Westerner religious feelings with Orientally tinged motives."[34] That is as much as Goldmark writes on this subject in "Thoughts about Form and Style." But in his memoirs, the composer goes one step further in distancing himself from those Orientally tinged motives. "I was never in the East," he writes, "but intuition helped me over that."[35]

[31] Ed. H. [Eduard Hanslick], "Hofoperntheater," *Neue Freie Presse*, June 24, 1874; adapted for Eduard Hanslick, *Die moderne Oper: Kritiken und Studien* (Berlin: A. Hofmann, 1875), 247–55 (at 250). Hanslick's preference for *Aida* over *Die Königin von Saba* stems in part from his conviction that, unlike Goldmark, Verdi limited his use of musical local color to a subordinate role.

[32] Goldmark, in *Neue Freie Presse*, June 4, 1911.

[33] For critics from across the spectrum, that cloth had, so to speak, the makings of Hasidic dress, as triplets quickly became code for "Jewish music," as we have seen.

[34] Goldmark, in *Neue Freie Presse*, June 4, 1911.

[35] Goldmark, *Erinnerungen*, 117; *Notes from the Life*, 210. Here Goldmark is perhaps setting himself apart from his fellow orientalist Félicien-César David, who, as he noted in his review of the latter's *Le désert* in 1862, had lived for several years in the Near East.

EXAMPLE 8.5a Goldmark, *Die Königin von Saba*, op. 27, Act II, Temple Scene, excerpt

E - wig, e - wig währt sei - ne Gü - te

e - wig, e - wig währt sei - ne Gü - te

EXAMPLE 8.5b Goldmark, *Sakuntala*, op. 13, first theme, beginning

EXAMPLE 8.5c Goldmark, *Die Königin von Saba*, op. 27, Act I, Queen's Entrance March, excerpt

For traditional liberal nationalist critics such as Hanslick and Speidel, writing in 1875 at the time of the opera's première, Goldmark's Orientalist signifiers may have been, as I have argued, too reminiscent of the "Jewish particularisms" that a properly acculturated, German-speaking Jew ought to have left behind. For the antisemitic critics who came at the end of the century, by contrast, Goldmark was indelibly marked by those "particularisms" and could never leave them behind. Goldmark will have none of any of this. He positions himself as a German composer who, in various dramatic contexts, represents a range of Others, thereby confounding as well Wilhelm Goldbaum and other sympathetic commentators who—adopting a late-nineteenth-century racialist assumption but with a positive take— insisted the composer's music must somehow have inscribed his Jewish soul. By donning the mantle of musical Orientalist, Goldmark not only resists being reduced to an ethnic stereotype but also aims to thwart those racists who would deny him right of entry into the cultural enterprise known as *die heilige deutsche Kunst*.

Germans, Jews, and Czechs in Mahler's
Vienna

Hitherto the conflict has not at all been one of principle. The bone of contention
was initially {a village like} Cilli, or Weckelsdorf, or an appointment as Hofrat,
or a school or an office; ultimately it came to be all the public offices in Bohemia,
Moravia, and Silesia. The Czech civil service entered upon a struggle for the more
or less exclusive right to hold office. The German middle classes in Austria, which
only a few generations previously had provided the civil administration for all the
Habsburg domains and for the Holy Roman Empire of the German Nation, found
themselves squeezed out of the German Empire, out of Hungary, out of Galicia,
and finally even out of the lands of the Crown of Wenceslas and the Slavonic parts
of the Alps, and restricted to the small sphere of the ancient hereditary lands. The
material effect of this explains the violence of the defense mounted by the Germans.
　　　　　　　　　　—Synopticus [Karl Renner], *Staat und Nation* (1899)

PROMPTED BY THE success of *Die verkaufte Braut* in the spring of 1893
at the Theater an der Wien, Wilhelm Jahn delayed no longer in introducing Smetana at the Court Opera, where one of the composer's works
was staged in German translation during each of the director's last three
seasons: *Der Kuß* (*Hubička* [*The Kiss*], 1894), *Das Geheimnis* (*Tajemstvi* [*The*

Secret], 1895), and finally *Die verkaufte Braut* itself (in 1896). Although Jahn continued to steer clear of Dvořák, Hans Richter remained very much in the composer's corner during these years, and in the conductor's final four seasons at the helm of the Philharmonic the orchestra programmed his music as never before, performing eight new compositions between December 1894 and December 1897, including the concert overtures *V přírodě* (*In Nature's Realm*), *Karneval* (*Carnival*), and *Othello*; the "New World" Symphony and Cello Concerto; and two symphonic poems, *Vodník* (*The Water Goblin*) and *Polednice* (*The Noon Witch*), from a set of four based on gruesome Czech fairy-tale ballads by Karel Jaromír Erben.[1] It was not only the works of Smetana and Dvořák that filled the bills with Czech music as the century drew to its end. In the 1896–97 season alone, Viennese audiences heard no fewer than twelve works by Czech composers, including, in addition to Smetana and Dvořák, also Zdeněk Fibich, Oskar Nedbal, and Josef Suk, not only in the concerts of the Philharmonic and Gesellschaft der Musikfreunde but in chamber music concerts given by the Rosé, Hellmesberger, and Bohemian quartets.[2]

None of this activity escaped the notice of Otakar Hostinský, the eminent Czech critic, aesthetician, and Smetana advocate who was commissioned to write the essay on "Music in Bohemia" published in the *Kronprinzenwerk* in 1896.[3] Although Hostinský was concerned primarily with musical life within the crown land itself, near the end of his account he cast an eye toward Vienna. After reporting on the successful performances of stage works by Smetana, Dvořák, and Fibich during the International Music and Theater Exhibition held four years earlier in the Wiener Prater, he concluded with an expression of great patriotic pride in his compatriots' musical triumphs:

> Further Viennese successes are coming to the three composers in the
> realms of the chamber style and orchestral music, so that the chapter

---

[1] For a brief discussion of these works' reception, see Brodbeck, "Dvořák's Reception in Liberal Vienna," 119–20, and McColl, *Music Criticism in Vienna*, 178–96 *passim*.

[2] For a selection of reviews with commentary, see McColl, *Music Criticism in Vienna*, 88–100. McColl focuses on the reception found in the German nationalist press (*Deutsche Zeitung, Deutsches Volksblatt*, and *Ostdeutsche Rundschau*) and seems somewhat surprised by the political awareness evinced by the "critics of a more tolerant liberal stripe, who normally kept clear of politics" (ibid., 90). As we have seen, the tensions between Germans and Czechs during the last twenty years of the century were never far from the surface in anyone's reviews.

[3] "Otakar Hostinský, "Musik in Böhmen," in *Die österreichisch-ungarische Monarchie in Wort und Bild*, vol. 15: *Böhmen*, part 2 (Vienna, 1896), 1–60.

"Music in Bohemia" can hardly be closed more appropriately than with this impressive evidence of the amends, if only belated, which the music-loving Imperial Capital has made in so full a measure to Czech music, blossoming since the rise of national culture in the 60s and yet scarcely noticed abroad.[4]

This may have seemed a fitting way to end an essay that was written, after all, for an encyclopedia designed to foster "collective patriotism" among the many national groups of the Habsburg Monarchy. Yet in the following year, August Püringer gave a very different take of the situation in his review of the season-opening Gesellschaft concert of November 14, 1897, which offered a complete performance of Dvořák's oratorio *St. Ludmilla*. Indeed, this reads like a German-nationalist rejoinder to Hostinský's expression of Czech pride. After pointedly (if unconvincingly) disclaiming any national chauvinism and professing his high esteem for Smetana and his more-than-passing interest in Tchaikovsky and even Dvořák, Püringer gets down to complaining about the recent "flooding" of the city's musical life with Slavic works:

> The Czechs raise their heads ever more boldly in our homeland, in our native city, claim German soil for themselves, and cast a covetous eye on our schools and political representation. At this point in time the two nations are opposed in bitter conflict and the waves surge high. Was it really an urgent necessity at this moment to open a concert season with a major work by a Czech composer, which deals to boot with a Czech national subject?[5]

Obviously, Hostinský and Püringer are viewing the same subject through two very different lenses. In what follows, we shall have a look primarily through the German-nationalist lens and attempt to make sense of what we see.

The Cilli Crisis and Die verkaufte Braut

As I have argued, Vienna's German-nationalist critics had generally praised Smetana's music, both on account of its obvious stylistic debts to Wagner

---

[4] Ibid., 60.

[5] Hagen [August Püringer], "Erstes Gesellschaftskonzert," *Ostdeutsche Rundschau*, November 17, 1897; translation adapted from McColl, *Music Criticism in Vienna*, 89–90, where the date of the review is erroneously given as November 17, 1896, and without attribution to Püringer.

and Liszt and also because unlike, say, that of Brahms or Goldmark, it offered a laudable model for what properly *deutschnational* composers might hope to achieve. Thus Püringer's review of the comic opera *Der Kuß*, introduced at the Court Opera on February 27, 1894, begins by extolling Smetana for being "the first to find a place for Czechdom among the other nations in the realm of music" and for not "limiting himself to the national tradition [but] also [making] the tenets of the new German art as created by Wagner a part of his own."[6] And if the German-nationalist critics were in agreement that *Das Geheimnis*, which followed on the Court Opera stage on March 27, 1895, was not a successful work, Püringer at least still found a way to praise its composer by attributing the waning creative power evinced in this late opera, written after the onset of his total deafness, not only to the social isolation imposed by this affliction but also to the unjust "injuries" that Smetana, precisely because he was a composer with stylistic affinities for Wagner and Liszt, had suffered at the hands of the very Czech countrymen "to whom he had brought the greatest renown in the field of art."[7]

Signs of a narrowing in attitude, however, are evident in the German-nationalist reception of *Die verkaufte Braut* when it was staged at last at the Court Opera on October 4, 1896.[8] Here again we may use a striking political episode to form the basis for a nuanced understanding of contemporary musical culture. Following Taaffe's resignation as minister-president in November 1893, Polish and German conservative holdovers from the Iron Ring formed a new government that also included moderates from the United German Left. Although German liberals had adopted an increasingly nationalist rhetoric in their long years in opposition, especially in the years since 1885, the more radical elements of the left had always questioned the nationalist commitment of the moderate party leaders. That these suspicions were well founded became clear in the spring of 1895, when the finance minister, Ernst von Plener, one of the two liberal members

---

[6] Hagen [August Püringer], "Hofoperntheater," *Ostdeutsche Rundschau*, March 4, 1894. See also Hans Puchstein, "Hofoperntheater," *Deutsches Volksblatt*, March 1, 1894.

[7] Hagen [August Püringer], "Das Geheimnis," *Ostdeutsche Rundschau*, March 30, 1895.

[8] On the Court Opera's production of *Die verkaufte Braut*, see Reittererová and Reitterer, *Vier Dutzend rothe Strümpfe*, 73–80. An extensive selection of reviews is provided in ibid., 292–385. My concern here is limited to the reception of Smetana's opera in the German-nationalist press, which takes on a different tone from what we saw in the coverage by those papers of the earlier Viennese performances from 1892 and 1893. Since, by contrast, the discourse used by reviewers who wrote for the more traditional liberal papers does not differ significantly from that which we have seen before, we need not examine it here.

of the cabinet, agreed to provide funding for a Slovene-language Gymnasium in Cilli, a small South Styrian town in which German speakers outnumbered Slovene speakers by about three to one. As Judson notes, since Cilli lay in an overwhelmingly Slovene-speaking region, this act of placing "a Slovene-language [school] in an 'embattled' German town (that is, one perceived to be surrounded by a Slovene hinterland) was an act of expropriation, a gratuitous gift of *Nationalbesitzstand* made to the enemy."[9] When Plener's outraged fellow liberals withdrew their support of the government, the coalition came undone, and in September 1895 the emperor turned to Count Casimir Badeni, a Polish aristocrat, to head a new cabinet. The liberals never again sat at the cabinet table.

We can see something of the same rhetoric of expropriation in the German-nationalist reception of *Die verkaufte Braut* in the following year. Although the moderate Theodor Helm praised the work in terms that recall his earlier assessments from 1892 and 1893, he did at least question the wisdom of scheduling a performance of this "expressly Slavic national work" on what was in fact the "nameday of the monarch in German Vienna."[10] Writing in the *Deutsches Volksblatt*, Camillo Horn took a more radical tack. He reproached "the leadership of the first German Court Opera" for being slow to introduce worthy new German works while instead "still giv[ing] preference to foreign art."[11] Here, then, it is not merely the city of Vienna that is claimed as *Nationalbesitzstand*—Hanslick might well have agreed with some modified version of that claim—but rather an institution of the Habsburg monarchy itself, whose domain, after all, was a multinational state. And it is a "foreign" work by the Czech Smetana that, in Horn's view, had no business enjoying preference at such an important German institution. To recall Judson's account of the Cilli crisis, here Horn has charged the leadership of the Court Opera with giving *Nationalbesitzstand* to the enemy. From the point of view of this and like-minded Viennese critics, things were about to get worse.

Mahler and the Court Opera

Six months later, Gustav Mahler, a Germanized (and recently baptized) Jew from the Czech crown lands, was appointed to the conducting staff of the

---

[9] Judson, *Exclusive Revolutionaries*, 249.

[10] I have quoted here from Helm's brief initial report (h–m [Theodor Helm], "Hofoperntheater," *Deutsche Zeitung*, October 5, 1896). The opera was then the subject of a feuilleton that appeared the next day as Theodor Helm, " 'Die verkaufte Braut' in Hofoperntheater," *Deutsche Zeitung*, October 6, 1896.

[11] Camillo Horn, "Die verkaufte Braut," *Deutsches Volksblatt*, October 6, 1896.

Court Opera with the tacit understanding that he would soon be named Jahn's successor as Court Opera director. Things moved quickly in the months that followed. Exhausted after seventeen years at the helm and nearly blind from cataracts, Jahn was soon eased into retirement, and on October 8, 1897, Mahler was indeed named to replace him.[12]

In achieving this long-sought goal, Mahler benefited in part from the support of Vienna's aging liberal cultural establishment. Brahms was on his deathbed at this time—he passed away on April 3—but his high regard of the younger man's conducting was well established. Goldmark had been present for—and much pleased by—Mahler's performances in Hamburg of *Das Heimchen am Herd* the previous November. In a series of letters that ensued, Mahler capitalized on this feeling of good will, encouraging Goldmark to take steps on behalf of his candidacy in Vienna.[13] The latter may well have done nothing in this regard, but word of his support, like that of Brahms, would surely have made its way into the court. Indeed, already in a testimonial letter of January 10, 1897, to the Imperial and Royal Court Councilor Josef von Bezecny, the distinguished Hungarian politician Count Albert Apponyi made known the high opinion both composers had formed of Mahler's conducting during his earlier tenure at the Royal Hungarian Court Opera in Budapest.[14]

In a feuilleton of March 27, 1897, Hanslick shared his view that the Vienna Court Opera was in need of new direction, laying the blame on Jahn for both "the poverty of the repertoire and the gaps in personnel."[15] If in this way the critic Hanslick made an implicit, public plea for new blood at the Opera, later that day Hofrat Hanslick articulated explicit, private support of Mahler's appointment in a letter that was probably intended for Bezecny. Hanslick's advocacy may well have been decisive, for a few days later Mahler

---

[12] For a fine account of Mahler's rise to the position of Court Opera director, see Jens Malte Fischer, *Gustav Mahler*, trans. Stewart Spencer (New Haven and London: Yale University Press, 2011), 282–302.

[13] Mahler's letters to Goldmark are discussed and quoted in Karpath, *Begegnung mit dem Genius*, 22–27 passim.

[14] Apponyi's letter is quoted in Kurt Blaukopf, *Gustav Mahler*, trans. Inge Goodwin (London: Futura, 1975), 133.

[15] Ed. H. [Eduard Hanslick], "Hofoperntheater," *Neue Freie Presse*, March 27, 1897. This feuilleton also paid tribute to Goldmark upon the recent one-hundredth performance of *Die Königin von Saba* at the Vienna Court Opera. In a letter of March 27, Goldmark not only thanked the critic for his kind remarks but also acknowledged certain shortcomings in the performance, which had taken place six days earlier, seemingly agreeing in this way with Hanslick's view of the state of the institution. Unpublished letter housed

arrived in Vienna from Budapest and, on April 4, came to terms with Bezecny on an initial contract.[16]

All parties were agreed that Jahn's best days were behind him and that the Court Opera was in need of dynamic new leadership. The liberal critics welcomed Mahler's appointment and praised his early performances, and even the conductor's detractors at first acknowledged his musical gifts.[17] Still, the antisemitic newspapers naturally opposed the appointment of any Jew—even a Catholic convert—to a position of such cultural influence and power in "German Vienna."[18] That Francis Joseph finally gave way and installed the antisemite Lueger as Vienna's mayor on April 16, one day after Mahler signed his contract, of course, adds considerable irony to the situation. Herta Blaukopf has even suggested the court may have approved Mahler's appointment as a way of setting a good example in a city rife with antisemitism, citing the Lord Chamberlain Prince Liechtenstein's reported response to the news that Mahler was a Jew: "Things have not yet become so bad for us in Austria that anti-Semitism is the crucial factor in matters such as this."[19] That is not to say Mahler's conversion was not a condition sine qua non for the appointment, but rather merely that the court did not subscribe to racialist antisemitism, which was an entirely different matter. The Jews, after all, were the Habsburg monarchy's most loyal supporters. However that may be,

in the Miklós Rózsa Collection of Music Letters, Photographs, and Other Materials, Special Collections, University of Southern California Libraries, Los Angeles.

[16] Hanslick's previously unpublished letter to Bezecny is quoted in Fischer, *Gustav Mahler*, 290. In it, Hanslick made a concerted attempt to show how Mahler was better suited for the position than Felix Mottl, Cosima Wagner's choice and the only other serious candidate. Mahler's memorandum of acceptance of the contract terms is given in Blaukopf, *Mahler: A Documentary Study*, 210.

[17] See Herta Blaukopf, "Mahler's First Season as Director at the k.k. Hofoperntheater: The Composer Waits in the Wings," in *Perspectives on Gustav Mahler*, ed. Jeremy Barham (Aldershot, UK, and Burlington, VT: Ashgate, 2005), 327–43; a number of reviews from Mahler's first months at the Opera are included in the discussion of this period in Henry-Louis de la Grange, *Mahler*, vol. 2: *Vienna: The Years of Challenge (1897–1904)* (Oxford and New York: Oxford University Press, 1995), 24–53. See also the relevant entries in Max Kalbeck's diary from 1897 quoted in Sandra McColl, "Max Kalbeck and Gustav Mahler," *19th-Century Music* 20 (1996): 169.

[18] See the notice in the *Reichspost*, quoted in *Mahler: A Documentary Study*, 210, as well as the reports in the *Deutsche Zeitung, Ostdeutsche Rundschau*, and *Deutsches Volksblatt* quoted in McColl, *Music Criticism in Vienna*, 100–7.

[19] H. Blaukopf, "Mahler's First Season as Director at the k.k. Hofoperntheater," 334. As lord chamberlain, Liechtenstein was the ultimate authority for all matters related to the Court Opera. Liechtenstein's reported comment on the matter of whether Mahler's

Blaukopf is surely correct in noting how the antisemitic critics immediately began to pit the "Jewish" Mahler against the "Teutonic" Richter, who stayed on as first Kapellmeister at the Opera until 1900.

Mahler's first *Ring* cycle in Vienna, made up of a series of repertory productions given together at the end of August 1897, brought forth a particularly instructive example of this kind of racialized way of seeing things. This occurs in Hans Puchstein's review of September 1 for the *Deutsches Volksblatt*. It is clear from the context that Puchstein was reacting at the outset to a pair of notices that had appeared in the *Neue Freie Presse* five days earlier. The first was a brief unsigned report—presumably written by Richard Heuberger, who was increasingly taking over the regular reviewing duties for this paper from the semi-retired Hanslick—of Mahler's performance of *Die Walküre*. This opera had first been given in Vienna twenty years earlier, but, as the author noted, "none of the artists who took part in the first performance [was] active any longer, and not even Hans Richter sat at the [conductor's] desk as usual, but rather Herr Mahler, who with his profound seriousness and great enthusiasm shows himself to be the equal of the greatest masters of his art." The second notice cited several well-sourced reports that Mahler would soon be named Jahn's replacement.[20] Reacting in anger, Puchstein began by noting that with no previous Viennese presentation of the *Ring* had so much fuss been made in the local press, and this only because a "young Capellmeister who was completely unknown to our public sat at the conductor's desk in place of the battle-hardened Field Marshall [Richter], to whom Richard Wagner, in the great decisive battle at Bayreuth in 1876, had entrusted the command of the troops he had summoned and drilled."[21] Puchstein goes on to complain scornfully about unnamed critics of "the Mahler clique" who had never before shown any appreciation for the *Ring* but who now, as a way of lending support to Mahler's candidacy for the position of Court Opera director, had suddenly had a change of heart. With a tacit reference to

---

Jewish origin should preclude his appointment is given in Mahler's letter of January 25, 1897, to the composer Ödön von Mihalovich, quoted in ibid. The letter itself is found in K. Blaukopf, ed., *Mahler: A Documentary Study*, 208.

[20] *Neue Freie Presse*, August 27, 1897.

[21] Hans Puchstein, "Der Nibelungen-Cyclus an unserer Oper," *Deutsches Volksblatt*, September 1, 1897, from which the next several quotations likewise are taken. See also A. L–ch [Albert Leitich], "Hofoperntheater," *Deutsche Zeitung*, August 26, 1897, where Mahler is similarly pitted unfavorably with Richter. Leitich (1869–1908), a founding member of the New Richard Wagner Society, was more in step than the older Helm with the antisemitic editorial policy taken by the *Deutsche Zeitung* after 1894. Leitich also wrote for the *Deutsches Volksblatt*.

Heuberger, a composer as well as critic, Puchstein suggests that one reason for this change was that the critics who were also composers wished to curry favor with the person whom they assumed would soon be the director and therefore in a position to affect their careers.

But rather than pursue that line, Puchstein turns instead to what is his main concern, namely, defending the idea that Mahler, notwithstanding his recent conversion to Catholicism and regardless of the musical merits, should be denied appointment as director of the Opera purely on racial grounds, on account of "his belonging to Judaism on the basis of his race" [*auf seine Racenzugehörigkeit zum Judenthum*]. He continues:

> I regard it as obviously improper that a Jew should be appointed to head the first German opera institution and am also convinced that the same gentlemen whose colleagues now call for a boycott of Pilsner beer and Prague ham would logically have to cry bloody murder if one now wanted to make a Czech the director of the Court Opera. The reproaches I must raise on these grounds are just as obviously not directed against Herr Mahler, whom one naturally cannot blame if he does not refuse a well-paid post in Vienna if it is offered to him, but rather against the persons who called him here and in so doing contributed to the gradual robbery of our Court Opera's German character.

It is notable that Puchstein refers to the German character of "our" Court Opera, stressing the racial rather than cultural element of *Nationalbesitzstand*. We have seen evidence of this alleged robbery of national property not only in the post-Cilli, German-nationalist reception of *Die verkaufte Braut* but also in the contemporaneous antisemitic reception of Kauders's *Walther von Vogelweide* and Goldmark's *Das Heimchen am Herd*. Mahler's imminent appointment to head the Opera, welcomed by liberals as the best way to reinvigorate a languorous institution, could only be seen by the antisemites as an imminent threat. Noting that the recently announced new season included no performances of Peter Cornelius's *Der Cid* or Hugo Wolf's *Der Corregidor*, the unnamed author of an article entitled "The Change of Direction at the Court Opera," which appeared in the *Deutsche Zeitung* on August 27, attempted to put the best face on his objection "to the appointment of a non-German, and indeed a Jew, to the leadership of a German institute" by claiming the need to stand up for works by German composers he seems to assume that Mahler would never favor with a performance.[22] Yet this implicit demand for

[22] "Der Direktionswechsel in der Hofoper," *Deutsche Zeitung*, August 27, 1897.

performance of more German operas was something of a smokescreen. After all, responding to Mahler's election in the following year as Richter's replacement at the head of the Vienna Philharmonic, the same newspaper expressed its objection more baldly: "In our view, in a German city only a German appears qualified to interpret German music, a condition that Mahler is just not able to fulfill."[23]

It lies beyond the scope of this book to pursue Mahler's tumultuous career in Vienna much further, a subject unto itself that has suffered from no lack of scholarly attention.[24] But by way of concluding, let us take up one last case study of how "music got mixed up in politics." Although this involves Mahler, the controversy had less to do with racial origins than with the alleged expropriation of *Nationalbesitzstand*.

The Badeni Crisis and Dalibor

On April 5, 1897, Count Badeni issued a controversial pair of language ordinances for Bohemia and Moravia. Designed to placate the Young Czechs in the Reichsrat, these decrees mandated that, beginning in July 1901, internal as well as external bureaucratic matters in the affected regions were to be transacted in whatever language, German or Czech, a case had first been brought. This, of course, meant that all German-speaking bureaucrats subject to the mandate

---

[23] *Deutsche Zeitung*, September 27, 1898; translated in K. M. Knittel, " 'Polemik im Concertsaal': Mahler, Beethoven, and the Viennese Critics," *19th-Century Music* 29 (2006): 289. See also E. Th., "Das jüdische Regime an der Wiener Oper," *Deutsche Zeitung*, November 4, 1898, which appeared on the day before Mahler's first concert with the Philharmonic. According to Natalie Bauer-Lechner, this article was written by a disgruntled member of the Court Opera Orchestra and accepted for publication without the knowledge of the newspaper's music critic; Bauer-Lechner is referring here to Theodor Helm. See Natalie Bauer-Lechner, *Recollections of Gustav Mahler*, trans. Dika Newlin, ed. Peter Franklin (Cambridge: Cambridge University Press, 1980), 121.

[24] For a useful overview, see Leon Botstein, "Gustav Mahler's Vienna," *The Mahler Companion*, ed. Donald Mitchell and Andrew Nicholson (Oxford: Oxford University Press, 1999), 6–38. For a more detailed study, see La Grange, *Mahler*, vol. 2: *Vienna: The Years of Challenge, 1897–1904*, and vol. 3: *Vienna: Triumph and Disillusion, 1904–1907* (Oxford and New York: Oxford University Press, 1995). The literature on Mahler's treatment by the Viennese critics (some of it, but by no means all, colored by antisemitism) is extensive. For the most recent study, see Knittel, *Seeing Mahler*; Knittel's work is problematic precisely because it views the critical writings almost exclusively through the lens of antisemitism. Notley's account ("Musical Culture in Vienna," 42–50), although brief, is far more balanced and nuanced.

would now be required to become proficient in Czech. (The Czech-speaking bureaucrats already spoke German as a matter of course.) These so-called Badeni Decrees set off a surge in German-nationalist sentiment, not only among the likes of Schönerer's radical All Germans but also among the various factions of the old "German left," even those for whom social and economic concerns had traditionally trumped nationality.[25] It was not merely a question of language, as sensitive an issue as ever, nor even one of economic opportunity or social standing. Badeni's decrees implied an indivisible Bohemia, which was tantamount to ceding the Young Czechs' claim of Bohemian state right. And the German Bohemians knew that under the terms of any constitution that might follow from this claim, they would inevitably be submerged in a Slavic state. (This explains the boycott of Pilsener beer and Prague ham that Puchstein suggested was supported even by the liberal press.)[26] By the end of November obstructionist tactics in the Reichsrat, coupled with violent street protests in Vienna and elsewhere, had brought about a retraction of the ordinances along with Badeni's resignation.[27]

It was in this charged atmosphere that Mahler, on October 4, 1897, conducted Vienna's first German-language performance of Smetana's *Dalibor*.[28] For the second year in a row, then, the emperor's nameday was marked by the performance of a new opera by Smetana, a circumstance that would raise eyebrows, as we shall see. Whereas *Die verkaufte Braut* is a simple rustic comedy, *Dalibor* tells the tragic story of a legendary knight of the fifteenth century, who kills the Burgrave of Ploškovice to avenge the death of his best friend, Zdeněk, who had fallen to the Burgrave in battle. Although Milada, the Burgrave's sister, testifies against Dalibor during his trial, she is so impressed by the man's courage that she eventually decides to help him. Disguised as a male musician, she comes to him in his prison cell to hatch a plan to secure his rescue. Through an act of betrayal, the opera ends with the separate

[25] See the concise but incisive commentary in Judson, *Exclusive Revolutionaries*, 254–58.

[26] On the use of nationalist boycotts, see Catherine Albrecht, "The Rhetoric of Economic Nationalism in the Bohemian Boycott Campaigns of the Late Habsburg Monarchy," *Austrian History Yearbook* 32 (2001): 47–68.

[27] For a good account, see Whiteside, *The Socialism of Fools*, 160–87.

[28] For a selection of reviews of performance in 1897 with commentary, see McColl, *Music Criticism in Vienna*, 93–98, 114–18. I refer to some of the same reviews as McColl in what follows, as well as others that she does not cite, but translations are generally my own and where her citations are erroneous I give the corrected dates. See also Julie Dorn Morrison, "Gustav Mahler at the Vienna Hofoper: A Study of the Reception in the Viennese Press (1897–1907)" (Ph.D. diss., Northwestern University, 1996), 160–76.

deaths of Milada, killed trying to liberate the knight, and Dalibor, felled in the ensuing battle with the victorious royal troops.

Despite a storyline that could easily be read in nationalist terms, Czech audiences reacted coolly to the opera when it was introduced in Prague in 1868. With its plot similarity to *Fidelio* and its many stylistic affinities for Wagner and Liszt, *Dalibor* was judged to be insufficiently "Czech," and the composer himself was described as the "Germanizer of Czech music." Indeed, the opera did not break through with Czech audiences until two years after the composer's death, when, in December 1886, František A. Šubert revived it at the Czech National Theater in Prague. As we have seen, *Dalibor* was well received, in turn, when Šubert and his visiting troupe performed it during their Viennese residency in the spring of 1892. Nevertheless, Jahn steered clear of it when he subsequently began to introduce Smetana's works at the Court Opera, turning first instead to the comic operas *Der Kuß, Das Geheimnis*, and *Die verkaufte Braut*. Only with Mahler's production of *Dalibor* in 1897 was one of Smetana's three operas based in Czech legend and history put on the boards there.

Dalibor was for many years close to Mahler's heart, although he later cooled on it. He first conducted the opera in Hamburg in February 1896 and spared no pains in preparing it the following year for Vienna, even corresponding with Šubert on matters of costume and staging.[29] Not only did he make numerous minor changes to the score; he also recomposed the opera's ending, seeking to improve on the work's main dramatic flaw by eliminating the final scene in which Dalibor is killed by the royal troops and closing instead with Milada's funeral song and a moment of quiet tenderness.

Artistically, as nearly everyone agreed, Mahler's *Dalibor* was a clear triumph and seemed to presage an exciting new era at the Court Opera. Hanslick put it thus:

> Herr Mahler...has earned our special gratitude by performing *Dalibor*. He shares with Wilhelm Jahn the valuable ability to direct his attention not just to the score but also to the stage picture, in every case contributing sensitively to the work's dramatic and musical impact. Mahler has rehearsed *Dalibor* with keen understanding and meticulous care. No one familiar with the work will have failed to notice the way in which he brings out every subtlety of the score, while maintaining the harmonious unity of the whole and now and then enhancing its effectiveness by means of a modest cut

[29] LaGrange, *Mahler*, 2: 65n.

or interpolation. Young, experienced and ambitious, he is, we hope, the man to breathe new life into our opera, which has recently grown weary and sleepy. The production of Smetana's *Dalibor* was without doubt a debt of honour that Austria's leading opera house needed to pay, both Hamburg and Munich long since having beaten us to the post. It will not be the last debt of honour that we shall have to thank Herr Mahler for paying off.[30]

In earlier years, as we have seen, Hanslick had by no means refrained from making explicit reference to Cisleithania's nationalities politics from a liberal nationalist point of view. In 1880, in his review of Smetana's *From My Life* Quartet, he expressed satisfaction that the composer's work gave evidence that, in music, German remained the *landesübliche Sprache*. In 1890, he took advantage of the opportunity presented by the Vienna Philharmonic's performance of Smetana's *Vltava* to insist on the same language rights for German music lovers in Vienna as proposed for Czechs in Prague under the terms of Taaffe's Bohemian Compromise. And in 1893, although he did not make open reference to the language controversy, his poetic reading of Smetana's *Vyšehrad* was unmistakable in the position it took on a "lost Prague" that was once a city of Germans. Now, in his review from 1897 of *Dalibor*, he evinces a subtle but significant change. Nowhere in his feuilleton is any mention made of Badeni or of the crisis that had ensued from his language decrees. At a moment of great social unrest, Hanslick seems to stand squarely with the Habsburg supranational ideal by referring to the debt of honor paid by *Austria*'s leading opera house to a composer by one of her own sons, Smetana. We cannot help being reminded that Hanslick was one of those "new men" who, in Gellner's view, were the monarchy's staunchest defenders.

Unlike Hanslick, the younger liberal critic Albert Kauders makes a frank reference to the increasingly tense political situation from the very first lines of his review:

The Bohemian master Smetana's new procession into the proud palace of art . . . is not taking place under favorable circumstances. Five years ago, when German Vienna afforded an . . . unexpected triumph to Czech art in the Exhibition Theater, those of an idealistically inspired

[30] Ed.H. [Eduard Hanslick], "Hofoperntheater," *Neue Freie Presse*, October 6, 1897, rpt.in Hanslick, *Am Ende des Jahrhunderts*, 57–65. I have taken my translation from Fischer, *Mahler*, 300.

nature tied this artistic event to political hopes both beautiful as well as bold. One expected nothing less than a solution to the Bohemian question, which persisted despite all the best efforts and diplomatic finesse of the Count of Reconciliation [*Versöhnungsgraf*].[31] It was to be loosened up through the artistic magic of a Bohemian Orpheus, succumb, and die away in harmony. Unfortunately we do not live in the best of worlds. . . . The shawms of peace have long since gone quiet, and the fanfares of national strife are resounding more stridently than ever. Therefore we say it again: the knight Dalibor does not arrive at the Opera Ring under favorable circumstances or at the best of times.[32]

Kauders regrets that *Dalibor* had not been performed in Vienna's "palace of art"—his way of referring to the Court Opera—in an earlier, less fraught time, for no other opera by Smetana, in his view, is more fitting of performance in German Vienna because none is more kindred and sympathetic to German feeling. Kauders's Smetana "speaks to the German spirit" in a manner befitting of Weber or Wagner. And the critic does not hesitate to remind his readers that Smetana had been scorned in his own homeland when *Dalibor* was introduced there on account of its Germanizing tendencies, a historical circumstance that he sees as an injustice done to the very composer "who [had] founded that art [in the first place] and immediately elevated it to an astonishingly thrilling echelon." Notably, though Kauders questioned the wisdom of going forward with a production of *Dalibor* at this time, he did not (nor, of course, did Hanslick) question the propriety of the Court Opera's decision to do so. His concern seemed to lie solely in what would be best to ensure the success of a work that confirmed his (no less than Hanslick's) own cultural project.

The German nationalists, by contrast, took a different point of view, even while they, too, praised the German qualities of Smetana's score. Thus writing in the *Deutsche Zeitung* on October 5, Theodor Helm puts in at least a token defense of the Court Opera as *Nationalbesitzstand*:

As we willingly grant this posthumous triumph to the Manes of the highly talented Czech composer who was little known in his lifetime, so it seems provocative that the Imperial Court Opera in German Vienna undertook to celebrate the Emperor's nameday with such an

---

[31] This was a clear reference to Count Taaffe's attempt to reconcile the Czechs and Germans of Bohemia by means of his ill-fated Compromise.

[32] Albert Kauders, "Hofoperntheater," *Neues Wiener Journal*, October 5, 1897.

expressively Czech national work. And this even in the era of the language decree! It showed rare moderation on the part of our public not to mount the slightest hostile demonstration. Indeed, not even the exuberant enthusiasm of the late composer's fellow countrymen who applauded as one [in the audience] was allowed to spoil the joy of the opera's many musical beauties.[33]

In the feuilleton that followed the day after, Helm snidely remarked that only a Czech chauvinist could take any pleasure from Josef Wenzig's dramatically ineffective libretto, whose many weaknesses Max Kalbeck could not overcome in his German adaption and translation. (Every critic agreed this was the work's weak link.) But for Smetana's musical setting, Helm had nothing but praise.[34] After enumerating the many, mostly German, composers whose influence, in his view, could be traced in Smetana's opera—Wagner and Liszt, of course, but also Beethoven, Weber, Schubert, Schumann and even Chopin—Helm stressed that Smetana avoided slavish imitation, never lost his individuality, and indeed learned as one master learns from another. Although near the end of the feuilleton Helm made another half-hearted defense of the Court Opera as *Nationalbesitzstand*, at least on the emperor's nameday, he leaves no doubt of his opinion that *Dalibor* was nevertheless a deserving addition to the institution's repertory.[35]

By the current standards of the *Deutsche Zeitung*, Helm was a moderate. More representative was a polemic that soon appeared in the same newspaper under the title "The Czechs and the Viennese Performance of *Dalibor*."[36] This article was published without the author's name revealed, but it was likely penned by the same person who had written "The Change of Direction at the Court Opera" a few months earlier. Both are concerned above all with the defense of *Nationalbesitzstand* that is conceived in racial terms. In the first

---

[33] Helm, in *Deutsche Zeitung*, October 5, 1897. Not surprisingly, the first performance was well attended by Vienna's resident Czech community, ranging from delegates to the Reichsrat to a large contingent of boisterous students sitting in the fourth gallery. Helm was not alone in expressing surprise that the national exuberance that was so evident in the students' boisterous cheering at every opportunity did not spark a counterdemonstration on the part of any Germans in the audience. See also the reports in the *Neue Freie Presse*, October 5, 1897, and the *Neues Wiener Tagblatt*, October 5, 1897.

[34] Theodor Helm, "Hof-Operntheater," *Deutsche Zeitung*, October 6, 1897.

[35] Ibid.

[36] "Die Tschechen und die Wiener Aufführung von *Dalibor*," *Deutsche Zeitung*, December 7, 1897.

article, the author's concern had been with the appointment of a "non-German" (i.e., the Jew Mahler) to the head of the institution and ostensibly with what he feared this boded for future repertorial choices. The implication, of course, was that Mahler would favor works contributing to the further "Jewification" of the programs. Now in the second article, with the new season announced, he expressed concern in so many words about a comparable "slavification" of the repertory: "Our protest against the growing denationalization of the *German* Court Opera has, at least in the case of *Dalibor*, borne no fruit."[37] Remembering that *Die verkaufte Braut* was performed on the emperor's name-day in 1896, the author predicts sarcastically that Smetana's *Libussa* would surely follow in 1898. Moreover, he complains that two other Slavic works, Tchaikovsky's *Eugen Onegin* and *Iolanthe*, were already on the schedule for the season at hand. With a pointed jab at Hanslick, he wonders why the "Court Opera of German Vienna," having cleared its debt to Smetana, does not now seem to feel obliged to pay a "debt of honor" to the neglected operas of German composers such as Cornelius, Wolf, and Richard Strauss.

If anything, the racial element associated with *Nationalbesitzstand* is even more clearly expressed in Theodor Antropp's largely favorable review of *Dalibor* for the *Ostdeutsche Rundschau*. Antropp, too, alludes to Hanslick when he acknowledges that with this performance "an artistic debt of honor was paid with compound interest." And he also seems to allude to the anonymous author of "The Czechs and the Viennese Performance of *Dalibor*" when he adds, "Now it is said that German debts of honor—and these are much greater and more urgent—should be cleared as soon as possible if our Court Opera wants to be for us what she should be in the German city of Vienna: a German artistic institution."[38] For Antropp this does not mean that worthy art by non-German composers does not deserve to be heard. Still, "blood must be thicker than water. One must beware of cultivating the greatness of the art of a foreign people in the midst of forsaking one's own artworks,

---

[37] Ibid. (emphasis added). When later that month, in the wake of the performances of *Dalibor* and *St. Ludmilla*, Max Kalbeck "hoped that it will not occur to anyone to be outraged at the slavification of the Vienna Court Opera and Vienna's concert halls," he was two and a half months late. See Max Kalbeck, "Anton Dvorak's [*sic*] 'Heilige Ludmilla'," *Neues Wiener Tagblatt*, November 17, 1897, cited in translation in McColl, *Music Criticism in Vienna*, 91. Here I have corrected McColl's bibliographical citation.

[38] McColl assumes it was this review in the *Ostdeutsche Rundschau* that drew attack in the *Deutsche Zeitung* on the question of settling debts (ibid., 95–96). In fact, as suggested, the writers for both these papers were making reference to Hanslick's review.

if otherwise one does not wish to play the sad role of a shirtless beggar in a purple cloak."[39]

Exacerbating the situation for the radical German nationalists was the Viennese première of Puccini's *La bohème* at the Theater an der Wien on the day following the opening of *Dalibor* at the Court Opera. This confluence of two new foreign operas in Vienna in two days' time drew a predictably outraged response from Hans Puchstein, who saw in it corroboration of his claim that non-German artists continued to enjoy an inappropriate preferential treatment in Vienna's artistic life. The jeremiad that follows is almost breathtaking in its vehemence:

> Two days ago at the Opera the long planned demonstration for the Czech Smetana and yesterday enthusiastic homage for the Italian Puccini, and all this to celebrate the nameday of a monarch of the one people of the polyglot empire whose intellectual work opened up the expanse of the dynasty to modern culture, without whose tremendous achievements in the various fields of activity of the human spirit itself all the other peoples of this empire with the exception of the Italians—the Poles, Czechs, Croats, Slovenes, etc., not to forget the imaginary Magyars—would even today find themselves on a cultural level barely higher than that which can be observed in the Cossacks, Kyrgyz, and Tatars.

Although the sharper-key rhetoric displayed in the foregoing diatribe would never have occurred to a refined soul such as Hanslick, the passage that follows makes a claim with which he and his fellow liberal nationalists would likely have agreed:

> On its own, without the help of German cultural missionaries, not one of these [non-German] peoples would have achieved its present-day culture, the Czechs especially are fortunate that their people, through the hand of fate, was given its homeland in the midst of the German tribes and not among their "Slavic brothers."

What is this if not a reiteration by a radical German nationalist and antisemite of the old liberal nationalist imperative to project German cultural hegemony over all the peoples of Austria?

---

[39] Th. A. [Theodor Antropp], "Dalibor," *Ostdeutsche Rundschau*, October 7, 1897. Antropp (1864–1923) was the newspaper's theater critic.

Yet Puchstein immediately goes on to do what a moderate liberal nationalist like Hanslick or even a moderate German nationalist like Helm does not: make the German case to the exclusion of all else.

> Far be it from me, as I write these sentences, to wish to transfer the nationality strife from the political realm to that of art, as I have already been accused of doing by the Czechs and liberals. No, certainly not, but I think it is a national duty of every German whose position gives him the opportunity to speak to wide popular circles, to ensure that in these [circles] the sense of pride about what German masters have created in the realm of art remains alive. How often in recent years has the German population of Vienna on the liberal side been accused of laxity in national issues. But how, I ask, are the Viennese, who are not at all directly affected by the incessant struggle of their people for its national existence, as it rages everywhere on the language border, to learn a sense of pride about belonging to the German people when our theaters—and theaters are supposed to be national educational institutes—present one foreign work after another, and when the allegedly German press breaks out at every such performance in hymns of jubilation, without pointing out that our people too possess a series of masters who do not need to avoid the comparison with foreign [ones], indeed are in many cases superior to them.

It is for precisely this reason that it is so important to Puchstein to make the case against "expropriating" the Court Opera—and by extension Vienna's other musical venues—to the "enemy":

> Of course we should not undervalue that which is foreign because it is not German, but our theaters must be forbidden to perform any foreign work as long as a German work that is just as good remains unknown by our public, and the German journalist who does not cooperate with all his strength in fulfilling this postulate makes himself guilty of a serious offense against his people.

To Puchstein, such a journalist would scarcely be German at all.[40]

As for Smetana, Puchstein reminds his readers that he was, despite the stylistic trappings of Wagner and Liszt, and despite his old reputation among

---

[40] Here Puchstein is more likely to have in mind someone like Helm than Hanslick or any of Vienna's "Jewish" critics.

the Czechs as the "Germanizer of Czech music," first and foremost a Czech nationalist. That had not been a bad thing among the *deutschnational* activists in 1890, when, for example, Puchstein heralded *Vltava* in part because its nationalism could serve as a salutary model for German composers. Things were different now in 1897. The perceived neglect of new German works in favor of Czech ones—this slavification of Vienna's musical life—brought out something like the fears awakened by Badeni's language decrees. Prerogatives that were due to the Germans on the basis of their assumed superior culture were under attack and on the verge of defeat by a cultural inferior.

So Puchstein works to discredit the music of Smetana and his fellow Czechs. While he concedes that the Czechs could take justifiable pride in *Die verkaufte Braut*, he holds it to be the right and obligation of every German to place a higher value on *Der Freischütz*. Similarly, *Dalibor* falls short in any comparison with a German predecessor, be it Weber's *Oberon,* Beethoven's *Fidelio*, or Wagner's *Lohengrin*, not to speak of the later music dramas. "The Czechs," he writes, "cleverly emulate German examples without achieving the brilliance of their model." In its own way, this recalls Wagner's claims about the inability of even supremely accomplished Jewish composers such as Mendelssohn to penetrate to the essence of German music, whatever their ability to imitate its outer features. In short, for Puchstein, Czech composers and German composers now stand in a clear hierarchical arrangement on the basis of "race," and the former can never hope to achieve the higher plane of the latter. We would be hard-pressed to find a clearer illustration of how the old liberal nationalist project, exemplified in Hanslick's implicit claim that Smetana and Dvořák (and Goldmark, too, despite his penchant at times for musical exoticism) had earned the right to be considered acculturated German composers through their surpassing musical accomplishments had come to be usurped by the equally exclusivist but very different project of German ethno-nationalism.

It cannot be said that the radical *deutschnational* music-critical discourse I have considered here carried all that much weight in the day-to-day workings of musical life at the end of the century. From Mahler's appointment as Court Opera director and his election as the conductor of the Philharmonic players, for example, it is obvious that it held little sway in determining cultural appointments.[41] And despite *deutschnational* harangues about musical venues

---

[41] Indeed, as Leon Botstein notes, Mahler was a "wildly successful and lionized" figure among the Viennese, not only as a conductor and public celebrity but also even to some degree as a composer of what was undoubtedly highly challenging music. Leon

as *Nationalbesitzstand*, the Czechs Smetana and Dvořák and the Germanized Jew Goldmark made out quite well in Mahler's Vienna. The conductor led *Dalibor* in no fewer than twenty-two performances during his first seven seasons at the Court Opera, and in December 1900 he led a performance with the Philharmonic players of Smetana's *Vltava* and the Overture to the opera *Libussa*. If his plans for a performance at the Court Opera of Dvořák's *Rusalka* came to naught, at the Philharmonic Mahler continued Richter's practice of performing the Czech composer's works in nearly every season, including the symphonic poems *Píseň bohatýrská* (*A Hero's Song*) and *Holoubek* (*The Wood Dove*) in December 1898 and 1899, respectively.[42] By contrast, Mahler did not favor Goldmark in his programming with the Philharmonic, although he did include the orchestral showpiece *Im Frühling* in the subscription concert of March 18, 1900, and took it on tour with the orchestra to Paris that June. But at the Court Opera he scheduled numerous performances of *Das Heimchen am Herd*; gave the première, in 1899, of Goldmark's new opera, *Die Kriegsgefangene* (*The Prisoner of War*); and staged a lavish new production of *Die Königin von Saba*, in 1901.[43] So it is true: we should not overestimate what day-to-day music criticism can tell us about musical life per se.

Botstein, "Witnessing Music: The Consequences of History and Criticism," *Musical Quarterly* 94 (2011): 5.

[42] These performances came about as a result of Mahler's request of Dvořák, shortly after being elected to the post, to send any suitable new works that might be included in his programs. Mahler's side of the ensuing correspondence between the conductor and composer on this matter is found in *Korespondence a dokumenty*, vol. 8: *Korespondence přijatá 1896–1904* [Correspondence Received 1896–1904] (2000): 91–92, 100–101. For a brief discussion of the Viennese reception of the two symphonic poems, see Brodbeck, "Dvořák's Reception in Liberal Vienna," 121–22. On Mahler's subsequent effort to stage *Rusalka* at the Court Opera, see Milan Kuna, "Dvořák und Mahler: Über die in Wien nicht stattgefundene Inszenierung der *Rusalka*," in *Dvořák-Studien*, ed. Klaus Döge and Peter Jost (Mainz: Schott, 1994), 197–203.

[43] All this, of course, only confirmed in certain minds the diagnosis of a lamentable "Judaization" of Vienna's cultural life. For one particularly biting notice, prompted by the new production of *Die Königin von Saba*, see H.P. [Hans Puchstein], "Hofoperntheater," *Deutsches Volksblatt*, April 30, 1901, partially quoted in Robert Werba, "'Königin' für 277 Abende: Goldmarks Oper und ihr wienerisches Schicksal," *Österreichische Musikzeitschrift* 34 (1979): 199. Mahler clearly favored *Die Königin von Saba* over the composer's other works; see Peter Revers, "Karl Goldmark's Operas During the Directorship of Gustav Mahler," in *The Great Tradition and its Legacy: The Evolution of Dramatic and Musical Theater in Austria and Central Europe*, ed. Michael Cherlin, Halina Filipowicz, and Richard L. Rudolph (New York and Oxford: Berghan Books, 2004), 227–36.

From the broader political and cultural historical perspective, however, the crux of the matter is that one critical aspect of contemporary political ideology—who and what counted as German in late Habsburg Austria—forever rose to the surface in the discourse of roughly three generations of Viennese music critics. The traditional German liberal nationalism of Hanslick and Speidel was forged in the crucible of 1848. Helm's more nationally inflected liberalism reflected the tensions between Germans and Czechs that began to flare up during the Czech Awakening of the 1860s. The radical student politics of the 1880s, with its embrace of Schönerer's racialist antisemitism and irredentist German nationalism, just as surely shaped the discourse of young educated bourgeois critics such as Püringer and Puchstein. What makes the end of the century so fascinating is that all three generations are operating at once. And so, clearly, there are many answers to the question of how, in the musical culture of Liberal Vienna, to define *Deutschtum*. It depends on whom you ask. Yet it is easy enough to discern something of a continuum of exclusivity on this question, from a conception of Germanness that was rooted in social class and cultural elitism to one based in blood. By the time of Mahler's return to Vienna in 1897, the old liberal-nationalist ideology of 1848 was no longer very liberal, and the national had been reimagined in terms almost entirely racial.

Published Correspondences

Alexius Meinong und Guido Adler: Eine Freundschaft in Briefen. Edited by Gabriele
Johanna Eder. Amsterdam and Atlanta: Rudopi, 1995.

Antonín Dvořák: Korespondence a dokumenty: kritické vydání [Correspondence and
Documents: Critical Edition]. 10 vols. Prague: Supraphon, 1987–2004.

Avins, Styra, ed. *Johannes Brahms: Life and Letters.* Translated by Josef Eisinger and Styra
Avins. Oxford and New York: Oxford University Press, 1997.

Billroth und Brahms im Briefwechsel. Edited by Otto Gottlieb-Billroth. Berlin: Urban &
Schwarzenberg, 1935.

Briefe von Theodor Billroth. 2nd ed. Edited by Georg Fischer. Hannover and
Leipzig: Hannchen, 1896.

Briefe von Theodor Billroth. 4th ed. Edited by Georg Fischer. Hannover and
Leipzig: Hannchen, 1897.

Briefe von Theodor Billroth. 5th ed. Edited by Georg Fischer. Hannover and
Leipzig: Hannchen, 1899.

Briefe von Theodor Billroth, 7th ed. Edited by Georg Fischer. Hannover and
Leipzig: Hannchen, 1906.

Der intime Theodor Billroth: Die Billroth-Seegen Briefe. Edited by Karel B. Absolon,
with Ernst Kern. Rockville, MD: Kabel, 1985. English translation, *The Intimate
Billroth: The Billroth-Seegen Letters.* Edited by Karel B. Absolon. Rockville,
MD: Kabel, 1985.

Höslinger, Clemens. "Eduard Hanslick in seinen Briefen." In Antonicek, Gruber, and
Landerer, *Eduard Hanslick zum Gedenken,* 123–38.

Johannes Brahms Briefwechsel. 19 vols. to date. 16 orig. vols. Rev. eds., Berlin: Deutsche
Brahms-Gesellschaft, 1912–22. Reprint, Tutzing: Hans Schneider, 1974. *Neue Folge*
consisting of 3 vols. to date. Tutzing: Hans Schneider, 1991–.

*Theodor Billroth: Chirurgische Briefe aus den Kriegs-Lazarethen in Weissenburg und Mannheim,
1870.* Berlin: August Hirschwald, 1872.

Theodor Herzl: Briefe und Tagebücher. 7 vols. Edited by Alex Bein et al. Frankfurt am
 Main: Ullstein; Berlin: Propyläen, 1983–c. 1996. English translation, *The Complete
 Diaries of Theodor Herzl.* Edited by Raphael Patai. Translated by Harry Zohn. 3 vols.
 New York and London: Herzl Press and Thomas Yoseloff, 1960.
Wiesenfeldt. Christiane. "Johannes Brahms im Briefwechsel mit Eduard Hanslick."
 In *Musik und Musikforschung: Johannes Brahms im Dialog mit Geschichte*, edited by
 Wolfgang Sandberger and Christiane Wiesenfeldt, 275–348. Kässel, Basel, London,
 New York, and Prague: Bärenreiter, 2007.

Books, Articles, and Dissertations

Absolon, Karel B. *The Study of Medical Sciences, Theodor Billroth and Abraham Flexner: An
 Analysis form Past to Present.* Rockville, MD: Kabel, 1986.
Absolon, Karel B. *The Surgeon's Surgeon: Theodor Billroth, 1829–1894.* 3 vols. Lawrence,
 KS: Coronado Press, 1979–1987.
Adler, Guido. *Wollen und Wirken: Aus dem Leben eines Musikhistorikers.*
 Vienna: Universal-Edition, 1935.
Agnew, Hugh LeCaine. "Czechs, Germans, Bohemians? Images of Self and Other in
 Bohemia to 1848." In Wingfield, *Creating the Other: Ethnic Conflict and Nationalism
 in Habsburg Central Europe*, 56–77.
Aigner, Thomas. "Die Bestimmung der Skizzen, Entwürfe und Frühfassungen der
 Oper Die Königin von Saba von Carl Goldmark—Grundlage zur Geschichte der
 Entstehung des Werks." Thesis, University of Vienna, in cooperation with the
 Österreichische Nationalbibliothek, 2006.
Albrecht, Catherine. "The Rhetoric of Economic Nationalism in the Bohemian
 Boycott Campaigns of the Late Habsburg Monarchy." *Austrian History Yearbook* 32
 (2001): 47–68.
Ambros, August Wilhelm. *Geschichte der Musik.* Vol. 1, *Die Musik des griechischen
 Altertums und des Orients* (1862). 3rd rev. ed. Leipzig: Leukart, 1887.
Anonymous. "Deutsch-böhmische Briefe." *Grenzboten* 46/1 (1887): 145–52; 258–66;
 401–8; 561–69; and 624–31; and ibid., 46/2 (1887): 49–57, 102–10, 193–99,
 302–10, and 456–64.
Anonymous. "The Jewish Background of Victor and Friedrich Adler: Selected
 Biographical Notes." *Leo Baeck Institute Yearbook* 10 (1965): 266–76.
Antonicek, Theophil, Gernot Gruber, and Christoph Landerer, eds. *Eduard Hanslick
 zum Gedenken: Bericht des Symposions zum Anlass seines 100. Todestages*, Tutzing: Hans
 Schneider, 2010.
Aschheim, Steven E. *Brothers and Strangers: The East European Jew in German and German
 Jewish Consciousness, 1800–1923.* Madison: University of Wisconsin Press, 1982.
Aschheim, Steven E. " 'The Jew Within: The Myth of 'Judaization' in Germany'." In his
 *Culture and Catastrophe: German and Jewish Confrontations with National Socialism and
 Other Crises*, 45–68. Houndmills, Basingstoke, Hampshire, and London: Macmillan,
 1996.
Avenary, Hanoch, Walter Pass, and Nikolaus Vielmetti, eds. *Kantor Salomon Sulzer und
 seine Zeit: Eine Dokumentation.* Sigmaringen: Jan Thorbecke, 1985.
Avins, Styra. "Brahms the Godfather." In Frisch and Karnes, *Brahms and His World*,
 41–56.

Bachrich, S[igismund]. *Aus verklungenen Zeiten: Erinnerungen eines alten Musikers*. Vienna: Paul Knepler, 1914.

Banti, Alberto Mario. "Deep Images in Nineteenth-Century Nationalist Narratives." *Historein* 8 (2008): 1–9.

Bauer-Lechner, Natalie. *Recollections of Gustav Mahler*. Translated by Dika Newlin. Edited by Peter Franklin. Cambridge: Cambridge University Press, 1980.

Beckerman, Michael, ed. *Dvořák and His World*. Princeton: Princeton University Press, 1993.

Beckermann, Michael. "In Search of Czechness in Music." *19th-Century Music* 10 (1986–87): 61–73.

Beckerman, Michael. "The Master's Little Joke: Antonín Dvořák and the Mask of Nation." In Beckerman, *Dvořák and His World*, 134–54.

Beetz, Wilhelm. *Das Wiener Opernhaus 1869 bis 1945*. Zurich: Central European Times Verlag, 1949.

Behr, Johannes. "Brahms als Gutachter und Preisrichter." In *Bruckner—Brahms: Urbanes Milieu als kompositorische Lebenswelt im Wien der Gründerzeit*, edited by Hans-Joachim Hinrichsen and Laurenz Lütteken, 145–53. Kassel: Bärenreiter, 2006.

Bein, Alex. *The Jewish Question: Biography of a World Problem*. Translated by Harry Zohn. Cranberry, NJ: Associated University Presses, 1990.

Belgum, Kirsten. *Popularizing the Nation: Audience, Representation, and the Production of Identity in Die Gartenlaube*. Lincoln and London: University of Nebraska Press, 2008.

Beller-McKenna, Daniel. *Brahms and the German Spirit*. Cambridge, MA, and London: Harvard University Press, 2004.

Beller, Steven. *Antisemitism: A Very Short Introduction*. Oxford: Oxford University Press, 2007.

Beller, Steven. *Francis Joseph*. London and New York: Longman, 1996.

Beller, Steven. *Herzl*. London: Peter Halban, 1991.

Beller, Steven. "Hitler's Hero: Georg von Schönerer and the Origins of Nazism." In *In the Shadow of Hitler: Personalities of the Right in Central and Eastern Europe*, edited by Rebecca Haynes and Martyn Rady, 38–54. London: Taurus, 2011.

Beller, Steven. Review of Pieter M. Judson, *Exclusive Revolutionaries: Liberal Politics, Social Experience, and National Identity in the Austrian Empire, 1848–1914*, in *Central European History* 33 (2000): 558–61.

Beller, Steven. *Vienna and the Jews, 1867–1938*. Cambridge: Cambridge University Press, 1987.

Bendix, Regina. "Ethnology, Cultural Reification, and the Dynamics of Difference in the *Kronprinzenwerk*." In Wingfield, *Creating the Other: Ethnic Conflict and Nationalism in Habsburg Central Europe*, 149–66.

Bertagnolli, Paul A. *Prometheus in Music: Representations of the Myth in the Romantic Era*. Aldershot, Hampshire: Ashgate, 2007.

Beveridge, David R. "Dvořák and Brahms: A Chronicle, an Interpretation." In Beckerman, *Dvořák and His World*, 56–91.

Beveridge, David R., ed. *Rethinking Dvořák: Views from Five Countries*. Oxford: Clarendon Press, 1996.

Beveridge, David R. "Romantic Ideas in a Classical Frame: The Sonata Forms of Dvořák." Ph.D. diss., University of California at Berkeley, 1980.

Biba, Otto. "Antonín Dvořák im Wiener Musikleben seiner Zeit." In *Colloquium "Dvořák, Janáček, Their Time" Brno 1984*, edited by Rudolf Pečman, 51–55. Brno: Česká hudební společnost, 1985.

Billroth, Theodor. *Aphorismen zum "Lehren und Lernen der medicinischen Wissenschaften."* Vienna: Carl Gerold's Sohn, 1886. English translation, Absolon, *The Study of the Medical Sciences*, 39–83.

Billroth, Theodor. *Chirurgische Klinik, Wien 1871–1876: nebst einem Gesammt-Bericht über die chirurgischen Kliniken in Zürich und Wien während der Jahre 1860– 1876: Erfahrungen auf dem Gebiet der practischen Chirurgie.* Berlin: Hirschwald, 1879.

Billroth, Theodor. *Prof. Dr. Th. Billroth's Antwort auf die Adresse des Lesevereines der deutschen Studenten Wien's.* Vienna: Carl Gerold's Sohn, 1875.

Billroth, Theodor. *Über das Lehren und Lernen der medicinischen Wissenschaften an den Universitäten der deutschen Nation nebst allgemeinen Bemerkungen über Universitäten: Eine culturhistorische Studie.* Vienna: Carl Gerold's Sohn, 1876. Abridged English translation, *The Medical Sciences in the German University: A Study in the History of Civilization.* Translated by William H. Welch. New York: Macmillan, 1924.

Blaukopf, Herta. "Mahler's First Season as Director at the k.k. Hofoperntheater: The Composer Waits in the Wings." In *Perspectives on Gustav Mahler*, edited by Jeremy Barham, 327–43. Aldershot, UK, and Burlington, VT: Ashgate, 2005.

Blaukopf, Kurt. *Gustav Mahler.* Translated by Inge Goodwin. London: Futura, 1975.

Blaukopf, Kurt, ed. *Mahler: A Documentary Study.* New York and Toronto: Oxford University Press, 1976.

Boisits, Barbara. "'diese gesungenen Bitten um Emancipation' – Akkulturationsdiskurse am Beispiel von Salomon Sulzers Wirken am Wiener Stadttempel." In Borchard and Zimmermann, eds., *Musikwelten – Lebenswelten: Jüdische Identitätssuche in der deutschen Musikkultur*, 91–107.

Bohlman, Philip V. "Composing the Cantorate: Westernizing Europe's Other Within." In *Western Music and Its Others: Difference, Representation, and Appropriation in Music*, edited by Georgina Born and David Hesmondhalgh, 189–212. Berkeley and Los Angeles: University of California Press, 2000.

Bohlman, Philip V. "Musical Life in the Central European Jewish Village." In *Modern Jews and their Musical Agendas*, edited by Ezra Mendelsohn, 17–39. New York and Oxford: Oxford University Press, 1993.

Bohlman, Philip V. *Music, Nationalism, and the Making of the New Europe.* London: Routledge, 2011.

Borchard, Beatrix, and Heidy Zimmermann, eds. *Musikwelten – Lebenswelten: Jüdische Identitätssuche in der deutschen Musikkultur.* Cologne, Weimar, and Vienna: Böhlau Verlag, 2009.

Botstein, Leon. "Brahms and Nineteenth-Century Painting." *19th-Century Music* 14 (1990): 154–68.

Botstein, Leon. "The Consequences of History and Criticism," *Musical Quarterly* 94 (2011): 1–8.

Botstein, Leon. "Gustav Mahler's Vienna." In *The Mahler Companion*, edited by Donald Mitchell and Andrew Nicholson, 6–38. Oxford: Oxford University Press, 1999.

Botstein, Leon. "The Jewish Question in Music." *Musical Quarterly* 94 (2012): 1–15.

Botstein, Leon. "Music and Its Public: Habits of Listening and the Crisis of Musical Modernism in Vienna, 1870–1914." Ph.D. diss., Harvard University, 1985.

Botstein, Leon. "Music in History: The Perils of Method in Reception History." *Musical Quarterly* 89 (2007): 1–16.

Botstein, Leon. "Time and Memory: Concert Life, Science, and Music in Brahms's Vienna." In Frisch and Karnes, *Brahms and His World*, 3–25.

Boyer, John W. *Political Radicalism in Late Habsburg Vienna: Origins of the Christian Social Movement, 1848–1897.* Chicago and London: University of Chicago Press, 1981.

Braunthal, Julius. *Victor und Friedrich Adler: Zwei Generationen Arbeiterbewegung.* Vienna: Wienervolksbuchhandlung, 1965.

Brodbeck, David. "*Ausgleichs-Abende*: The First Viennese Performances of Smetana's *Bartered Bride*." *Austrian Studies* 17 (2009): 43–61.

Brodbeck, David. "Brahms, the Third Symphony, and the New German School." In *Brahms and His World*, edited by Walter Frisch, 65–80. Princeton: Princeton University Press, 1990.

Brodbeck, David. "Brahms, the Third Symphony, and the New German School." In Frisch and Karnes, *Brahms and His World*, 95–116.

Brodbeck, David. "Dvořák's Reception in Liberal Vienna: Language Ordinances, National Property, and the Rhetoric of *Deutschtum*." *Journal of the American Musicological Society* 60 (2007): 71–132.

Brodbeck, David. "Hanslick's Smetana and Hanslick's Prague." *Journal of the Royal Musical Association* 134 (2009): 1–36.

Brodbeck, David. "Notes from the Lives of Two Viennese Composers." *American Brahms Society Newsletter* 32/1 (Spring 2014): 1–5.

Brodbeck, David. "Hanslick's Smetana and Hanslick's Prague." *Journal of the Royal Musical Association* 134 (2009): 1–36.

Brodbeck, David. " 'Poison-flaming Flowers from the Orient and Nightingales from Bayreuth': On Hanslick's Reception of the Music of Goldmark." In Grimes, Donavan, and Marx, *Rethinking Hanslick*, 132–59.

Brubaker, Rogers. "The Manichean Myth: Rethinking the Distinction Between 'Civic' and 'Ethnic' Nationalism." In *Nation and National Identity: The European Experience in Perspective*, edited by Hanspeter Kriesl, Klaus Armingeon, Hannes Siegrist, and Andreas Brimmer, 55–71. Chur and Zurich: Verlag Rüegger, 1999.

Buklijas, Tatjana. "Surgery and National Identity in Late Nineteenth-Century Vienna." *Studies in History and Philosophy of Biological and Biomedical Sciences* 38 (2007): 756–74.

Burghauser, Jarmil. *Antonín Dvořák: Thematic Catalogue.* Prague: Bärenreiter, 1996.

Chamberlain, Houston Stewart. *Die Grundlagen des neunzehnten Jahrhunderts.* 2 vols. Munich: F. Bruckmann, 1906,

Christianowitsch, Alexander. *Esquisse historique de la Musique Arabe.* Cologne: M. Dumont-Schauberg, 1863.

Clapham, John. *Dvořák.* New York: Norton, 1979.

Clapham, John. *Dvořák: Musician and Craftsman.* New York: St. Martin's Press, 1966.

Clapham, John. "Dvořák's Relations with Brahms and Hanslick." *Musical Quarterly* 57 (1971): 241–54.

Clapham, John. "Dvořáks Aufstieg zum Komponisten von internationalem Rang: Einige neue Entdeckungen." *Die Musikforschung* 30 (1977): 47–55.

Coen, Deborah R. *Vienna in the Age of Uncertainty: Science, Liberalism & Private Life.* Chicago and London: University of Chicago Press, 2007.

Cohen, Gary B. "Citizenship and Nationality in Late Imperial Austria." In *Nation, Nationalitäten und Nationalismus im östlichen Europa: Festschrift für Arnold Suppan zum 65. Geburtstag,* edited by Marija Wakounig, Wolfgang Mueller, and Michael Portmann, 201–24. Vienna and Berlin: Lit Verlag, 2004.

Cohen, Gary B. "Cultural Crossings in Prague, 1900: Scenes from Late Imperial Austria." *Austrian History Yearbook* 45 (2014): 1–30.

Cohen, Gary B. *Education and Middle-Class Society in Imperial Austria, 1848–1918.* West Lafayette, IN: Purdue University Press, 1996.

Cohen, Gary B. "Ideals and Realities in the Austrian Universities, 1850–1914." In *Rediscovering History: Culture, Politics, and the Psyche,* edited by Michael S. Roth, 83–101. Stanford: Stanford University Press, 1994.

Cohen, Gary B. "Neither Absolutism nor Anarchy: New Narratives on Society and Government in Late Imperial Austria," *Austrian History Yearbook* 29 (1998): 37–61.

Cohen, Gary B. *The Politics of Ethnic Survival: Germans in Prague, 1861–1914.* 2nd., rev. ed. West Lafayette, IN: Purdue University Press, 2006.

Conway, David. *Jewry in Music: Entry to the Profession from the Enlightenment to Richard Wagner.* Cambridge: Cambridge University Press, 2012.

David-Fox, Katherine. "Prague-Vienna, Prague-Berlin: The Hidden Geography of Czech Modernism." *Slavic Review* 59 (2000): 735–60.

Deaville, James. " 'Die Wacht an der Donau'?!? The Wiener akademischer Wagner-Verein, Wiener Moderne and Pan-Germanism." In *Wien 1897: Kulturgeschichtliches Profil eines Epochenjahres,* edited by Christian Glanz, 49–84. Frankfurt am Main: Peter Lang, 1999.

Döge, Klaus. *Antonín Dvořák: Leben, Werke, Dokumente.* 2nd ed. Zurich and Mainz: Atlantis Musikbuch-Verlag, 1997.

Döge, Klaus, and Peter Jost, eds., *Dvořák-Studien.* Mainz: Schott, 1994.

Efron, John M. *Medicine and the German Jews: A History.* New Haven and London: Yale University Press, 2001.

Eppel, Peter. *"Concordia soll ihr Name sein…" 125 Jahre Journalisten- und Schriftstellerverein "Concordia": Eine Dokumentation zur Presse- und Zeitgeschichte Österreichs.* Vienna, Cologne, and Graz: Böhlau, 2004.

Evans, R. J. W. "Language and State Building: The Case of the Habsburg Monarchy." *Austrian History Yearbook* 35 (2004): 1–24.

Ewen, David. *Hebrew Music: A Study and an Interpretation.* New York: Bloch, 1931.

Fischer, Jens Malte. *Gustav Mahler.* Translated by Stewart Spencer. New Haven and London: Yale University Press, 2011.

Fischer, Jens Malte. *Richard Wagners "Das Judentum in der Musik": eine kritische Dokumentation als Beitrag zur Geschichte des Antisemitismus.* Frankfurt: Insel, 2000.

Fleischer, Oskar. *Die Bedeutung der internationalen Musik- und Theater-Ausstellung in Wien für Kunst und Wissenschaft der Musik.* Leipzig and New York: Internationales Verlags- und Kunstanstalt, 1894.

Frankel, Jonathan, and Steven J. Zipperstein, eds. *Assimilation and Community: The Jews of Nineteenth-Century Europe*. Cambridge: Cambridge University Press, 1992.

Freigedank, K. [Richard Wagner]. "Das Judenthum in der Musik." *Neue Zeitschrift für Musik* 33 (3 September 1850): 101–7 and (6 September 1850): 109–12.

Friedjung, Heinrich. *Ein Stück Zeitungsgeschichte*. Vienna: Genossensc hafts-Buchdruckerei, 1887.

Friedmann, Aron, ed. *Lebensbilder berühmter Kantoren. Teil I: Zum 100. Geburtstage des verdienstvollen Oberkantor der Breslauer Synagogengemeinde weiland Moritz Deutsch*. Berlin: C. Boas Nachf., 1918.

Friedmann-Album: Zur bleibenden Erinnerung an die Feier des 25-jährigen Amtsjubiläum des Herrn Moritz Friedmann, Obercantors der israelitischen Religionsgemeinde Pest. Budapest: Chorin & Co., 1877.

Frisch, Walter, and Kevin C. Karnes, eds. *Brahms and His World*. Rev. ed. Princeton: Princeton University Press, 2009.

Furness, Raymond. *Wagner and Literature*. Manchester: Manchester University Press, 1982.

Gabrielová, Jarmila. "Antonín Dvořák und Johannes Brahms: Bemerkungen zur Kompositionsproblematik der Symphonie Nr. 6 D-Dur, Op. 60." In *Colloquium: Die Instrumentalmusik (Struktur—Funktion—Ästhetik) Brno 1991, Ethnonationale Wechselbeziehungen in der mitteleuropäischen Musik mit besonderer Berücksichtigung der Situation in den böhmischen Ländern*. Brno: Masarykova Univerzita, 1994.

Garver, Bruce M. *The Young Czech Party 1874–1901 and the Emergence of a Multi-Party System*. New Haven: Yale University Press, 1978.

Geehr, Richard S. *Karl Lueger: Mayor of Fin-de-Siècle Vienna*. Detroit: Wayne State University Press, 1990.

Gellner, Ernest. *Language and Solitude: Wittgenstein, Malinowski and the Habsburg Dilemma*. Cambridge: Cambridge University Press, 1998.

Gilman, Sander L. *The Jew's Body*. New York: Routledge, 1991.

Gilman, Sander L. *Jewish Self-Hatred: Anti-Semitism and the Hidden Language of the Jews*. Baltimore and London: Johns Hopkins University Press, 1986.

Glassheim, Eagle. "Between Empire and Nation: The Bohemian Nobility, 1880–1918." In Judson and Rozenblit, *Constructing Nationalities in East Central Europe*, 61–88.

Glettler, Monika. "Minority Culture in a Capital City: The Czechs in Vienna at the Turn of the Century." In *Decadence & Innovation: Austro-Hungarian Life and Arts at the Turn of the Century*, edited by Robert Pynsent, 49–60. London: Weidenfeld and Nicolson, 1989.

Goldbaum, Wilhelm. *Entlegene Kulturen: Skizzen und Bilder*. Berlin: A. Hofmann, 1877.

Goldbaum, Wilhelm. *Literarische Physiognomieen*. Vienna and Teschen: Karl Prochaska, 1884.

Goldmark, Josephine. *Pilgrims of '48: One Man's Part in the Austrian Revolution of 1848 and a Family Migration to America*. 1930. Reprint, New York: Arno Press, 1975.

Goldmark, Karl. *Erinnerungen aus meinem Leben*. Vienna: Rikola Verlag, 1922. English translation, *Notes from the Life of a Viennese Composer*. Translated by Alice Goldmark Brandeis. New York: Albert and Charles Boni, 1927.

Gombrich, Ernst. *The Visual Arts in Vienna circa 1900: Reflections on the Jewish Catastrophe*. London: Austrian Cultural Institute, 1997.

Gomperz-Bettelheim, Caroline von. *Ein biographisches Blatt*. Vienna: Carl Fromme, 1905.

Gooley, Dana. "Hanslick and the Institution of Criticism." *Journal of Musicology* 28 (2011): 289–324.

Graf, Harald. "Carl Goldmark: Studie zur Biographie und Rezeption." Master's thesis, University of Vienna, 1994.

Graf, Max. *Composer and Critic: Two Hundred Years of Musical Criticism.* London: Chapman & Hall, 1947.

Graf, Max. *Legend of a Musical City*. New York: Philosophical Library, 1945.

Grey, Thomas S. "The Jewish Question." In *The Cambridge Companion to Wagner*, edited by Thomas S. Grey, 203–18. Cambridge: Cambridge University Press, 2008.

Grey, Thomas S. "Masters and Their Critics: Wagner, Hanslick, Beckmesser, and *Die Meistersinger*." In *Wagner's* Meistersinger: *Performance, History, Representation*, edited by Nicholas Vazsonyi, 165–89. Rochester: University of Rochester Press, 2004.

Grey, Thomas. "Wagner and the 'Makart Style'." *Cambridge Opera Journal* 25 (2013): 225–60.

Grimes, Nicole. " 'Wordless Judaism, Like the Songs of Mendelssohn?' Hanslick, Mendelssohn and Cultural Politics in Late Nineteenth-Century Vienna." In *Mendelssohn Perspectives*, edited by Nicole Grimes and Angela R. Mace, 49–62. Farnham, Surrey and Burlington, VT: Ashgate, 2012.

Grimes, Nicole, Siobhán Donovan, and Wolfgang Marx, eds. *Rethinking Hanslick: Music, Formalism, and Expression*. Rochester: University of Rochester Press, 2013.

Grimm, Ines. *Eduard Hanslicks Prager Zeit: Frühe Wurzeln seiner Schrift Vom Musikalisch-Schönen*. Saarbrücken: Pfau, 2003.

Gunter, Ann C. *Greek Art and the Orient*. Cambridge: Cambridge University Press, 2012.

H[arten], U[we]. "Wiener Tonkünstler-Verein." *Oesterreichisches Musiklexikon*. 5 vols. Vienna: Verlag der Österreichischen Akademie der Wissenschaften, 2006; 5: 268–69.

Haacke, Wilmont. *Feuilletonkunde: das Feuilleton als literarische und journalistische Gattung.* 2 vols. Leipzig: K. W. Hiersemann, 1943–44.

Hacohen, Malacai Haim. *Karl Popper, The Formative Years, 1902–1945: Politics and Philosophy in Interwar Vienna*. Cambridge: Cambridge University Press, 2000.

HaCohen, Ruth. *The Music Libel Against the Jews*. New Haven and London: Yale University Press, 2011.

Haddenhorst, Gerda. *Die Wiesbadener Kaiserfestspiele*. Wiesbaden: Selbstverlag der Historischen Kommission für Nassau, 1985.

Haider, Markus Erwin. *Im Streit um die österreichische Nation: Nationale Leitwörter in Österreich 1866–1938*. Vienna, Cologne, and Weimar: Böhlau, 1998.

Hanslick, Eduard. *Am Ende des Jahrhunderts {1895–1899} (Der "modernen Oper" VIII. Teil.)* Berlin: Allgemeiner Verein für Deutsche Litteratur, 1899.

Hanslick, Eduard. *Aus dem Concertsaal: Kritiken und Schilderungen aus den letzten 20 Jahren des Wiener Musiklebens 1848–1868*. Vienna: Wilhelm Braumüller, 1870.

Hanslick, Eduard. *Aus dem Tagebuche eines Musikers. (Der "modernen Oper" VI. Theil).* Berlin: Allgemeiner Verein für Deutsche Litteratur, 1892.

Hanslick, Eduard. *Aus meinem Leben*, 2 vols. Berlin: Allgemeiner Verein für deutsche Litteratur, 1894.

Hanslick, Eduard. *Aus neuer und neuester Zeit. (Der "modernen Oper" IX. Theil.)*
Berlin: Allgemeiner Verein für Deutsche Litteratur, 1900.

Hanslick, Eduard. *Concerte, Componisten und Virtuosen der letzten fünfzehn Jahre.*
1870–1885. Berlin: Allgemeiner Verein für Deutsche Literatur, 1886.

Hanslick, Eduard. *Fünf Jahre Musik {1891–1895} (Der "Moderne Oper" VII.*
Theil): Kritiken. Berlin: Allgemeiner Verein für Deutsche Litteratur, 1896.

Hanslick, Eduard. "Johannes Brahms: The Last Days, Memories and Letters." In Frisch
and Karnes, *Brahms and His World,* 307–37.

Hanslick, Eduard. "Musik." In *Wien 1848–1888: Denkschrift zum 2. Dezember 1888.*
Edited by the Gemeinderathe der Stadt Wien, 2 vols.; 2: 303–42. Vienna: Carl
Konegan, 1888.

Hanslick, Eduard. "Die Musik in Wien." In *Die österreichisch-ungarische Monarchie in Wort*
und Bild. Vol. 1 (1886), *Wien und Niederösterreich,* part 1: *Wien,* 123–38.

Hanslick, Eduard. *Musikalische Stationen. (Der "Modernen Oper" II. Theil)*
Berlin: Allgemeiner Verein für Deutsche Literatur, 1885.

Hanslick, Eduard. *Musikalisches Skizzenbuch (Der "modernen Oper" IV. Theil): Neue Kritiken*
und Schilderungen. Berlin: Allgemeiner Verein für Deutsche Literatur, 1888.

Hanslick, Eduard. *Sämtliche Schriften: Historisch-kritische Ausgabe, I/i: Aufsätze und*
Rezensionen 1844–1848, ed. Dietmar Strauß. Vienna, Cologne and Berlin, 1993.

Harrandt, Andrea. "Bruckner in Vienna." In Williamson, *The Cambridge Companion to*
Bruckner, 26–37.

Harrandt, Andrea. "Students and Friends as 'Prophets' and 'Promoters': The Reception
of Bruckner's Works in the *Wiener Akademische Wagner-Verein.*" In *Perspectives on*
Anton Bruckner, edited by Crawford Howie, Paul Hawkshaw, and Timothy Jackson,
317–27. Aldershot: Ashgate, 2001.

Harten, Uwe, ed. *Max Kalbeck zum 150. Geburtstag.* Tutzing: Hans Schneider, 2007.

Haselböck, Lukas. "Dvořáks 6. Sinfonie: Ein 'intertextueller' Kommentar zu Brahms'
2. Sinfonie?" *Hudební veda* 41 (2004): 341–54.

Hasner, Leopold von. *Denkwürdigkeiten: Autobiographisches und Aphorismen.*
Stuttgart: Cotta, 1892.

Havránek, Jan. "The Development of Czech Nationalism," *Austrian History Yearbook* 3
(1967): 223–60.

Hein, Annette. *"Es ist viel 'Hitler' in Wagner": Rassismus und antisemitische*
Deutschtumsideologie in den "Bayreuther Blätter" (1878–1938). Tübingen: Max
Niemeyer, 1996.

Hein, Robert. *Studentischer Antisemitismus in Österreich.* Vienna: Österreichischer Verein
für Studentgeschichte, 1984.

Heine, Heinrich. *Ludwig Börne: A Memorial.* Edited and translated by Jeffrey
L. Sammons. Rochester, NY: Camden House, 2006.

Hellsberg, Clemens. *Demokratie der Könige: Die Geschichte der Wiener Philharmoniker.*
Zurich, Vienna, and Mainz: Schweizer Verl.-Haus, 1992.

Helm, Theodor. *Fünfzig Jahre Wiener Musikleben (1866–1916): Erinnerungen eines*
Musikkritikers. Edited by Max Schönherr. Vienna: Im Verlag des Herausgebers,
1977.

Herzog, Hillary Hope. *"Vienna is Different": Jewish Writers in Austria from the Fin de Siècle*
to the Present. New York and Oxford: Berghahn, 2011.

Hess, Jonathan M. "Jewish Emancipation and the Politics of Race." In *The German Invention of Race*, edited by Sara Eigen and Mark Larrimore, 203–12. Albany: State University of New York Press, 2006.

Hess, Jonathan M. "Leopold Kompert and the Work of Nostalgia: The Cultural Capital of German Jewish Ghetto Fiction." *Jewish Quarterly Review* 97 (2007): 576–615.

Heuberger, Richard. *Erinnerungen an Johannes Brahms*. Rev. ed. Edited by Kurt Hofmann. Tutzing: Hans Schneider, 1976.

Heuberger, Richard. "My Early Acquaintance with Brahms." In Frisch and Karnes, *Brahms and His World*, 339–48; originally published as "Aus der ersten Zeit meiner Bekanntschaft mit Brahms," *Die Musik* 5 (1902): 223–29.

Hevesi, Ludwig. "Ludwig Speidel." *Biographisches Jahrbuch und deutscher Nekrolog (1906)*, edited by Anton Bettelheim, 193–223. Berlin: Reimer, 1908.

Hevesi, Ludwig. *Ludwig Speidel: Eine literarisch-biographische Würdigung*. Berlin: Meyer & Jessen, 1910.

Höbelt, Lothar. *Kornblume und Kaiseradler: Die deutschfreiheitlichen Parteien Altösterreichs 1882–1918*. Vienna: Verlag für Geschichte und Politik; Munich: R. Oldenbourg Verlag, 1993.

Höbelt, Lothar. "'Well-Tempered Domestic Discontent': Austrian Domestic Politics." In *The Last Years of Austria-Hungary: A Multi-National Experiment in Early Twentieth-Century Europe*, rev. ed., edited by Mark Cornwell, 47–74. Exeter: University of Exeter Press, 2002.

Hofmann, Kurt. *Die Bibliothek von Johannes Brahms: Bücher- und Musikalienverzeichnis*. Hamburg: Karl Dieter Wagner, 1974.

Honolka, Kurt. *Dvořák*. Translated by Anne Wyburd. London: Haus, 2004.

Horn, Friedrich. *Offener Brief an Herrn Hofrath Dr. Theodor Billroth*. Vienna: Alfred Hölder, 1876. English trans., Absolon, *The Study of Medical Sciences, Theodor Billroth and Abraham Flexner*, 97–101.

Hostinský, Otakar. "Musik in Böhmen." In *Die österreichisch-ungarische Monarchie in Wort und Bild*. Vol. 15 (1896), *Böhmen*, (Part 2), 1–60.

Houtchens, Alan. "From the Vistula to the Danube by Way of the Vltava: Dvořák's Vanda in Vienna." In Beveridge, *Rethinking Dvořák*, 73–80.

Houtchens, [Henry] Alan. "A Critical Study of Antonín Dvořák's." Ph.D. diss., University of California at Santa Barbara, 1987.

Idelsohn, A[braham] Z[evi]. *Jewish Music in its Historical Development*. New York: Holt, 1929.

Imber, Jonathan B. "Review of M. B. Hart, *The Healthy Jew: The Symbiosis of Judaism and Modern Medicine*." *Sociology* 46 (2009): 97–99.

Jacobs, Jack. *On Socialists and "the Jewish Question" After Marx*. New York and London: New York University Press, 1992.

Jenks, William A. *Austria Under the Iron Ring, 1879–1893*. Charlottesville: University Press of Virginia, 1965.

John, Michael. "'We Do Not Even Possess Our Selves': On Identity and Ethnicity in Austria, 1880–1937." *Austria History Yearbook* 30 (1999): 17–64.

Judson, Pieter M. *Exclusive Revolutionaries: Liberal Politics, Social Experience, and National Identity in the Austrian Empire, 1848–1914*. Ann Arbor: University of Michigan Press, 1996.

Judson, Pieter M. "Frontier Germans: The Invention of the *Sprachgrenze*." In *Identität Kultur Raum: Kulturelle Praktiken und die Ausbildung von Imagined Communities in Nordamerika u{n}d Zentraleuropa*, edited by Susan Ingram, Markus Reisenleitner, and Cornelia Szabó-Knotik, 85–99. Vienna: Turia + Kant, 2000.

Judson, Pieter M. "Frontiers, Islands, Forests, Stones: Mapping the Geography of a German Identity in the Habsburg Monarchy, 1848–1900." In *The Geography of Identity*, edited by Patricia Yaeger, 382–406. Ann Arbor: University of Michigan Press, 1996.

Judson, Pieter M. *Guardians of the Nation: Activists on the Language Frontiers of Imperial Austria*. Cambridge, MA, and London: Harvard University Press, 2006.

Judson, Pieter M. "Inventing Germans: Class, Nationality and Colonial Fantasy at the Margins of the Habsburg Monarchy." In *Nations, Colonies and Metropoles*, edited by Daniel A. Segal and Richard Handler, special edition of *Social Analysis* 33 (1993): 47–67.

Judson, Pieter M. " 'Not Another Square Foot!': German Liberalism and the Rhetoric of National Ownership in 19th-Century Austria," *Austrian History Yearbook* 26 (1995): 83–97.

Judson, Pieter M. "Rethinking the Liberal Legacy." In *Rethinking Vienna 1900*, edited by Steven Beller, 57–79. New York and Oxford: Berghahn, 2001.

Judson, Pieter M. *Wien brennt! Die Revolution von 1848 und ihr liberales Erbe*. Vienna and Cologne: Böhlau, 1998.

Judson, Pieter M., and Marsha L. Rozenblit, eds. *Constructing Nationalities in East Central Europe*. New York and Oxford: Berghahn, 2005.

Jütte, Daniel. "Der jüdische Tenor as Éléazar: Heinrich Sontheim und die *La Juive*-Rezeption im 19. Jahrhundert." In *Judenrollen: Darstellungsformen im europäischen Theater von der Restauration bis zur Zwischenkriegszeit*, edited by Hans-Peter Bayerdörfer, Jens Malte Fischer, and Frank Halbach, 41–55. Berlin and New York: Walter de Gruyter, Max Niemeyer, 2008.

Kaiser, Nancy A. "Berthold Auerbach: The Dilemma of the Jewish Humanist from *Vormärz* to Empire." *German Studies Review* 6 (1983): 399–419.

Kalbeck, Max. *Johannes Brahms*. Rev. ed. 4 vols. in 8. Berlin: Deutsche Brahms-Gesellschaft, 1915–21. Reprint, Tutzing: Hans Schneider, 1976.

Kalbeck, Max. "Karl Goldmark." *Deutsche Dichtung* 1 (1886–87): 204–6.

Kann, Robert A. *A History of the Habsburg Empire, 1526–1918*. Berkeley and Los Angeles: University of California Press, 1974.

Kann, Robert A. *The Multi-National Empire: Nationalism and National Reform in the Habsburg Monarchy 1848–1918*. 2 vols. New York: Columbia University Press, 1950. Reprint, New York: Octagon Books, 1964.

Karnes, Kevin C. *Music, Criticism, and the Challenge of History: Shaping Modern Musical Thought in Late Nineteenth-Century Vienna*. Oxford: Oxford University Press, 2008.

Karpath, Ludwig. *Begegnung mit dem Genius*. 2nd ed. Vienna: Fiba-Verlag, 1934.

Kecskeméti, István. "Goldmarkiana: Unbekannte primäre Quellen in Ungarn." In *Musica Conservata: Günter Brosche zum 60. Geburtstag*, edited by Josef Gmeiner, Zsigmond Kokits, Thomas Leibnitz, and Inge Pechotsch-Feichtinger, 131–47. Tutzing: Hans Schneider, 1999.

Kecskeméti, István. "Liturgical Elements in the Opera *Die Königin von Saba* (1875) by Karl Goldmark." In *Essays in Honor of Hanoch Avenary*, special edition of *Orbis musicae* 10 (1990/91): 229–40.

Kernmayer, Hildegard. *Judentum im Wiener Feuilleton (1848–1903): Exemplarische Untersuchungen zum literarästhetischen und politischen Diskurs der Moderne.* Tübingen: Max Niemoyer, 1998.

Kieval, Hillel J. *The Making of Czech Jewry: National Conflict and Jewish Society in Bohemia, 1870–1910.* New York and Oxford: Oxford University Press, 1988.

Kieval, Hillel J. "The Social Vision of Bohemian Jews." In Frankel and Zipperstein, *Assimilation and Community,* 246–83.

King, Jeremy. *Budweisers into Czechs and Germans: A Local History of Bohemian Politics, 1848–1948.* Princeton: Princeton University Press, 2002.

Klein, Dennis B. *The Jewish Origins of the Psychoanalytic Movement.* New York: Praeger, 1981.

Knepler, Hermann. *Der Prozeß Goldmark aktenmäßig dargestellt vom Vertheidiger.* Vienna: Herzfeld & Bauer, 1868.

Knittel, K. M. "'Ein hypermoderner Dirigent': Mahler and Anti-Semitism in Fin-de-Siècle Vienna." *19th-Century Music* 18 (1995): 257–76.

Knittel, K. M. "'Polemik im Concertsaal': Mahler, Beethoven, and the Viennese Critics." *19th-Century Music* 29 (2006): 289–317.

Knittel, K. M. *Seeing Mahler: Music and the Language of Antisemitism in Fin-de-Siècle Vienna.* Burlington, VT: Ashgate, 2010.

Kohn, Hans. *The Idea of Nationalism.* New York: Macmillan, 1941.

Kohut, Adolph. *Berühmte israelitische Männer und Frauen in der Kulturgeschichte der Menschheit: Lebens- und Charakterbilder aus Vergangenheit und Gegewart.* 2 vols. Leipzig-Reudnitz: A. W. Payne, 1900–1901.

Konje, Todd. *German Orientalisms.* Ann Arbor: University of Michigan Press, 2004.

Kornberg, Jacques. "Vienna, the 1890s: Jews in the Eyes of their Defenders (Der Verein zur Abwehr des Antisemitismus)." *Central European History* 28 (1995): 153–73.

Kornberg, Jacques. "Vienna in the 1890s: The Austrian Opposition to Antisemitism, the Verein zur Abwehr des Antisemitismus." *Leo Baeck Institute Year Book* 41 (1996): 161–96.

Korstvedt, Benjamin. "The Critics and the Quintet: A Study in Musical Representation." In *Anton Bruckners Wiener Jahre: Analysen—Fakten—Perspektiven. Wiener Bruckner-Studien 1,* edited by Renate Grasberger, Elisabeth Maier, and Erich Wolfgang Partsch, 145–66. Vienna: Musikwissenschaftlicher Verlag, 2009.

Korstvedt, Benjamin. "Reading Music Criticism Beyond the Fin-de-siècle Vienna Paradigm." *Musical Quarterly* 94 (2011): 156–210.

Kralodworsky Rukopis: Zbjrka staročeskych zpiewo-prawnych basnj, s niekolika ginymi staročeskymi zpiewy / Königinhofer Handschrift: Sammlung altböhmischer lyrisch-epischer Gesänge, nebst andern altböhmischen Gedichten. Discovered and edited by Waclawa Hanky/Wenceslaw Hanka. Translated by Waclawa Aloysia Swobody/Wenceslaw Aloys Swoboda. Prague: J. G. Calve, 1829.

Kravitz, Edward. "Mahler, Victim of the 'New' Anti-Semitism." *Journal of the Royal Musical Association* 127 (2002): 72–94.

Krebs, Michael. "Theodor Helm (1843–1920): Ein Musikschriftsteller im Umkreis von Anton Bruckner." Ph.D. diss., University of Vienna, 1999.

Kretschmann, Theobald. *Tempi passati: Aus den Erinnerungen eines Musikanten.* 2 vols. Vienna: K. Prochaska, 1910–13.

Kuna, Milan. "Dvořák und Mahler: Über die in Wien nicht stattgefundende Inszenierung der *Rusalka*," in Döge and Jost, *Dvořák-Studien*, 197–203.

Kuna, Milan. "Dvořák's Slavic Spirit, and His Relation to Tchaikovsky and Russia." In Beveridge, *Rethinking Dvořák*, 143–53.

Kuna, Milan. "Umelecká stipendia Antonína Dvořáka," *Hudební veda* n.s., 4 (1992): 293–315.

Kwan, Jonathan. *Liberalism and the Habsburg Monarchy, 1861–1895*. London: Palgrave Macmillan, 2013.

Kwiek, Marek. "Revisiting the Classical German Idea of the University (On the Nationalization of the Modern Institution)." *Polish Journal of Philosophy* 2 (2008): 1–24.

La Grange, Henry-Louis de. *Gustav Mahler*. Vol. 2, *Vienna: The Years of Challenge (1897–1904)*. Oxford and New York: Oxford University Press, 1995. Vol. 3, *Vienna: Triumph and Disillusion (1904–1907)*. Oxford and New York: Oxford University Press, 1999.

Leigh, Jeffrey T. "Public Opinion, Public Order, and Press Policy in the Neo-Absolutist State: Bohemia, 1849–52." *Austrian History Yearbook* 35 (2004): 81–89.

Lesky, Erna. *The Vienna Medical School of the 19th Century*. Baltimore and London: Johns Hopkins University Press, 1976.

Librett, Jeffrey S. *The Rhetoric of Cultural Dialogue: Jews and Germans from Moses Mendelssohn to Richard Wagner and Beyond*. Stanford: Stanford University Press, 2000.

Locke, Brian S. *Opera and Ideology in Prague*. Rochester: University of Rochester Press, 2006.

Locke, Ralph P. "Cutthroats and Casbah Dancers, Muezzins and Timeless Sands: Musical Images of the Middle East." *19th-Century Music* 22 (1998): 20–53.

Loeffler, James. "Wagner's 'Jewish Music': Antisemitism and Aesthetics in Modern Jewish Culture." *Jewish Social Studies: History, Culture, Society* n.s. 15, no. 2 (Winter 2009): 2–36.

Lomnäs, Bonnie, Erling Lomnäs, and Dietmar Strauß. *Auf der Suche nach der poetischen Zeit: Der Prager Davidsbund: Ambros, Bach, Bayer, Hampel, Hanslick, Helfert, Heller, Hock, Ulm. Zu einem vergessenen Abschnitt der Musikgeschichte des 19. Jahrhunderts*. 2 vols. Saarbrücken: Pfau, 1999.

Lotar, Peter. *Eine Krähe war mit mir*. Stuttgart: Deutsche Verlags-Anstalt, 1987.

Ludvová, Jitka. *Dokonalý antiwagnerián Eduard Hanslick*. Prague: Supraphon, 1992.

Ludvová, Jitka. "Několik pražských reálií k biografii Eduarda Hanslicka." *Miscellanea theatralia: Sborník Adolfu Scherlovi k osmdesátinám*, edited by Eva Šormová and Michaelou Kuklovou, 379–90. Prague: Divadelní ústav, 2005. German translation, "Einige Prager Realien zum Thema Hanslick." In Antonicek, Gruber, and Landerer, *Eduard Hanslick zum Gedenken*, 163–79.

Ludvová, Jitka. "Zur Biographie Eduard Hanslicks," *Studien zur Musikwissenschaft* 37 (1986): 37–46.

Luft, David S. "Austrian Intellectual History and Bohemia." *Austrian History Yearbook* 38 (2007): 108–21.

Luft, David S. *Eros and Inwardness in Vienna: Weininger, Musil, Doderer*. Chicago and London: University of Chicago Press, 2003.

Luther, Martin. *Luther's Lieder und Gedichte*. Edited by Wilhelm Stapel. Stuttgart: Evangelisches Verlagswerk, 1950.

Marchand, Suzanne L. *German Orientalism in the Age of Empire*. Cambridge: Cambridge University Press, 2009.

Markel, Howard. *An Anatomy of Addiction: Sigmund Freud, William Halstead, and the Miracle*. New York: Pantheon, 2011.

Marr, Wilhelm. *Der Sieg des Judenthums über das Germanenthum: Vom nichtconfessionellen Standpunkt aus betrachtet*. 2nd ed. Bern: Rudolph Costenoble, 1879.

Marr, Wilhelm. *Wählet keinen Juden! Der Weg zum Siege des Germanenthums über das Judenthum: Ein Mahnwort an die Wähler nichtjüdischen Stammes aller Confessionen, mit einem Schlußwort: "An die Juden in Preussen."* Berlin: Hentze, 1879.

McColl, Sandra. "Max Kalbeck and Gustav Mahler." *19th-Century Music* 20 (1996): 167–84.

McColl, Sandra. *Music Criticism in Vienna 1896–1897: Critically Moving Forms*. Oxford: Clarendon Press, 1996.

McGrath, William. *Dionysian Art and Populist Politics in Austria*. New Haven and London: Yale University Press, 1974.

Meißner, Alfred. *Geschichte meines Lebens*. 2 vols. Vienna: K. Prochaska, 1884.

Mendes-Flohr, Paul. *German Jews: A Dual Identity*. New Haven and London: Yale University Press, 1999.

Meyer, Michael A., ed. *German-Jewish History in Modern Times*. 4 vols. New York: Columbia University Press, 1996–98.

Mikoletzky, Lorenz. "Johannes Brahms und die Politik seiner Zeit." In *Brahms-Kongress Wien 1983: Kongressbericht*, edited by Susanne Antonicek and Otto Biba, 387–96. Tutzing: Hans Schneider, 1988.

Mikovec, Ferdinand B. *Záhuba rodu Přemyslovského*. Prague: Pospíšil, 1851.

Molisch, Paul. *Geschichte der deutschen Hochschulen in Österreich von 1848 bis 1918*, 2nd ed. Vienna and Leipzig: Wilhelm Braumüller, 1939.

Móricz, Klára. *Jewish Identities: Nationalism, Racism, and Utopianism in Twentieth-Century Music*. Berkeley, Los Angeles and London: University of California Press, 2008.

Morrison, Julie Dorn. "Gustav Mahler at the Vienna Hofoper: A Study of the Reception in the Viennese Press (1897–1907)." Ph.D. diss., Northwestern University, 1996).

Mosse, George L. "Jewish Emancipation: Between *Bildung* and Respectability." In *The Jewish Response to German Culture from the Enlightenment to the Second World War*, edited by Jehuda Reinharz and Walter Schatzberg, 1–16. Hanover and London: University Press of New England, 1985.

Nagel, Martin, Karl-Ludwig Schober, and Günther Weiß. *Theodor Billroth: Chirurg und Musiker*. Regensburg: ConBrio, 1994.

Die Nationalitäten—, das ist: Sprachenfrage in Oesterreich. Ein Vorschlag zu ihrer Lösung von einem Deutsch-Oesterreicher. Vienna: Verlag von L. Rosner, 1881.

Newmarch, Rosa. "The Letters of Dvorák [*sic*] to Hans Richter." *Musical Times* 73 (1932): 605–7.

Niekerk, Carl. *Reading Mahler: German Culture and Jewish Identity in Fin-de-Siècle Vienna*. Rochester, NY: Camden House, 2010.

Nietzsche, Friedrich. *The Birth of Tragedy and The Case of Wagner*. Translated with commentary by Walter Kaufmann. New York: Random House, 1967.

Notley, Margaret. "Brahms as Liberal: Genre, Style, and Politics in Late Nineteenth-Century Vienna." *19th-Century Music* 23 (1993): 107–23.

Notley, Margaret. "Bruckner and Viennese Wagnerism." In *Bruckner Studies*, edited by Timothy L. Jackson and Paul Hawkshaw, 545–71. Cambridge: Cambridge University Press, 1997.

Notley, Margaret. *Lateness and Brahms: Music and Culture in the Twilight of Viennese Liberalism.* Oxford and New York: Oxford University Press, 2007.

Notley, Margaret. "Musical Culture in Vienna at the Turn of the Twentieth Century." In *Schoenberg, Berg, and Webern: A Companion to the Second Viennese School*, edited by Bryan R. Simms, 36–71. Westport, CT: Greenwood Press, 1999.

Notley, Margaret. "'Volkskonzerte' in Vienna and Late Nineteenth-Century Ideology of the Symphony." *Journal of the American Musicological Society* 50 (1997): 421–53.

Novotný, Jan. "Zu den Beziehungen der slawischen Politiker zur Wiener Regierung während der Revolution 1848–1849." In *L'udovít Štúr und die slawische Wechselseitigkeit: Gesamte Referate und die integrale Diskussion der wissenschaftlichen Tagung in Smolenice 27.–29. Juni 1966*, edited by L'udovít Holotík, 152–64. Bratislava: Verlag der Slowakischen Akademie der Wissenschaften, 1969.

Nuland, Sherwin B. *The Masterful Spirit—Theodor Billroth.* Birmingham, AL: Classics of Surgery Library, 1984.

Nußbaumer, Martina. "Identity on Display: (Re-)Präsentationen des Eigenen und des Fremden auf der Internationalen Ausstellung für Musik- und Theaterwesen in Wien 1892." *Historische Anthropologie. Kultur, Gesellschaft, Alltag* 13 (2005): 45–60.

Nußbaumer, Martina. *Musikstadt Wien: Die Konstruktion eines Images.* Freiburg i. Br., Berlin, and Vienna: Rombach Verlag, 2007.

Okey, Robin. *The Habsburg Monarchy c. 1765–1918: From Enlightenment to Eclipse.* New York: Palgrave Macmillan, 2001.

Osbourne, Charles. *Richard Wagner: Stories and Essays.* London: Owen, 1973.

Die österreichisch-ungarische Monarchie in Wort und Bild. 24 vols. Vienna: Druck und Verlag der kaiserlich-königlichen Hof- und Staatsdruckerei, 1886–1902.

Paces, Cynthia, and Nancy C. Wingfield. "The Sacred and the Profane: Religion and Nationalism in the Bohemian Lands, 1880–1920." In Judson and Rozenblit, *Constructing Nationalities in East Central Europe*, 107–25.

Painter, Karen, and Bettina Varwig. "Mahler's German-Language Critics." In *Mahler and His World*, edited by Karen Painter, 267–378. Princeton and Oxford: Princeton University Press, 2002.

Palacký, František. *Geschichte von Böhmen: Grössentheils nach Urkunden und Handschriften.* 5 vols. Prague: Kronberger und Weber, 1836–67.

Pauley, Bruce F. *From Prejudice to Persecution: A History of Austrian Anti-Semitism.* Chapel Hill: University of North Carolina Press, 1992.

Paupié, Kurt. *Handbuch der österreichischen Pressegeschichte 1848–1959.* 2 vols. Vienna: Wilhelm Braumüller, 1960.

Pazi, Margarita. "Berthold Auerbach and Moritz Hartmann: Two Jewish Writers of the Nineteenth Century." *Leo Baeck Institute Yearbook* 18 (1973): 201–18.

Peck, Clemens C. "'Paralysis progressiva': Zur Figuration des Bildungsproletariats in Jakob Julius Davids Wien-Roman Am Wege sterben." *Internationales Archiv für Sozialgeschichte der deutschen Literatur* 35 (2010): 37–60.

Perger, Richard. *Denkschrift: Zum Feier des fünfzigjährigen ununterbrochenen Bestandes der Philharmonischen Konzerte in Wien 1860–1910*. Vienna and Leipzig: Carl Fromme, 1910.

Pinter, Charlotte. *Ludwig Speidel als Musikkritiker*. Ph.D. diss., University of Vienna, 1949.

Potter, Pamela M. "Race in German Musical Discourse." In *Western Music and Race*, edited by Julie Brown, 49–62. Cambridge: Cambridge University Press, 2007.

Prohaska, Norbert. *Der Schulverein: Beiträge zum 120. Gründungstag*. Vienna: Österreichische Landsmannschaft, 2000.

Pulzer, Peter. "Legal Equality and Public Life." In Meyer, *German-Jewish History in Modern Times*, vol. 3: *Integration in Dispute 1871–1918*, edited by Steven M. Lowenstein, Paul Mendes-Flohr, Peter Pulzer, and Monika Richarz, 153–95.

Pulzer, Peter. "The Return of Old Hatreds." In Meyer, *German-Jewish History in Modern Times, vol. 3: Integration in Dispute 1871–1918*, edited by Steven M. Lowenstein, Paul Mendes-Flohr, Peter Pulzer, and Monika Richarz, 196–251.

Pulzer, Peter. *The Rise of Political Antisemitism in Germany and Austria*. Rev. ed. Cambridge, MA: Harvard University Press, 1988.

Reinwarth, Julius, ed. *Gedichte von Friedrich Bach*. Prague: Calve, 1900.

Reiss, Johannes. "Geschichte der Juden und jüdische Geschichte im Burgenland." In *Juden in der Stadt*, edited by Fritz Mayrhofer and Ferdinand Opll, 1–19. Linz: Donau, 1999.

Reitterer, Hubert. "Josef Adolf Hanslik jako knihovník a satiric." *Hudebni veda* 43 (2006): 385–406. German translation, "Josef Adolf Hanslik als Bibliotheksbeamter und Satiriker." In Antonicek, Gruber, and Landerer, *Eduard Hanslick zum Gedenken*, 139–62.

Reittererová, Vlasta, and Hubert Reitterer. *Vier Dutzend rothe Strümpfe... Zur Rezeptionsgeschichte der Verkauften Braut von Bedřich Smetana in Wien am Ende des 19. Jahrhunderts*. Vienna: Verlag der Österreichischen Akademie der Wissenschaften, 2004.

Renan, Ernst. *Nouvelles considérations sur le caractère général des peuples sémitiques, et en particulier sur leur tendance au monothéisme*. Paris: Imprimerie Imperial, 1859.

Revers, Peter. "Karl Goldmark's Operas During the Directorship of Gustav Mahler." In *The Great Tradition and its Legacy: The Evolution of Dramatic and Musical Theater in Austria and Central Europe*, edited by Michael Cherlin, Halina Filipowicz, and Richard L. Rudolph, 227–36. New York and Oxford: Berghan Books, 2004.

Riegert, Jr., Leo William. "Negotiating the German-Jewish: The Uncomfortable Writing of Karl Emil Franzos." Ph.D. diss., University of Minnesota, 2004.

Rose, Paul Lawrence. *German Question/Jewish Question: Revolutionary Antisemitism from Kant to Wagner*. New Haven and London: Yale University Press, 1992.

Rose, Paul Lawrence. "One of Wagner's Jewish Friends: Berthold Auerbach and his Unpublished Reply to Wagner's Antisemitism (1881)." *Leo Baeck Institute Yearbook* 36 (1991): 219–28.

Rosenkranz, Karl. *Die Poesie und ihre Geschichte: Eine Entwicklung der poetischen Ideale der Völker*. Königsberg: Gebrüder Bornträger, 1855.

Roses, Daniel F. "Brahms and Billroth." *American Brahms Society Newsletter* 5/2 (Spring 1987): 1–5.

Roth, Joseph. "Die Juden von Deutschkreuz und die Schweh-Khilles" [1919]. In *Joseph Roth Werke*, i: *Das journalistische Werk, 1915–1923*. Cologne: Kipenheuer & Witsch, 1989), 115–16.

Rozenblit, Marsha L. "Jewish Assimilation in Vienna." In Frankel and Zipperstein, *Assimilation and Community*, 225–45.

Rozenblit, Marsha. *The Jews of Habsburg Austria During the First World War*. Oxford: Oxford University Press, 2001.

Rozenblit, Marsha L. "The Jews of the Dual Monarchy." *Austrian History Yearbook* 23 (1992): 160–80.

Rürup, Reinhard. "Progress and Its Limits: The Revolution of 1848 and European Jewry." In *Europe in 1848: Revolution and Reform*, edited by Dieter Dowe, Heinz-Gerhard Haupt, Dieter Langewiesche, and Jonathan Sperber, translated by David Higgins, 749–64. New York and Oxford: Berghahn, 2001.

Sagarra, Eda. "Social Types and Social Reality in the Narrative Fiction of Ferdinand von Saar." In *Ferdinand von Saar: Ein Wegbereiter der literarischen Moderne*, edited by Karl Konrad Polheim, 150–57. Bonn: Bourvier Verlag Herbert Grundmann, 1985.

Salomon, Gotthold. *Israels Erlösung aus Druck und Knechtschaft, oder auf welchem Wege können wir zu einer würdigern Stellung in der bürgerlichen Gesellschaft gelangen*. Hamburg: Hartwig & Müller, 1829.

Sayer, Derek. *The Coasts of Bohemia: A Czech History*. Princeton: Princeton University Press, 1998.

Schoenberg, Arnold. "New Music, Outmoded Music, Style and Idea." In *Style and Idea: Selected Writings of Arnold Schoenberg*, edited by Leonard Stein, translated by Leo Black, 113–24. Berkeley and Los Angeles: University of California Press, 1985.

Schonberg, Harold C. "Brahms Spoke Up—To Knock the Jew." *New York Times*, March 22, 1970.

Schorske, Carl E. *Fin-de-siècle Vienna: Politics and Culture*. New York: Vintage Books, 1981.

Schorske, Carl E. "Generational Tension and Cultural Change." In *Thinking with History: Explorations in the Passage to Modernism*, 141–56. Princeton: Princeton University Press, 1998.

Schüler, Winfried. *Der Bayreuther Kreis von seiner Entstehung bis zum Ausgang der Wilhelminischen Ära*. Münster: Aschendorff, 1971.

Scott, Derek. "Orientalism and Musical Style." *Musical Quarterly* 82 (1998): 309–35.

Scott, Derek. "Postmodernism and Music." In *The Routledge Companion to Postmodern Thought*, edited by Stuart Sim, 122–32. 2nd ed. New York: Routledge, 2005.

Seebacher, Felicitas. *Das Fremde im 'deutschen' Tempel der Wissenschaften: Brücke in der Wissenschaftskultur der Medizinischen Fakultät der Universität Wien*. Vienna: Verlag der Österreichische Akademie der Wissenschaften, 2011.

Seebacher, Felicitas. "'Der operierte Chirurg': Theodor Billroths Deutschnationalismus und akademischer Antisemitismus." *Zeitschrift für Geschichtswissenschaft* 54 (2006): 317–38.

Seiler, Martin. "Kurt Blaukopf und Robert Zimmermann: Spuren altösterreichischer Philosophie im Werk eines Musiksoziologen der Gegenwart." In *Weltanschauungen des Wiener Fin de siècle 1900/2000: Festgabe für Kurt Rudolf Fischer zum achtzigsten Geburtstag*, edited by Gertraud Diem-Wille, Ludwig Nagl, and Friedrich Stadler, 185–94. Frankfurt am Main: Peter Lang, 2002.

Šmahel, František. "The Hussite Movement: An Anomaly of European History?" In *Bohemia in History*, edited by Mikuláš Teich, 79–97. Cambridge: Cambridge University Press, 1998.

Sorkin, David. *The Transformation of German Jewry, 1780–1840*. Oxford: Oxford University Press, 1987.

Šourek Otakar, ed. *Antonín Dvořák, Letters and Reminiscences*. Translated by Roberta Finlayson Samsour. Prague: Artia, 1954.

Specht, Richard. *Johannes Brahms*. Translated by Eric Blom. New York: Dutton, 1927.

Spector, Scott. "Another Zionism: Hugo Bergmann's Circumscription of Spiritual Territory," *Journal of Contemporary History* 34 (1999): 87–108.

Stachel, Peter. "'Mit wärme und lebhafter Anschaulichkeit': Eduard Hanslicks Anteil am 'Kronprinzenwerk'." In Antonicek, Gruber, and Landerer, *Eduard Hanslick zum Gedenken*, 215–32.

Stachel, Peter. "Eine 'vaterländische' Oper für die Habsburgermonarchie oder eine 'jüdische Nationaloper'? Carl Goldmarks *Königin von Saba* in Wien." In *Die Oper im Wandel der Gesellschaft: Kulturtransfers und Netzwerke des Musiktheaters in Europa*, edited by Sven O. Müller, Gesa zu Nieden, Philipp Ther, and Jutta Toelle, 197–218. Vienna, Cologne, and Weimar: Böhlau, 2010.

Stephenson, Kurt. *Johannes Brahms und die Familie Beckerath*. Hamburg: Christians, 1979.

Stöckl-Steinebrunner, Karin M. "Der unbequeme Dvořák: Reaktionen der Musikkritik auf die ersten Aufführungen der Sinfonischen Dichtungen im deutschsprachigen Raum," in Döge and Jost, *Dvořák-Studien*, 190–96. Translated by David R. Beveridge as "The 'Uncomfortable' Dvořák: Critical Reactions to the First Performances of his Symphonic Poems in German-Speaking Lands." In Beveridge, *Rethinking Dvořák*, 201–10.

Stölzl, Christoph. *Kafkas böses Böhmen: Zur Sozialgeschichte eines Prager Juden*. Munich: Hans Pribil, 1975.

Storck, Christopher P. *Kulturnation und Nationalkunst. Strategien und Mechanismen tschechischer Nationsbildung von 1860 bis 1914*. Cologne: Wissenschaft und Politik, 2001.

Stourzh, Gerald. *Die Gleichberechtigung der Nationalitäten in der Verfassung und Verwaltung Österreichs 1848–1918*. Vienna: Verlag der Österreichischen Akademie der Wissenschaften, 1985.

Stříteckỳ, Jaroslav. "Eduard Hanslick und die tschechische Musik." In *Festival Česká hudba / Musica bohemica: Problémy a metody hudební historiografie*, edited by Rudolf Pečman, 85–93. Brno, 1974.

Šubert, Fr[antišek] Ad[olf]. *Das Böhmische National-Theater in der ersten internationalen Musik- und Theater-Ausstellung zu Wien im Jahre 1892*. Prague: Im Verlage des Nationaltheater-Consortiums, 1892.

Sullivan, Elizabeth Way. "German Nationalism and the Reception of the Czech String Quartet in Vienna." In *Nineteenth-Century Music. Selected Proceedings of the Tenth International Conference*, edited by Jim Samson and Bennett Zon, 296–313. Aldershot, Hants, England; Burlington, VT: Ashgate, 2002.

Sunderman, F. William. "Theodor Billroth as Musician." *Bulletin of the Medical Library Association* 25/4 (1937): 209–20.

Synopticus [Renner, Karl]. *Staat und Nation: Zur österreichischen Nationalitätenfrage*. Vienna: J. Dietl, 1899.

Taruskin, Richard. *The Oxford History of Western Music*. Vol. 3, *The Nineteenth Century*. Oxford and New York: Oxford University Press, 2005.

Taylor, A. J. P. *The Habsburg Monarchy, 1809–1918: A History of the Austrian Empire and Austria-Hungary*. Chicago: University of Chicago Press, 1948.

Teuber, Oscar. "Das Ausstellungs-Theater und seine Thaten." In *Die internationale Ausstellung für Musik- und Theaterwesen Wien 1892*, edited by Siegmund Schneider, 305–9. Vienna: Perles, 1894.

Treadwell, James. *Interpreting Wagner*. New Haven: Yale University Press, 2003.

Treitschke, Heinrich von. *Ein Wort über unser Judenthum*. Berlin: G. Reimer, 1880.

Varga, Péter. "Deutsch-Jüdische Identitäten in Autobiografien ungarischer Juden des ausgehenden 19. Jahrhunderts." In *Mehrdeutigkeit: Die Ambivalenz von Gedächtnis und Erinnerung*, edited by Moritz Csáky and Peter Stachel, 105–21. Vienna: Passagen, 2002.

Varga, Péter. "'Wo gehörte ich eigentlich hin?': Deutsch-jüdisches Leben im Ungarn des 19. Jahrhunderts." In *"Swer sinen vriunt behaltet, daz ist lobelich": Festschrift für András Vizkelety zum 70. Geburtstag*, edited by Márta Nagy and László Jonácsik, 549–55. Budapest: Piliscsaba, 2001.

Vick, Brian. "Arndt and German Ideas of Race: Between Kant and Social Darwinism." In *Ernst Moritz Arndt (1769–1860): Deutscher Nationalismus–Europa–Transatlantische Perspektiven*, edited by Walter Erhart and Arne Koch, 65–76. Tübingen: Max Niemayer, 2007.

Vysloužil, Jiří. "Hanslick 'Für und Wider' Dvořák: ein Diskurs zur Ästhetik der Orchester Musik im 19. Jahrhundert." In *Bruckner Symposien: Orchestermusik im 19. Jahrhundert*, 101–5. Linz: Anton Bruckner Institut, 1992.

Wagner, Cosima. *Cosima Wagner's Diaries*. Edited by Martin Gregor-Dellin and Dietrich Mack. Translated by Geoffrey Skelton. 2 vols. New York: Harcourt Brace Jovanovich, 1978–80.

Wagner, Manfred. "Bruckner and Hanslick." In Antonicek, Gruber, and Landerer, *Eduard Hanslick zum Gedenken*, 309–15.

Wagner, Richard. *Das Judenthum in der Musik*. Leipzig: J. J. Weber, 1869.

Wagner, Richard. *Gesammelte Schriften und Dichtungen*. 10 vols. Leipzig, 1887–1911.

Wagner, Richard. *Religion and Art*. Translated by William Ashton Ellis. Lincoln and London: University of Nebraska Press, 1994.

Walter, Edith. *Österreichische Tageszeitungen der Jahrhundertwende: Ideologischer Anspruch und ökonomische Erfordernisse*. Vienna, Cologne, and Weimar: Böhlau Verlag, 1994.

Welti, Heinrich. "Die Zukunft der Märchenoper." *Die Nation* 13 (1896): 607–8.

Werba, Robert. "'Königin' für 277 Abende: Goldmarks Oper und ihr wienerisches Schicksal." *Österreichische Musikzeitschrift* 34 (1979): 192–201.

Werner, Eric. *A Voice Still Heard... The Sacred Songs of the Ashkenazic Jews*. University Park, and London: Pennsylvania State University Press, 1976.

Whiteside, Andrew G. *The Socialism of Fools: Georg Ritter von Schönerer and Austrian Pan-Germanism*. Berkeley and Los Angeles: University of California Press, 1975.

Wiese, Christiane. "'Let His Memory be Holy to Us!': Jewish Interpretations of Martin Luther from the Enlightenment to the Holocaust." *Leo Baeck Institute Year Book* 54 (2009): 93–126.

Williamson, John, ed. *The Cambridge Companion to Bruckner*. Cambridge: Cambridge University Press, 2004.

Wingfield, Nancy W., ed. *Creating the Other: Ethnic Conflict and Nationalism in Habsburg Central Europe*. New York and Oxford: Berghahn, 2003.

Winkler, Gerhard J. "Carl Goldmark und die Antisemitismus." *Burgenländische Heimatblätter* 60 (1998), H. 3: 128–34.

Winkler, Gerhard J. "Carl Goldmark und die Moderne." In *"Denn in jenen Tönen lebt es": Wolfgang Marggraf zum 65. Geburtstag*, ed. Helen Geyer, Michael Berg, and Matthias Tischer, 229–43. Weimar: Hochschule für Musik Franz Liszt, 1999.

Winkler, Gerhard J. "Joseph Joachim, Carl Goldmark—Zwei parallele jüdische Musikerbiographien aus dem historischen Westungarn." In *Musik der Juden im Burgenland*, ed. Gerhard J. Winkler, 79–100. Eisenstadt: Amt der burgenländischen Landesregierung, 2006.

Winkler, Gerhard J. " 'Multikulturalität' und 'Heilige deutsche Tonkunst': Komplementäre und parallele Lebensläufe aus dem historischen Westungarn." In Borchard and Zimmermann, eds., *Musikwelten–Lebenswelten: Jüdische Identitätssuche in der deutschen Musikkultur*, 267–85.

Wistrich, Robert S. *The Jews of Vienna in the Age of Franz Joseph*. Oxford: Oxford University Press, 1989.

Wladika, Michael. *Hitlers Vätergeneration: die Ursprüng des Nationalsozialismus in der k. u. k. Monarchie*. Vienna, Cologne, and Weimer: Böhlau Verlag, 2005.

Wolf, Hugo. *Hugo Wolfs Kritiken im Wiener Salonblatt*. 2 vols. Vienna: Musikwissenschaftlicher Verlag, 2002.

Wurzbach, Constant von. *"Ferdinand Bogelislaw/Mikowec."* In *Biographisches Lexikon der Kaiserthums Oesterreich*, viii: 283–87. Vienna, 1868.

Wyklicky, Helmut. *Unbekanntes von Theodor Billroth: eine Dokumentation in Fragmenten*. Vienna: Österreichische Akademie der Wissenschaften, 1993.

Zistler, Alfred. "Geschichte der Juden in Deutschkreuz." In *Gedenkbuch der untergegangenen Judengemeinden des Burgenlandes*, edited by Hugo Gold, 57–74. Tel Aviv: Olamenu, 1970.

Zubatý, Josef. *Anton Dvořák: Eine biographische Skizze*. Leipzig: Gebrüder Hug, 1886.

Zudrell, Petra. *Der Kulturkritiker und Schriftsteller Max Nordau: Zwischen Zionismus, Deutschtum und Judentum*. Würzburg: Königshausen & Neumann, 2003.

Autograph Materials Cited

Archive, Leo Baeck Institute, New York: Carl Goldmark Family Collection
Family letters and other primary sources

Handschriftensammlung, Wiener Stadt- und Landesbibliothek, Vienna
Letters from Carl Goldmark to Ludwig Speidel
Letter from Solomon Sulzer to Eduard Hanslick

Historisches Archiv der Wiener Philharmoniker, Vienna
Minutes of the meetings of the Executive Committee

Hungarian State Opera, Budapest: Carl Goldmark
Autograph manuscript of "Eine Ansicht über Fortschritt"
Autograph manuscript of "Über musikalischen Fortschritt: 'Eine Mahnung' "
Autograph manuscript of "Gedanken über Form und Stil (Eine Abwehr)"

Miklós Rózsa Collection of Music Letters, Photographs, and Other Materials,
    University of Southern California Libraries, Los Angeles
    Two letters from Carl Goldmark to Eduard Hanslick

National Széchényi Library, Budapest: Carl Goldmark
    Autograph manuscript of *Erinnerungen*
    Autograph full score *Sakuntala*

Rare Book and Manuscript Library, Columbia University: Goldmark Family Papers
    Letters and other primary sources

Verein für Geschichte der Arbeitbewegung. Vienna: Victor Adler
    Draft of a speech by Victor Adler to the *Leseverein der deutschen Studenten Wiens*

Contemporary Periodicals (All Published in Vienna Except as Otherwise Noted)

Allgemeine Deutsche Musik-Zeitung. Leipzig
Allgemeine Kunst-Chronik
Die Bombe
Constitutionelle oesterreichische Zeitung
Dalibor. Prague
Deutsche Kunst- und Musik-Zeitung
Deutsche Musik-Zeitung
Deutsche Zeitung
Deutsches Volksblatt
Der Floh
Freies Blatt
Fremden-Blatt
Die Gegenwart. Berlin
Illustrirtes Wiener Extrablatt
Musikalisches Wochenblatt
National Zeitung. Berlin
Neue Freie Presse
Neues Wiener Journal
Neues Wiener Tagblatt
Ostdeutsche Rundschau
Pester Lloyd. Budapest
Prager Zeitung. Prague
Die Presse
Signale für die musikalische Welt. Leipzig
Der Tag
Das Vaterland
Wiener Abendpost
Wiener Allgemeine Zeitung
Wiener Salonblatt
Wiener Sonn- und Montags Zeitung
Wiener Tagblatt
Wiener Zeitung

racialist antisemitism (*Cont.*)
  German nationalism and, 123–24
  and Mahler as Court Opera director,
    315–18
  of Wagner, 115–16
Radnitzky, Franz, 153–54
Radnitzky Quartet, 153–54
Rákóczy March (Smetana), 259
Reading Society of Vienna's German
    Students, 111n11, 126
religion, importance of, to *völkisch* parties,
    190n117
"Richard Wagner and the Self-Respect of
    the Jews" (Auerbach), 112n13
Richter, Hans
  commissions Dvořák symphony, 146–47
  Hanslick on, 152
  and performance of Dvořák's Rhapsody
    No. 3, 169
  and performance of Dvořák's Symphony
    No. 6, 156–58, 162
  and Philharmonic's refusal to play certain
    composers, 170n61
  Püringer on, 246
  Symphony No. 6 dedicated to, 172
Ring cycle, 316–17
Rosé, Arnold, 239
Rosenkranz, Karl, 92–93
Roth, Joseph, 53
Rozenblit, Marsha, 9, 128n58
Rubinstein, Anton
  Die Maccabäer, 79
  Der Thurm zu Babel, 78–79, 81–83ex.
Rudolf von Habsburg, Crown Prince, 2–3

Saar, Ferdinand von, 286
Sabina, Karel, 31
Sakuntala (Goldmark)
  composition and reception of, 72
  critical reviews of, 74–79
  description of, 72–74
  differentiation of style in, 307
  influences on, 71–72
Salomon, Gotthold, 45–47
Šárka (Smetana), 253
Sayer, Derek, 28n4
scales, in Oriental music, 303–5
Schelle, Eduard, 86, 87, 169
Scherber, Ferdinand, 302n24
Scherzo capriccio (Dvořák), 185–86, 194–95

Schir Zion (Sulzer), 94–100, 99ex.
Schönerer, Georg von, 160, 209–10, 212
Schubert, Franz, 171n63
Schumann, Robert, 102
Scott, Derek, 306
Seebacher, Felicitas, 113
Seegen, Hermine, 110, 132
Seegen, Josef, 109, 132
"Sensitiven" (Bach), 287
Serenade for Winds (Dvořák), 145, 146, 152
Seven Weeks' War (1866), 7
Siebert, August, 153–54
Simrock, Fritz, 144–45, 147, 195
Škroup, Johann Nepomuk, 26, 42n42
Slavonic Dances (Dvořák), 144–45
Slavonic Rhapsodies (Dvořák), 145
Slavonic Rhapsody No. 2 (Cowen), 164–69
Slavonic Rhapsody No. 2 (Dvořák), 183–84
Slavonic Rhapsody No. 3 (Dvořák), 146–51,
    167
Smetana, Bedřich
  critical acclaim of, 253–58, 311–12
  Dalibor, 268–69, 318–27
  dropped from Vienna Philharmonic's
    1885–86 season, 185–86
  emergence of, 152–54
  From My Life, 153–55, 274–75, 321
  Das Geheimnis, 312
  Helm on Dvořák and, 259
  Kauders on identity and nationality of,
    271–72
  Der Kuß, 312
  Libussa, 255
  Má vlast, 153–54, 191–94, 253–58
  Piano Trio in G minor, 153
  Prodaná nevěsta, 268–73, 274
  Rákóczy March, 259
  Šárka, 253
  Die Verkaufte Braut, 275–80, 310, 312–13
  Vltava, 192–94, 253–56, 258, 321
  Vyšehrad, 253, 281–89
  works of, in Court Opera program,
    309–10
  Z českých luhů a hájů, 253
  Z mého zivota, 153
social class
  antisemitism based on, 43–44
  distinction between Jews based on,
    46–47
  language as marker of, 25–26, 28